Defying
Disfranchisement

Defying Disfranchisement

Black Voting Rights Activism in the Jim Crow South, 1890–1908

R. VOLNEY RISER

Louisiana State University Press
Baton Rouge

Published by Louisiana State University Press
Copyright © 2010 by Robert Volney Riser II
All rights reserved
Manufactured in the United States of America

Designer: Laura Roubique Gleason
Typeface: Adobe Caslon Pro

LIBRARY OF CONGRESS CATALOGING-IN-PUBLICATION DATA

Riser, R. Volney.
    Defying disfranchisement : Black voting rights activism in the Jim Crow South,
1890–1908 / R. Volney Riser.
        p. cm.
    Includes bibliographical references and index.
    ISBN 978-0-8071-3638-6 (cloth : alk. paper)
1. African Americans—Suffrage—Southern States. 2. Voter registration—Southern States.
3. African American political activists. 4. African Americans—Civil rights—Southern States—
History—19th century. 5. African Americans—Civil rights—Southern States—History—20th
century. 6. Southern States—Politics and government—1865–1950. I. Title.
    JK1929.A2R57 2010
    324.6'208996073075—dc22
                                    2009048364
ISBN 978-0-8071-5010-8 (pbk. : alk. paper) — ISBN 978-0-8071-3741-3 (pdf) —
ISBN 978-0-8071-4607-1 (epub) — ISBN 978-0-8071-4608-8 (mobi)

Portions of chapters 3 and 4 appeared previously, in different form, as " 'The Milk in the Cocoanut': Booker T. Washington, Theodore Roosevelt, and the Fear of Conspiracy in Alabama's 1901
Constitutional Ratification Referendum," *Southern Historian* 26 (Spring 2005): 30–54; and "Disfranchisement, the U.S. Constitution, and the Federal Courts: Alabama's 1901 Constitutional
Convention Debates the Grandfather Clause," *American Journal of Legal History* 48, no. 3 (August 2006): 237–79.

The paper in this book meets the guidelines for permanence and durability of the Committee
on Production Guidelines for Book Longevity of the Council on Library Resources. ∞

For my grandmothers

Myrtle Breland Hollifield
and
Lucille Childers Riser

Contents

Defying
Disfranchisement

Prologue
April 27, 1903

Hushed by the marshal's cry of "Oyez! Oyez! Oyez!" the crowd stood and watched as nine men clad in silken black robes filed onto the dais. It was a decision day in the U.S. Supreme Court. The chamber fell silent, and the marshal admonished "all persons having business" before the Court to "draw near and give their attention, for the Court is now sitting." This was a Friday, and there was anticipation that the justices planned to reveal their long-awaited opinion in the closely watched Alabama voting rights case of *Giles v. Harris.* As the justices assembled, the audience waited and wondered if this was indeed the day the Supreme Court would swing a cudgel against disfranchisement. "God save the United States and this honorable Court," the marshal intoned, and then he withdrew.

Jackson W. Giles, president of the nascent Colored Men's Suffrage Association of Alabama, had filed a mandamus petition in federal court to force the Montgomery County Board of Registrars to register him and five thousand other black Montgomerians as voters. Through some very clever lawyering, Giles's attorney, Wilford Smith, with the cooperation of the registrars' attorney, Alabama's attorney general, and a U.S. district judge, had engineered an expedited Supreme Court appearance. *Giles v. Harris,* technically, was nothing more than a simple jurisdictional inquiry, the question being whether a U.S. district court could hear Giles's petition. But Giles's attorney implored the Court to explore the merits of his client's claim and settle the question once and for all. The justices accepted that invitation.

The county boards of registrars were creatures born of Alabama's 1901 constitutional convention, which had brought disfranchisement to the state. The boards implemented Alabama's new suffrage restrictions, and black activists statewide had threatened lawsuits designed to force their fair application (and thus destroy disfranchisement). Not surprisingly, the Montgomery county registrars didn't administer them fairly; in a countermove, Giles lent his name to a test case.

Giles v. Harris was the first of three U.S. Supreme Court cases linked to Giles's organization. The "Alabama Case," as the press sometimes described it, was the first of the antidisfranchisement cases argued on Fifteenth Amendment grounds before the U.S. Supreme Court, and black activists nationwide had placed their faith in Giles's effort, hoping it would rein in the southern disfranchisers.

April 27, 1903, was indeed the day of decision, as the curious crowd soon realized, when newly appointed Justice Oliver Wendell Holmes Jr. spoke for the Court. He read the opinion from the bench (the printed text would not be available for a week), and the decision was confusing. Holmes first said that the federal courts *did* have jurisdiction to hear cases like Giles's—a victory! Had Holmes stopped there, *Giles v. Harris* would have been celebrated as a landmark advance in African Americans' long struggle for civil rights, opening wide the doors of federal courthouses to voting rights plaintiffs. But Holmes did not stop. He accepted Wilford Smith's invitation to venture into the case's merits. Even if Giles's constitutional rights had been violated, Holmes reasoned, there was nothing the U.S. Supreme Court could do about it. If the registrars' actions had rendered Alabama's new constitution fraudulent, he asserted, ordering Giles registered would make the Court party to that fraud. Then Holmes asserted that courts were the wrong place for Giles. If Giles wanted redress for a "political wrong," he insisted, he should look to Congress or the Alabama legislature. The Montgomery County Board of Registrars' decision stood: Giles would not be registered as a voter.[1]

Reading the opinion's plain text only made things seem worse. Justices John Marshall Harlan and David Brewer offered vigorous dissents, but those were of no avail and little comfort. All that really mattered was that the Court had declared itself impotent in the face of disfranchisement. The crushing result drew immediate comparisons to the 1857 *Dred Scott* decision, which had denied the very notion that blacks could be U.S. citizens. Overnight, *Giles* became a "second *Dred Scott*" and Holmes a "second Roger Taney." The decision's effect, the *Boston Guardian* cried, was that the "Negro still has no rights that white men are bound to respect."[2]

On that Friday, the twenty-seventh of April, the U.S. Supreme Court erected *Plessy v. Ferguson*'s twin pillar, completing the legal structure upon which Jim Crow stood. The problem was not simply that Giles lost that day—*how* he lost was the real trouble. Holmes's opinion was too technical, too clever, too obviously a dodge for many Americans, black Americans in particular, to take. "Mr. Giles," the *Indianapolis Freeman* offered on May 2, had "taken his goose to a very poor market." Considering the opinion's bizarre claim of impotence, and two strident and contradictory dissents, the paper thought that Giles should count himself lucky were he to succeed "in recognizing himself sufficiently to get home again." Continuing, the *Freeman* offered that "he may be very thankful that he is alive after the mill he has gone through." Holmes said that the Court had jurisdiction but no power, that politics rather than the Constitution had dictated his decision, and that a contrary ruling would make the Court party to a fraud. The dissenters only added to the confusion. Justice Harlan insisted that the Court had no jurisdiction, but had the Court jurisdiction, he added, he would order Giles registered. Justice Brewer, with Justice Henry Brown (who had written the *Plessy* decision) concurring, insisted that the Court *did* have jurisdiction and that Giles *should* be registered. The Supreme Court "has decided all around him," the *Freeman* lamented, concluding, "Yes, Mr. Giles, you are lucky to be alive." A week later, the *Freeman*'s cartoonist sketched his own take on *Giles*. The Supreme Court and the southern disfranchisers had teamed up to humiliate Uncle Sam. With pistols and a switch, they made him dance for his life: "Putting the Constitution Under Foot They Make Him Dance to Their Tune."[3]

Jackson Giles was in the Supreme Court because, as bad as things were, many southern blacks were fighting back, insistent that they could preserve African Americans' civic dignity by protecting their voting rights. Blacks were losing the ballot because southern white Democrats ascribed their own sins to black voting. It was, Algernon Sidney Crapsey told a mass meeting at Washington's Metropolitan AME Church in 1901, the "excuse of the criminal who pleads his own crime as bar to his punishment." But African Americans would not passively accept the transferred guilt. Many tried to resist, aware that they hadn't much else to lose. Voting was everything, AME bishop Alexander Walters declared in 1909, because it is "the badge of political equality, the insignia of one's citizenship." Disfranchisement robbed African Americans of the protections that full citizenship brings, leaving them vulnerable to segregation, economic and social subjugation, and Judge Lynch.[4]

The value of full and unfettered citizenship was the lesson taught by Rev. Francis Grimké in his 1905 sermon "The Negro and his Citizenship," based upon Acts 22:22–30. The passage chronicles the Apostle Paul's return to Jerusalem several years after Christ's death and the public outcry and scapegoating that led to his arrest. He was immediately imprisoned, and as his captors prepared him for flogging, Paul reminded them that he was no ordinary resident of the Roman Empire: He was a citizen. Any unjustified assault upon a Roman citizen was an attack upon all of Rome. The *Civis Romani* could not be abused or tried for crime without established cause and had the right to demand a trial in the imperial capital with an appeal to Caesar. When Paul invoked these prerogatives with the locution "I am a Roman!"—*Civis Romanus sum*—the guard immediately warned the jailers. They had better take care. Suddenly afraid for their lives, the panicked captors hastily prepared a hearing so that Paul might know the charges against him. Citizenship afforded Paul these special protections, Grimké illustrated. Voting was the ultimate insignia of American citizenship, and disfranchisement degraded blacks and left them defenseless. If blacks were to guard themselves against demagogues and public persecution, if blacks were to control their destiny, "if we are to be sovereign citizens of the Republic," Grimké continued, "the right to vote must be preserved."[5]

Stripping African Americans of their voting rights damaged the entire nation, Archibald Grimké, Francis Grimké's brother, wrote in a 1904 essay, "Why Disfranchisement Is Bad." Disfranchisement was bad and had damaged the South, degraded the region industrially, "and fixed for her likewise a place of permanent economic inferiority and subordination." He did not stop there. If disfranchisement was bad for the South, he continued, "it is bad for the rest of the nation. For whatever injures the part injures the whole." Degraded citizenship hurt everyone, and some African Americans fought in the courts of law and public opinion. John Hope, writing in 1904, believed that the nation might yet be persuaded to act on blacks' behalf, but he believed just as strongly that blacks must not wait any longer: "Why *delay* voting in the hope of better things; better *welcome* disfranchisement as *men* than *suffer* from it as *cowards*."[6]

African American voting rights had steadily eroded since Reconstruction, but things accelerated rapidly in the 1890s. African Americans quickly grew impatient and disillusioned with Congress' and the presidency's failures and saw the U.S. Supreme Court as their last best hope. And so from the early 1890s through the early 1900s, they launched initiatives that were designed to yield a direct Supreme Court review of disfranchisement. In that period they gave the Court twelve chances to make things right. Twelve times, the Court disappointed them.

This body of disfranchisement era voting rights litigation does not rise to the level of a "movement." These voting rights initiatives were very individualized and did not offer, as Neil McMillen wrote of resistance in this nadir period among Mississippi African Americans, the "high drama . . . of the later civil rights revolution." Street marches and voter registration drives did not happen. Strong advocacy organizations never took hold and thus could not provide the institutional support that any real "movement" required. Fears of white violence and retribution clearly played a role, as did malaise and confusion. "This disfranchisement came upon the negro like the shock of an earthquake. It came suddenly and violently," AME bishop James Walker Hood explained in 1903. "Some are only waiting," Hood continued, "to see just how greatly they are damaged before making a move." So the campaigns emerged slowly, and even then they were loosely connected and small, and often for the worst possible reasons—pride and vanity—and primarily served their organizers' egos and political careers. Worse still, the various state-level organizations competed for money and glory.[7]

The antidisfranchisement activists learned the hard way that they needed something bigger, an institution that could sustain a broader fight. None other than Booker T. Washington, who himself participated (privately) in antidisfranchisement campaigns in Louisiana and Alabama and underwrote the Alabama litigation, recognized that imperative. Addressing the National Sociological Society's 1903 meeting in Washington, D.C., he declared that "the crying need of the Negro is organization"—this after thirteen years of failed efforts on the part of himself and others to fill that void. Washington was neither the first nor the last to identify this problem. Oswald Garrison Villard (grandson of legendary abolitionist William Lloyd Garrison), addressing "The Need of Organization" before the National Negro Conference of 1909, demanded that whatever his fellow attendees decided upon (and they decided to create the National Association for the Advancement of Colored People or NAACP), they had to provide for a permanent legal department. Villard had witnessed the Supreme Court's evasions in the antidisfranchisement cases, and demanded that the "political and civil rights bureau should have at its disposal sufficient money to employ the highest legal talent obtainable and to pay the heavy cost" of "case after case" before the Supreme Court. They would be able to do what the antidisfranchisement litigators could not—force that "shifting and evasive body . . . to decide whether there shall be two degrees of citizenship in the country." Taking another lesson from the antidisfranchisement litigators, whose efforts often accompanied or masqueraded as political campaigns, Villard envisioned this "political and civil rights bureau" as nonpartisan, confining "itself [to] battling for principles, for civil rights, for an untarnished Constitution."[8]

Disputatious, disorganized, and underfunded, the antidisfranchisement activists of 1890–1908 lost, and badly, for their repeated and infuriating defeats did not simply leave the status quo in place but actually made things worse. By 1908, when the last of the original flight of antidisfranchisement cases was decided, some of those involved no doubt questioned why they had ever pledged themselves to this Sisyphean task. Sadly, most probably never realized that some good had come from their attempts. Regardless of their mistakes, the antidisfranchisement organizers and attorneys brought attention to the problem, identified the legal questions and procedural difficulties facing blacks, and motivated a second generation of activists. They laid the foundation upon which Moorefield Storey, Charles Houston, Thurgood Marshall, and other twentieth-century civil rights litigators built. Those early activists, Marshall wrote of his disfranchisement era forebears, "identified the inequalities in the legal order and [began] to lay the foundation for social change. In storefront offices, over kitchen tables, and on porch steps," Marshall continued, "they worked diligently to expand the rights of African-Americans and to ensure, case by case, that justice would not be forever delayed."[9]

This book ends in 1908, before the NAACP's inception, because that event changed everything. Black civil rights activism after the NAACP's founding must be judged differently than that which preceded it. In terms of size and scale, and efficacy, there just is no direct comparison to be made. Indeed, the NAACP was so essential and timely that accounts of its inception cannot but overshadow everything that came previously.[10]

The NAACP's founders' initial, overriding goal was to salvage black voting rights. At the National Negro Conference in 1909 (the meeting that led to its founding), suffrage received the most attention. Oswald Garrison Villard addressed it, as did Albert Pillsbury and AME bishop Alexander Walters, both of whom were veterans of the earlier antidisfranchisement campaigns. W. E. B. Du Bois also targeted voting rights, and he targeted disfranchisement in a speech titled "Politics and Industry." Du Bois wanted direct, "frank agitation" that might prevent racial and economic conflict. "The voteless negro is a provocation," he eloquently warned, "an invitation to oppression, a plaything for mobs and a bonanza for demagogues." Until southern blacks regained the ballot they would suffer as pawns, Du Bois continued, "to distract attention from real issues and to raise fools and rascals into political power."[11]

Before the year was out, the nascent organization was proselytizing and publishing tracts. One of the first it released was "The Disfranchisement of Negroes," penned by Rev. John Haynes Holmes. "What can we do about it?" Holmes asked. They could crusade, he answered, "we can agitate, discuss, denounce, trouble, America to-day, as Elijah of old troubled Israel." Just as Elijah troubled Israel for worshiping Baal, Holmes intended to trouble the United States for tolerating disfranchisement. Keep "this abomination before the people," he demanded.[12]

Within a few decades, the NAACP had seemingly lost any institutional memory of the litigation and protest campaigns that had preceded its founding. With regard to disfranchisement, this condition seemed particularly acute. Herbert Hill, the NAACP's labor secretary, published a 1957 essay, "A Review of Negro Disfranchisement," that simply wrote away the antidisfranchisement cases and most of the pre-1909 period, replacing it with a narrative that conflated the NAACP's establishment with the genesis of black voting rights activism. After reviewing southern disfranchisement's course, from Mississippi's 1890 constitutional convention onward, Hill intimated that disfranchisement faced no serious legal challenge until 1915, when Moorefield Storey and the NAACP Legal Defense Fund made their first Supreme Court appearance, in the case of *Guinn v. United States,* which challenged grandfather clauses adopted by the state of Oklahoma and the city of Annapolis, Maryland. In a striking departure, the Court struck down the device as unconstitutional and touched off a minor tempest across the South.[13]

Guinn was, the *Birmingham Age-Herald* reported, "probably one of the most important race decisions" in the Supreme Court's history. It was so important, the paper's editor believed, that he trotted out the former president of Alabama's 1901 constitutional convention, John B. Knox, "one of the best informed constitutional lawyers in the south," for his expert analysis. *Guinn* was exciting, Knox conceded, but he thought it would have "no effect whatever" on Alabama or any jurisdictions beyond the state of Oklahoma and the city of Annapolis. Elsewhere, the grandfather clauses had been time limited and had already expired. Further, *Guinn* corrected nothing that had been done to black voters over the previous twenty-five years. Still, it marked the first occasion when the Court invalidated *anything* the southern disfranchisers had done. The fact of that victory best explains the historical amnesia surrounding the antidisfranchisement cases. Victories, even superficial ones such as *Guinn,* soothe hurts. For all that it did not do, *Guinn* certainly helped assuage the repeated, numbing U.S. Supreme Court defeats of 1895–1908.[14]

The antidisfranchisement cases were a testing ground for civil rights activism and were the often overlooked "other side" of the disfranchisement saga. The southern disfranchisement campaigns, and the court challenges that they provoked, were components of a single historical episode—a "momentous drama," as the *Washington Post* described them contemporaneously. The players all believed that they had the U.S. Constitution on their side. The disfranchisers insisted that the Constitution gave them virtually limitless authority over voting qualifications, which, they claimed (or hoped), Congress and the federal courts would never and could never circumscribe. But Congress and the federal courts, so African American voting rights activists and antidisfranchisement litigators believed (or hoped), *would* intervene and enforce the Constitution on behalf of disfranchised blacks.[15]

The disfranchisers and the antidisfranchisement crusaders were unevenly matched in the political arena. It would be erroneous to suggest that there was a match at all. The courts, activists believed, were another matter. Blacks could not vote disfranchisement down and they could not persuade whites to vote it down for them. Still, they could take their pleas to the Great Equalizer, the U.S. Supreme Court, whose power the antidisfranchisement litigators intended to turn to their advantage. The disfranchisers also recognized and respected the Court's power and spent the better part of a decade defending against lawsuits and trying to convince themselves and one another that their fears of judicial scrutiny were unwarranted. Each group realized that the Supreme Court could settle the question in one fell swoop.

Disfranchisement, and African American resistance thereto, unleashed torrents of cliché, much of it shopworn and most of it cloying. The disfranchisers struggled with the enormity of their task (the successful evasion of the Fourteenth and Fifteenth Amendments) and derived comfort from metaphorical references to rocks and hard places, and the devil and the sea. They festooned their rhetoric with poetic, high-brow, and often ill-applied literary allusions, Shakespeare and Homer were particular favorites, even among those who probably never read either. Their critics, white as well as black, tossed out metaphors just as freely. Biblical references abounded.

From the mouths and pens of the disfranchisers, clever, lettered witticisms cannot but seem trite, if not offensive. But from the mouths and pens of their victims—the poor, Republicans and Populists, and especially African Americans—these things can seem poignant.

Variations on "Katy, bar the door!"—an obscure expression of even murkier origin—surfaced more than once in the disfranchisement era. As a rhetorical device, it warns of doom, and Rev. Anderson McEwen, editor of Mobile's *Southern Watchman* (a prominent black paper), put the turn-of-phrase to arresting use when he explained that Supreme Court intervention was the only hope for African Americans. They had to drag the disfranchisers before the nation's highest bench, and if they failed in that endeavor, he warned in 1901, if the Court did not make things right, "it is katy with the Negro, mark our prediction."[16]

As the Gilded Age waned and the Progressive era waxed, Jim Crow's sun approached its zenith and the southern states stripped African American men of the vote, thus robbing them of their civic dignity. Combined with the indignity of segregation and the terror of Judge Lynch, this set the stage for the nadir period of the African American experience. But even at this darkest hour, many black political leaders and attorneys and preachers and activists fought back, desperate to save their ballots and their citizenship rights, and sustained that fight for the better part of two decades. As was mentioned previously, none of these disfranchisement era voting rights campaigns either constituted or inspired a movement. However, that resistance, which resulted in the antidisfranchisement cases, constituted a small, necessary, and instructive prelude to the civil rights movement.

Historians have neglected this story, but it is an important one nonetheless, and it is one of those stories that matters simply because it happened at all. Black protest campaigns and voting rights test cases always attended disfranchisement, but those protests and test cases languish at the margins of historical scholarship. Historians of the American South are aware that some of the antidisfranchisement cases happened, but these efforts are never presented as anything other than footnotes to the larger story of disfranchisement. Social and political historians of the United States have afforded them only passing mention. With rare exceptions, constitutional historians also have overlooked this episode. *Defying Disfranchisement,* however, rescues these cases and the activists that launched them from faded memory and restores them to the fore.

Constitutional and political historians and legal scholars may be disappointed to find that I've dabbled only lightly in theory. Social historians may be equally concerned that I have delved so deeply into the Latinate technicalities of constitutional law and of common-law civil procedure. However, as this project matured, I grew ever more convinced that this story has been forgotten (or at least underappreciated) because social and political historians do not understand the constitutional issues involved here and constitutional scholars know too little of these cases' grass-roots origins and the limitations and constraints those origins imposed upon this story's protagonists. So I sought the middle ground and have constructed a narrative history of black voting rights activism in the disfranchisement era around the story of the antidisfranchisement cases of 1895–1908.

Defying Disfranchisement begins in Mississippi and then follows the story through South Carolina, Louisiana, North Carolina, Alabama, and Virginia. But one state saw antidisfranchisement activity on a scale that exceeded the others—Alabama—and its story fills roughly half of these pages. Alabama yielded the single most important antidisfranchisement case, *Giles v. Harris,* Alabama had the best lawyer, Wilford Smith, and Alabama had Booker T. Washington. Washington was also involved in the Louisiana effort, but after 1900 he withdrew and focused on his home state. For Jackson Giles and Alabama's other antidisfranchisement activists, Washington's involvement meant better funding, better lawyering, and better contacts in the North.

The Alabama litigation far surpassed any other state's, and for that reason alone Alabama would command the most attention. But in this case, Washington's personal papers, both the fourteen volumes that Louis Harlan edited and the originals held by the Library of Congress (much of which were never published), preserve the only complete record we have of an antidisfranchisement campaign. Washington's papers similarly illumine much of the Louisiana story and fragments of Virginia's.

Beyond the Booker T. Washington Papers and other manuscript collections, court records (the actual papers and briefs collected by judges at that state and federal level), in addition to published appellate opinions, were obviously indispensable to this study. Then there are the newspapers, news magazines, and opinion journals. In many instances, newspapers provide the only remaining record of a particular event. Newspapers and other periodicals, however, can be problematic. Representative samples are hard to capture, susceptible as we historians are to judgments made long ago by librarians and archivists. Anyone who has ever tried to locate copies of southern African American newspapers can attest to that. Editors' and reporters' unspoken prejudices are always a concern, too, and I combated those by reading broadly and deeply. I cast a wide net, examining several hundred newspapers (published at the national, regional, state, and county levels) and scores of news magazines and journals (secular as well as religious), published in all regions and all states, and every extant African American publication. The coverage was extensive, revealing voices that, as often as possible, I have let speak for themselves.

Activists launched the antidisfranchisement cases to force the federal government's hand, hoping that it would bring southern disfranchisers to heel. The effort failed miserably. Presidents Benjamin Harrison, Grover Cleveland, William McKinley, and Theodore Roosevelt offered saccharine platitudes about the sanctity of the ballot and the need to treat all men fairly, irrespective of race. Yet they did not stem disfranchisement's advance. Republican senators and representatives consistently denounced disfranchisement. However, Congress fled from the issue. Then there was the U.S. Supreme Court. That august assembly resorted to extraordinary and embarrassing dodges, desperate to avoid any direct approach or firm declaration. The three branches of the U.S. government were veritably impotent when confronted by southern disfranchisement. Federal officials were too afraid of fickle constituents, and far too self-conscious about their limitations, to bring their power to bear against the forces of institutionalized white supremacy.

From their wallets, from their personal accounts, and into collection plates passed at revivalistic mass meetings, African Americans gave tens of thousands of their dollars to their fight. Most were of meager means and led lives of exhausting toil and material hardship, blighted by racist indignities. Still, they believed this to be a vital and necessary enterprise, a sound investment of money and time. They spent so much money and so much time on a losing proposition that it all could be seen as pointless. But it did not seem pointless to them.

I

We Must Either Fight or Submit

Phase One Begins

> We must either fight or submit.
> —*Beaufort (S.C.) New South,* March 7, 1895

Robert Sproule had campaigned hard to be Warren County, Mississippi's tax assessor, but when officials opened the ballot boxes and tallied the results of the 1892 county election, his opponent, R. A. Fredericks, prevailed by eight votes. Whispers flew furiously. Something was rotten in the Brunswick precinct. Seventy votes were cast there and all had an *X* by Fredericks's name. Apparently, many of those came from illiterate blacks. Col. B. G. Kiger, who supervised Brunswick, was later charged by Sproule of marking those ballots for Fredericks and colluding with his fellow precinct officials in depositing them in the Democratic ballot box. Sproule believed that a total of forty-one fraudulent ballots had been cast at Brunswick, but he proffered only seventeen as evidence. The other twenty-four did not matter; striking just those seventeen would guarantee Sproule a nine-vote victory.[1]

This was postdisfranchisement Mississippi, a place where black men's votes were not supposed to decide elections and where no illiterate men of any complexion were supposed to vote. Yet in Warren County black men's votes had just decided an election and at least forty-one illiterates had apparently cast ballots at one backwater precinct. That meant that disfranchisement's meaning and scope remained contested, and if those things remained unsettled, if what had happened at Brunswick proved to be in any way permissible under the new state constitution, it also meant that black Mississippians might yet mount a counterattack, or at least retain a political foothold in the face of the new constitution's restrictions and prohibitions.

For his part, Robert Sproule believed that Mississippi's 1890 constitution—the first of the disfranchisement constitutions adopted in the Jim Crow era—had settled things and that by helping illiterate men mark their ballots (or even letting them into the polling place), Colonel Kiger had defied the 1890 constitutional convention's clear intent. Sproule refused to stand aside quietly and let Fredericks have the office. He lawyered up, collected his evidence, and marched into court. In time, this gave rise to the first judicial examination of one of the southern states' disfranchisement constitutions.

Sproule's lawyer, state representative Lawson Magruder, had witnessed both disfranchisement's conception and birth. He was a member of the 1890 Mississippi legislature, which had approved a constitutional convention, and then was elected to the convention as an at-large delegate and helped disfranchise the state's blacks and poor whites. Democratic leaders—and Magruder was among them—billed disfranchisement as a miracle elixir, an antidote for elections fraud, ensuring that thenceforth only the best men (i.e., the best white men) would vote. The enfranchisement of the "negro race," convention president Solomon S. Calhoon reminded Magruder and the other delegates after they completed their work, had brought "stagnation, the enslavement of woman, the brutalization of man, animal savagery, [and] universal ruin." Calhoon was preaching to the choir. Mississippi's constitution made all of those things right, delegate after delegate proudly boasted. Mississippi was the first state to attempt such a thing—the effective nullification of the Fourteenth and Fifteenth Amendments—and more than one politician, and a host of editors and observers, doubted that it would work. They insisted that Mississippi would surely face congressional and federal judicial wrath for the violence they had done to the U.S. Constitution. But they need not worry, Calhoon reassured them. In closing the registration books to African Americans (or "the negro," as he always put it), they did so "with his full cooperation, and with his rights and franchises, as guaranteed by the organic Federal Compact, not only unimpaired, but fully protected." Calhoon's postmortem was transparent sophistry, a puerile and ludicrous confection, but it was exactly what Magruder and the others needed and wanted to hear and believe.[2]

The 1890 Mississippi constitution ensured, Magruder, Sproule, and nearly all other white Mississippians understood, that black men's votes would no longer decide elections—not because black men had voted freely before but because white partisans had always manipulated black men's votes as they saw fit. The situation had degenerated completely by the late 1880s, and the 1890 constitution was advertised as a corrective measure. With its adoption, Democratic victories would not require on-the-fly tricks, the mutilation of ballots, and ballot box molestation. Instead, elections registrars would handle all of the dirty work. They could register or dismiss whomever they chose.

The registrars' wide authority was derived from what the 1890 constitution had not said; the convention had not said exactly what the registrars could and could not do and who they could or could not register. The idea was to eliminate the old-time methods but not to outlaw them per se. Thus the voting provisions in Mississippi's 1890 constitution were opaque—at once detailed and vague—and again, this was deliberate. Any explicit proscriptions would likely have brought them into open conflict with the Fourteenth and Fifteenth Amendments to the U.S. Constitution. However, and despite all of this, seventeen illiterate black men had somehow tipped an election in R. A. Fredericks's favor and his opponent, Robert Sproule, was a sore and angry loser and sued him.[3]

The 1892 election was the first held under the new state constitution, but even so, Mississippi blacks were slow to react. There had been no widespread protests during the 1892 voter registration period, during the election, or in the election's aftermath. This was not just apathy; there were real reasons for Mississippi blacks' apparent nonresponse. For one, disfranchisement was incomplete in Mississippi. What happened at the Brunswick precinct demonstrated as much. Further, blacks continued to win Mississippi elections in the 1890s (though with as much frequency as angels' visits), they continued to register, and some sizable number actually voted, all of which undercut sweeping arguments that the 1890 constitution violated the U.S. Constitution. That would change in a few years' time, when Mississippi blacks tried to mobilize for an antidisfranchisement fight. In the immediate short term, it remained to be seen what Mississippi courts might do with Sproule and Fredericks and what that might mean for black Mississippians.

The case moved rapidly through the county circuit court and then on to the state supreme court. At trial in Vicksburg, Warren County's seat, Fredericks insisted that the Brunswick elections officers had done no more than what the new constitution permitted. The circuit court judge ruled in his favor. The judge also excluded Sproule's evidence of fraudulent ballots, and Sproule appealed to the Mississippi Supreme Court. Magruder repeated Sproule's original claims before the state supreme court and revisited the 1890 constitution's framing and adoption. There was a great deal of "gray" in the Mississippi constitution, and that was no accident. Elections officers had to have virtually unfettered authority to achieve what Mississippi's constitution could not state expressly: Black men's votes would not decide elections. But unfettered authority was just that—unfettered. It could work either way. Though the constitution prescribed a literacy test, it fixed no literacy standard. "Literacy," according to the 1890 constitution, was left so vague as to be meaningless and thus meant whatever any particular registrar, on any particular day, said it meant. Further, the 1890 constitution allowed any man who "understood" the privileges and nature of citizenship to register to vote. Then there was a provision that allowed elections officials to "assist" voters in the preparation and deposit of their ballots. These were all designed to give the appearance of allowing illiterate whites to register (and thus temper white opposition to the new constitution), but they could also be used by illiterate blacks. That appeared to have happened at the Brunswick precinct.[4]

Though it cannot but seem humane to have an official on hand to aid voters, that is not why Mississippi or any other southern state allowed (or forbade, in some cases) such assistance. Rather, "assistance" was just the door through which Democratic Party ballot thieves entered the polling place. They purchased or stole illiterate black men's ballots and marked them per the highest bidding candidate's instruction. Southern elections, as novelist John Henry Wallace described them in *The Senator from Alabama*, his fictionalized account of a disfranchisement era campaign, typically devolved into a "Carnival of the Ballot Box Stuffers." In Wallace's melodrama, Democratic operatives were "vampires that grew fat and slick as they smacked their lips and licked their gory chops," and through their frenzied manipulation of the ballot boxes, they "drank the life blood of all that was noble, grand and patriotic in the Democratic party." Black southerners also noted the presence of thieves. Ned Cobb, son of a black Alabama sharecropper, later recalled in his pseudonymous autobiography *All God's Dangers* that before his father was disfranchised, the old man had always sold his vote. Whites had not wanted the elder Cobb to be an informed citizen and did all they could to keep him ignorant and pliant and easily bought. "He was kept out of the knowledge of knowin'," his son recalled, "so that he would want to sell his vote because that was the only advantage he could get from votin.'" Other black men just wanted to make sure that no one thought that they had ever done such a thing. Louis Hamilton, a ninety-year-old former slave in Fredericktown, Missouri, told a 1930s Works Progress Administration (WPA) interviewer that no one had ever tried to keep him from voting, that he had cast his first vote for Theodore Roosevelt, and that "I been voting ever since." He was proud of his record and made it clear that the historical record showed that he had resisted the temptations of ballot fraud artists. "Lots of dem have told me how to vote," Hamilton continued, "but I never sold my vote." [5]

Mississippi's constitutional framers talked a lot about elections fraud, but fraud per se was not why they had holed themselves up in the stuffy, sweltering statehouse in Jackson in the late summer of 1890. Cleaning up elections would have required only that state officials crack down on the graft and violence that blighted elections in the black majority counties. But clean elections would be fair elections, and if Mississippi elections were fair, blacks would likely command a near-majority of state legislative seats. Instead, the disfranchisers would regulate the foul work of carrying elections for the Democracy. They could have attempted some sort of statutory revision, but they wanted something more permanent, something that would not be left in the hands of popularly elected sheriffs and state officials. Thus they chose to reform state elections through constitutional revision, altering the terms of state citizenship.

Some other southern states limited black voting rights through statutory revision, and it is common to view these efforts as part of the disfranchisement movement, even if they were not technically the same thing. Those statutory revisions were simply impediments and altered no fundamental right. Further, they typically targeted the conduct of elections rather than individual voters. Tennessee was the leader in this regard, and that state's Dortch Law targeted anyone who offered "assistance" to illiterate, ill-informed, or confused voters in the state's four urban counties.

The Dortch Law faced a Tennessee state supreme court challenge one year before *Sproule v. Fredericks*. Tennessee's Dortch Law, just as with Mississippi's 1890 constitution, also faced its first legal challenge courtesy of a white man. Julius Cook, a white man and a purported ballot thief, was indicted and prosecuted for marking the ballots of several illiterate *white* voters at the 1890 congressional election in Memphis. Cook challenged his indictment on grounds that the Dortch Law violated both the Tennessee state constitution's and the Fourteenth Amendment's privileges and immunities and equal protection clauses. Both Cook and his attorney understood and even alluded to the fact that the law targeted illiterate blacks. The Dortch Law only applied to the four counties that contained the state's four major cities—Shelby (Memphis), Hamilton (Chattanooga), Davidson (Nashville), and Knox (Knoxville)—which were home to most of Tennessee's black residents. Still, Cook's counsel paid relatively little attention to the racial motive behind the law. Instead, he emphasized the constitutional rights of illiterate men. Cook was a white man, after all, accused of marking ballots for other white men. In any event, the Tennessee Supreme Court was not impressed and sustained Cook's conviction.[6]

Like Tennessee's legislators two years earlier, Mississippi's disfranchisers talked a good game about reining in graft, and all of this emerged before the state supreme court. Unlike their Tennessee counterparts, however, they did not bother with the pretense of outlawing ballot fraud. They targeted blacks more directly, though they could not express that in terms without violating the Fourteenth and Fifteenth Amendments to the U.S. Constitution. This led them to adopt a literacy test and their infamous understanding clause, devices that let registrars exclude black voters and include whites however and whenever they saw fit.

The ministerial discretion that the Mississippi constitution allowed, Magruder and Sproule insisted, had been abused at the Brunswick precinct. The alleged rot, Fredericks countered, was permissible according to the 1890 constitution's text. What had happened, Magruder maintained, violated the spirit of its framers. He demanded that the state supreme court construe the constitution in light of its framers' promises and, unlike in the Tennessee case, confronted the convention's racial considerations squarely. The 1890 constitution provided leeway for the registrars as a way for them to admit more whites and exclude more blacks. This had been no secret, so "who can deny," Magruder's brief asked, that its purpose was to "relieve the white intelligent race . . . from the danger of ignorant . . . unlettered rule?"— unlettered and *black* rule, to be more precise. The 1890 constitutional convention had promised to discriminate against African Americans—Lawson Magruder was part of that promise, after all—and Sproule was determined to redeem that guarantee.[7]

That this case ever arose at all is remarkable, but it took a bizarre turn with Fredericks's reply. He could not defeat Sproule's evidence and did not bother to try. Instead, he lobbed a bombshell: The 1890 constitution was invalid. The constitution had never been ratified by the people of Mississippi, and, he continued, the convention's disfranchising efforts violated the 1870 congressional act readmitting Mississippi to the Union, which required that the state maintain a republican form of government (a primary of feature of which is a written constitution). Thus Mississippi's first disfranchisement case became its very first antidisfranchisement case as well, albeit far different from what we might have expected.[8]

R. A. Fredericks surely cared little about black voters beyond their capacity to supply him with pliant votes, yet the effect of his argument might have
worked—temporarily—in their favor. Still, Fredericks's claim amounted to
a desperate, victory-saving gambit, and Mississippi's unimpressed state supreme court justices swatted it away. "With confidence," Justice Woods
wrote, the court rejected his assertion as "unsound." Fredericks's counsel
argued that the constitution was invalid because it had not been ratified,
an assertion that the justices considered "imaginary and fanciful." Then he
argued that the constitution violated the 1870 readmission act, and the justices disposed of that as "manifestly untenable." Suffrage, they intoned, was
the exclusive province of the states. Having made short work of Fredericks's
stunt, the justices considered Sproule's evidence. It seemed persuasive, they
agreed, it was certainly germane, and the trial judge should have allowed it.
They reversed the lower court judge and remanded the matter. They did not
examine the framers' intent, the constitution's purpose, or the questions surrounding those seventeen ballots. With that, disfranchisement's courtroom
debut ended. It passed so quickly that almost no one noticed.[9]

The first two elections cases of the disfranchisement era had been initiated
by competing white men arguing over what one another had or had not
helped ostensibly disfranchised black men do. That is not what we would
expect to find; that is not what we would want to find; but that is what happened. As matters of law, *Sproule v. Fredericks* and *Cook v. State* were of little
consequence. As historical artifacts, however, both are instructive. This is
not because they are necessarily instructive but rather because of the questions they raise, questions about why no African American plaintiffs had yet
filed suit and whether blacks would or even could marshal a response.
    Blacks simply were not prepared to make a fight when Tennessee
amended its state statutes to restrict black voting in 1889 and when Mississippi imposed disfranchisement via its 1890 constitution. Many may not
have recognized or understood the need. Stunned by what was happening,
Mississippi's black community reacted slowly. And then once they did react,
they found that they did not necessarily know how to make a fight. No one,
actually, whether white or black, would have known how to do this. Voting rights activism of the kind needed here, voting rights litigation, and
the broader field of civil rights protest generally are art forms unto themselves. Southern blacks, once they awakened to what disfranchisement really meant, would have to discover that themselves, learning how to do these

things as they went and taking their lessons from defeat upon crushing defeat.

The heyday of antidisfranchisement activity came between 1894 and 1904. By 1894 groups of black activists in Mississippi and in South Carolina were making noises about mounting challenges to disfranchisement and those had run their course by 1898. Though every state's activists faced a steep learning curve, the incline was steeper and slicker for the Mississippians and South Carolinians. Together, the activity seen in those two states comprised Phase One of blacks' Jim Crow era fight to preserve their voting rights.

The false starts, halting progress, and bewildering strategic miscues that these first antidisfranchisement crusaders made are at once maddening and entirely understandable. Yet despite that, and though the two groups never collaborated, they shared three unmistakable traits. First, these initiatives were state centered and inward looking. There was no attempt to mobilize black southerners in general, and the only external support the principals cultivated was that of national Republican Party leaders. Second, these were almost exclusively Republican affairs, organized and conducted by African American GOP politicians and organizers. In South Carolina, a few Low Country conservative Democrats briefly lent their aid but played no sustained role. They cared only for their own power, engaged as they were in an ongoing intraparty quarrel with the radical Up Country "Reformers" led by Ben Tillman. In Mississippi, African American activists briefly flirted with Populists but nothing durable ever came of these half-hearted courtships. Third, test cases were always their initial goal and the story of black voting rights activism in the disfranchisement era is largely a story of the courts.

Whether the various groups of antidisfranchisement activists intended for judges to rectify things or whether they thought suits might provoke some congressional rescue of blacks' voting rights was often unclear. They sometimes apparently sought both and in other instances seemed unconcerned about which came first. Regardless, courtrooms—federal courtrooms especially—were always the favored venue. Courts were the best (or just the least bad) option available to them, but having made that choice they too often found their initiatives buried by a mass of Latinate technicalities. They lived by the courts, which meant that they would perish in the courts, and their labors typically died bloodless, juridical deaths wrought by a muffled succession of petitions, averments, and demurrers. Further, by taking the fight off of the streets and into courtrooms, activists risked losing (and did lose) the support of the rank and file, who were alienated by arcane legal protocol, confused by obscure forms of common-law practice, and disheartened by the glacial pace of appeals and the frozen countenances of appellate judges.

The South Carolinians were the first to make it into court. Under the leadership of former congressman George Washington Murray, one of the last African Americans to represent the South in Congress in the nineteenth century, blacks mounted a preemptive assault against that state's disfranchisers that originated with the 1894 state elections. In its initial stages, it exploited a division between Conservatives and Ben Tillman's Reformers. That year's election was dominated by Tillman's U.S. Senate campaign against the incumbent, Matthew C. Butler, by Tiliman's efforts to install Gary Evans as his gubernatorial successor, and by his crusade to elect a pro-disfranchisement legislature. Black South Carolinians, along with Tillman's nemeses, opposed his triple ambitions, and the Tillmanites' efforts to suppress black votes were well documented by subsequent congressional investigations.[10]

After Tillman defeated Matthew Butler in the Democratic primary, Butler initiated a series of suits to invalidate the 1894 general election results. Butler brought two cases to the South Carolina Supreme Court, one in his own interest and the other on behalf of Sampson Pope, an unsuccessful Democratic gubernatorial candidate. The cases, styled as *Ex parte Lumsden* and *Butler v. Ellerbe*, each challenged an 1893 revision of South Carolina's elections laws and each failed.[11]

In challenging that 1893 statute, which was much akin to Tennessee's Dortch Law, Matthew Butler was not concerned for African Americans' voting rights per se. Like Robert Sproule and Lawson Magruder in their Mississippi case of one year earlier, Butler's primary interest lay in resuscitating his own political career. And he, like Sproule and Magruder and so many other long-serving southern Democratic politicians of that era, relied, to a great extent upon a large, disadvantaged pool of African American voters whose ballots could, when needed, be manipulated by corrupt and well-connected Democratic elections managers. Likewise, Congressman Murray would not have been as interested in Matthew Butler's senatorial tenure as in protecting his and other black politicians' own interests (something about which Senator Butler certainly cared little). Murray, a Republican, represented a heavily black district in eastern South Carolina. He also needed a large population of black voters, though for a different reason. Butler simply wanted to use them; Murray could not win office without their support because white South Carolinians were not going to send a black man to Congress. Thus Butler's cases demonstrate nothing more than a simple convergence of interests.

Matthew Butler was a three-term U.S. senator and owed his eighteen-year tenure to the very same system he now challenged, something no one overlooked. Tillmanites scoffed, dismissing his efforts as "a futile attempt to retain his seat," and Butler, when pressed to explain he was motivated by conscience or convenience, pled ignorance. "To tell you the truth," he said of the 1893 election laws, "I never read them or knew what was in them until very recently." Butler then revealed that his problem was not so much the 1893 statutes (or the ones they replaced, which were no less antiblack) as the idea that someone like Ben Tillman controlled them. "For years things ran along very smoothly," he explained, "until the Tillmanites . . . got hold of the machinery." After those first three cases failed to yield fruit, Butler invited a U.S. Senate investigation of the 1894 senatorial and gubernatorial contests. No investigation was immediately forthcoming. Butler's work was done. Yet though his cases had failed, the fight had not ended, and South Carolina black leaders stepped to the fore.[12]

Meanwhile, Tillman's forces moved with alacrity. On Christmas Eve 1894, the new state legislature passed an enabling act for a constitutional convention, scheduled a delegates election for the summer of 1895, and created special voter registration requirements for the same. The latter was designed as a way to pack as many sympathetic whites as possible onto (and bar as many blacks as possible from) the voting rolls. Time was short. Thus there was far greater urgency than the previous fall, when *Lumsden* and *Butler* had been filed. So activists lined up and raised monies for an antidisfranchisement effort organized and led by Congressman Murray. Murray's chief lieutenants in this work were the preachers, and they conducted their work zealously. The newspapers, too, quickly fell into line and demanded, according to the *Beaufort New South*'s editor, that "we must either fight or submit."[13]

The South Carolina fight moved in a blur. There were no pauses, no delays; the whole thing swept along in a spirited rush. Inspired by Murray's organization, African Americans first resisted the convention and the special registration by trying to register as voters, and not surprisingly, Tillmanite registrars held their ground. Blacks were turned away in droves, and in due course there were a series of challenges filed against local registration boards. When those too failed, they gave rise to a substantial legal test—the first that African Americans had initiated.[14]

The first of three federal cases owing to Murray's efforts, *Wiley v. Sinkler*, asked for money damages from the state elections officials who had blocked Daniel Wiley's voting in the 1894 congressional elections. Wiley demanded compensation for an infringement of his Fourteenth Amendment rights and could only succeed by persuading a federal judge that South Carolina's voting restrictions violated the U.S. Constitution and that a dollar value could be placed on a man's vote. Though money damages were the ostensible aim of this suit, its real object was a court review of South Carolina's election laws. Wiley would only win, and claim those damages, if he persuaded a court that the South Carolina statute violated the U.S. Constitution. The case did not receive an immediate hearing, did not reach the U.S. Supreme Court until late 1898, and did not yield a satisfactory result. The Court dismissed Wiley's suit as moot (because the congressman elected in 1894 had completed his term) but also affirmed that disfranchised voters could bring claims for damages to the federal courts. It was a small victory, but one saddled by a larger loss. There never was a full airing of Wiley's constitutional claims.[15]

The more virile and consequential South Carolina case was the second that resulted from Murray's labors. *Mills v. Green* attacked disfranchisement by attempting to derail the 1895 convention itself. *Mills* was preemptive and aggressive and dramatic, but it was also indirect. It did not question whether South Carolina could revise the suffrage; it did not examine potential suffrage restrictions. Instead, it targeted the Christmas Eve 1894 enabling act and the special registration prescribed therein.

The act's practical effect, attorneys Henry Obear and Charles Douglass (the same two white lawyers from Winnsboro who had handled Senator Butler's two suits) argued, was to nullify the Fourteenth Amendment's due process and privileges and immunities clauses. The Tillmanites designed the statute to preclude blacks from the delegates election, Obear and Douglass insisted. Prospective voters had to show that they had registered *and* voted in each state election held since they reached voting age or settled in the state. It was difficult enough for any man to document his entire voting history. It was harder still for a poor or working-class man (who more likely than not was black) to do so given the often transient nature of farm labor and shift work. That had been the whole point of the new law.[16]

Mills v. Green, like *Wiley v. Sinkler,* involved the Fourteenth Amendment alone, which at first glance seems counterintuitive. It is not that the Fourteenth seems to have no relevance, but the Fifteenth Amendment was, after all, intended as a protection for African American men's voting rights. Yet the antidisfranchisement litigators did not find it useful, primarily because it had not been litigated extensively, unlike the Fourteenth Amendment.

The Fourteenth Amendment (with regard to voting) had succeeded to the extent that no state dared to adopt voting qualifications that turned explicitly on race. Literacy tests, understanding clauses, poll taxes, and the like did not necessarily offend the late-nineteenth-century American civic sensibility and were employed nationwide. Southern states, however, used those tests as racial proxies to a degree and with an effect not seen elsewhere. Central and eastern European immigrants in the Northeast and Asian immigrants in the West were expressly targeted by these restrictions, but their situation was not exactly analogous to that of southern blacks.[17] They were most certainly "differentiated others," to use the academic term of art, but they were a different kind of "other." Those immigrant groups were recent arrivals, spoke different languages, and carried wildly divergent cultural traditions. African Americans, however, were Americans by birth. They had been in North America as long as white Americans, and amendments to the Constitution had been drafted for their especial protection. At the same time, and as a matter of law and of constitutional interpretation, these impediments to voting were the same and none had been subjected to extensive judicial review. Thus, as the disfranchisement era dawned, the Supreme Court had never yet decided whether the inexplicit racial and cultural proxies embodied in various states' statutory and constitutional voting regulations violated either the Fifteenth Amendment's explicit prohibitions or the Fourteenth Amendment's broader mandates. Until the Court did decide, those proxies violated neither as a matter of law.[18]

Armed with their Fourteenth Amendment–based briefs, Obear and Douglass requested an injunction from the U.S. district court in Lawrence Mills's name on April 13, 1895. Mills was a twenty-six-year-old resident of Richland County, a tailor by trade, living in Columbia's Fourth Ward. He had not registered to vote in 1888, the year reached voting age, and thus, per the statute, he could not register. He had tried to register several times but was never allowed to make the attempt. The registration office always closed before he (and presumably many other blacks) could file an application. Mills, and Obear and Douglass, believed that this violated the Fourteenth Amendment and gave him standing to challenge the decision in federal court, and they duly asked for an injunction to block further voter registration.[19]

Mills v. Green was a strong case, made even more so because of an extremely solicitous federal judge. Ordinarily it would have come before U.S. District Judge Charles Simonton of Charleston, but Simonton and Mills's attorneys preferred that he not hear the matter. They deferred instead to Judge Nathan Goff of the Fourth U.S. Circuit Court of Appeal, though "not from any suggestion of my part yet with my full consent," Simonton explained to Goff. Simonton and the lawyers were afraid that any decision of his adverse to Tillman would have disastrous political implications. Judge Simonton (a scion of the state's conservative Democratic establishment) had previously clashed with Tillman in a battle over the state's dispensary laws (which regulated the sale and purchase of alcohol) and Tillman, Simonton continued, "has poisoned the minds of his people so much that they look upon any decisions as controlled by a partisan devotion to the 'Antis.'"[20]

Goff, a West Virginia Republican, had come to Columbia to referee the ongoing dispensary dispute between Tillman and his conservative Democratic enemies (involving the state dispensary laws) and really could not refuse. He received Mills's initial complaint on April 19, and on April 20 he enjoined Green from administering the 1894 enabling act. Columbia's *State*, in an editorial titled "Honesty's Hope," welcomed Goff's inquiry but regretted that state affairs had reached such a low point. The *State* was a Democratic paper, but it was no friend of the Tillmanites. "We have been imbued with an earnest devotion to the principle of State Rights," the editor explained, but he believed that the enabling act was "a State Wrong." He regretted that "this appeal . . . is made in the name of Republicans and negroes," but thought it would ultimately benefit Democrats and white men. Goff subsequently scheduled a hearing that South Carolina governor Gary Evans promised to treat "with the contempt it deserves." Irrespective of Goff's decision, he vowed, he would enforce the laws of the state, including the special registration statute. "If I am in contempt of Judge Goff," Evans continued, self-satisfyingly, "he must make the most of it." Of the hearing it was said that Henry Obear and Charles Douglass "riddled the laws with legal shot from no end of authorities." South Carolina Attorney General William Barber did not impress, and confined himself to trite arguments about federal jurisdiction. Goff was not moved.[21]

This was all new. There were no controlling precedents either to guide or constrain Goff and he relished this free hand. He could have begged off. Judges of inferior courts typically defer to superior appellate courts in situations such as this, especially when confronted with such a charged social and political issue. The American legal system depends upon precedent. Lawyers and judges compass their work according to higher court opinions, and unlitigated statutes or constitutional provisions provide no such direction. Judges do not like to fill jurisprudential voids, especially a void as controversial as this. Not so Nathan Goff. He attacked directly, basing his decision upon the Fourteenth Amendment's history and adoption. Congress designed the amendment, he remembered, for the freedmen's protection, and by virtue of their offices, United States judges must enforce Congress' design.

Goff never doubted that South Carolina's legislature had flouted the Fourteenth Amendment. This was not because the briefs necessarily showed that this had happened, but rather because he understood the situation as an observer of South Carolina politics. That was an extraordinary thing for a late-nineteenth-century judge to do. The formalist doctrines that they operated under eschewed judicial knowledge of the facts of case, demanding that judges adhere to truths that were "revealed" through close study of statutes, constitutions, sundry well-worn and universally relied-upon treatises, and established precedent. Disregarding all of that, Goff *knew* that the revised statute could not but disadvantage black applicants and he observed that even "our most intelligent voters would dread this ordeal," since with "crushing force . . . must it strike the weaker race, which is thus made to suffer by the stronger." As for the claims of Attorney General Barber and the governor that his was a "foreign court," Goff retorted that "this is as much a court of the state of South Carolina as is the circuit or supreme court of that state." That the U.S. Circuit Court for the District of South Carolina "should be regarded" as foreign, he wrote of the case and the larger political drama unfolding around him, "is wonderful in the extreme, and as strange as is the story relative to which it is about to enter its decision."[22]

"Slaying the Vulture" was how the *State* began the headlines for its coverage of the injunction. Goff had, at least temporarily, restrained the winged beast "Which Has Been Tearing at the Vitals of the Fraud-Fettered Body of Carolina." Wherever there were opponents of Ben Tillman, and wherever there were friends of African Americans and the U.S. Constitution, there was rejoicing over Goff's decision. Down in Savannah, Georgia, the *Tribune* (an African American paper) rejoiced that the "South Carolina conspirators" who had plotted against the Fourteenth and Fifteenth Amendments "have received a slap in the face which they richly merited."[23]

Goff may as well have stepped right out of the antidisfranchisement activists' dreams, and his bold and daring decision occasioned thanksgiving from South Carolina's black community. Blacks regarded the decision, the *Raleigh News and Observer* complained, "as in the nature of a new emancipation." They raised Goff's name heavenward over and again in the following weeks. At Centenary Church in Columbia, a mass meeting thanked God for Nathan Goff and adopted a series of celebratory resolutions. They offered hosannas for George Washington Murray and his allies too, of course, but in Goff's decision, they declared, "we recognize the hand of God." There was political praise as well. A West Virginia U.S. senator, Stephen B. Elkins, launched a favorite son presidential boomlet for the judge in late May, and in August a "large negro convention" met in Columbia to "nominate" Goff for president in 1896. Rev. E. H. Hart did the nominating, describing Goff as the "savior of the negro race." The convention, one news account reported, "went wild at the mention of Goff's name."[24]

When given a chance to pen the next line of this, in his words, "strange story," Nathan Goff insisted that Congress designed the Fourteenth Amendment for the especial benefit of the freedmen and their descendants and that states could not void its purpose. His political résumé qualified him to speak for the so-called Radical Republicans, who had pushed for its adoption. Nathan Goff was himself a bona fide Radical Republican. He had been active in Republican Party politics since Reconstruction and had won the West Virginia Republican Party's gubernatorial nomination twice (and lost the general election twice) and served in the West Virginia legislature and on the national level as U.S. Attorney for West Virginia, navy secretary under President Rutherford Hayes, U.S. representative, and judge of the Fourth U.S. Circuit Court of Appeal. Goff remained on the bench until 1912, when West Virginia voters sent him to the U.S. Senate. When he traveled to Columbia in the spring of 1895 and was confronted with South Carolina's constitutional convention enabling act, he remained true to his Republican roots when he ruled in Lawrence Mills's favor.[25]

Goff made his injunction permanent, restraining Briggs Green (and with him all of South Carolina's registrars) from enforcing the registration provisions of the 1894 enabling act. Nathan Goff wrote the first federal judicial word on southern disfranchisement and had placed his court squarely behind disfranchised blacks. "No such blow to state's rights," *Outlook* magazine

editorialized, had "been given in years," and that ensured renewed white an-
tipathy toward Goff, federal courts, and black voters. Democrats rushed to
stop him. They fought him in appellate courts and the court of public opinion, and some simply wanted him removed. Had Goff or any other federal
judge attempted such a thing twenty years earlier, *Raleigh News and Observer* editor Josephus Daniels surmised, Congress would have impeached
him—and, Daniels groused, "he ought to be impeached now."[26]

Governor Evans and Senator Tillman, upon learning of Goff's decision,
flew into an apoplectic rage and made vague threats of violent revolution.
Nathan Goff returned to his Clarksburg, West Virginia, home and offered
no public comment on his injunction. Privately, Judge Charles Simonton
reassured him that his *Mills* decision had been wise and welcomed. "Very
many believe," Simonton explained, making clear his anti-Tillman sentiments, that "your decree affords a chance of escape from a vulgar tyranny
which bids fair to dominate the State."[27]

The state immediately appealed Goff's ruling to the Fourth Circuit in
Richmond. Contrary to modern sensibilities regarding recusal and propriety, Goff could have presided over this appeal. There was no official prohibition against his doing so, but the extraordinary circumstances of this
case rendered his appearance problematic, just as when Judge Simonton re-
cused himself earlier, so he requested Chief Justice Melville Weston Fuller's
presence in his stead (Fuller was the Supreme Court justice assigned to the
Fourth Circuit). Fuller agreed but was decidedly nonplused. "I suppose the
case is important," he replied to Judge Goff. "I ought to do this if I can."
There would be three judges on the panel: Fuller, Robert William Hughes
of Virginia's Eastern District, and Sherrill Seymour of North Carolina's
Eastern District.[28]

Congressman Murray and his associates had thus far gotten exactly what
they wanted—a friendly federal judge, a lower court ruling that turned upon
federal questions, and a strong chance of a U.S. Supreme Court appeal, but
they mounted no sustained campaign of public pressure. Reporters were interested in the cases, lawyers were interested in the cases, but lay observers
and the black voters who had the most to gain (and lose) apparently fell silent. There were no rallies, no demonstrations in support of Lawrence Mills
or against disfranchisement. The activist ranks were sorely limited, and because this type of organization and activity was new, their actions were
limited as well. They had sought a court review, and once they had it they
ceded the stage. They were apparently content to let judges and lawyers find

the "right" answer on their own. So judges and lawyers took over and did what they do: trade in legalisms and technicalities. The voices of protest fell silent—for whatever reason—and so the story of *Mills* thenceforth became one of pleadings and counterpleadings and strained references to obscure precedents.

The merits of Mills's case received little attention in Richmond. Attorney General Barber argued that Goff had exceeded his jurisdiction and that the case presented no clear federal question; Obear and Douglass argued that the Fourth Circuit did not have jurisdiction over the appeal. Since Mills's petition concerned a South Carolina statute and its possible contravention of the U.S. Constitution, they asserted that only the U.S. Supreme Court was competent to hear the matter. What this all meant was that they clearly did not trust the Fourth Circuit. All involved agreed that the sooner a decision came down the better. "Our people are very much excited and exercised," Barber explained about Goff's injunction, over "this sudden annulling of the registration law." Yet there was no immediate decision.[29]

No one understood the judges' silence and all of the principals were frustrated by it. Given the great weight of the issue before them, some acknowledgment of its import was imperative, but Fuller remained staunchly silent for two weeks. On June 10, Fuller sent Judge Hughes a preliminary order in "accordance with our conclusion" that he wanted released immediately. The decree reversed Goff and untied the registrars' hands. Fuller's two-paragraph-long pronouncement offered nothing to clarify his reasoning. Since they did not know upon what he had based it, Mills's attorneys could not prepare a U.S. Supreme Court appeal, and this was a real danger because they wanted to get to Washington before the election occurred and before the convention was seated. The governor and attorney general, who knew they would have to defend against that appeal, were similarly disadvantaged.

When Judge Hughes released Fuller's preliminary order on June 11, he offered his own concurring opinion. Goff freely embraced things he himself knew to be true, but Hughes fell back upon formalist rationalizations about Mills's original complaint (he noted that nothing in the record "showed" that Mills was a "man of color," for example). Jurisdiction, however, was the primary tool employed by the Fourth Circuit. This was a political case and these judges did not want federal courts to involve themselves in political campaigns. Goff had wanted to wrap African Americans with the protection of judicial ermine, asserting his jurisdiction over the conduct of state elections when those elections were predicated upon unconstitutional enactments. Hughes allowed that a personal claim for damages from Lawrence Mills may have been another matter entirely, but enjoining a statewide election was out of the question. "I can imagine nothing more pernicious," Hughes stated, "than a direct participation by the judiciary . . . in the politics of the people." It sounded logical, but it was really just trite. Mills had not asked the federal judiciary to participate in a state election, he had asked that federal judges invalidate an unconstitutional state law.[30]

Hughes's statement was a direct repudiation of Goff, and Fuller, in his subsequent final order, agreed. The chief justice insisted that federal courts had to stay out of state and local politics and, also like Hughes, found Mills's evidence unpersuasive. It is likelier, frankly, that he did not *want* to be persuaded and concluded that Mills's complaint claimed "no threatened infringement of rights of property or civil rights," ignoring the fact that the very purpose of Mills's case was to ameliorate just such a threat. Where Goff was willing to act upon what he knew to be true, Fuller stubbornly, and to a degree conveniently, refused to do likewise. He said that Goff had not demonstrated any danger to his civil rights but gave no indication of what proper proof might look like. Reflecting Judge Hughes's rather odd concern with whether Mills had proven himself black, the chief justice invoked the Fifteenth Amendment when he complained that he had seen "no specific evidence" of "discrimination on account of race, color, or previous condition of servitude."[31]

Tillman, Barber, Evans, and other state officials were, of course, delighted. But not everyone was happy. Goff himself took the extraordinary step of writing a letter to Joseph Pulitzer's *New York World*, contending that his original injunction had been misunderstood (he claimed that he had not forbidden the delegates election) and that the Fourth Circuit had not questioned his findings of fact. Rather, the judge wrote, the Fourth Circuit had only taken issue with his use of the injunctive power and his decision to accept the claim in equity, as they believed that an adequate legal remedy already existed. This was a curious argument for Goff to make because the circuit court had taken exception with everything that he decided in *Mills* and it was evident to everyone that he had, in fact, forbidden the delegates election. The Fourth Circuit clearly objected to Goff's interference with a state election; that was exactly the effect of his injunction. Yet in his *World* letter, Goff claimed that he had not "enjoined the holding of an election in that State." Rather, he offered, he had only held that "all citizens of South

Carolina . . . were entitled to cast their ballots at such election, and that the illegal requirements of the registration laws of said State should not be used to prevent them from so doing." This was curious, because by enjoining registration for that election, he necessarily enjoined the election. The *World* had been extremely critical of Goff's original injunction and continued that criticism throughout the episode. As one of the nation's largest and most influential newspapers, the "Thrice Weekly *World*" was as good a place as any for a judge to explain himself, though choosing to explain himself was something that Judge Goff probably should not have done. The *World*'s editor quickly published the letter and a biting retort thereto—complete with direct quotations from Goff's original injunction. Goff's assertions in his letter were tortured at best. "To speak with entire frankness," the editor wrote, "unless the published reports of his decision are utterly wrong he now seriously misstates the facts." The judge, his home state's *Wheeling Register* offered, "has not improved his position by mixing himself up with the *New York World,* which seems to be pretty thoroughly posted on the subject." Still, the judge did not have to look far to find sympathizers. Judge Simonton, for one, wrote Goff to complain that "I can see no authority" for the Fourth Circuit's decision.[32]

The U.S. circuit court's decision had raised the ire of many legal observers and commentators. Beyond the evidentiary issues, there was the shocking notion that courts could not prevent otherwise justiciable injuries. "It is vain," the widely read *Central Law Journal* complained, "for a court to say that there is an adequate remedy at law when the injury will be completed before the remedy can be applied and when it is of an irreparable character." African Americans were the most dismayed of all. Concurring in the 1890s emigrationist impulse amongst many southern blacks, a group of prospective émigrés planned a meeting in Columbia to discuss a responsive exodus. "Propose to Emigrate: South Carolina Negroes Say They Must Move to Another State," an *Atlanta Constitution* headline explained.[33]

The Fourth Circuit's disposition of *Green v. Mills* highlighted a trio of concerns that would emerge in all antidisfranchisement litigation. These all had to do with legal practice, and all may seem impenetrable. This was heightened by the fact that there were as yet no prescribed rules of federal civil procedure). These cases were all conducted through common-law forms (averments, demurrers, etc.) and under common-law rules of evidence that were literally, in some cases, medieval. First, there was the problem of hypotheticals, of showing that an enactment was unconstitutional based upon how state officers *could* misuse it rather than demonstrating that something unconstitutional had actually happened. Any attempt to preempt disfranchisement would trigger this. In *Mills,* Fuller (and Hughes and Seymour) certainly understood what South Carolina intended to do, but the complaint itself showed no specific evidence of discrimination. Indeed, it could not have: The point of *Mills* had been to prevent discrimination rather than to correct a discrimination that had already occurred. Second, *Mills* relied upon context, of common knowledge of current news events, and the chief justice made clear that common knowledge was not enough to drag federal courts into a matter. There had to be "real" evidence for every claim—everything had to be documented somehow, even a man's claim of African ancestry. Third, federal judges (Nathan Goff excepted) did not want to interfere with either state elections or state constitutions, especially in connection with charged social questions. All of these obscured, and even heightened, the fundamental injustice involved, but these recurrent problems had to be addressed. Judges' aversion to preempting *possible* equal protection violations, their exacting yet ill-explained evidentiary demands, and the courts' refusal to interfere in state elections were higher hurdles than the pioneering antidisfranchisement litigators immediately understood or, arguably, could have anticipated.

Make no mistake—*Green v. Mills* was devastating, but it was not the end. Murray was determined to continue, and besides, it was only July. There was still time to launch a second challenge. A mass meeting sponsored by the Colored Ministerial Union had already been scheduled for July 10, and it was quickly reorganized. There reportedly was "a good deal of wild talk" from black officeholders and "some talk among colored politicians of a wholesale exodus of colored men" who wanted to threaten the state with the loss of their labor force. Congressman Murray and the preachers, however, worked to tamp that down and to reassure the faithful. *Mills* would still reach the Supreme Court, Murray noted in an open letter, and the "ablest lawyers in the land are at a loss to comprehend" the circuit court's decision. He assured his readers that the case was sound. He wanted all counties represented on July 10 because black South Carolinians in every precinct had to be "fully informed, so that each might do his full duty in the great battle now raging." As for those black politicians who were muttering about emigration, Murray demanded that they set aside personal ambition and "sink self out of sight," recognizing that in the grander scheme, in the face of this calamity, "they themselves are nonentities."[34]

Obear and Douglass would appeal Mills's case to the U.S. Supreme Court. In the meantime, a second attempt to obstruct the convention was prepared, and Obear and Douglass returned to Judge Goff with the case of *Joseph H. Gowdy v. W. Briggs Green.* Joseph Gowdy was an African American minister and, like most pastors, did not have complete control over his place of residence. He depended upon the congregations that called him to serve, and constant relocations meant that Briggs Green and other registrars could easily demand practically unattainable proof of residence. Without such proof, they could deny him registration, and did. In abstract terms, the sin in requiring proof of residence is not easily seen. However, the reason for adopting that requirement was to create yet one more way to disqualify poor and often itinerant blacks. By using Joseph Gowdy, the attorneys could also challenge the requirement as arbitrary and force the state to explain why preachers, for example, must be disfranchised on account of their chosen profession or economic condition. Gowdy's bill for injunction—a request that the election be blocked—was virtually identical to Mills's, except that, in light of what had happened before the Fourth Circuit in *Mills,* Obear and Douglass tried to show more specific evidence of racial discrimination (though no one yet knew how that was properly to be done). They delivered the injunction to Goff's chambers in Clarksburg, West Virginia, and he agreed to hear their arguments once more. He again enjoined Green and scheduled a hearing for August 5 in Richmond.[35]

The August 5 hearing took place as scheduled and Goff promised a decision the next day. The judge was no less sympathetic than he had been earlier that year. In the spring, he had been given the first shot at disfranchisement and had blasted away at its heart. But just weeks later he was overruled, and now another Latinate obstacle, stare decisis (the principle that courts must obey precedents set by superior courts), stood in his way. The judge's personal views of disfranchisement were well known (he elucidated them fully in *Mills*), but though he was bound by the Fourth Circuit's decision, that did not mean that he could not complain from the bench. He was "unable to find the reason or the authority for and by which" the Fourth Circuit dissolved his earlier ruling. Goff had studied Chief Justice Fuller's opinion and did not understand his reasoning: "I will not concede that it is proper to close the doors" of U.S. courts to "citizens who are complaining that they are deprived by the states of their rights and privileges guaranteed to them by the constitution of the United States." State courts, Goff surmised, could not be trusted to offer relief "from the outrages imposed by

the unconstitutional enactments of such states." Yet he concluded that had
to reject Reverend Gowdy's petition. Factually and legally, *Gowdy* was too
similar to *Mills*.[36]

Gowdy had turned out badly, the South Carolina Supreme Court had rejected *Lumsden* and *Butler,* and the Fourth Circuit had undone Mills's initial victory. The South Carolina litigation was still not over, however, since
Wiley was still alive (though stalled), and in September Lawrence Mills appealed to the U.S. Supreme Court. Obear and Douglass, in a letter made
public by Congressman Murray in mid-August, pleaded for financial assistance to cover the costs of the case. They admitted only to optimism and ral-
lied the troops: "Having embarked upon this sea of registration litigation let
us not rest until we reach the haven of a full decision by the Supreme Court
of the United States." Just weeks earlier, South Carolina had staged the delegates election, and by the time that the Court announced its decision in
Mills v. Green on November 25, the state's 1895 constitutional convention
had met, deliberated, written a new constitution, and adjourned. *Mills* only
challenged the delegates election and that canvass had already happened.
The state, responding to Mills's initial brief to the Court, moved for a dismissal on grounds of mootness: The very deed that Mills hoped to prevent
had already been done.[37]

In June, when the matter came before the Fourth Circuit, Chief Justice
Fuller reversed Goff's injunction because the delegates election had not yet
happened and thus had not injured Lawrence Mills. Now, subsequent to
that election, and subsequent to his injury, the Supreme Court turned down
his appeal because, it held, the registration requirements were dead letters.
Technically, the Court did not even review the substance of Mills's complaint. The South Carolina litigation had reached its effective end. There
was no "yea" or "nay" vote on disfranchisement. Instead, the justices sought,
and found, a dodge. Their decision was unanimous: The matter was moot.
As such, Justice Horace Gray explained, "even if the bill could properly be
held to present a case within the jurisdiction of the circuit court, no relief
could now be granted."[38]

As the *Natchez Brotherhood* (an African American paper) had editorialized several weeks earlier, South Carolina was "first in fanaticism and the
one-sided idea that the negro is fit only to be a slave." From far away in Mississippi, where disfranchisement had begun four years earlier, the *Brotherhood* maintained that the U.S. Constitution, "grand and glorious, venerable as it is, overshadows us all, and the Palmetto state cannot make it

a nullity, a sham and a reproach." Yet South Carolina's 1895 "disfranchising" constitution had done just that, and it took effect nine days after the Court announced *Mills*. The Palmetto State had nullified the U.S. Constitution, despite the *Brotherhood*'s prediction to the contrary, and despite the efforts of the South Carolina activists and Judge Goff, the U.S. Supreme Court had refused to stop it. The "wrongs and injustices done the negro will be righted," that editorial had concluded, "just as surely as God reigns in heaven." No such intervention seemed imminent, however, and it was not clear whether anyone in South Carolina would keep up the fight. Omaha, Nebraska's *Enterprise,* another African American paper, urged South Carolina blacks to press on, "to test the law," and demanded that "every colored man and liberty loving white man" lend their aid, but no test of South Carolina's 1895 constitution could be made until the new suffrage qualifications went into effect. Moreover, the South Carolina activists' energies seemed to have been sapped.[39]

There were few precedents upon which to build a legal crusade such as this and so it was very much a learn-as-you-go affair. Lessons came in threes for the antidisfranchisement litigators, and the next trinity emerged after the U.S. Supreme Court had disposed of *Mills*. These had to do with how the Court avoided unpleasant and controversial issues. Prior to 1925, the Supreme Court had to accept nearly all of the thousands of appeals sent its way. The justices could not simply decline review of a case and so they found ways to avoid appeals that either wasted their time, tried their patience, or threatened embarrassment. To avoid uncomfortable cases such as *Mills,* the Court strained to divine, devise, and seize convenient dodges.

First, *Mills* and *Gowdy* each violated the Political Questions Doctrine (PQD), introduced in 1803 by Chief Justice John Marshall in *Marbury v. Madison* and later perfected by the Taney court in 1849's *Luther v. Borden*. Under this doctrine, political questions (i.e., election disputes), the Court declared, were "to be settled by the political power." This meant that the Court would ignore (if it could) and wiggle away from (if it could not) electoral disputes. It might comment upon, or even attempt to settle, controversial political *issues* (*Dred Scott* being the most spectacularly disastrous example of this impulse), but it sought no part in political *campaigns*. This distinction will surely seem too fine to some, but it was no trifling matter for the antidisfranchisement fight was the very definition of a political question.

Accordingly, antidisfranchisement litigators would be forced into a bizarre sequence of footwork in order to dance around the PQD.[40]

Second, *Mills* ventured into relatively unknown territory. The boundaries and scope of the Fourteenth Amendment, regarding political rights, remained inchoate in 1895. Judge Nathan Goff believed that the Fourteenth Amendment should be construed in favor of disfranchised blacks, but he really could have ruled either way. Litigators and judges preferred to deal with precedents, but there were none to guide him; the Supreme Court had not yet decided how far it would, or would not, go to enforce the "equal protection," "due process," and "privileges and immunities" clauses of the Fourteenth Amendment with respect to the political process. In the South Carolina cases, it treated disfranchisement as a political campaign rather than as a political issue.

Third, there were evidentiary problems in both *Mills* and *Gowdy*, namely, the matter of proving as a matter of law that which everyone knew as a matter of common knowledge. Chief Justice Fuller, in the Fourth Circuit appeal, had noted Lawrence Mills's failure to show specific evidence of both racial discrimination and of an actual, remediable injury. He insisted that Mills had not proven either his race or that any injury resulted therefrom, but he did not indicate how that might be done.

As *Mills* met its end, in one of those creeping, shifting conclusions that typified the earliest antidisfranchisement efforts, the spotlight shifted to Mississippi, and the legal strategy behind antidisfranchisement test cases shifted as well. The Fourteenth Amendment remained the constitutional basis for attack, but the Mississippi litigation did not turn directly upon voting rights. The Mississippi cases harkened back to a line of Fourteenth Amendment–based landmark cases from the 1880s that forbade the exclusion of blacks from jury service. *Strauder v. West Virginia* and *Neal v. Delaware* were the two most significant of four 1880 cases treating the issue of black jury service. *Strauder* invalidated a state statute limiting jury service to whites on Fourteenth Amendment equal protection grounds; *Neal* (as well as the lesser-known *Ex parte Virginia*) saw the Supreme Court hold that practical exclusion, whether stated in terms or not, was no less an equal protection violation. These three were tempered, however, by a fourth 1880 decision—*Virginia v. Rives*—which held that blacks' absence from juries did not, of itself, amount to a constitutional violation. Mississippi chose jurors from voter lists. Because those lists were inextricably linked to the new disfranchisement scheme, Fourteenth Amendment jury challenges seemed a promising (though still indirect) avenue of attack.[41]

As was made clear by the South Carolina experience, the lack of controlling precedents posed serious problems for antidisfranchisement litigators, as did the federal judiciary's general aversion to "political" cases or to controversial issues. Administering this type of litigation raised a host of problems as well. As was noted earlier, the antidisfranchisement campaigns were state based and inward looking. While there was fault to found there, it is mitigated by the knowledge that as of 1895, no regional or national organization yet existed that was dedicated to protecting blacks' civil rights and liberties. But there did exist a small, loosely connected African American bar in the United States and its members typically initiated the sporadic civil and voting rights efforts that arose, locally, in the early to mid-1890s. This informal network had its nexus in Washington, D.C., and one of its members was Cornelius J. Jones of Issaquena County, Mississippi, who, largely unaided and daringly, initiated all three of the U.S. Supreme Court challenges to Mississippi's 1890 constitution.

Issaquena County, Mississippi, was the blackest county in America, according to the 1890 U.S. census, with a population of 11,623 African Americans and 692 whites, and that 17:1 ratio topped a survey of "census black spots" that appeared in Jackson's Populist newspaper, the *Mississippian*. Clinging to the Mississippi River's serpentine banks, tiny Issaquena is but a narrow twist of dry land. The county is one of the state's smallest, all of its towns and communities are small, and few were smaller than the hamlet of Ben Lomond. And in Ben Lomond lived one of Mississippi's few African Americans who did not live in complete subservience to the white minority. Cornelius Jones was a schoolteacher-turned-lawyer, and in 1889 he won election as Issaquena County's delegate to the Mississippi House of Representatives.[42]

Jones was born to Cornelius Jones Sr. and Hannah Donaldson Jones, both slaves, in Vicksburg in 1858, and by the time he reached school age, there were Freedmen's Bureau common schools for him to attend. He remained in those schools until age fourteen, when he left home for the newly opened Alcorn University at Rodney, Mississippi. Alcorn at that time was a liberal arts institution, and Jones stayed there until age twenty, when he graduated and became a schoolteacher in Louisiana. A freedman rarely made it through primary school, rarer still did he then attend and graduate from a university, and it was frankly exotic for him then to enter professional training. Cornelius Jones did all of this, however, and began reading law in 1880 under the tutelage of a former Louisiana Supreme Court justice.[43]

After two years with the justice, Jones came home to Mississippi. He married, he reentered the classroom as a teacher, and he returned to the law, resuming his studies with the McLaurin brothers of Brandon. Jones was not simply a black Mississippian who studied the law. He was studying under the wing of one of the state's best-connected firms, both professionally and politically. The eldest of the two McLaurin brothers, Anselm, was elected governor while Jones was his student and went on to serve in the U.S. Senate before taking a second turn as governor in the 1890s. There is no record of his time with the McLaurin's, he had obviously been an extraordinary young man and was extraordinarily well placed and, we may also infer, protected.

A charmed life was enjoyed by no nineteenth-century black Mississippian, but Cornelius Jones's experience was as close to charmed as it could possibly be. He left the McLaurin brothers in 1888, passed the state bar exam, and moved to Issaquena County. He hung his shingle in the little village of Ben Lomond and within a year won election to the state legislature. He was one of six African American legislators elected that year, all Republicans and all to the lower house.[44]

At only thirty-one, Jones had already attained far more than anyone born to his place and station could have dreamed. He had done everything right. He educated himself and established himself professionally. But this was the worst possible time for a black man in Mississippi to embark upon a political career. Calls for constitutional revisions, all injurious to African American interests, had dominated the 1889 state election. Issaquena County was a prime target, and so too black politicians such as Jones.

Jones owed his election to a fusion arrangement between white Democrats and black Republicans. Mississippi's brand of fusion was born after Redemption, in the 1870s, and before each election, the two parties' leaders doled out offices to black and white candidates. Make no mistake, the system only really worked for white Democrats. The only blacks who benefitted at all hailed from small cliques of Republicans with whom Democrats felt comfortable (because they posed no serious threat). Democrats always received the more powerful posts; black Republicans never claimed more than a minority of county offices and usually a legislative seat. These cozy arrangements, which Mississippi's most famous black politicians, U.S. Senators Blanche K. Bruce and Hiram Revels, and U.S. Representative John Roy Lynch, had pioneered, infuriated white-county leaders. The irritant was not black politicians as such but the disproportionate influence of white black-county politicians. Mississippi's legislature was apportioned on the basis of population—not voting strength—and thus those few whites in heavily black and black-majority counties were distinctly overrepresented in the legislature. A total of 44,500 white voters lived in black counties in 1890, 71,000 in the white counties. Sixty-eight black-county politicians (only a handful of whom were either black or Republican) sat in the Mississippi House of Representatives in 1890, compared to 52 from white counties. Black-county African American men voted in large numbers and their votes were used to support white political authority. Resentments hardened, and in the fall of 1889 white-county demands for constitutional reform, tax reform, and, above all else, the disfranchisement of black voters, dominated the election campaign.[45]

When the 1890 Mississippi legislature assembled in January, Jones, the other five black Republicans, and many white black-county representatives fought doggedly against the convention bill. Jones's efforts were especially well regarded. His address on the subject was noted in the press (though apparently never published); Jackson's *Daily Clarion-Ledger* characterized it as "eloquent and impressive" and, in a separate piece, the editor noted that his appeal had been "complimented by all who heard him." Jones was not alone. When state representative Absalom M. West proposed a petition to Congress calling for the Fifteenth Amendment's repeal, remarkably, the legislature's Committee on Federal Relations reported it favorably, two days after the convention bill passed, and this occasioned heated protest. One white committee member, J. H. Jones, complained that the measure seemed inappropriate, and then an African American committee member, George F. Bowles (the publisher of the *Natchez Brotherhood*), delivered an emotional minority report denouncing both the memorial and the just-passed convention bill. "It is not justice for the whites of the South to seek to bind . . . blacks to a condition little better than Mexican peonage," Bowles railed. "It would not be justice for a government after granting a proud and humane right to any class of its citizens, to alienate or recall that right because that class or race had not in twenty (or even fifty) years attained the wondrous civilization of the Anglo-Saxon Southerner." The efforts of Jones, Bowles, and their allies went for naught and that was no surprise. The bill had already passed the state house, it passed the senate shortly thereafter, and the governor promptly signed it. A new front had been opened in the war over African American suffrage.[46]

Mississippi's convention attracted little interest beyond the state. The Lodge Elections bill (which would have authorized federal supervision of congressional elections) and a new tariff bill were before Congress, and those garnered greater notice. National commentators vainly attempted to foment broader national outrage over the "Spectacle of Mississippi," as an *Independent* magazine editorial headline described the convention. "A most extraordinary condition of things is now on exhibition in Mississippi," the editor noted, "and nobody seems interested." But that referred to observers outside of the state. Back in Mississippi, the convention was a closely watched affair, by black and white alike.[47]

Immediate cries to fight disfranchisement and to foil the Democrats' convention plans arose from Mississippi's African American community, but bloody violence quelled that talk. Few blacks campaigned for convention seats and one of them, Jasper County's F. M. B. Cook, was apparently murdered for the offense. Adams County Republicans nominated state representative George Bowles of Natchez for the convention, but by mid-July they had rescinded his candidacy. According to the *New Orleans Crusader*'s "Natchez Letter," they realized that Bowles's bid "was not wise." [48]

Only one African American sat in the 1890 convention, Isaiah T. Montgomery, and he did not attack the Democrat's franchise proposal. In the end, he offered his endorsement, based upon his apparent belief that whites would abide by the letter and spirit of the new constitution in the conduct of elections. White Mississippians hailed him as a hero, many (but certainly not all) blacks claimed to wish that he had "never been born," and few of either group really ever acknowledged his actual, and incredibly limited, function in the convention. He was completely powerless, but after the convention did its work, what Montgomery had or had not done was of little concern. Montgomery's controversial endorsement also had carried a caveat: that the state had to enforce the new rules equitably. He did that because the new constitution's literacy test, good character provision, poll tax, and understanding clause did not preclude black political activity. Indeed, Montgomery believed (and he was not alone in this) that those provisions, the literacy test especially, might trigger a generalized movement among black Mississippians to better themselves in a material sense.[49]

Years later, some Mississippi whites pretended that blacks readily submitted to their disfranchisement. It was "accepted by the masses of the sons of Ham," J. S. McNeily claimed before the Mississippi Historical Society, "without show of sorrow or sign of resentment." But not all whites subscribed to that pretense. Frank Johnston, a revered Jackson attorney and future state attorney general, advised in an 1890 press statement that he saw no "disposition on the part of the negroes to acquiesce in the suppression of their votes or to retire from politics." Literacy was the standard that the disfranchisers prescribed for prospective voters, and just as Isaiah Montgomery seemed to have wished, several spontaneous educational efforts emerged, all designed to help blacks satisfy the new literacy test. These would, in time, yield intriguing results.[50]

Disfranchisement upended Cornelius Jones's political career and those of every other black officeholder in Mississippi. "One by one, as the roses fall," the *Brookhaven Leader* noted in late 1895, black legislators had vanished from the state capitol. There had been fifteen in 1883, seven in 1890, three in 1892, but in 1896 there would be "neither colored man nor Republican." Jones had not been reelected in 1892 and it is not clear that he even stood for election that year. After leaving the house, he became a full-time lawyer and, as one of only a handful of black attorneys in Mississippi's overwhelmingly black river and Delta counties, he found plenty to do. He continued to work within the Republican Party and some blacks continued to seek and win office in Mississippi. Blacks returned to the legislature in 1898 and 1900, but Jones sought no office in the first half of the decade.[51]

Jones spent the early 1890s traversing the Delta as a journeyman criminal defense attorney. There were prosperous black attorneys in Mississippi, but Jones was never among them. He seemed not to favor the unexciting civil work, pension applications, wills, and so on that guaranteed a steady income. Instead, he pursued trial work, both civil and criminal. Jones was a smart man—he could not have risen as far as he did otherwise—but he was by no means a gifted or diligent jurist. He was, however, ambitious, and as George Washington Murray's South Carolina antidisfranchisement effort wound down, Jones arrived in Washington, D.C., with two cases (entirely of his own design) that questioned Mississippi's 1890 constitution. These were appeals of the murder convictions of John Gibson and Charley Smith.

On January 9, 1892, John Gibson killed Robert Stinson, who managed the plantation where he worked as a wagoner. January 9 was payday, and when Gibson collected his wages, he discovered that Stinson had docked him twenty cents for "time lost." Gibson confronted Stinson at the plantation store, refuted the time-lost deduction, and demanded "satisfaction."

They argued there until the clerk ejected Gibson, who upon leaving promised that either he or Stinson "would go to Hell that night."[52]

Gibson left the store and headed for a saloon. "I stayed there a pretty good while," he testified. Besotted, he went to the planter's home and shouted his demand for "satisfaction" through an open office window. The plantation owner refused to intervene, but Stinson was there, too, and promised Gibson what he craved.[53]

They met at the sidewalk gate. Gibson was unarmed. Stinson bore a six-shot revolver in his left hand and a large stick in his right. Without hesitation or a single word, Stinson dropped Gibson to his knees with six quick blows to the head, and when Gibson struggled back, Stinson fired twice, and missed twice. Gibson grabbed Stinson's arm. They struggled. Shots three, four, and five followed, and then a pause. Witnesses then heard the sixth shot and saw Stinson crumple. Gibson ran, he later testified, first to Arkansas and then to Kansas City: "I heard that he was shot and was dead, and I thought I had better leave, that the white folks were after me and were going to kill me and I thought I had better leave."[54]

A homesick Gibson quietly returned from Missouri later that year and was promptly arrested and charged, indicted, tried, and convicted of murder, and sentenced to hang. The Washington County jury had been all white, but that was not the key issue on appeal. Robert Craig, Gibson's original lawyer, had lost a handful of early evidentiary motions, and on the basis of those, Gibson's new attorney, Cornelius Jones, successfully petitioned the state supreme court for a new trial.[55]

Jones was a little-known, former one-term state representative and no one within the white establishment seems to have understood what he was attempting. Gibson's second trial produced Jones's first antidisfranchisement test case. Unlike the South Carolina cases, and unlike *Sproule v. Fredericks,* this case involved neither a question of voter registration nor of an election contest. Instead, the Mississippi cases were built upon Fourteenth Amendment–based jury service precedents from the 1880s. This was a very good strategic choice on Jones's part. So too was his decision to launch facsimile cases. He could challenge multiple counties' juries at once and he could potentially crowd the state supreme court's docket. Additionally, he could force the state's legal officers to spread themselves thin in their defense. Unfortunately, Jones was a better politician than a lawyer. His performance was abysmal. The cases all failed, and his clients paid with their lives.

In the early going, all seemed well with Cornelius Jones's plan. The Mississippi Supreme Court remanded Gibson's case to Washington County and then Jones handed it back to Robert Craig. At this second trial, Craig moved to withdraw Gibson's not guilty plea and to quash his indictment on account of "race prejudice." Craig also wanted to remove Gibson's case to the U.S. district court. The judge denied Craig's motions, the trial continued, and a new jury reached the same verdict. For a second time, Gibson was sentenced "to be hung by the neck until he is dead," with his execution scheduled for August 2, 1894. The court postponed this pending a state supreme court appeal, where Jones would again step in as appellate counsel.[56]

John Gibson's second appeal had a companion on the October 1894 Mississippi Supreme Court docket—*Charley Smith v. State of Mississippi*. Smith was at a "country dance" in Bolivar County when he quarreled with another man and exchanged "some hot or unpleasant words." A melee ensued and someone "suggested that they go outside." The pugilists tumbled out into a violent thunderstorm and fought in the wind and rain. Shots were fired—many shots. No one knew by whom, no one knew from whence, and no one had been struck by the initial volley. Soon afterward "there were two shots fired into the house," and one of the attendees, Wiley Nesby, fell dead. Witnesses blamed Charley Smith for starting the original fracas and for firing the last two shots. Smith denied all of these accusations.[57]

Cornelius Jones represented Charley Smith at his trial in Rosedale and he moved immediately, just as had Robert Craig had done in Gibson's second trial, to quash the indictment. When that failed, he tried to remove Smith's trial to U.S. district court. "Quashing the indictment" meant setting it aside and the removal motion would have suspended the trial pending a federal district judge's review of the federal question (in this instance, those arising under the Fourteenth Amendment). Jones wanted to have his case in federal court because he, like the South Carolina litigators before him, believed that federal courts offered the best hope for redress. He would have been arguing for Charley Smith's life, yes, but he would do it by attacking the 1890 Mississippi constitution's elective franchise article, and he hoped to take this all the way to the U.S. Supreme Court. There were other ways of getting there, more straightforward ways, but this was potentially quicker, and would also prevent state officials from destroying his case. Smith's death would have ended the matter, as would a conviction and sentence that did not involve a federal question. If Jones lost in state court, there had to be a federal question involved if he ever wished to launch a federal appeal, but at the same time, Jones did not actually need to win on either motion and probably did not want to do so. Just by filing them, he established possible grounds for an appeal. Had he won either motion in the circuit court, he could not have taken the case any further.[58]

The circuit court denied both motions. Smith's trial went on and he was convicted and sentenced to be hanged. With Smith's execution scheduled for January 24, 1895, Jones appealed and won a stay, pending the Mississippi Supreme Court's decision. Neither Robert Craig nor Cornelius Jones presented evidence supporting their removal motions (beyond their clients' sworn affirmation of their respective briefs' assertions) and this made it easy for the Mississippi Supreme Court to reject both appeals. This in turn facilitated a further appeal to the U.S. Supreme Court, but the evidentiary issues cited by the Mississippi justices portended ill for Cornelius Jones.[59]

Jones delivered the two cases to the Supreme Court in late 1895, just as the Court was looking for a way out of *Mills*. At this stage he enlisted as his co-counsel Emanuel Molyneaux Hewlett. Hewlett was born in Brooklyn, New York, in 1850 but was raised in Boston, where he attended prep school and the Boston University Law School. He graduated in 1877 and practiced in Boston until the early 1880s, when he relocated to Washington, D.C. Hewlett was renowned for his work in criminal cases (he would appear as co-counsel in numerous criminal appeals filed on behalf of black southerners), and by 1890 his reputation was such that President Benjamin Harrison appointed him justice of the peace for the District of Columbia. He was reappointed by Presidents Grover Cleveland, William McKinley, and Theodore Roosevelt.[60]

Jurisdiction was the ostensible question in both *Gibson* and *Smith*. The Court had allowed jury challenges before, but they had to persuade the Court that federal courts should have jurisdiction to hear *these*. The jury case precedents provided an opening, but not a wide one. Mississippi's jury lists, as was the case with most states, were derived from voter registries, so any obstacle to voting also impeded jury service. So if Jones and Hewlett could show a racial motive in refusing potential black voters (and likewise potential black jurors), they would have a reasonably strong case.

The elements of a strong, jury-based antidisfranchisement case were in place for Jones and Hewlett and all that they really wanted was to have his case remanded to a U.S. district court. That might seem anticlimactic, but it would have meant that southern judges, sheriffs, and voting registrars would find themselves standing before federal district judges to justify their administration of jury selection and voter registration. In the immediate short term, there would almost surely be some benefit for disfranchised African Americans.

They argued the cases on December 13, 1895, and the Supreme Court announced decisions in *Gibson* and *Smith* on April 13, 1896, little more than one month before *Plessy v. Ferguson*. Justice John Marshall Harlan wrote both opinions and dismissed each case on jurisdictional grounds. The problem lay in the evidence, which was conspicuous by its paucity, a defect that had previously been cited by the Mississippi Supreme Court. Mississippi did not exclude blacks in terms, so *Strauder* was not triggered. *Neal* and *Ex parte Virginia* were the most relevant here because Mississippi had certainly excluded blacks, but *Rives* had made clear that blacks' absence from juries was not necessarily evidence of exclusion. There had to be proof, and Jones provided so little that the 1880s jury service precedents only barely came into play. The only supporting materials that he offered to the Washington and Bolivar County courts, the Mississippi Supreme Court, and then the U.S. Supreme Court, were the sworn affirmations of John Gibson and Charley Smith. John Marshall Harlan, who would earn his place among the immortals with his *Plessy* dissent, made short work of Cornelius Jones. Nothing in either of his cases, Harlan found, brought them under federal jurisdiction. In *Gibson,* Jones had not shown that Mississippi's courts committed "any error of law of which this court may take cognizance" or that his client's murder conviction "was due to prejudice of race." Harlan did likewise in *Smith.* The motion there, he wrote, was "unsupported by any competent evidence."[61]

Gibson and *Smith* do not count as dodges, though the Court likely would have tried to dodge the question if Jones had presented a better case. Jones had provided nothing more than perfunctory affidavits from John Gibson and Charley Smith as evidence and Harlan hammered him for that. Maybe it is unfair to judge Jones harshly at this stage. Maybe. Regardless, his work thus far had come to naught and John Gibson and Charley Smith each faced the executioner. The Washington County sheriff hanged Gibson on May 1, 1897. No record has been found of Smith's Bolivar County execution.[62]

Jones's attack on Mississippi's 1890 constitution received scant press mention. "No Colored Jurymen Allowed," headlined an October 27, 1895, *Washington Post* article about *Gibson* and *Smith*. Jones, the *Post* explained, had borne Smith's and Gibson's U.S. Supreme Court appeals to Washington. The cases were "of particular interest to the leading colored men of this city, and throughout the South, as the decision of the Supreme Court means much to the negroes in the prosecution of criminal cases." No comparison to *Mills v. Green* was offered, and it is highly doubtful that anyone made the connection. A dispatch to the *New Orleans Daily Picayune* noted that Jones addressed "an audience in one of the colored churches" about the cases, but like the *Post*, the *Picayune* correspondent missed the implication of a jury challenge involving the 1890 constitution. That misapprehension was widespread. The African American *Savannah Tribune* celebrated the fact that two African American lawyers had appeared before the Court but also seemed unaware of the cases' broader implications for disfranchisement.[63]

Neither the *Post*'s nor the *Daily Picayune*'s correspondents, nor the *Tribune*'s editor, mentioned, or likely understood, the potential effect of these cases upon disfranchisement. This could have been due to indifference but it was not. There was something far more exciting afoot in Mississippi that doubtless distracted attention from *Gibson* and *Smith* and promised, however briefly, to alter the course of Mississippi politics and possibly southern politics. It was a person, actually, former congressman John Roy Lynch, but his was not an entirely constructive contribution to this story. He stole the spotlight, was consumed by a longstanding, internecine feud, and very nearly derailed black Mississippians' antidisfranchisement efforts—a flurry of activity that yielded the infamous Supreme Court decision of *Williams v. Mississippi*.

2

If Thine Eye Be Evil

The Road to *Williams v. Mississippi*

> The light of the body is the eye: if therefore thine eye be single, thy
> whole body shall be full of light. But if thine eye be evil, thy whole
> body shall be full of darkness. If therefore the light that is in thee be
> darkness, how great is that darkness.
> —Matthew 6:22–23

In late August 1895, Indianola, Mississippi's *Sunflower Tocsin* printed po-
etry on its front page, offering readers an excerpt from E. C. Hudson's
"The Negriad." The first stanza began

> Come wake ye up, my people
>   And sing your sweetest song,
> Our harps from weeping willows
>   We'll take with courage strong.

The *Tocsin*—a white, conservative Democratic newspaper published deep
in the Delta's Sunflower County—identified Hudson as "a colored teacher
of this county" and explained that he was offering the thirty-six stanzas of
"The Negriad" "in pamphlet form for sale." Whether Hudson ever actually
did so is unclear because no such copy has survived. Only six stanzas made
it into the *Tocsin*. The best and most inspiring was the first, which concluded,

> O listen every nation
>   Every race and clan,
> While with the sweetest music
>   We will sing "The Colored Man."[1]

It is startling that "The Negriad" ever made it into the *Toscin*. White
Democrats in the Mississippi Delta in 1895 had neither any interest in nor
use for African American history and culture and surely cared little for Hud-

son's epic-style review of blacks' place in the Bible and in human history. But those are neither the only nor the most important reasons we might take notice of "The Negriad." As it turns out, Hudson's opening line—"Come wake ye up, my people"—preceded a much-delayed stir of sorts among black Mississippians. Eighteen ninety-five was an election year in Mississippi, and beginning that spring, white Mississippians would have heard of a curious uptick in black voter registration statewide. By late summer, when Hudson's poem surfaced, many whites had grown concerned about that surge and what it meant. When autumn arrived and brought with it former U.S. representative John Roy Lynch, they grew increasingly irritated, both by the registration numbers and by Lynch's announced intention to destroy the elective franchise provisions in Mississippi's 1890 constitution.

Lynch was the likeliest and most desired figure to lead black Mississippians in an antidisfranchisement fight. A legendary Reconstruction era politician, businessman, planter, and attorney, he towers over all other black Mississippians of the late Gilded Age. Though his tenure in public life dated to the 1870s, Lynch was so young when his political career began that he was only forty-three when disfranchisement came in 1890. The political tide had turned in Mississippi long before that and Lynch lost his U.S. House seat in the 1880s. Afterward, he sought admission to the Mississippi bar, failing the exam on his first attempt. He was licensed to practice in Washington, D.C., however, and he moved there and partnered with Robert Terrell (husband of famed activist Mary Church Terrell) and later accepted a U.S. Treasury post from President Benjamin Harrison. He had made a new life for himself, his wife, and daughter in D.C., but Lynch seemingly dominated Mississippi's Republican Party from afar, claiming as his residence the various plantations and businesses he owned in and around Natchez. But by the mid-1890s, Lynch was really only a quadrennial visitor, concerned largely with reestablishing his position and promising Mississippi's convention delegates to the "right" Republican presidential candidate.[2]

Before Lynch could set his antidisfranchisement plan in motion, however, he would have to reassert his effective authority over Mississippi's other African American political leaders. To outside observers Lynch appeared to control black politics in his home state. He was doubtless the predominant black Mississippi politician. At home, however, there were questions. From the 1880s onward, Lynch had controlled party patronage, and the role of patronage-master for either major party in *any* state was lucrative. Not surprisingly, he had rivals for the job, and with Lynch spending his time in Washington the opportunity was ripe for someone local to try to challenge him. Many black Mississippi Republicans simply resented the fact that Lynch did not live in Mississippi and yet presumed to dictate political affairs to those who did. In 1892, James Hill challenged Lynch, and the result was a badly divided party. Two Mississippi delegations traveled to the Republican national convention that year; Lynch's promises that he, with President Harrison's aid, would fight the 1890 constitution had not mollified the Hill faction. Both Mississippi delegations supported Harrison and then Harrison lost to Grover Cleveland. Not only would neither Hill nor Lynch be Mississippi's patronage boss, there would not be any Republican patronage in Mississippi for at least the next four years. In the election's wake, Lynch returned to his Washington law practice.[3]

Lynch showed up in September, and this would be unlike any of his previous tours. He had attacked it before, but at no time in the four years previous had the assault seemed to be an end unto itself. "He abused the Democratic party," the *Pascagoula Democrat-Star*'s editor noted of his appearance there, "and was down on the state constitution." The *Democrat-Star* was no fan of Lynch and so its analysis was skewed and in the expected direction. The paper correctly inferred that Lynch was not seeking office and that he was trying to cement his position in the party, but did not apprehend what was actually afoot and hastily assumed that it was just about lucre. "John was merely keeping himself before his party in the event the Republicans got in power next year," the editor insisted. A GOP victory in 1896 would create a fresh batch of patronage and if Lynch could fix his position among Mississippi Republicans, the editorial suggested, "he would be in line to get some more pie." This was not an entirely unfounded presumption, yet it is clear that Lynch was interested in something more than money and power. Lynch had arrived amid the 1895 state elections and coincident to increasingly frequent press reports and editorial commentary about African American voter registration. There were no black candidates of consequence on the ballot and the increasing numbers of black voters had to be what motivated Lynch that fall. They comprised a force that Lynch might yet marshal in a fight against the state constitution. As the balloting drew nearer, newspapers regarded the increasing numbers of black voters suspiciously, and it must be emphasized that in terms of real numbers, black voters remained astoundingly few, but the *rate* of increase was another story. In 1892 there had been 66,905 white voters and 9,036 black voters. By election day 1895 (though excluding three late-reporting counties), the *New Orleans Daily Pic-*

ayune calculated that there were 106,156 white voters and 16,965 black voters, reflecting an impressive 58.6 percent increase in white voter registration and an astounding 87.7 percent increase in black voter registration. From Adams County, Lynch's ostensible home, the *Natchez Daily Democrat* reported that there had been 637 white and 350 black voters in 1894. By 1895 the totals were 820 and 663, respectively, reflecting the statewide trend quantified in the *Daily Picayune* report. "The negroes are learning to read and write so rapidly," the wildly optimistic *Natchez Brotherhood* gushed, "that they will constitute a majority of the voters of the state."[4]

Blacks were nowhere near a majority of registered voters, were nowhere near a large fraction of it, and would be neither at any time in the near future. Still, African Americans were registering at a substantially higher rate than whites, which meant that they were *trying* to vote and for Democrats that was not good. It was a potential boon for John Roy Lynch, and as he progressed around the state, rumors flew that something larger was afoot. Only the wildest, most elaborate, and least credible theories gained credence: The October 27 *Memphis Commercial Appeal* headlines blazed with the horrifying news (for whites) that "Secret Bands of Nigs," commanded by Lynch, planned to mount a wholesale campaign against the 1890 constitution during the 1896 congressional elections. Mississippi Democrats, understandably, took sharp notice and obsessed over Lynch's every move and stalked him catlike, insisting all the while that they could care less and that the whole thing was a farce. The "tenacity with which this colored patriot clings to the wreck of Reconstruction," the *Vicksburg Commercial Herald* snorted, is "a marvel of blindness and Bourbonism." Determined to dismiss Lynch's attack, the *Commercial Herald* insisted that nothing would come of his "absurdities." "Reason and facts," the editor offered, "are the obstacles in the way of his schemes." Elsewhere, African American observers were simply glad to see that something was happening at all, though some questioned why this had been so long in coming. Of Lynch's planned challenges, Nebraska's *Omaha Enterprise* offered, "Why this was not done long ago we are at a loss to say."[5]

Lynch's plan—and there definitely *was* a plan—emerged in due time and was intended to yield test cases, but not of the regular sort. The plan was fairly complicated and its fulcrum would be the 1896 congressional races. Lynch, as leader of Mississippi's Republicans, would field a candidate in each of Mississippi's seven U.S. House districts and a complete slate of presidential electors. When they all lost, he would initiate seating challenges before the U.S. House of Representatives. The House, as he envisioned it, would then investigate Mississippi's 1896 elections and the constitution and statutes under which they were conducted. If that failed to trigger punitive measures, he would presumably file some sort of suit in federal court. Lynch was never clear about how this strategy would shift from Congress to the courts; federal courts do not have jurisdiction over the composition of Congress and thus he could not have sued the U.S. House.

Lynch's interest in congressional seating challenges is not in the least surprising. Nor was it an original idea. Just as the antidisfranchisement cases have received very little historical attention, there were a host of seating challenges filed against southern congressmen in the late nineteenth century. Lynch had once retained his own congressional seat through such a challenge, and Representative George Washington Murray initiated a series of similar efforts from South Carolina following the failure of *Mills v. Green*. Murray, in fact, would continue in this vein following the 1896 and 1898 elections. In all of these, there were congressional investigations of varying scope, and in some the U.S. House admitted that blacks had been disfranchised unconstitutionally. The problem, however, was that the House had only shown itself willing to, at the most, order new elections rather than seat black challengers. Given the paucity of options available to southern blacks, it seemed a worthwhile use of their time. With regard to Lynch's plans for Mississippi, where he hoped to launch tests of the 1896 congressional elections, he had already signed on as and was the attorney of record for a group of three Mississippi Populists who challenged their defeats in the 1894 congressional contest. From Lynch's perspective—that of a professional politician, Republican Party icon, and Washington "insider"—this all probably seemed promising, though to modern eyes it cannot but seem weak. On the one hand, some Republican congressmen remained interested in southern elections contests, but the GOP landslide in the 1894 midterm election demonstrated that the party did not necessarily need southern congressional seats to retain control of the House. Lynch thus could only hope to appeal to Grand Old Party members' morality and their consciences, both of which were far harder to arouse in politicians when it promised no immediate political gain.[6]

Despite the excited headlines indicating otherwise, Lynch's plan was never a secret, and there never were "secret bands" of anyone meeting anywhere to do anything. When Lynch launched his 1895 speaking tour of the state in September, an attack against the 1890 constitution had been his open intention. On a visit to Ohio to pay court to Mark Hanna and Republican presidential hopeful William McKinley, he candidly told a reporter there of his plans. That reporter, though, offered a hyperbolic account of "secret societies" and alluded to some vague collaboration with George Washington Murray (whose South Carolina initiative was making headlines simultaneously). On the heels of those initial accounts, Lynch visited the *Natchez Daily Democrat* offices to clarify his position. Lynch claimed not to understand why the Ohio reporter believed that he had inaugurated any "secret society" to fight disfranchisement. The "only allusion to secrecy was that some of our plans and methods . . . are party secrets." Secret or no, Lynch's plans attracted more and more interest as time passed and as he traveled around the state.[7]

Aside from his *Daily Democrat* interview, Lynch never described his intentions in any great detail, but his speaking schedule offered hints. He did not traverse the Delta and river counties (which were overwhelmingly black), concentrating instead on the white counties of north and east Mississippi. Those were Populist and agrarian strongholds; those were areas that had once agitated hard and long for disfranchisement and where there had been dramatic surges in black voter registration. Populists and agrarians, however, were badly burned by the new constitution and thus stood to gain from its destruction. Yet Populists and agrarians were not necessarily pleased by the recent spurt of black voter registration. Indeed, these areas had seen the largest proportion of new black voters. Remarking upon the 1895 registration figures, the *Daily Picayune's* Jackson correspondent noted that "the increase of negro registration in white counties is out of all proportion to the increase of negro registration in the Delta." Lynch would have to unite two disparate groups and so hoped to keep everyone focused on their common interest. He would have to keep them mindful of their shared complaint. As the *Eupora Sun* put it, "Mississippi has a state constitution that would not be tolerated by the people of some states."[8]

Lynch only ever emphasized his audiences' common bane, and he invited all disaffected Mississippi voters to make league with him and the Republicans. In Okolona, Meridian, and other eastern Mississippi locales, he drew throngs, and by the time he reached Sardis, talk was loud and long about a possible Republican-Populist fusion. Lynch expressly denied any such intent on his part, a relieved *Sardis Reporter* noted, but that paper was nonetheless worried about Lynch's plan for Congress to "intermeddle in our State affairs." Mississippi Democrats needed to take care, Democratic editors warned. Though Republicans themselves posed little threat, some Democrats might be tempted. "Considering the lukewarmness and apostasy" of many Democrats, the "lamentable tendency . . . to consort with the heterodox Populists," fusion was dangerous, the *Natchez Daily Democrat* believed. The editor disclaimed any alarmism but nonetheless urged Democratic leaders to remain alert—"on the qui vive"—and keep Republicans in their place.[9]

Democrats' anxieties about Lynch were heightened in late November, when the Mississippi Supreme Court finally admitted Lynch to the state bar. The *Natchez Daily Democrat* felt certain that it meant a real court test, and not just some campaign season stunt, was forthcoming. Nevertheless, the 1890 constitution would survive. The paper then offered a prediction: "We are rather inclined to believe that it will successfully resist all assaults made against it by Mr. Lynch and those who are backing him in this contention."[10]

Lynch wrote a lengthy autobiography late in life included a substantial discussion of disfranchisement and of Mississippi's 1890 constitution. Curiously, he penned nary a word about this antidisfranchisement assault. Further, it has never been discussed or noted by either his biographers or historians of Mississippi and the South. That Lynch never mentioned it himself accounts for the biographical and historical silences, but his own reticence likely owed to the fact that this episode was spectacularly disastrous on a personal level and began the end of influence in Mississippi Republican politics. Questions about school funding arose, which frightened and divided potential supporters, aided his opponents' cause, and gave entrée to his black and Republican rivals.

Lynch launched this program at a time of surging political activity among Mississippi African Americans and white Democrats would not let that go unchallenged. They had seen and considered the registration figures and had begun working to reverse the trend by removing the literacy incentive. The 1890 constitution had made literacy the standard for registering to vote and poll taxes were the price of voting. In light of that, blacks in some counties launched herculean efforts to promote and attain literacy, and many were learning to read in state-funded common schools whose sole state funding source was poll-tax revenues. The autumn of 1895, as it turned out, saw both Lynch's return and the beginnings of a movement to make poll taxes compulsory for all registered voters, whether or not they intended to vote, and to divide poll-tax receipts by race. Lynch, in short, was an accelerant for the potential conflagration, and the *Hazelhurst Courier* warned that the "negro had better keep clear of Lynch—let him severely alone" and issued veiled threats against the "education and future development" of black children. Poll-tax receipts amounted to $245,723.58 in 1893, $229,217.87 in 1894, and $223,291.43 in 1895, according to press reports. There were 594,000 men "liable for the poll tax," the *Memphis Commercial Appeal* estimated, but less than half actually voted (and thus paid the tax). The conversation always returned to the refrain that white men's poll taxes paid for teaching blacks to read and to Democrats' grousing about blacks' alleged ingratitude. Lynch and his supporters were "absolutely unmindful of the extremely liberal provision the hated constitution" made for black education, the *Vicksburg Commercial Herald* thundered. Invoking Scripture, the editor denounced Lynch just as Hosea had condemned Israel: His attacks seemed to offer "proof that Ephraim is still joined to his idols."[11]

Lynch's antidisfranchisement fight had contributed to an increasingly heated debate about school funding, prompting complaints from black leaders. "Endurance Has Its Bounds," a *Daily Picayune* editorial headline explained in early October. "Conservative negroes," a November report told, were alarmed. They fought Lynch's attack on the 1890 constitution, not because they supported it but because of school funding. This was shortsighted. School funding was already shockingly meager. Regardless, they were resolved to oppose Lynch's "mad attacks upon the state constitution, which cannot fail to prejudice many white men about how the school funds should be apportioned between whites and blacks." "In various ways the negroes of Mississippi are protesting," the *Memphis Commercial Appeal* noted in late November. In early December, state papers reported that the Colored Baptist State Convention, meeting in Vicksburg, had implored their parishioners to pay their poll taxes, "both as a duty and a pleasure."[12] Lynch had engendered what the *Commercial Herald* called a "Lusty Howl from the Negroes," and that did not bode well for his political future. But Lynch would not stop, the *Daily Picayune* observed. His tour, the report continued, which was "inciting the negroes . . . in defiance of the protest" of African American religious leaders "even though his course jeopardizes the public schools of his race, shows the length to which he will go." And it encouraged those white lawmakers who advanced their plans for compulsory poll-tax payments and a division of poll-tax receipts by race.[13]

Lynch's plan, as explained publicly, was simple enough, but the devil, as the cliché says, lay in the details. It was "far reaching . . . and on its face looks plausible," a hostile *Sunflower Tocsin* conceded, "but its premise is rotten." To the *Tocsin*'s editor, the "rot" was the idea that Mississippi would ever send Republicans or Populists to Congress. However, Lynch never thought that men of either stripe would necessarily win in 1896. His purpose was to build a test, "paved," the *Natchez Daily Democrat* reminded readers, "by putting out candidates in some of the districts to be made martyrs of." Yet no sooner had he animated it than the plan unraveled. Lynch had previously offended resident GOP leaders by his long-distance leadership, but school funding strained those relationships past breaking. Methodist and Baptist ministers had risen against Lynch and his schemes, as did his longtime antagonists Isaiah T. Montgomery, James Hill, and other lesser-known figures who represented the secular wing of the state's black community.[14]

What came next was a sad and sorry spectacle, one that effectively ruined Lynch politically and destroyed his antidisfranchisement plan. Hill and Lynch had tangled for control of the state party in 1892, and a rematch was guaranteed for 1896. When Lynch first reemerged in late 1895, the *Natchez Daily Democrat*'s editor quipped (only half in jest) that Hill carried "a knife up his sleeve for John R. Lynch." Lynch, while never mentioning his attack on the state constitution, devoted three chapters of his autobiography to the feud with Hill and seemed, even in the sunset of life, unable to believe that his adversary acted either of his own volition or with a pure heart. Hill was greedy, Lynch suggested, duped and bribed by GOP kingmaker Mark Hanna (who had a strained relationship with Lynch). "It was to be a life-and-death struggle," he remembered. "I knew that Hill and his friends had not the means with which to make very much of a fight" and yet a vigorous one had been made. And Hill won. Lynch and Hill fought over delegates to the state convention. And Hill won. Then they fought to control the state convention. And Hill won. Lynch responded by staging a convention of his own and, in the end, two delegations of Mississippi Republicans traveled to the national convention. As had happened four years earlier, each went before the credentials committee and demanded to be seated. And Hill won. That fall, Hill and Lynch launched competing slates of congressional candidates and presidential electors. This time, they both lost. The whole affair was just sad. Lynch never again wielded real power over Mississippi Republicans. Democrats giggled and tittered and then laughed out loud at the spectacle, relieved that the Republicans had destroyed themselves and possibly their test case ambitions. "Let 'em go at it," the *Sardis Southern Reporter* said of the Hill-Lynch quarrel, "it is not a Democratic fight or funeral."[15]

While Hill and Lynch fought one another, to neither man's credit and to the detriment of all Mississippi Republicans, the poll-tax issue continued to make headlines. Black leaders were pressed to choose between the two prospective GOP dons, and to mount some sort of defense of public education. They knew that they could not rely upon either Hill or Lynch. Leaders of various African American "religious bodies and societies" met in Jackson and pleaded, in personal meetings with the governor and state legislators, that poll-tax receipts not be divided by race. Desperate to protect their schools, they allied themselves with a proposal to make poll taxes (of two dollars annually) compulsory for all men of voting age, whether registered to vote or not. It was a clever strategy because, in the end, the bill to make poll taxes compulsory failed to pass the Mississippi legislature. The initiative had not died, however, and in late spring those state leaders who had supported the measure hatched a test case that might enable their forced collection. This was the matter of *W. J. Ratliff v. Ambus Beale,* which in time shaped the U.S. Supreme Court's eventual disposition of the widely cited, little-studied, and much misunderstood case of *Williams v. Mississippi,* the capstone decision of the antidisfranchisement cases' first stage.[16]

The prime mover behind the revived poll-tax discussion was Mississippi's newly elected attorney general, Wiley Nash. When the legislature failed to make the tax compulsory, Nash rose to the challenge. Armed with the state auditor's declaration that collecting unpaid poll taxes due from 1892 forward would net $50,000 to $80,000 and that annual collections from all voting age men would bring in roughly $500,000 thenceforth, Nash pressed forward. His predecessor, Frank Johnston, opposed the proposal, as did Solomon S. Calhoon and former U.S. Senator J. Z. George, the latter of whom had crafted the 1890 constitution's suffrage provisions. For many, most notably George, compulsory poll-tax payments promised increased black voter registration and increased black voting, things to be avoided at all costs. Nash's initiative, George maintained, would "work very injuriously to the interests and safety of the people of Mississippi. . . . It will . . . strike down one of the safeguards of good government." Johnston, Calhoon, and George could not dissuade Nash. He always insisted that compulsory payment did not necessarily mean increased black voting, and with the assistance of Hinds County sheriff and tax collector W. J. Ratliff and a pliant African American factory worker named Ambus Beale, he initiated a test.[17]

Ambus Beale lived in Jackson. He was a laborer and supported a wife and children. He owned no real estate. All that he had in the world were some rudimentary household furnishings. To wit: a bedstead, bed sheets, a small washstand, miscellaneous other pieces of furniture, and the clothing worn by himself and his family. Court documents described these as of a "cheap and plain quality, consisting of the most absolute necessities of life." None were considered taxable under Mississippi law, but Ambus Beale had not paid his poll tax for 1895, and to trigger review by state courts, Ratliff seized Beale's bedstead. Ratliff planned to auction the bed in pursuit of Beale's unpaid poll tax and initiated collection proceedings in the Hinds County chancery court. Beale was not alone among black Mississippians who saw their property seized in pursuit of poll-tax revenues. That July, an Illinois Central Railroad Company train was stopped at Sardis, where the Panola County sheriff seized the paychecks of twenty-five section hands. All twenty-five were black, and all had failed to pay any poll taxes. White taxpayers, a news account explained, "pay the burden of the taxes to keep up those negro schools and these negro section hands derive a benefit from the schools." Whether the case came from Jackson or Sardis, the state supreme court would have to settle the issue.[18]

Ratliff v. Beale, as Nash intended it, would settle the questions surrounding Mississippi's poll tax. Specifically, he wanted to know whether the poll tax was a revenue measure or a disfranchising instrument. Furthermore, Nash was serious about increasing revenues for public education—for whites. He was convinced that the poll tax had not worked as it should. The state supreme court, courtesy of Ratliff and Beale, was thus invited to settle a trio of pressing questions. First, was the poll tax purely optional for the state's voting age men? Second, could the state force payment of the poll tax? These gave rise to the third and most important question: What had been the 1890 constitutional convention's purpose in adopting the poll-tax measure? The answer would be of enormous consequence in subsequent antidisfranchisement litigation.[19]

Mississippi's best lawyers lent their talents. Nash and former state supreme court justice John H. Campbell represented Ratliff. Beale's legal team was no less impressive and included former senator J. Z. George, former attorney general Frank Johnston, former governor Robert Lowry, and an aged Solomon S. Calhoon.

In the Hinds County Chancery Court, Judge Campbell presented the state's case plainly. "The average member of the constitutional convention," he stated in a typed and hand-corrected brief, "must have understood" that the poll tax was compulsory. He querulously asked whether some other motive underlay the poll tax's adoption: "Can it be that the poll tax was imposed to exclude ~~niggers~~ negroes from voting?" "The constitution says it was to aid common schools," he continued, "is that a lie?" Campbell wanted the state to collect this tax from every voting age man, whether or not he intended to register or vote in order to support the common schools. Further, Campbell and Nash sought to detach voting from tax payments. By questioning the convention's intent, Campbell baited the justices into denying any racial motive. They surely would not state outright that black men were the targets of the poll tax; the justices would never flout the Fourteenth and Fifteenth Amendments so openly. The white common schools would win, Campbell believed, and ultimately so too would Mississippi's body politic. He and Nash insisted that forcing poll-tax payments would not create new voters. This would be achieved by flipping the process. For the first five years of the constitution's operation, registered voters could not vote without also paying the tax. To prevent electoral disaster, Campbell and Nash proposed that the state should pocket men's money before putting them through a gauntlet of registration tests. They believed that could work because the registrars, who possessed almost limitless discretion over the registration process, could make it work.[20]

In 1890, neither Solomon Calhoon nor any others among Mississippi's leading disfranchisers had been discreet about their intentions. They openly plotted, and candidly confessed, their plans to disfranchise black men. Yet by 1896 they had grown curiously circumspect. Calhoon replied sharply to Campbell's barbed allusions, insisting that the poll tax's purpose was to "exclude *ignorance* not *niggers*." Calhoon's brief was concise and extraordinary. It was drafted in cramped handwriting, and at first glance it seems purely defensive. Read closely, however, it confirms the evil genius that underlay the 1890 constitution that he (and opposing counsel) had framed. The convention targeted blacks—there was no point in Calhoon's attempting to deny that—but it did far more. Mississippi's disfranchisers advertised the tax as a boon for public education, but if that tax were not collected, common schools would suffer, ignorance would be maintained and even deepened, and the electorate would shrink inexorably. And shrinking the electorate had been the whole point of the 1890 constitution.[21]

Calhoon, George, and other convention leaders were the watchmakers, and the mechanism they had designed was tick-tocking away beautifully. That is what Calhoon was really defending—not black schools and not any paternalistic notion of fairness. He may have wished that his motives were noble, but only the most credulous of observers could grant him that conceit. As he bade farewell to the convention delegates six years earlier, he blithely decreed that the educational funding provision (i.e., the poll tax) "reflects the generosity for which our State is justly famed, and if erroneous, is along the lines of noble and magnanimous endeavor." However, he continued, "if the pockets of our impoverished people can bear the draft, you are right, and they will never complain." Solomon Calhoon well understood that poverty begets ignorance and he also well understood that the pockets of a great many Mississippi men could not bear the draft. That was the whole idea, after all. Further, when in *Ratliff v. Beale* he protested that the poll tax was a way to fight "*ignorance* not *niggers*," he was serious. The poll tax would get rid of poor black voters as easily as it would poor white voters, and tying poll-tax receipts to school funding was a way to make sure that relatively few of either group escaped that condition. Moreover, Calhoon had known in 1890 just as he knew in 1896 that targeting ignorance affected blacks disproportionately. Neither did he shed tears for white illiterates. Calhoon and others like him were content to let poor white men— men with what he and those of his mien viewed as an unfortunate proclivity for reform movements—excuse themselves from public affairs. Despite the recent flurry of activity on black Mississippians' part, there was every reason to believe that voting age men would continue to disappear from the voting rolls as the second hand continued its inexorable march. Thus, to Calhoon's mind, the 1890 constitution was working perfectly.[22]

The chancery judge ruled in Beale's favor in early August, paving the way for the state high court's review. The Mississippi Supreme Court announced its decision in November 1896. *Sproule v. Fredericks,* from four years earlier, had been the court's first review of the 1890 constitution's suffrage provisions, and *Ratliff* was just the second, and far more serious. Examining the circumstances of the 1890 convention, Chief Justice Tim E. Cooper wrote candidly that "within the field of permissible action under the . . . federal constitution, the convention swept the circle of expedients to obstruct the exercise of franchise of the negro race." This was no easy task, Cooper explained, and so "restrained by the federal constitution from discriminating against the negro race, the convention discriminated against its characteristics and the offenses to which its weaker members were prone." That passage later found its way into that most infamous of all the antidisfranchisement cases, *Williams v. Mississippi,* but in the short term it was only part of a broader construction that preserved the existing poll-tax arrangement. Cooper admitted John Campbell's point: Yes, the poll tax was a tax, but it was not just a tax. It was also, and primarily, a disfranchising instrument. In our opinion," Cooper wrote, "the clause was primarily intended . . . as a clog upon the franchise, and secondarily and incidentally only as a means of revenue." Nash had lost. There would be no judicially mandated poll-tax revision. Mississippi sheriffs and tax collectors would auction no man's personal property to pay poll taxes. "It is safe to say," the *Sardis Southern Reporter's* disappointed editor offered, "that the white people in the hill counties will have to put up larger contributions for the education of the negroes in the bottom."[23]

Ratliff v. Beale was important in historical terms for how it would later be used by the U.S. Supreme Court, but the case had also inadvertently advanced the antidisfranchisement cause in legal terms, if only the activists behind it would seize the chance. Cooper's opinion was significant in that regard because it contained a frank and legally binding admission of what the 1890 convention intended. Convention proceedings, and legislative deliberations, were not, in the late nineteenth century, readily admissible in either state or federal courts. They *could* be used, theoretically, but judges embraced them only rarely. If, say, a court were asked to decide some controversial issue (like disfranchisement) on the basis of legislative intent, the court would likely reject such evidence for fear of judicial overreach. Because of how the Mississippi Supreme Court decided *Ratliff v. Beale,* and because it involved an open exploration of the Mississippi framers' motives, evidence of those motives was therefore potentially admissible in all Mississippi courts. Further, everything in the state supreme court's opinion—simply because it was there—was admissible before the U.S. Supreme Court. That unpleasant fact did not escape Mississippi newspaper editors. "With no disposition to criticize . . . the Supreme Court in the poll tax case," the *Clarion-Ledger* cautioned, "this decision will yet be used . . . in an effort to nullify the franchise article" of the Mississippi Constitution.[24]

The Mississippi Supreme Court announced *Ratliff v. Beale* at the close of an exceptionally exciting election year. On the national level, Republican presidential candidate William McKinley turned back the "Commoner"—Democratic nominee William Jennings Bryan. Bryan's nomination caused a split within the Democratic Party nationally, undercutting whatever chance he may have had of winning. In Mississippi, the campaign had been no less exciting due to the unsavory fracturing within African American and Republican ranks.

After he lost control of the state party to James Hill, John Roy Lynch chose to ignore defeat and tapped his own slate of congressional candidates and presidential electors, all of whom campaigned against the Hill wing's nominees. Lynch, and the Lynch candidates, were made objects of ridicule by Democrats, James Hill, and the Hill men. Nothing had worked for Lynch that year. The seating challenges he brought on behalf of three unsuccessful Populist congressional candidates from 1894 failed, and the House Elections Committee declined to even make a full investigation. Lynch's campaign to be a presidential elector fared little better. For most of that autumn, he battled with Adams County officials and Governor Anselm McLaurin for a place on the ballot. They insisted that he was not a resident of the state, fought it out in court, and Lynch eventually won, but it was a hollow victory.[25]

Throughout the summer and fall, black Mississippians appeared more engaged politically than usual (in relative terms) and seemed evenly divided between the Hill and Lynch candidates, which made their split that much sadder. Sadder still, and more tragic, were the charges and countercharges leveled about the two men's stances toward the 1890 constitution. Hill, according to a "Lynch Faction Ukase," as the *Daily Clarion-Ledger* described the document, "supports and defends the iniquitous understanding clause of our present state constitution, under the provisions of which over ninety per cent of the Republicans have been disfranchised."[26]

Forgotten in all of this was the enterprising attorney and politician from Issaquena County, Cornelius J. Jones. The poll-tax business, and Lynch's headline-grabbing perambulations around Mississippi, came as South Carolina staged its widely watched constitutional convention and as the U.S. Supreme Court handed down *Mills v. Green*. Little wonder, then, that Cornelius Jones's appeals on behalf of John Gibson and Charley Smith went unnoticed in Mississippi and were barely noted anywhere else. Their potential effect upon disfranchisement was not readily apparent, in all likelihood, to anyone other than Jones. Despite all of the flash and thunder surrounding Lynch's proposed machinations the previous fall and through the spring and then the summer, Cornelius Jones was the only man in Mississippi who was actually doing something concrete to reverse, or just slow, blacks' disfranchisement, but his work was completely overshadowed by the continuing debate over poll taxes, by Lynch's promised attack on the state constitution, and by the bitter and tragic internecine feud that gripped Mississippi's Republican Party—until the late summer of 1896.

The most significant Republican campaign in Mississippi in 1896 came from the state's third Delta district, where the incumbent Democrat, Thomas C. Catchings, was targeted by the only black man who had yet attacked the voting-related provisions of Mississippi's constitution, Cornelius J. Jones. Jones, who was the nominee of the James Hill faction of Mississippi Republicans, launched his canvas of the district that August, inviting Civil War veterans (black Union veterans, presumably) and "every Republican who voted before he was disfranchised" to "rally around the flag" and join his campaign. It would be, he promised, the "grandest ratification rally ever witnessed." Participants met at the masonic hall, and a number of luminaries appeared, including Isaiah T. Montgomery. Jones was the man from whom they all wished to hear and he did not disappoint. He spoke at length on the subjects of presidential nominee William McKinley, vice-presidential nominee Garret A. Hobart, and the twin evils of free silver and bimetallism. "More enthusiasm was manifested," a *Greenville Times* reporter noted, "than has been usual at such occasions." Records are scarce, but Jones campaigned thoroughly and hard. He lost, but the campaign showed that blacks' political enthusiasm seemed to be growing. Politically active (or at least politically curious) blacks turned out across the Delta to hear and see Jones and, down river at Natchez, a "Colored Political Club" was born. All of its members were young, all urban, and their participation demonstrated blacks' reluctance to accede to their civic emasculation.[27]

It surprised no one when Jones contested the election, but the vitriol that greeted the announcement is striking. "Jones vs. the State" headlined a long-winded outburst from the *Greenville Times*. The seating challenge annoyed the *Times* and the editor thought that Jones's repeated earlier defeats "should have taught any head less thick than that of an African that he was wasting his time." Jones could not be fighting for principle, the editor asserted. Instead, he charged, it was the "double temptation of lucre and prestige . . . that actuates this chronic contestant." Jones stood to receive two thousand dollars from the U.S. House of Representatives to cover the costs of his case, a significant sum, and the *Times* wanted to believe that this was Jones's only motivation: "The pockets of Mr. Jones promptly gape for the coveted windfall." Whether Jones ever won a single cent was not what really bothered the *Times*. Jones was no mere gadfly and that was the problem. Mindful of renewed black political activity in 1896, the editor sensed something larger afoot. Jones, he decided, was acting on someone else's behalf, maybe Lynch, maybe the Republican National Committee, maybe some other body. He could not believe that Jones alone was really preparing the challenge; its wording suggested, he continued, "the presence of a far shrewder power." Unable to accept that Jones could conceive and execute this, he dared not guess "who the monkey is behind the cat's paw" and warned that some more ominous and "determined assault" lay in the offing.[28]

Cornelius Jones soldiered on and began taking testimony in mid-January. This was the best chance Mississippi Republicans would have in a long time to do *anything* about the hated 1890 constitution, but not even that fact could knit the Hill and Lynch factions back together. Lynch, in fact, spoke out against Jones (who was a Hill man, after all) and his contest, so the *Vicksburg Commercial Herald* noted. There was no more hostile paper in Mississippi than that venerable Vicksburg organ, whose editor was delighted to see even more fissures developing in within Mississippi's ranks of black politicians. Jones was doing exactly what Lynch had hoped to do himself but that seemed not to matter; according to this account, Lynch had told friends that Jones was not up to the task and that his elections contest could not succeed, never mind that it was exactly what Lynch himself had proposed. Picking up the story from Vicksburg, the *Memphis Commercial Appeal,* which had consistently denounced Lynch throughout the previous year, seemed now to consider him a statesman, and smugly headlined the piece "Lynch Takes No Stock in Jones." Jones never replied in kind and left no record to suggest that he was concerned in the slightest.[29]

Cornelius Jones's most important work in 1896 was done before the Mississippi Supreme Court, where he argued two new criminal appeals, one of which was *Williams v. Mississippi.* The cases were argued simultaneously to *Ratliff v. Beale,* and the latter was the only one that Mississippians noticed. Only one report, in fact, has been found that alludes to any sort of African American initiative to test the state's constitution in the courts. A brief comment in the *New Orleans Daily Picayune* described an "organization of negroes to test the state's franchise plan," insisting that the effort is "rather to be welcomed." The account suggested that the initiative owed to Lynch, but that seems unlikely. Lynch would have publicized such a thing far more widely had he any hand in it. It is likelier, though still uncertain, that this referred to Jones's cases. None of that mattered to reporters. They cared only that the question might be settled soon. "Nothing is gained through delay," the *Daily Picayune* report concluded. The 1890 constitution's franchise article, whether due to its poll-tax provision or its dubious constitutionality, was a recurrent topic of discussion throughout 1896. Black Mississippians and Populists always derided it; Democrats universally exulted in it. It was, an anonymous Jackson attorney gushed that June in the *Daily Clarion-Ledger*'s "Street Talk" column, "one of the greatest documents ever framed." Cornelius Jones had initiated a test, but the lawyer was surely unconcerned because, as he described it, the "Constitution of Mississippi is a great and wise one" that "will stand through the ages."[30]

Jones had prepared two appeals for the Mississippi Supreme Court. *Williams,* though more famous by far, was originally secondary to its companion—*John Henry Dixon v. Mississippi.* On May 15, 1896, John Henry Dixon slung a loaded shotgun over his shoulder and stormed furiously down a country road outside Greenville. When he reached the home of Eliza Minor, a school-aged boy, "Jake," who lived in Eliza's care asked John Henry where he was going. John Henry threatened to kill the boy if he asked that question again. So the precocious child repeated his question, whereupon John Henry raised the gun to his shoulder and fired two warning shots. Eliza's neighbor and daughter, Lavinia, heard the shots and confronted John Henry. He reloaded his gun and fired on Lavinia twice, wounding her seriously and Nancy Minor (another of Eliza's daughters) mortally. Dixon's intended destination that day had, in fact, been Lavinia's house. He went there to claim the young woman he wanted to marry, Felina Minor (Eliza's granddaughter). Felina and John Henry had once been engaged, but she broke it off and he had not taken it well. Enraged, he threatened to kill his former intended, and she sought refuge with her Aunt Lavinia. Dixon was arrested that day and arraigned on May 29. This was a crime of passion and that was the defense presented by his attorney, Cornelius Jones, after a motion to quash and a removal petition were denied during his June 15 trial. The defense failed and the Washington County circuit court sentenced Dixon to lifetime imprisonment in the state penitentiary at Jackson.[31]

The removal motion's failure came as no surprise. Jones had needed it to fail. Mindful of his losses in *Gibson* and *Smith,* he made some show of satisfying Justice Harlan's evidentiary demands. Here, though, Cornelius Jones showed that his ambition exceeded his acumen. He was not the attorney for this job. He apparently regarded Justice Harlan's dictates as pro forma, presenting no exhibits and no data to support his motions and pleas. All he offered the circuit court were shoddy affidavits from himself, John Henry Dixon, and his other client—Henry Williams.

Affidavits alone were acceptable under Mississippi practice, but since he intended all along to enter federal court with these cases, he should have anticipated what federal courts—the U.S. Supreme Court, in particular— might demand in addition to the state rules. Again, those additional demands had been made clear in *Gibson* and *Smith*. Jones's own affidavit was significant because he had been in Mississippi's legislature when it debated whether to call a constitutional convention in 1890 and thus he knew full well what the intent had been. Even so it was brief but not nearly so short as Dixon's, which basically stated that he agreed with Jones's assertions, or as Williams's, which simply seconded Dixon's. Still, the *Dixon* affidavits appear positively exhaustive when compared with those presented in the prosecution of Eliza Brown's murderer, Henry Williams, who also stood trial on June 15, 1896.

Theophilus Brown awoke on the morning of December 27, 1895, and he could not find his favorite pants. He thought they might be at his sister Eliza's house (who worked as a laundress) so he went there looking for them. Her house quiet, he let himself inside, came upon a large pile of dirty laundry, and dug through it in search of the missing trousers. He never found the pants, though he did find Eliza. Her body was hidden beneath the heap, cold and covered with small feathers. Washington County's medical examiner concluded that she "was choked to death."[32]

Brown had last seen his sister alive on Christmas Day, which also was the last time her family and friends recalled having seen Henry Williams, her live-in paramour. Williams had suspected Eliza of cheating long before that fateful Christmas day. He had told his friend Gus Miles of rumors about Lizzie; gossip was circulating that she had "taken a man." Henry worked hard and gave Eliza his money, he fumed, "and she was lying around with another man." He was furious, Miles remembered: "The God dam bitch he was going to fix her, and leave her." Williams actually suspected Miles, who, of course, denied the accusation. Gus Miles had not been the only person whom Henry Williams confronted about Lizzie's alleged infidelity, and when she was found slain, the suspicious lover became a suspected murderer.[33]

On December 27, 1895, when Theophilus Brown found his sister's body, Henry Williams was nowhere to be found. He had left Greenville in a hurry and the Washington County sheriff posted a reward for his capture. Williams turned up a few weeks later and was promptly arrested. His captor found him in the rafters of a southern Washington home, where he climbed (according to varied testimony) to either evade capture or to steal a cache of pecans squirreled away there by a group of local children. In any event, he did not resist arrest and while waiting for the train to Greenville, Williams confessed—plied with alcohol, or so he claimed. A grand jury promptly indicted and arraigned him and he was readied for trial. Cornelius Jones was his attorney and, as had happened in *Dixon,* he filed a pretrial removal petition and motion to quash. As had also happened in *Dixon,* the circuit court denied both.

At trial on June 16, Williams never denied that he killed Eliza Brown and even volunteered that he had wanted her dead. He stated under cross examination: "I did not say I killed her at all, I do not know whether I killed her or not, I tried to do it." When he arrived at Eliza's house on December 25, he claimed to have seen another man leaving "with his hat in his hand." Too, Henry claimed that Eliza wished to see him dead. He unlocked the door, stormed in, and Eliza grabbed a pistol, threatening him: "You God dam son of a bitch I told you days and days before I was going to kill you."[34]

Henry Williams was not a sophisticated man and there was never a doubt as to how his trial would turn out. His best hope was to cast the episode as self-defense. It was a desperate claim and he did himself no favors with his tortured and rambling testimony. Williams never made clear who tried to kill whom first. Eliza raised her gun and told Henry she was going to kill him, he stated:

> And I said what for, I had not been paying no attention to her, she says I have told you if you ever run on me with a man I am going to kill you and today you run on me she says prepare yourself to die, because when I go to kill you I am going to kill myself so that the law won't have no hold on me and she made at me with the pistol and I struck her with my hand on the side of the neck.

It all happened atop the feather-stuffed mattress that Eliza and Henry had shared as lovers. It was a violent struggle and the bedding ripped and disgorged its downy stuffing. A pair of pants found at the scene—Henry's pants—were covered from the knees down with the same downy feathers that adhered to Eliza's body. Someone other than he (though Henry claimed not to know whom) had carried her from the bed, laid her on the floor, and hid her under the wash.[35]

Cornelius Jones's motions in Henry Williams's case were identical to those filed on John Henry Dixon's behalf and supported by the same three affiants: himself, Williams, and Dixon. Though it hardly seems possible, the *Williams* affidavits were more perfunctory and shoddier than those in *Dixon*. Jones's eight-line-long affidavit stated his support for the motions, Williams endorsed Jones's endorsement, and Dixon seconded Williams. He was convicted and sentenced to death. Williams was scheduled to be hanged on July 30, 1896.[36]

Macabre and risky though it may seem at first glance, Jones needed to lose at the circuit level, and given that these were murder cases death sentences were the probably outcome. The apparent truth is that John Henry Dixon's and Henry Williams's lives were not his concern. This was not a desperate bid to spare them—it was a gamble. But the gambler would not have to cover the loss. That burden fell upon his indigent and desperate clients. The *Greenville Times,* in its "Jones vs. the State" editorial decrying Jones's congressional seating challenge, had also attacked these repeated criminal appeals. Jones cared only to enrich himself and gain "prestige with his own race," the editor sneered. In all four cases, "the negroes of the surrounding country were stirred up to a sort of religious fervor by appeals of their preachers and leaders." Those appeals yielded contributions "solicited from the pockets of cooks and washerwomen," but the greatest sacrifice came from his clients, for, as the *Times* editor pointed out, "each appealed case paid a capital fee." "Jones vs. the State" was in no way fair. Jones was never going to receive reasoned treatment from the *Times* or any other Democratic organ. Still, the editor's point was, on some level, valid. Jones's ultimate goal was noble, but his chosen route and the decision to go it alone were undeniably dangerous and arguably reckless.[37]

Jones carried Dixon's and Williams's appeals to Jackson in late summer. Unlike in *Gibson* and *Smith,* it was readily apparent that *Dixon* and *Williams* were attempts to undermine disfranchisement. The court and Attorney General Wiley Nash raised their guard and *Dixon* drew the closest attention. Jones was trying to overturn the state constitution with these murder appeals and was trying to make legislative intent the issue. Though *Dixon* and *Williams* were argued simultaneous to *Ratliff v. Beale,* and though in the latter Nash freely indulged explorations of legislative intent, Nash resolved to close that avenue to Jones. "Such an effort, such an attempt," Nash fumed of Jones's claims about legislative intent, was "unprecedented in legislative, or judicial history, in this or any other civilized country, and such an idea will not be entertained for one moment." Chief Justice Tim Cooper, writing for the court, was not quite as exercised as Nash, though he was no more receptive to Jones's plan. Further, he could simply dance away from the question on account of the quality of Jones's briefs. His opinion was substantial. Cooper reviewed the state's constitution and its statutory jury and elections provisions at some length. Having done so, Cooper brushed aside Jones's hurried brief and barely consequential evidentiary affidavits. Jones offered nothing but an argument, the chief justice surmised, providing "some facts, many inferences, and deductions" to suggest that broad swaths of Mississippi's 1890 constitution violated the Fourteenth Amendment. But there was no evidence to persuade the court, even if the court had wanted to be persuaded.[38]

There had been absolutely no chance that Jones might win, and at the circuit court level, Jones really did not want to. If he won, he could not carry these appeals to Washington, D.C., but it did not have to be this easy for the state of Mississippi. His hasty and shallow presentation made things too simple for the Mississippi Supreme Court, which used the U.S. Supreme Court's *Gibson* and *Smith* decisions against him. Their critique was devastating. "We have searched the record in vain," Chief Justice Cooper wrote, for evidence of official malfeasance. "The motion contains much irrelevant matter," he noted, "set up with great prolixity, and in involved obscure language." There was "no suggestion in the motion that the jury commissioners were guilty of fraud" and "we can discover nothing in the record which shows that the appellant . . . has been denied" a fair trial. The court affirmed Dixon's conviction and so too that of Henry Williams, whose appeal merited only a per curiam opinion, a terse explanation that the *Williams* decision was the same as that in *Dixon*. The Mississippi Supreme Court had done great violence to Jones's cases, but they remained alive.[39]

Jones wanted to bring more U.S. Supreme Court challenges to Mississippi's 1890 constitution and he had them, but *Gibson* and *Smith* controlled *Dixon* and *Williams* and that portended ill. Jones had responded to John Marshall Harlan's evidentiary demands with three affidavits and no sort of exhibits. Worse, those affidavits were poor and pro forma. Jones did not know it, but he had botched things. He faced overwhelming odds, they stacked the deck against him, his was an uphill struggle, one hand was tied behind his back, and so on, but no patronizing cliché excuses poor law-yering.

The Mississippi Supreme Court revealed its rulings in *Dixon* and *Williams* on November 9, 1896. Williams's execution was scheduled for December 11. The state supreme court postponed Williams's hanging and then formally certified writs of error (which explain the particular questions raised on appeal) on December 13. For reasons unknown, Jones did not file *Williams v. Mississippi* until December 10, 1897. He never did appeal John Henry Dixon's case to Washington, D.C., and nothing in the historical record explains why that case reached an end or whether Dixon had met his.

Little was heard about *Williams* until March 15, 1898, at the height of Louisiana's 1898 "disfranchising" constitutional convention, when the *Daily Picayune* reported that the Supreme Court had certified Henry Williams's appeal. The paper anticipated that its eventual decision would "have an important bearing on the suffrage amendment of the Louisiana constitution." That did not happen. Something else had intervened, ensuring that *Williams* went virtually unnoticed: the Spanish-American War. With a war raging, there was little national interest in a Mississippi voting rights case argued by an obscure black attorney on some convicted black murderer's behalf.[40]

Jones told the U.S. Supreme Court that it should overturn Henry Williams's death sentence because the grand jury that indicted him and the petit jury that convicted him were products of unconstitutional suffrage restrictions. The three specific assignments of error to the Supreme Court were (1) the trial court should have quashed the indictment and accepted the removal petition, (2) the trial court should have granted a new trial and should not have levied the death penalty, and (3) the Mississippi Supreme Court erred when it affirmed the trial court's decision. The 1890 constitution, Jones contended, was invalid, and thus too the jury selection statutes adopted subsequently. It violated the Fourteenth Amendment and the 1870 congressional act readmitting Mississippi to the United States. Mississippi's framers, Jones told the Court, had intended to discriminate "on account of race, color, and previous condition of servitude, *and their enforcement has so resulted*." The phrase "their enforcement has so resulted" was problematic because Jones thereby burdened himself with proving intent, and with proving voting officials' maliciousness, and with his failure to show either any textual deficiency or how the texts themselves had led to an unconstitutional result.[41]

Some years ago, historian J. Morgan Kousser aptly characterized Jones's

Williams brief as "bluster." It was but eighteen pages long, and for evidence Jones offered nothing beyond the briefs and affidavits he had previously submitted to the Washington County circuit court and Mississippi's supreme court. Those were filed as part of the transcript of record from the lower courts and were shockingly substandard and insubstantial. Given that his client could already feel a coarse rope tightening around his neck, Jones's work on Henry Williams's behalf was nothing short of reckless.[42]

Of the infamous "understanding clause," Jones complained that it granted officials the "full power . . . to ask all sorts of vain impertinent questions," but he offered no evidence, anecdotal or otherwise, of what a "vain impertinent question" looked like. Jones complained of the registrars' broad discretion, but he offered nothing to show why broad discretion violated either the Constitution or laws of the United States. Jones complained that a county's voting officer was the "sole judge" of an applicant's fitness but, again, offered nothing to support his contention. Regarding intent, and to his credit, Jones suggested that the Court examine *Ratliff v. Beale* and spent several pages arguing that the justices had authority to review state constitutions. As for the evidentiary burden that Justice Harlan elucidated in *Gibson* and *Smith,* Jones simply stated that the evidence he presented in the state courts was in accord "with the law and practice" of Mississippi courts. Continuing in that vein, he dared the Court to disagree with Mississippi practice: "We contend that if the facts alleged . . . are true, which is admitted by the State Supreme Court, then this court is bound to assume that the facts are true." Whatever may be said of his talents as a lawyer, Jones was an educated man, and an earnest and ardent spokesman for black Mississippians. "The principles invoked in this cause are as firm as our great government," he insisted. Henry Williams's plea, which was a bid for his life, was "no technicality, but an appeal to the judiciary of the country that the vindication of the Federal Constitution and laws should be most emphatic for its generosity and unswerving constancy."[43]

Charles B. Mitchell of Pontotoc, an agrarian Democrat, a former speaker of the Mississippi House of Representatives, Cornelius Jones's colleague in the 1890 legislature, a prime mover behind the 1890 constitutional convention, argued the state's case. Mitchell, of course, carefully answered Jones's arguments, but because supporting evidence was essentially nonexistent, his was not a hard task. Jones had failed to attack the text of either the constitution or state statutes, which allowed Mitchell to posit that "nothing can be found, not a line or word, which in any manner whatever discriminates against any citizen." "Not a word or line in either," he continued, "by any reasonable construction, can be deemed obnoxious to any part of the Constitution of the United States or any law thereof." He went through the precedents Jones cited one by one, methodically dismissing every contention, and reproduced much of the Mississippi Supreme Court's decision in *Dixon*. Just as the state court had brushed aside Jones's contentions as mere verbiage, Mitchell concluded that "it is true that plaintiff in error has a good deal to say as to the motives which actuated the framers of these laws." Mitchell insisted that, in the absence of contrary evidence, the Supreme Court should stick to those laws' plain text. They thus must not consider anything that Jones had laid before them. "We think," he wrote, "the surest way to arrive at their motive is by a proper Construction and interpretation of the laws themselves."[44]

During the 1890 constitutional convention, in the years following, and then again in the *Williams* briefs, Mississippi officials openly admitted that they had wanted to eliminate as many black voters as possible. There was never any suggestion otherwise. Yet they also insisted that they had really only targeted illiteracy, poverty, and criminal proclivities—not skin color. They knew that all three would affect black voters especially hard because the constitution identified all of the crimes committed disproportionately by blacks. Still, illiterate and poor whites suffered too, and this, it was always argued, rendered the document "constitutional." The disfranchisers would go after personal characteristics rather than complexion, and Mississippi's supreme court had said in *Ratliff v. Beale* that personal characteristics fell "within the field of permissible action under the limitations imposed by the federal constitution."[45]

Once in operation, there was nothing benign or color blind about the 1890 constitution. There was never supposed to be, and few seriously believed otherwise. If Jones wanted to prove racial animus, he could have done better than he did. Basic, rudimentary evidence—voter registration tables, records of the convention, substantive affidavits, and so on—was what he needed. John Marshall Harlan had specifically demanded that Jones show evidence in his *Gibson* and *Smith* opinion and the best we can presume is that Jones misunderstood Harlan. He could not hope to impress the U.S. Supreme Court with evidence that he did not offer. He simply failed to do *anything* that might prevent the Court from resorting to syllogisms and technicalities.

California's Joseph McKenna wrote the *Williams v. Mississippi* decision.

He borrowed liberally from *Ratliff v. Beale,* explaining that Mississippi's framers, operating "within the field of permissible action . . . swept the circle of expedients to obstruct the exercise of the franchise by the negro race." The Court similarly and unanimously swept aside Jones's case. Focusing on the texts of the state constitution and statutes, the justices concluded that the Mississippi constitution disadvantaged white men as much as it did black men; Mississippi's voting restrictions were neutral on their face since "whatever is sinister in their intention, if anything, can be prevented by both races." The justices had ducked disfranchisement for the fourth time in three years and McKenna laid down his now-infamous declaration that Mississippi's suffrage restrictions "do not on their face discriminate between the races, and it has not been shown that their actual administration was evil; only that evil was possible under them."[46]

An important precedent cited by McKenna was *Yick Wo v. Hopkins,* which involved a San Francisco city ordinance that targeted the Chinese without stating as much. *Yick Wo* had said that if a statute's enforcement produced an unconstitutional discrimination (as the San Francisco ordinance did), then it would be held void. Mississippi's 1890 constitution produced a discrimination, one that certainly seemed to fail the *Yick Wo* test for constitutionality, but the Court found that the California case presented clear evidence of discrimination while the Mississippi case did not. Indeed, the single most important line in *Williams* followed Justice McKenna's application of the *Yick Wo* test. Regarding Mississippi's suffrage regulations, McKenna concluded, "it has not been shown their actual administration was evil." Conveniently, the Court did not indicate what kind of evidence could prove racial discrimination.[47]

Historians, with rare exceptions, have presented *Williams v. Mississippi* as having offered explicit and final approval for southern disfranchisement, but it did not, and it invited further litigation.[48] It had settled nothing, one way or another. Frank Dake was among *Williams'* earliest critics and he complained about it to the *Albany Law Journal's* editor in 1904. Southern states had devised all sorts of ruses to obscure the true nature of their suffrage restrictions and Dake thought it was time that the Court return to *Yick Wo* and presume that effects had causes. He believed that if the justices could not stand on their own precedents then they might consider the Bible. "Long ago," Dake recalled from the Gospel of Matthew, "the world's greatest teacher said: "'if thine eye be evil, thy whole body shall be full of darkness.'"[49]

Williams garnered more notice than had *Gibson* and *Smith,* but it was not a landmark event, even in Mississippi. The Spanish-American War was foremost in the popular mind, and the Court's ruling barely rose above the din. The war, the *Nation* complained, had allowed the decision "to pass almost unnoticed." There were sporadic, localized efforts to rouse wider interest—among Boston's religious community, for example. That city's *Congregationalist,* writing in the summer, wondered whether the "radical decision" would provoke any sustained inquiry, though "as yet it can scarcely be said to have been noted by the people of the country." Boston's Methodists shared the Congregationalists' concern. Their organ, *Zion's Herald,* doubted whether the "careful legislation of a whole generation was ever before so effectively wiped out by a single decision of any court." Summer lapsed into fall, fall into winter, and still no stronger reaction arose. The *Congregationalist* finally concluded that it had been a slow year in American courts but that *Williams* had been the "most pregnant decision" by far.[50]

Jones did make two applications for reargument in *Williams.* The first, dated May 12, 1898, attempted to address the Court's concerns about the lack of hard evidence in his briefs. He insisted that the Court erred in demanding anything beyond the lower court record. His affidavits were acceptable under state practice, he continued to insist. In the Mississippi Supreme Court, "the averment and proof supporting the pleadings were considered ample, and dealt therewith upon the assumption that they were true." The May 12 application failed (though no formal expression of that survives) and Jones subsequently filed a second, undated application. The second one was more strident than the first and more strident than even the original briefs. Yet the argument itself did not change. It was nothing but argument, really, and that had been the problem all along. Cornelius Jones consistently missed the point. The U.S. Supreme Court had not denied the brief's validity, it had said that argument was not enough. What he needed to have done, at the trial level, was anticipate the Supreme Court's demands. He had intended all along to get his case to Washington, D.C., and he should have anticipated the need for something more than the minimum required by state practice. This was not too much to expect of a late-nineteenth-century lawyer.[51]

Cornelius Jones's 1898 congressional campaign also failed, and he buried himself in another seating challenge. He could, though, derive some small comfort from the fact that he fared better than any other black candidate in Mississippi that year, garnering 15 percent of the vote. African Americans in the district remained unusually active, the *Belen Quitman Quill*'s concerned editor had noted just ahead of the election, and if Democrats did not turn out in full force, "we might be represented in the next Congress by a colored Republican." That did not happen, of course, and afterward Jones effectively retired from politics.[52]

After the original case and the two applications for reargument failed, Jones made no further effort to save Henry Williams's life. The man whose name would forever be connected with southern disfranchisement was hanged on September 28, 1899. His ill-fated appeal ended the antidisfranchisement litigation's first phase. By the time that the Supreme Court announced *Williams*, disfranchisement had changed and with it the opposition. The grandfather clause had debuted. With that, the second phase began.[53]

3
The Grandfather Clause
Phase Two Begins

> The brain of a lawyer never devised anything more ingenious than
> the "grandfather clause" of the Louisiana constitution.
> —*Edinburgh Review,* 1905

Good registrars were hard to find. Their task was delicate and thankless and dirty, and in Mississippi, that state's disfranchisers would have been nothing without men like Jim Brown. W. J. "Jim" Brown Jr. oversaw the city of Jackson's voter registration, and as the *Jackson Daily Clarion-Ledger* reported in October 1896, he "not only makes a good and careful registrar but he really gets a barrel of fun out of his job most every day." Brown was described as a "very conscientious man," one with "religious scruples against letting names of objectionable voters get on the books." But his was not a sacerdotal office, though he apparently regarded voter registration as sacramental. The Mississippi constitution was his Scripture and the understanding clause was his primary tool. "Can you read," he would ask a "clerical looking darkey," and "Oh, yes sir" was given as the "usual response, but seldom is it done satisfactorily." [1]

In 1897 Alex Gates, a Mississippi black man who had failed an understanding test similar to those administered by Brown, offered his experience as testimony in a congressional seating challenge:

REGISTRAR: What is the Congress?
GATES: Congress is the people.
REGISTRAR: What is the Congress?
GATES: Congress is Congress.
REGISTRAR: What are the duties of Congress?
GATES: Well, they make speeches, and pow wows, and play cards, and get drunk, and rides on the trains, and draws salaries. That is all I see in the papers.

Gates's story was eventually published in order to both make fun of him and make light of public perceptions of the duties and responsibilities of congressmen. In that respect it surely succeeded. It also showed that the understanding clause, and the understanding tests that followed from it, were jokes, but ones that only qualified as gallows humor.[2]

When queried during these the ill-defined understanding tests, few applicants could offer the correct shibboleths in reply because they were not supposed to be able to do so. The registrars' pleasure was the fulcrum in this enterprise, and disfavored men simply could not tilt things their way—no matter how many correct answers they did or did not give. To wit, as the *Daily Clarion-Ledger*'s piece on Brown concluded, "Failure to explain and elucidate" the Mississippi and the United States constitutions to the "satisfaction of the conscientious registrar settles the would-be voter." Clearly, Jim Brown was the very model of a Mississippi registrar.[3]

Mississippi Democrats were glad to have found a few men like Jim Brown and praised them. Disfranchisement was not easy. Disfranchisement was not pretty. Disfranchisement was not for the fainthearted. Jocular though Jim Brown may have seemed, he bore a heavy burden. The Democracy depended upon him to do the party's dirty work, and he carried Mississippi's electoral frauds upon his shoulders, protecting the many from their taint.

Jim Brown did his dirty deeds with surgical precision, yet few other state's disfranchisers seemed eager to rely upon any Jim Browns of their own. South Carolina had welcomed "Jim Brown" in 1895 and adopted a modified "Mississippi Plan," but by 1898 that formula was falling from favor. Several more southern states were clamoring for disfranchising constitutions of their own, but none turned to Mississippi, at least not openly. The "Mississippi Plan" for disfranchisement featured literacy and property tests and the infamous understanding clause. That understanding clause, which was Mississippi's primary innovation, was just a fancier way to steal, and Mississippi Democrats *knew* how to steal. Though no other state's disfranchisers doubted its efficacy, and appreciated that it would be difficult to attack in court, there were widespread reservations, namely, that it did not actually end ballot fraud. It only transferred ballot fraud into the hands of registration boards and individual registrars such as Jim Brown.

The disfranchisers who emerged after 1895, like those before, hungered to disfranchise blacks and Republicans, and sometimes Populists—anyone who threatened conservative, white Democratic hegemony. They were no less hungry to "purify" elections; they sought an end to the fraud and theft and violence of the thirty years previous. Louisiana was the first of this new group to act and that state resolved not to follow Mississippi's model. In 1898, Louisiana's disfranchisers searched furiously for a better, cleaner way, some self-executing loophole that could exempt whites who stood to suffer under the newly heightened regulations.

By abandoning the Mississippi Plan, disfranchisers in Louisiana and succeeding states lurched toward an explicit violation of the Fourteenth and Fifteenth Amendments. Mississippi's disfranchisers argued about the U.S. Constitution in 1890, as did South Carolina's in 1895, and the devices those two states adopted exploited a national trend toward restricted suffrage. These restrictions may not have been bulletproof, and few contemporaries actually believed that they operated fairly, but they *looked* fair and their framers advanced clever arguments in their defense.

Appearances were everything in the business of disfranchisement. Appropriately, contemporaneous analyses trended toward the superficial. Many national observers found themselves caught between disdain for southern states' malign intentions and support for new elections regulations. Thus they fell prey to the South's deft rhetorical trap and conceded that they could not criticize southern states for adopting educational tests when many northern states had already done likewise. Ahead of Louisiana's 1898 convention, the *Pointe à la Hâche Plaquemines Protector* reviewed northern newspaper coverage and deduced that the country's editors sympathized with what Mississippi and South Carolina had done and what Louisiana was about to do. Unanimity did not exist nationally, of course, but "every intelligent Northern paper," the *Protector* claimed, "raises no objection to the contemplated action of the Louisiana convention to disfranchise the negroes." That was a stretch. National papers approved of ballot reform, yes, but whether that extended to the particular methods the southern states used was another matter.[4]

One of the disfranchisers' strangest qualities, and the hardest to accept and appreciate, was that when they complained of fraud and crime, and begged for relief, they meant it. This reflected a genuine and genuinely twisted concern that things had gotten out of hand. They did not mind that conservative Democrats had retained power as a result of this malfeasance. They only minded that their frauds and crimes had become so flagrant and overt.

When the movement reached Louisiana, few Louisianans wanted anything to do with Mississippi's understanding clause because it was more of the same: it was dishonest, and did not resolve the problem of political corruption. They denounced Mississippi's "cure" as worse than the disease and demanded some new remedy that would not require systematic manipulation. That, the *Abbeville Meridional* editorialized in January 1898, was "where the shoe pinches." Louisiana voters had already agreed to stage a constitutional convention and the *Meridional* wanted it to protect as many white voters as possible, though there must be "no juggling, no shibboleth scheme or gauzy fraud" such as that in Mississippi. Accordingly, the *Meridional* was pleased to hear Ernest Kruttschnitt's criticism of Louisiana's disfranchising forebears. Speaking in January 1898, Kruttschnitt (who would preside over Louisiana's constitutional convention) declared that "we can do better than the state of Mississippi." Mississippi's plan, he thought, "means the crystallization of fraud in the organic law." He surmised that South Carolina had done better by making its understanding clause temporary, where Mississippi's was permanent. "It was an improvement," he explained, because "Mississippi's fraud is eternal." The only hope for an alternative lay in innovation, and Kruttschnitt declared that "the time is ripe for the experiment we are about to make." Enter the grandfather clause.[5]

Though it came to represent all that was foul about southern disfranchisement, the grandfather clause was not of southern nativity and, in its purest form, was innocuous. The term "grandfather," in legalese, indicates that a particular statute or provision thereof is self-executing. Grandfather provisions typically suggest a fixed expiration date (e.g., "this subsection shall remain operative until . . ."). They may also create an exemption so that a previously qualified licensed class (voters, teachers, physicians, etc.) does not suffer under heightened or more onerous qualifications. Licensees are thus "grandfathered" past the stricter standard. Nor were grandfather clauses to suffrage restrictions especially novel. Massachusetts, for example, adopted one in 1857. Article XX of the Massachusetts Constitution, ratified on May 1, 1857, established a literacy test but also exempted older voters: "The provisions of this amendment shall not apply to any person . . . who now has the right to vote, nor to any person who shall be sixty years of age or upwards at the time this amendment shall take effect." Again, loopholes such as that were self-executing, and no mere registration board member decided who qualified—sixty years old was sixty years old. By contrast, nothing in the Mississippi constitution operated of its own statutory volition. Every disfranchising state relied to a great degree upon steely-eyed, cold-blooded registrars; some measure of discretion was always necessary to achieve that which could never be spelled out in terms. In Mississippi, however, everything was left to the registrars and Ernest Kruttschnitt wanted no such thing for Louisiana.[6]

A grandfather clause solved the self-execution problem for the Louisianans and quelled whites' fears about the strict literacy and property tests. South Carolina had briefly entertained the concept of a grandfather clause, but none other than Ben Tillman had deemed it unworkable and risky and quashed it. Louisiana's disfranchisers were willing to take that risk, though they had to wrestle with one very thorny question: How, exactly, would they word it? They could not say "no black man may benefit" or "no white man of Democratic proclivities need fear disqualification." However phrased, their clause had to stand a court test and there *would* be one. Of that, everyone was certain.

The Louisiana convention made its grandfather clause very literal. Like that of Massachusetts, Louisiana's exempted voters of a certain age, but it also protected younger men based upon the person of their grandfather. The provision allowed illiterate and impoverished men to register if their father or grandfathers had voted anywhere before January 1, 1867—before passage of the Reconstruction Act, which provided for adult male suffrage—and therefore excluded nearly all blacks. Additionally, Louisiana's grandfather clause embraced all applicants, but those claiming it had to first prove that they or some male ancestor had registered as a voter somewhere in the United States before Reconstruction: "No male person who was on January 1, 1867, or at any date prior thereto, entitled to vote under the Constitution or statutes of any State of the United States, wherein he resided, and no son or grandson of any such person not less than twenty-one years of age at the date of the adoption of this Constitution, . . . shall be denied the right to register and vote in this State by reason of his failure to possess the educational or property qualifications."[7]

Lurking all the while behind this complex verbiage were those inevitable legal challenges. Louisiana's disfranchisers knew they were playing a dangerous game and hoped to outfox litigators by mooting their cases. To that end, they built a second grandfather clause into the grandfather clause, a self-destruct mechanism set to detonate on September 1, 1898. If no one filed suit case before that date, a plaintiff would be in the difficult position of asking a court to either invalidate or enjoin something that did not exist as a matter of law. Further, the 1898 constitution forbade judicial appeals of unsuccessful registration attempts. That would not affect any federal cases, but the Louisiana framers thought they had prevented any use of the state's district courts. It also was unclear whether federal courts even possessed jurisdiction, and thus any U.S. district court proceeding would necessarily be a drawn-out affair.

Louisiana's grandfather clause meant that parish-level registrars, registration boards, and elections managers would not have to commit the same frauds as their Mississippi and South Carolina counterparts. There was still a clear fraud involved, but their role in the fraud was simply ministerial, rather than practical or discretionary. They would not have to "do" much of anything to sneak whites onto the voting rolls, and black men too might theoretically use it. The thing was just weird; "Peculiar and Unique" was how a *Portland Morning Oregonian* headline described it.[8]

Disfranchisers embraced the clause because it "was ingenious," Charles Chesnutt wrote in his novel *The Marrow of Tradition*, "but it was not fair." Fair or not, however, the grandfather clause did not mention race and as such it facilitated lame paeans to racial neutrality. Yet many leading disfranchisers and sympathetic observers believed that it was not enough, that the grandfather clause revealed too much, would provoke judicial and congressional wrath, and that it was unseemly, medieval even, for its suggestion that voting capacity could be transferred through blood. In that vein, a prominent delegate to Alabama's 1901 constitutional convention characterized the instrument as a "creature of the thirteenth century, born out of time, whose great-grandfather lives in the State of Louisiana." In an 1899 *Harvard Law Review* essay, Providence attorney and Rhode Island state legislator, Amasa Eaton, concluded that the clause could never withstand the U.S. Supreme Court's scrutiny. During the 1890s and early 1900s, Eaton made a hobby of studying the new southern constitutions for the *Review* and through prodigiousness became a leading disfranchisement expert. "Can we doubt," he asked of Louisiana's innovation, that U.S. Supreme Court justices would reject it after examining its "true intent, real meaning, and actual operation?" Still, it was so novel that predictions were difficult, and devotees and detractors alike always returned to its ingenuity. The thing was undeniably and devilishly clever. Charles Chesnutt had seen that, as did the *Edinburgh Review,* which wryly concluded that the "brain of a lawyer never devised anything more ingenious than the grandfather clause of the Louisiana constitution."[9]

Ingenious, but also igneous, Louisiana's grandfather clause ignited a fiery controversy that blazed through the convention hall and consumed editorial pages. The state's press corps deemed it ridiculous and fumed—with neither a wink nor a nod—that it besmirched the integrity of Louisiana politics. For all of the talk about finding something better than Mississippi's plan, the delegates had left editors and opinion leaders nonplused. Mississippi and South Carolina editors too had complained just as loudly about those states' understanding clauses, but to little avail. Louisiana editors nonetheless tried to dissuade their state's convention. Alexandria's *Daily Town Talk* was incredulous and blunt: It would be "better to beat the negro as it has been done in the past than to do it by endeavoring to break down" the nation's organic law with "something that a school boy can see will not stand when carried before the United States Supreme Court."[10]

Louisiana's disfranchising turn initially seemed destined to garner far more notice than either Mississippi's or South Carolina's. But outside events constantly intruded, distracting outside observers. Those distractions are essential to understanding what happened that spring in New Orleans and why the nation reacted as it did (or rather did not). In New Orleans, the convention coincided with Mardi Gras and Rex and his merry courtiers provided better copy than the preening politicos who populated the convention hall. National papers cared more about things like the sensational Émile Zola libel trial across the ocean in France and a simmering diplomatic dispute with Spain. On February 8, local newspapers reported that the battleship USS *Maine* would not come for Mardi Gras as previously planned. Instead it remained in the Caribbean. One week later, the *Maine* exploded in Havana Harbor, and at least one editor thought that the convention should suspend its work or simply change course. "In view of the threatened war with Spain," the *Monroe Bulletin* complained, "now is a pretty time to be disfranchising citizens who are expected to fight for Louisiana." But the Populist *Bulletin*'s plea fell on deaf ears, and attention began to turn away from the convention.[11]

While the nation throbbed to the tocsin's beat, Louisiana's framers trotted out the grandfather clause. State observers had been furious—as furious as they were about Spain's alleged sneak attack on the *Maine*. Then another sort of torpedo struck the grandfather clause. State papers buzzed. "Ordinance No. 205 of the Suffrage Committee was 'blown up from the outside,'" an excited *Daily States* exclaimed. "The mine was placed unerring below Section 5 and the explosion . . . caused the almost immediate sinking of the same ordinance." The device had been planted by Louisiana's U.S. senators, Donelson Caffery and Samuel D. McEnery, who announced that they would not and could not defend the grandfather clause in the Senate. The senators unsettled the delegates. "Nothing of recent date," the *Opelousas Courier* believed, "had been so startling . . . and so prostrating to studied modes of constitutional circumvention as the terse and concurrent opinions" of Caffery and McEnery "recently wired to the savants of our unconstitutional convention." [12]

Instead of arguing with Caffery and McEnery, the convention majority contrasted their proposal with those adopted in Mississippi and South Carolina, schemes that convention president Ernest Kruttschnitt again criticized as "replete with opportunities for fraud." Kruttschnitt noted the limitations that circumscribed the convention's options: Louisiana could not confer the suffrage upon white men and exclude blacks "without coming into conflict with the fifteenth amendment of the federal constitution." That said, he insisted that the grandfather clause satisfied that demand and reiterated his absolute conviction that courts would let the new constitution alone. Judge Adolphe Valery Coco was one of those delegates who contended that Section 5 exceeded the Fifteenth Amendment's limits: "One needs only to compare the bill with the amendment to reach that conclusion." Beyond that, Coco believed the clause was a "weak and transparent subterfuge, an unmanly evasion of the constitution of the United States." Still, the majority ignored Coco's and all others' objections and adopted the grandfather clause overwhelmingly and "in spite of all attacks." The horrified editor of the *Morgan City Independent Democrat* was left to conclude that the convention had worked so hard and so long simply to convince the "intelligent voter that there are more fools to the square inch" in the Louisiana Democratic Party "than any other place in the United States." [13]

Louisiana adopted the grandfather clause at a time when much of the nation was not looking, when war fever gripped the public, and when few cared about black suffrage and electoral propriety. Still, that war fever would someday pass and the nation and Congress and the federal courts might yet turn their attention to disfranchisement. In 1900, the *Chicago Record-Herald's* Frank Putnam began a correspondence with Joseph Leveque, editor-publisher of a New Orleans literary magazine, the *Harlequin,* because he thought that "the South will shortly be 'called to the bar'" over disfranchisement. "While I have no thought of calling anyone to the bar (except for the gentle pursuit of cooling liquors)," Putnam teased, he was certain that the prospective court case bided ill for Louisiana. Leveque met Putnam's jibe with a defense of the new constitution written by Lieutenant Governor

Bob Snyder. Having read "Friend Snyder's exposition," Leveque retorted, "it would appear that Louisiana is ready for refreshments." Leveque's sparring was entertaining but not entirely convincing. Louisiana had to be ready, and not everyone was as glib as Monsieur Leveque. Glibness concerned Shreveport's *Daily Times* in June 1898: The new constitution "with the radical suffrage clause therein, makes it absolutely necessary that Louisiana's congressmen should be men of profound learning and unquestionable legal ability." Since both of Louisiana's U.S. senators hated the clause and had vowed not to defend it, the state's House delegation was key. Any Louisiana congressman, the *Daily Times* continued, would "have to contest with giants, and we must not send pigmys [*sic*]." Though no one knew when, whence, or by whom, Louisiana's grandfather clause *would* be called to the bar and pygmies would not do then, either.[14]

When disfranchisement came to North Carolina ten months later, commentators and policymakers there resurrected the Louisianans' demand for straightforward, self-executing, and court-proof suffrage restrictions. "We want it distinctively understood we are opposed to all sorts of trickery and jugglery," the *Beaufort Evening Messenger* editorialized. North Carolina would not have a constitutional convention. Instead, the 1899 legislature was going to prepare an amendment to the state constitution, one that would have to be ratified by the state's voters in August 1900. Whatever the legislature devised, Dunn's *County Union* insisted, it had to be "thoroughly prepared so that it will stand the tests of the courts." The amendment, the paper continued "must be faultless." Those were just the opening and familiar salvos. With no war to distract attention, and a long delay for completion of the amending process, North Carolina's grandfather clause fight was longer, louder, and far harder than Louisiana's had been.[15]

In every southern state, disfranchisers warned of "Negro rule," but North Carolina was the only one where what Democratic disfranchisers called "negro rule" came closest to actually happening. North Carolina Republicans and Populists, with a fusion ticket that mixed candidates of both parties, won a fair number of statewide offices in 1896, and they had relied upon the support of black voters. The *Raleigh Gazette,* an African American paper, had cautioned readers that Democrats would use race baiting and violence to sway those 1896 elections, issuing "A Warning" in an editorial column that black voters must avoid trouble at all costs, but another editorial published that same day demanded that blacks "Keep Up the Fight." "Bury Democracy," the editor chanted, and while it may not have been "buried," the Democracy suffered a cataclysm that election day in North Carolina.[16]

North Carolina Democrats' indignant reaction surprised no one, but the vicious and vitriolic responses of white North Carolinians in general did. No one was more alarmed or disappointed than the *Raleigh Gazette* when even the white churches inveighed against black voters. "It is clear that the negro is an obstacle; clear that inevitably the Southern country must be retarded in her political progress so long as he is an obstacle," the *Raleigh Biblical Recorder*, a white Baptist organ, declared in October 1897. Therefore, disfranchisement was "the only hope." The *Gazette*'s editor had expected as much from secular Democratic mouthpieces, "but when the journal of a great and powerful religious denomination gives such advice, then indeed are the rights and privileges of the negro as a voter in danger." "Danger Ahead," the editorial headline had warned.[17]

The *Biblical Recorder* maintained its call for disfranchisement through that autumn, driving the *Gazette*'s editor to respond that they must be worshiping a different savior. Of the *Recorder*'s reigning deity, the *Gazette* concluded that "such a God . . . we do not wish to serve." White Democratic sentiment was coalescing, and fast. By early 1898, the *Gazette* could only plead that Republicans and Populists be given a little time: "all that [they] want or need is a fair trial at running the State." That the *Gazette* even had to ask was an answer unto itself. No such "fair trial" would be forthcoming.[18]

What ensued was the vile and vicious election season that is now known as the White Supremacy Campaign of 1898. The name captured the sole issue in contention, but as James K. Vardaman observed from far away in Mississippi, white supremacy was never endangered in the Tarheel State. "The trouble in North Carolina is republicanism" Vardaman wrote, "not the negro," offering Mississippi up as an example of racial harmony courtesy of the 1890 constitution. But among southern Democrats, "Republican" and "negro" were synonyms, and that would not be corrected, not even by the likes of Vardaman, amidst a political campaign.[19]

The 1898 campaign was long, detestable, and infamous and need not be recounted at length here. North Carolina blacks resisted as much they could and pleaded their case, though it was a hopeless effort. The Baptist State Convention, an African American organization, lamented the "heated and most bitter political campaign" and begged that "colored people, our people, restrain themselves from excessive anger." No charge was too scurrilous to gain currency. "Negroes Buying Guns: A Negro Office-Holder

Visits Norfolk and Baltimore to Make Purchases," a *Raleigh News and Observer* November 1, 1898, front-page headline screamed in oversized type and set off in a special inset box. He purchased those guns, the report explained, "for the opening of the ball," which the anonymous and probably imaginary politician supposedly predicted "would be a lively one when it started." A second box story that day warned, cryptically, "WITH RIFLES" and stated that Republicans would take the election even if it required bayonet-tipped rifles. Even U.S. Representative George Henry White's wife and daughter came under attack that day. A third inset, placed above the other two, was evidently the most frightening of all, warning, "NEGRO WOMEN ACTIVE" and accusing Cora Cherry White of importing rifles into the state—she was said to have "received an express package containing rifles, name of shipper withheld." The younger Miss White, it was claimed, had initiated an effort "asking colored women to refuse to work for white people." Whichever was worse, the paper did not make clear, but reassured readers that the "white people are ready and prepared for any emergency," either martial or domestic, presumably. Sticking to the theme of election-day terror, the second page of the November 1 *News and Observer* contained a harrowing tale of "fusion with the negro in power." Moses West, a black man, allegedly accosted a poor white woman near the town of Ross' Church and told her, "I am your fellow." Ballot fever, of course, was said to have caused this, and the *News and Observer* reminded readers that the "Democratic party is the only party that promises to keep the home of the poor man safe from the negro." For good measure, the article contained yet more talk of black men and firearms. Richard Biggs, a black man of twenty-two, the account explained, reportedly told a meeting at "St. Matthews colored church" that "the negroes were getting on top" of whites and that "they would carry the state this time if it took guns to do it."[20]

Every report or news item that suggested any threat to Democrats' plans stoked the furor. Congressman White's wife and daughter were made villains, as was President William McKinley. That autumn, the armies raised for the fight with Spain were coming home and those in the South, North Carolina's Democratic press insisted, were not being mustered out—they were being massed for some intervention in North Carolina's election. Things had devolved so rapidly and thoroughly that the *Biblical Recorder* rejoined the debate, regretting that "it has come to this." Residents of heavily African American eastern North Carolina were especially afraid, the report explained, "restless, perturbed, and fearful." "With a sense of dread," the *Recorder* wrote, "our people look forward to election day."[21]

The campaign produced a new Democratic-majority legislature, and in 1899 that body flatly rejected the restrictions adopted in Mississippi and South Carolina. The legislature instead took Louisiana as its model. Democratic editors were especially excited by the device. The *Raleigh News and Observer* editor, Josephus Daniels, was among North Carolina's (and the South's) most rabid disfranchisers. After a research tour of Louisiana, he came home rhapsodizing about the grandfather clause. "All Want the Louisiana Law," Daniels reported on January 13, 1899, and a month later the general assembly submitted its version of Louisiana's grandfather clause to North Carolina voters.[22]

Because North Carolina's legislature adopted the suffrage amendment so quickly, and because nearly twenty months would elapse before the August 1900 ratification referendum, there was ample time to argue about the grandfather clause. For more than eighteen months, North Carolinians heard that the grandfather clause was constitutional, that it was unconstitutional, that it would eliminate all black voters, that it was a trick to ensnare poor and working-class whites, that it was designed to protect white men, and that it had nothing to do with race. North Carolina voters even read that Louisiana's disfranchisement scheme was not so much an effort to maintain white supremacy as an attempt to rein in La Cosa Nostra. This came from another of Josephus Daniels's widely distributed interviews with prominent Louisianans. Disfranchisement in Louisiana, Daniels reported in 1900, was ultimately a nativist movement. Italians, not blacks, were the real targets "on account of the lawlessness of these people and the murders and other crimes perpetrated by the secret bands known as the Mafia." "No one," he continued, "who has read the accounts of the atrocities perpetrated by these secret, oath-bound law transgressors and defiers and stiletto wielders" could criticize Louisiana. Despite the rhetorical sideshows, the argument always returned to questions about the U.S. Constitution and what would happen whenever a federal court reviewed the grandfather clause.[23]

Beyond Louisiana and North Carolina, nationally as well as regionally, commentators wished that there would be some judicial review of the South's disfranchising constitutions—the grandfather clause, in particular. "We do not believe the United States supreme court would give a single vote in favor of its constitutionality," Massachusetts' *Springfield Republican* offered. Commenting upon Louisiana's first elections held under the 1898 constitution, the *Minneapolis Journal* thought that "the democrats are nice people to pose as guardians of human liberty and human rights" despite having constrained "the negro vote in two or three states by enacting laws distinctly indefensible constitutionally." There was broad agreement that a judicial resolution was needed and soon. The *Birmingham Age-Herald* too noted that "it would be well to have a decision" from the courts "before many more States" adopted grandfather clauses. Though "wealthy negroes" in Washington, D.C., had promised a court test, none had yet emerged, and North Carolina's ratification campaign rolled along.[24]

Unfortunately and predictably, much of what was said and written in North Carolina about the United States Constitution and the grandfather clause's constitutionality was strikingly unsophisticated when it was not simply ridiculous. North Carolinians wanted to know what federal courts might do, but no court, either state or federal, had ever examined anything like the grandfather clause. Predictably, the clause's champions steadfastly maintained that the courts posed no danger. North Carolina's disfranchisers propagated the delightfully specious argument that because there had been no challenge to the Louisiana constitution in court, there neither could nor ever would be. U.S. Representative William Kitchin of North Carolina boasted that no case had been brought to challenge the device and, therefore, the state's "ablest lawyers . . . have entire confidence in its constitutionality." A broadside circulated throughout the Old North State echoed Kitchin, its boldface, excessively capitalized title insisting that "THE LOUISIANA AMENDMENT THE SAME AS OURS!" The flyer proclaimed, "No test has been made of the question in the courts," ignoring the simple fact that there really had not been time to mount a challenge.[25]

The silly proposition that because Louisiana's grandfather clause had not been challenged it could never be reached its zenith when Democrats boiled it down for an "Explanation of the Amendment" published in newspapers throughout North Carolina. The "Explanation" consisted of sixteen breezy question-and-answer exchanges, the bulk of which dealt with the grandfather clause's constitutionality:

(#5) Q: Has this amendment been adopted and tried anywhere else?
       A: Yes. It is the law of the State of Louisiana today.
(#6) Q: Has the law worked in Louisiana?
       A: Splendidly. The white people there are delighted with it. It has

solved the negro problem there and established white supremacy permanently.

(#8) Q: Did the negroes in Louisiana register under it?
       A: Not many.

Louisiana Republicans had also claimed that the clause was unconstitutional, the "Explanation" explained, and the people there had ignored them.
Of course there had been no ratification referendum in Louisiana and so the
people's options were rather constrained. However, there had already been a
state election under the new restrictions:

(#12) Q: And the Republicans did not take it into Court?
        A: Why dear men, no. They knew the law was all right and that it
            had been investigated by the greatest lawyers in the State and
            pronounced sound and good.
(#13) Q: Has the constitutionality of the amendment been thoroughly
            investigated by our North Carolina lawyers?
        A: Yes. Thoroughly, fully, and exhaustively.

North Carolina's disfranchisers had thus recast Louisiana's grandfather
clause as a tried and true landmark of American constitutional development.[26]

North Carolina Democrats found that they could not outargue opponents who charged that the grandfather clause would be struck down, leaving white men defenseless from the heightened suffrage restrictions. It was
cast as a conspiracy and depicted as such in a *Raleigh Caucasian* editorial
cartoon The grandfather clause would fall, the *Caucasian* cartoon suggested,
and the North Carolina People's Party 1900 platform insisted, and thereby
leave poor and illiterate whites unprotected, "disfranchising . . . fifty or sixty
thousand white voters." Democrats, rather than reassure the conspiratori-
ally minded, only resisted half-heartedly when People's Party (Populist) and
Republican Party campaigners threatened "to carry [the grandfather clause]
to the Supreme Court," so Democratic leader Furnifold Simmons recalled
in his memoir. This was definitely a mixed message; whether or not they
wished to see the clause invalidated was unclear. Regardless, Republicans
and Populists aroused so much anti-amendment sentiment that the Democrats had no choice but to respond.[27]

The response that Simmons recalled had been an amendment redraft.

Democrats convened a special legislative session and altered the proposal to make the grandfather clause inseparable from the other suffrage restrictions. If a court invalidated the grandfather clause, the entire amendment would be invalid and the legislature would have the power to correct the defect as they saw fit. This was really just a trick, and although it may have reassured uneasy and less-than-discerning voters, it did not impress opposition leaders. They never let up.[28]

Disfranchisement's opponents typically warned of federal opposition and potential federal interference. The federal government—by which is meant the powers that be in Washington, D.C.—did not interfere in North Carolina's ratification campaign. However, federal officials within the state did interfere, and with spectacular results. This was done on behalf of black voters, and suggested that the U.S. government might back up any effort to foment large-scale African American resistance.

Republicans held the White House in 1899–1900, and thus Republicans occupied all U.S. attorneys' offices. At an early stage, those officials attempted to prosecute Democrats for their behavior in the 1898 congressional elections. At Greenville, a number of Democratic officials were hauled before U.S. commissioners (the equivalent of modern-day U.S. magistrate judges), indicted, and arraigned for harassing black voters. U.S. commissioners really could not do anything other than arraign defendants and have them bound over for trial. These were very low-level proceedings, but Democrats responded with full-blown, furious, indignation. They amounted to "Vile Maliciousness," a *Greenville King's Weekly* headline screamed, since "White Men Lurk Behind Negroes in Nefarious Political Prosecutions." Nothing came of the matter, other than to provide Democrats with an inflammatory campaign cry. There would be more. In July 1900, just as North Carolina Democrats prepared to rewrite the amendment, U.S. marshals in Winston arrested a Forsyth County registrar, John Thompson. The U.S. attorney and a U.S. commissioner charged him under the Reconstruction era Enforcement Acts, based upon affidavits from black men whom Thompson had refused to register. They eventually secured a twenty-four-count indictment against Thompson, which was unsealed in the campaign's closing weeks. Then, in Transylvania County, J. L. Aiken was indicted and arraigned on identical charges. Further such episodes unfolded that involved Cherokee Indians. At Bryson City, the Swain County registrars refused to register Cherokees, "even those who can read and write," and one of their number, Lloyd Owl, reportedly instituted a suit to force his registration. In

Jackson County, a registrar allegedly refused to register three Cherokee men, all of whom subsequently threatened to involve the U.S. attorney. Democrats howled with outrage, but nothing could have been finer for them, as it turned out to be a godsend for North Carolina's disfranchisers.[29]

Reports of Thompson's and Aiken's arrests, and the Swain and Jackson County incidents, blended with standing rumors and charges that blacks had threatened violent attacks against elections officials. Republicans and Populists, of course, were said to have hatched these plots. In Vance County, gossip spread that two Populist leaders had urged blacks that they should "take a stick and burst his brains out" if any registrar turned them away. Violence was not the only imaginary concern weighing upon white and Democratic North Carolinians' minds. The *Rockingham Anglo-Saxon* excitedly reported on a "conference of negroes" that would meet in Raleigh to "devise ways and means to defeat the amendment." According to the account, that vaguely described conference planned to resettle blacks from outside the state in North Carolina to "swell the negro vote" against the amendment. That report had come in 1899, and such stories only proliferated over the next year and steadily gained currency. By 1900 the tales had become more specific and worries about anti-amendment immigration and violence melded into one: Wild warnings swirled about, claiming that fiendish bands of armed blacks had sneaked in from Virginia to register as voters who could defeat the amendment. The Democrat-manufactured horrors did not stop there. Registrars at Honeycutts Township, Sampson County, shared their harrowing experience of being forced to enroll obviously unqualified black men as voters. But they could not actually identify these vote-crazed fiends for after registering to vote in Sampson County, the new voters inexplicably erased their own names. It all was utterly ridiculous, but never comical, because, sickeningly, people believed it. None of these exciting stories can be verified beyond newspaper accounts. Nevertheless, they poisoned the Carolina air that summer. It was exactly what the North Carolina Democratic Party needed to keep their flock interested, angry, and afraid.[30]

Responding to the North Carolina amendment campaign (and reports that some blacks actually supported the Democratic Party there, even as that party proposed to disfranchise them), the *American Banner,* an African American paper published in Bay Minette, Alabama, remarked in 1899 that the "democratic party of the south reminds us of Uncle Ned's old mule. They are tricky." The *American Banner* did not know the half of it. North Carolina Democrats had gone way beyond tricks and now trafficked in vile and incendiary threats and chicanery. The state's black and Republican press, as would be expected, countered these tales, but to little avail. The *Littleton True Reformer* publicized evidence of one such hoax—"this deceitful sheet"—to "let our people see what kind of fakes live among us." The document was a letter written to a local doctor, supposedly from a black resident, warning that "the Colored People ame . . . to do great Dammage to all the white People, & that soon." "While I am a Negro," the anonymous letter writer explained, "I dont think it is right to do this, & to kill all the little childon, as the [*sic*] might do." In closing, the letter advised the doctor that "you had better let all the Towns know this at once. GIT REDY." The frenzied campaign disturbed the devil himself. "Satan Devil" was a regular columnist for the staunchly Republican *Moravian Falls Yellow-Jacket* and wrote in his July 26, 1900, "Devil's Letter" that "if you hear anybody say that the North Carolina democratic legislature beats the devil tell them I admit it." He followed North Carolina politics from Hades and professed to be "fully disgusted" with his Democratic minions. They had gone too far: "I'm heartily ashamed of the boys," Satan declared, and "have a good notion to withdraw my support from the campaign and let the republicans wipe the boys off the face of the earth." [31]

Black voters may have understood that the hoaxes and rumors and lies were just that. White Democrats, however, did not want to believe that, and seem not to have. Reflecting upon that summer's incendiary reports, Raleigh's *Biblical Recorder* continued its unfortunate role in disfranchisement by publicly lamenting, and thus validating, the wilder tales of black violence. The paper claimed to regret that "certain negroes" have made such threats, and that they had been published, but "we can not doubt that they have been made." Hope was prayerfully expressed that "prompt and unselfish intercession" would yet save North Carolina. "Blessed are the peace-makers," the *Biblical Recorder* intoned in closing, dragging Christ and his Sermon on the Mount down into the mire. "Blessed are the peacefully-minded; blessed are the pure-in-heart; blessed are the men of good intentions; blessed are the lovers of righteousness." The clear implication, too, expressed only between the lines: "And blessed are the disfranchisers." [32]

North Carolina voters approved the amendment handily. Charles Aycock was swept into the governor's chair on the disfranchising tide and he was always happy to defend the grandfather clause. Addressing the annual dinner of New York City's North Carolina Society in May 1901, Aycock explained, benignly, that "we think that those who have exercised the privilege of suffrage and those descended from such people are more likely to exercise that suffrage beneficially than the men upon whom suffrage was cast as a gift." He could not have made it sound more innocent.[33]

As Governor Aycock took the rostrum that May evening, Alabama's constitutional convention delegates were assembling in Montgomery and readying themselves for a disfranchising initiative of their own. On May 22, two days after Aycock's New York speech, the Alabamians chose John Barnett Knox as their convention president. Upon claiming his gavel Knox delivered an address that he may have taken straight from the mind of Ernest Kruttschnitt, and that would have made Governor Aycock proud. Just as Kruttschnitt had done three years earlier, Knox attacked the Mississippi and South Carolina plans. He was far kinder toward Louisiana and North Carolina. The grandfather clauses those states adopted were "justified in law and in morals" because, he claimed, they did not discriminate "on account of race, but on account of . . . intellectual and moral condition. There is a difference," Knox continued, "between the uneducated white man and the ignorant negro."[34]

Alabama gave the South another grandfather clause in 1901, and by then things had changed dramatically. Alabama, for many reasons, dominates the story of black voting rights activism in the disfranchisement era. By the time of Alabama's constitutional convention, black men were preparing to drag the clause into court. This was going to be a far different fight than the furtive efforts launched by George Washington Murray, John Roy Lynch, and Cornelius Jones. The target appeared easier to hit, the fighters were better prepared, and the scale was bigger. And this time, Booker T. Washington threw his weight into the effort. Washington engaged the issue early and, beginning with the reaction to Louisiana's grandfather clause, his role in the antidisfranchisement fight expanded rapidly.

As disfranchisement accelerated in the 1890s, those on both sides of the question tried to enlist Booker T. Washington into their respective camps, especially after 1895. That year brought Washington's elevation to superstar status, the combined result of Frederick Douglass's death and his widely celebrated speech before Atlanta's Cotton States Exposition. Widely denigrated by his critics as the "Atlanta Compromise Address," Washington's performance that September afternoon cemented his new position in American public affairs. Public men and women hailed him as a "negro Moses" and southern white audiences reveled in their deliberately incomplete readings of his demand that southern blacks "cast down their buckets" and his claim that whites and blacks could live together happily and as "separate as the fingers on the hand." Those white audiences, and Washington's black and white critics, did not fully appreciate that he had asked as much of whites as blacks. He intended whites to perform their side of the contract and, whenever he saw fit, he publicly chided and privately challenged them. Those challenges are perhaps the least-known and least-understood aspect of Washington's career.[35]

Washington gave his Atlanta address at roughly the same time that Cornelius Jones was preparing his *Gibson* and *Smith* cases, which tested Mississippi's constitution, and that the U.S. Supreme Court was deliberating its decision in *Mills v. Green.* The South Carolina convention was well underway by the time of the address, and before it had decided upon anything, a *New York World* correspondent, James Creelman, urged Washington to speak out. Creelman urged Washington to draft an open letter to U.S. Senator Ben Tillman (who was directing South Carolina's disfranchising convention), a letter that Creelman envisioned as "a ringing appeal to the nation."[36]

Washington had not expected the reception he received after Atlanta. "The reception," he wrote to Francis Grimké, an African American scion of the famous Grimké family (the South Carolina–born white abolitionists Sarah and Angelina Grimké were his half-sisters) and a widely known African American leader, "has been a revelation to me. . . . The heart of the whole South now seems to be turned in a different direction." Given the rapidly deteriorating state of southern race relations, Washington's "revelation" about the "heart of the South" seems frankly odd. If anything, the southern heart was darkening, and when Creelman asked him to "speak" to Ben Tillman, Washington believed that he might do some good. The letter appeared in the *World* on November 5, and there is no indication that Tillman paid it the slightest attention. It is probably that he just ignored it. South Carolina newspapers also ignored it and, the *World* aside, so did other national publications.[37]

"I am no politician. I never made a political speech, and do not know as I should ever make one"—thus began Washington's political debut. He sweetened the document with paeans to interracial cooperation and amity: how blacks and whites had to love one another, how they should treat one another, and so on. Alongside his saccharine platitudes, Washington worked in a specific appeal for black education. Tillman, as he proposed an educational test for the suffrage, insisted upon closing black schools—which were already scarce and poorly funded. Washington naïvely claimed to believe that Tillman was "too great and magnanimous to permit this." He had no idea just how small and penurious Tillman was. Aside from the pointlessness of any appeal to Tillman, the letter displayed a reticence and temerity that Washington would have to overcome.[38]

Over the following months, Washington honed his skills. By spring, his public pronouncements grew more forceful. They remained measured and always would be, but he was definitely developing a style. Writing about the recent *Plessy v. Ferguson* decision, Washington first wanted to disarm whites. He was not going to attack segregation outright and even suggested that it might have some merit. "This separation may be good law," he wrote, though he immediately followed with a critique: "But it is not good common sense." Then he ridiculed all the various distinctions the decision made possible: separate cars for yellow-skinned people, the sunburned, the bald, and so forth. Only then did he arrive at his point: Any injury inflicted upon African Americans was equally injurious to whites and "such an unjust law injures the white man and inconveniences the negro." *Plessy* was more than a chance to address segregation. It was a vehicle for addressing other, more pressing concerns for African Americans, namely, disfranchisement and lynching. "If a white man steals a negro's ballot," he stated, "it is the white man who is permanently injured." As for lynching, "physical death" visited the black victim, but "death of the soul" came to his lynchers. Washington was honing his public voice, and by the time of Louisiana's 1898 constitutional convention, he had acquired some daring as well.[39]

"Daring," as a descriptor for Booker T. Washington, does not mean that he was outspoken, blunt, or the least bit obvious. It means daring *for him;* it means that his entreaties still conveyed a recognizable message. His open letter to Ben Tillman had been difficult to penetrate, choked as it was by fulsome flattery; his open letter to Louisiana's constitutional convention was definitely sugary. "I am no politician," he began, as he had with Tillman's letter three years earlier, and he immediately reassured the delegates "that he valued "good citizenship, rather than . . . mere political agitation." He told them that he would speak to a question of "civilization," as it affected the two races, and placed it on the elemental level of "man to man, Christian to Christian."[40]

Washington sanctioned the idea that there was a "race question" and that it needed a solution. Restricted suffrage was necessary, he then offered, and this was an extremely dangerous concession on his part. Speaking broadly, the principle of universal manhood suffrage was attacked broadly in the late nineteenth century. There were few public voices raised in support of that ideal. So in an abstract sense it was not so unusual for Booker T. Washington or anyone else to say that the suffrage must be restricted to only capable and well-informed citizens. However, whenever suffrage was restricted, those restrictions always disproportionately affected blacks, immigrants, the poor, and other differentiated groups. Washington apparently believed that some restrictions would be fine as long as they were applied equitably and so long as the new standards were attainable for all men who so desired.[41]

So he made this dangerous bargain and told the Louisiana delegates that an intelligent electorate would benefit everyone. For thirty years the South had traveled a political road "strewn with thorns and thistles," the result of the sudden enfranchisement of roughly one million freedmen. They were ill prepared for citizenship, Washington stated, making an additional concession to one of the disfranchisers' bedrock contentions. He promised that there was a "highway that will lead both races out into the pure, beautiful sunshine. . . . I believe," he said, stroking the delegates' egos, "that your Convention will find this highway." They would not get there with anything unfair, unequally applied, or beyond the reach of African Americans. The "pure, beautiful sunshine" could only be theirs if they adopted a new constitution that "will be absolutely just and fair to white and black alike." Washington was every bit as accommodating and conciliatory as his critics have described over the past century. However, these open letters and other carefully prepared pronouncements are only half of the story. By 1898 Washington had taken his first steps toward protest, and he and his associates and followers believed they could force the fair application of voting regulations. Their first target was Louisiana.[42]

By early summer 1898, Washington became involved in discussions of a court challenge to Louisiana's constitution. John F. Patty was among the many men whom Washington approached about the possible litigation. On the Fourth of July, Patty wrote to say, "I will be glad to assist you in having the action of the Constitutional Convention tested by the proper tribunal." The prospective test case had no form as yet. Neither had it a plaintiff nor a sponsor. Nevertheless, Patty wanted an outline of what Washington thought "ought to be done" and he recommended a number of men for invitations to join "this good work."[43]

Washington left a staggering collection of papers, but relatively few examples of outgoing correspondence survive. We cannot always determine what projects he initiated or when, and so whether he dreamed this test case up himself is unknown. But in advancing a court test, Washington was simply fulfilling an oft-expressed prophecy. The Mississippi constitution had been dragged into court, as had South Carolina's, but only through the isolated and ultimately unsuccessful efforts of George Washington Murray and Cornelius Jones. When the Louisiana convention embraced the grandfather clause, disgusted delegates and outraged commentators railed against it because it invited broader and more virulent challenges. Most political observers recognized that it was only a matter of time. That court test came, after two years' time, courtesy of Washington and a brand-new national organization he helped create, the National Afro-American Council (AAC).[44]

Washington's involvement in the Louisiana action was as important as this new organization's role. The AAC's presence marked the first time that any national organization attempted to challenge southern disfranchisement. Organized at Rochester, New York, in September 1898, the AAC was an interracial effort to establish, an advocacy organization designed to fight for the civil and political rights of African Americans. The council elected Bishop Alexander Walters as its first president and scheduled a second meeting for late December in Washington, D.C. The December meeting's program read like a who's who of African American leadership. George Washington Murray and John Roy Lynch spoke about "Our Progress in Business," George Henry White discussed the "Protection of American Citizens," Ida Wells-Barnett presented a paper on "Mob Violence and Anarchy," Booker T. Washington lectured on "Industrial Education," and Cornelius Jones examined "Our Place in the Politics of the Country." For the AAC and its leadership, disfranchisement was issue number one. Notably, the first official history of the organization, written in 1902 by Cyrus Field Adams, gave primary emphasis to suffrage and showcased AAC efforts to drag Louisiana's constitution into court.[45]

The AAC membership soon learned that forming a group and defining a mission were easy, but the "doing" was far harder. Little happened with their antidisfranchisement project until early 1901. Though the council was immediately beset by internal difficulties, it went ahead and announced its plans for an attack on Louisiana's constitution. The "strongest legal talent in the country will be employed," Edward Cooper of the *Colored American* and the council's executive committee announced, for "it is our intention to push the matter until it can be passed upon by the supreme court of the United

States." Louisiana's Democratic establishment had always known that this would happen, the *Daily Picayune*'s editor reassured readers, but the "ablest leaders in the state" had been consulted during the drafting and were prepared for a defense. But nothing could happen without a plaintiff, and the AAC had yet to offer one. While the public and Louisiana's disfranchisers waited for a suit, the council asked African Americans to gird themselves for the coming court battle. An AAC proclamation announced that June 2, 1899, was to be set aside as a day of prayer and fasting. After a detailed elegy, the document called upon African Americans to appeal to a judge who was not earthbound for help and relief. "If United States courts proved unwilling" to offer their aid, it explained, they would appeal to the "bar of infinite power and justice, whose judge holds the destinies of nations in his hands."[46]

There were many prominent African Americans involved in the Afro-American Council, but Booker T. Washington stood out above all others and the AAC's ebb corresponded to the oscillating flow of Washington's power and renown. It could not do anything without him, because by 1898 no such organization would enjoy any public credibility without Washington's sanction. Yet Washington, even as he flexed his newfound influence, could not win. Had he stayed out of the AAC, he would be criticized. Had he been more open about his involvement, he would be criticized. Had he pursued a middle-of-the-road tack, he would be criticized. No one, and no constituency, really, was ever happy with Washington, and that was a function of the singular position he held in American society.

When Chicago's city fathers staged their National Peace Jubilee in October 1898, they wanted only the best for their oratorical program. President William McKinley was the guest of honor and it was a distinctly ecumenical occasion. There were four speakers: a priest, a rabbi, a Presbyterian minister, and Booker T. Washington. Prayers and hosannas were sent up, an audience of twelve thousand cheered and murmured "Amen," and the evening's program built toward Washington's closing address. Washington was supposed to praise the president, which he did. Washington was supposed to praise the great military victory over Spain, which he did. He was not there to speak truths about American society, however, which he did anyway. The Spanish-American War was a glorious triumph, Washington declared, but warned that another battle lay ahead, one against racial prejudice at home. Until America's "race problem" was solved and solved equitably, he stated, "we shall have, especially in the southern part of the country, a can-

cer gnawing at the heart of this republic that shall one day prove as dangerous as an attack from an army." His Chicago audience cheered, but at home
he touched off a nasty controversy and he spent the next few weeks explaining and defending himself.[47]

White southerners took his attack on racial inequality as a call for social
equality, something they could not handle. Rather than simply comment on
the honor of the invitation, he was forced to explain over and over that "social equality" did not interest him. "What is termed social recognition," he
insisted, "is a question I never discuss." Even W. E. B. Du Bois noted the
conundrum Washington faced after his Chicago address. Washington was
"dealing with the one subject of deepest sensitiveness to that section," Du
Bois wrote in *The Souls of Black Folk,* and the Chicago episode was one instance where "Southern criticism has been violent enough to threaten seriously his popularity." His popularity was no minor concern. Washington's
influence was a product of his celebrity. If he was not celebrated, he would
have no power to wield. He could get nowhere by suggesting to white southerners that there was, or had ever been, a race problem and, of course, his
critics railed against him whenever he did not.[48]

Booker T. Washington did not want to bow out. He would not decline
his turn on the stage because he stood where no other African American
ever had. Not even Frederick Douglass ever had such a pulpit at his disposal.
Everyone wanted to use him, and at the turn of the last century, disfranchisement was very often the reason.

Washington was convinced that his chosen course was the one true path,
and there were successes—always minor—that he took as affirmation. One
of these came in Georgia, where a particularly mean-spirited proposal to restrict the suffrage statutorily went up in flames. In 1899, Washington, along
with several other southern black leaders (including the young Atlanta University professor, W. E. B. Du Bois, and Bishop Henry McNeal Turner),
helped defeat the Hardwick bill, introduced by state representative Thomas
W. Hardwick.[49]

Thomas Hardwick proposed that Georgia adopt a literacy test by statute then provide a grandfather clause loophole for whites. The problem for
Hardwick was that in Georgia, black suffrage had already been all but wiped
out by a poll-tax provision that dated back to Reconstruction. Georgia had
been the only state to include a poll tax in its Redemption constitution, and
the effect was devastating upon blacks and poor whites. Thus there was no
great imperative in Georgia Democratic circles for any further restriction.

In the states that did adopt new statutory suffrage restrictions in the 1890s, blacks and Republicans (and sometimes Populists) posed an actual, potential threat to Democratic control. In the states that took the next step, and resolved to actual disfranchise a large portion of their citizenry, racial antagonism and political furor were driven to a fever pitch. That was not the case in Georgia in 1899.[50]

In Georgia there was precious little support for any new suffrage restrictions, much less a new disfranchising constitution. Hardwick was consumed by a degree of race hatred that was not uncommon elsewhere in the South but was distinctly unfashionable in Georgia's legislature. In the setting in which Hardwick operated, he was really nothing more than a crank and a rogue who commanded virtually no support. His bill, which proposed restrictions that were entirely in line with those adopted in Louisiana and North Carolina, failed a roll call vote of 137 to 3. There just never was the slightest chance that it might succeed. Still, Washington, Du Bois, and the others had mounted a dogged lobbying campaign, both public and private, to thwart the measure. When the legislature defeated the bill, those African Americans who actively fought it took credit for their efforts. That was deserved, because it was personally dangerous for any black man to protest against anything that any white man proposed. Washington seemed more convinced than any of the others that these methods—the sort of lobbying they undertook in Georgia—would work elsewhere. The truth is that what had happened in Georgia in 1899 did not really matter. They had helped defeat something (the Hardwick Bill) that had never stood a chance of succeeding, and Georgia would have disfranchisement a few years down the road. Nevertheless, Washington was heartened, perhaps a bit emboldened, and he pressed onward.[51]

If an enterprising social activist or policymaker had anything to offer regarding "ballot reform," whether a critique or a proposed "solution," they carried it to Washington. White Democrats outdid everyone in the scramble for his blessing, but his Republican friends rushed in and demanded that there was only one "right" choice. In 1899, for example, Washington was inclined to endorse the proposal of a former Democratic West Virginia governor, William MacCorkle, to "solve" the "race problem" with a uniform educational qualification for suffrage. But West Virginia's Republican incumbent governor, Edward Atkinson, warned Washington that MacCorkle's initiative was dangerous. "The more I think of the scheme . . . the more I am opposed to it," Atkinson wrote. Atkinson believed "it is only a trap" that promised the "practical disfranchisement" of all blacks, educated or not. Governor Atkinson advised Washington that he was popular among Democrats only "because . . . they think they can use you." Atkinson, who considered MacCorkle "a warm friend," nevertheless insisted that Washington reject the proposal. MacCorkle and others like him posed a recurrent temptation for Washington, and their proposals were constantly strewn across his perilous path.[52]

Washington simply did not, even at this late date, appreciate the situation and more than once arguably made things worse. He and those few other blacks who had managed to establish a foothold among the educated and professional and upwardly mobile petit bourgeois often concerned themselves with making league with their white peers (in an economic sense). Washington's relationship with middle-class white disfranchisers apparently led him to believe that they did not object to literate, propertied, and prosperous black men, and thus he seemed willing to jettison the illiterate, the propertyless, and the poor. Washington believed the disfranchisers' rhetoric about protecting the "better" class of black men.

Governor Atkinson recognized Washington's dangerous miscalculation and demanded that he disabuse himself of the notion. There was no such distinction in the disfranchisers' minds, Atkinson insisted. Whether educated, wealthy, or Booker T. Washington, black men were just black men as far as the Democratic disfranchisers were concerned and their votes were in jeopardy. Washington stubbornly tried persuading Atkinson otherwise, but the governor held firm. It was true, Atkinson later agreed, that blacks were already "practically disfranchised" but that was because "they are robbed . . . by the white people of the South, by their dictum, and not by authority of law." MacCorkle and other white Democrats, Atkinson maintained, coveted Washington's endorsement as if it were a dispensation. If Democrats wanted disfranchisement, Governor Atkinson advised, Washington must offer them no quarter: "It took a revolution to enfranchise the colored people, and nothing short of a revolution should disfranchise them." Atkinson won the point and so MacCorkle did not win Washington's imprimatur. Still, Booker T. Washington did not fully heed Atkinson's advice, at least not publicly. Though he did not endorse MacCorkle's proposal, Booker T. Washington publicly maintained that increased suffrage restrictions, if fairly enforced, would benefit all southerners.[53]

Washington meant to see those new suffrage restrictions enforced equitably, through legal action if necessary, and by early 1900, he was deeply involved in the nascent court test of Louisiana's constitution. This was an AAC affair but Washington often conducted himself as if it were his personal project. When he sought his wealthy white friends' aid, he couched it as a favor. They gave freely, and then Washington asked that they wring funds from their own larger circle of friends and associates and they did, as a personal favor to Booker T. Washington. "It will require $2,000 to take the case up through the Supreme Court," Washington advised Francis Garrison in March in a typical solicitation. Though these missives were distinctly personal, Washington did not deceive and he passed along what little he knew about the AAC's plans. He explained to Garrison, a scion of the famed abolitionist family, that they would file a case in Louisiana state court and, if things went according to plan, it would soon reach the U.S. Supreme Court. There, the impending Louisiana case would be argued by former U.S. senator George Edmunds of Vermont.[54]

Washington's friends seemed enthusiastic about the effort but the plan soon frayed. Apparently, Washington's name was the only concrete aspect of the AAC's preparations, but his name was not theirs to use. They needed to act quickly. While the AAC dithered, a white New Orleans attorney, A. C. Gusman, crossed the Mississippi River into neighboring Jefferson Parish and launched a legal effort on his own initiative. Gusman mounted his attack upon the back of Samuel Wright (a.k.a. Sam Wright, Martin Wright, and Nathan Wright), a black man facing a death sentence for a conviction of attempted rape (a crime that existed in Louisiana law). Gusman sued Sheriff Lucien H. Marrero, claiming that the 1898 constitution was invalid for a host of reasons, not the least of which was the state's deliberate violation of the Fifteenth Amendment. He persuaded the U.S. district court to hear his claim, which was not a habeas corpus petition but rather a personal claim filed on Wright's behalf, and won a delay.[55]

Gusman's valiant effort only made things more confusing for those who were privy to the AAC's plans. Their concern began to grow. Richard Thompson, editor of Washington, D.C.'s *Colored American,* advised Washington that "some of us" had doubts. He suggested further study: "it is well to understand the issue thoroughly, before going to battle." They were also concerned about Washington's absolute refusal to have his name attached to the AAC's public fund-raising appeals. Whether Washington himself shared or understood Thompson's misgivings is unclear. However, he did not confine his antidisfranchisement legal activities to council channels.[56]

A generation ago, Washington biographer Louis Harlan concluded that he chose to become a solo operator because the Louisiana effort failed, but the reality is more complicated. Washington, in fact, never officially broke with the AAC. Instead, he quietly branched out on his own. This all happened unbeknown to the AAC and revolved around his introduction to Wilford H. Smith, an unassuming, ambitious, and brilliant African American attorney from Galveston, Texas.[57]

In the late spring of 1900, Washington's private secretary and consigliere, Emmet J. Scott, had begun consulting Smith as to the shape and strategy of potential antidisfranchisement litigation. Initially, Scott wished to have Smith handle the New Orleans efforts and nudged Washington in that direction. However, Smith was never actually recommended to the AAC, the AAC never considered him, and he, with Scott and Washington, eventually staged the most significant of the antidisfranchisement cases, those the trio launched from Alabama. Smith entered the antidisfranchisement scene, however, through an audition for the New Orleans litigation, but rather than win Washington's endorsement for the AAC job, it is likelier that Smith's superb analysis of that case simply proved the futility of the New Orleans effort and persuaded Washington to reconsider his role.[58]

Wilford Smith is unknown today, but his peers, the African American lawyer and historian Fitzhugh Lee Styles wrote in 1937, "considered [him] one of the most astute legal experts on the law involving the rights of the Negro under the United States Constitution." The NAACP's Moorefield Storey and other Legal Defense Fund attorneys dominate early 1900s civil rights legal history, but in fact, Styles noted, "long before such stalwarts as Moorefield Storey, Louis Marshall, and Samuel Leibowitz appeared, Smith was called from his office . . . to take the case of *Seth Carter v. Texas*." That 1900 victory, in which the Supreme Court affirmed the right of blacks to sit on juries, made Smith the first black attorney to win a U.S. Supreme Court case.[59]

Smith was born in 1860 in the tiny Delta community of Leota Landing, some thirty miles south of Greenville in the swamps and bends of rural Washington County. We do not know who his parents were other than that his father was from Virginia and his mother from Kentucky. No details of his early life are known, but he likely received at least a respectable education because he graduated from Boston University's law school in 1883. Smith came home to Mississippi and opened shop in Greenville. A contemporary of Cornelius Jones, Smith always shunned excitement. He stayed far away from controversy and unlike Jones found material success. He rapidly built a practice handling Civil War pension applications for veterans and their widows and was soon the highest-paid black lawyer in Mississippi.[60]

Smith was a remarkable man who enjoyed notable careers in both law and business. In the latter, he became a player in Harlem real estate as a founder of the Afro-American Realty Company. As an attorney, he built a lucrative practice and served as private counsel for African American luminaries, first for Booker T. Washington and later Marcus Garvey, but his personal life is an absolute mystery. The most significant personal detail that can be found is the record of his marriage. He married Laura Compton in Greenville on New Year's Eve 1885. Like her husband, Laura Compton Smith is a mystery, and all that is known of her comes from U.S. census records. She was a mulatto, born in 1864 in Mississippi. Her mother was born in Alabama and her father in Kentucky. By 1880 Laura Compton was possibly orphaned, and lived with her grandmother, Eliza Kane, two younger sisters, and her grandmother's household servants in Greenville. By 1894 Smith had departed Greenville and settled in the booming seaport of Galveston, Texas. It is unclear whether Laura accompanied her husband, as is whether they ever had children.[61]

Smith's Galveston clientele was both black and white and his business exceeded that of many white attorneys. He only spent six years in Galveston but made a lasting impression. His technical prowess was superb, but more important, his low-key personality ensured that he did not threaten whites. Smith was intensely discrete, both professionally and personally. He disclaimed politics, avoided overt participation in public controversies, and his modest demeanor as much as anything else won him entreé into Booker T. Washington's inner circle.[62]

Wilford Smith first came to Booker T. Washington's attention when Emmet Scott secured for Smith an invitation to a "Negro Conference." Scott arrived in Tuskegee in 1897, fresh from a stint as editor of the *Houston Freeman*. As prominent African Americans in neighboring cities, it was only natural that Scott and Smith crossed paths. They moved in the same Texas circles and Scott had come to know Smith quite well and he was impressed. Once ensconced at Tuskegee, Scott moved quickly to bring Smith into Washington's inner orbit. The Negro Conference invitation was Scott's initial overture and Smith reciprocated with an invitation for Washington to appear in Galveston. In these early years, Scott remembered Smith to Washington at every possible opportunity and Scott was always trying to use Washington's influence to advance his friend's career. In July 1898,

Washington, who had never met Smith, recommended him to Liberia's consul general, who needed to appoint a port consul for Galveston. Smith won the post. This was a major station in one of the United States' largest ports, and Liberia's newest port consul hurried to thank Washington. Smith gushed over the "very great honor of your personal recommendation" and promised "that my friends shall have no reason to regret having secured my appointment."[63]

Emmet Scott was not the only friend who helped Smith along. Another was Emanuel Hewlett, the D.C. attorney who collaborated with Cornelius Jones on the cases of *Gibson v. Mississippi* and *Smith v. Mississippi*. Hewlett, a fellow Boston University alumnus, was Smith's link to that group of African American lawyers in D.C. They were few in number and offered one another what they usually could not find where they lived: the professional fellowship of a bar association. As for Smith, Hewlett was his early collaborator in the defense of Seth Carter, a murder defendant in Galveston.

Seth Carter's case made a star out of Wilford Smith. An all-white jury had indicted Carter on November 26, 1897, two days after he allegedly murdered his girlfriend. Hewlett represented Carter at trial and then Smith made his appeal before the Texas Court of Criminal Appeals. Smith won. The court overturned Carter's conviction on grounds that the trial court improperly excluded evidence. At the second trial, Smith moved to quash the indictment because no blacks were selected for the grand jury even though they comprised one-quarter of Galveston County's electorate. The judge refused to entertain the motion, Carter was tried, and an all-white petit jury convicted him of first-degree murder. Following this reconviction, Smith made a second appeal to the court of criminal appeals, which he lost. This was what he wanted because it created a U.S. Supreme Court appeal. It bears mention, too, that as of 1900, no black attorney had ever won an appeal to the U.S. Supreme Court and only two others had ever made oral arguments—Cornelius Jones and Emmanuel Hewlett.[64]

Cornelius Jones's Mississippi cases had all been jury challenges and they attempted to build upon landmark jury decisions from 1880. Jones's cases all failed, and even though the earlier precedents had not been overruled or impugned, they seemed weakened as a result. Wilford Smith had a chance to correct that and he did.

Texas officials always claimed that the absence of blacks from the grand and petit juries was coincidental, but this did not impress the Court. Then there was the trial court's refusal to hear the motion to quash. Counsel for Texas complained that Carter's attorneys had submitted no evidence in support of the motion, even though the trial judge refused to allow Carter's lawyer to present that same evidence. The U.S. Supreme Court rejected this specious logic. Smith's evidence was the key factor. Justice Horace Gray, writing for a unanimous Court, thought "the necessary conclusion is that the defendant has been denied a right duly set up and claimed by him under the Constitution and laws of the United States." The indictment was set aside, the case remanded to Galveston County, and the 1880 decisions were tacitly reaffirmed. Wilford H. Smith's first appearance before the supreme bench had been a resounding success. The *A.M.E. Church Review* echoed Scott's praise. That Smith "has been the means to bring about the action of the Texas courts in this case," the *Review* declared, "is to make him the instrument of honor in the uplift of the race."[65]

Smith's victory came amid preparations for the Louisiana case. No attorney had as yet been hired and Emmet Scott immediately advanced Smith's name. Scott reminded Washington that he had recommended Smith to the Liberians two years earlier. "He is a splendid man and has much tenacity in fighting his way in the courts," Scott wrote of his Texan friend. There was "no bluster about him . . . he is a quiet worker." Several months later, amid the case preparations, Scott was more emphatic, stating that "the race owes Wilford H. Smith of Galveston a debt of gratitude which it will never pay, as it pays none of those who labor and sacrifice in its behalf. That was a blatant appeal to Washington's vanity, of course, but Scott was determined to see Smith in charge of the Louisiana litigation.[66]

In June 1900, Washington dispatched Scott to New Orleans for a first-hand investigation of case preparations because the AAC had neither a plaintiff nor a lawyer. Nor, it seems, did they have a plan. They could either find a black man whom the registrars had denied registration or challenge a jury indictment or conviction (because in Louisiana as in all other states prospective jurors were selected from the pool of registered voters). Scott's report suggested that a jury-based case was under serious consideration, explaining local AAC members' assessment of A. C. Gusman's "Wright case," which Gusman wanted the council to adopt. Washington had somehow heard of the matter and Scott informed him that a scion of a prominent abolitionist family, Arthur Birney, had joined Gusman on the case and together they were preparing a U.S. Supreme Court appeal. Birney may also have been advising the AAC informally, but the AAC did not want a test case associated with rape. Wright's case had other serious problems, Scott explained, namely, Gusman himself, the contingency fee he had proposed, and the fact that the Louisiana "constitution's validity [was not directly] involved." The matter would have to bounce around through several rounds of federal and state hearings before Louisiana's suffrage scheme became an issue, if it ever did, and no one in New Orleans believed it would.[67]

Scott explained to Washington that A. C. Gusman had literally rescued Wright from the gallows, out of "humanity's impulse," but local AAC planners doubted Gusman's utility (not to mention the Wright case's propriety). He was respectable enough personally but possessed of no special legal talent, a "man of little weight and prestige and without any substantial standing in the community." Col. James Lewis (one of the AAC's local leaders) and others pitied the impoverished Gusman, Scott found, and tried to "do something to keep him in food and clothing." When Gusman heard of the AAC's plans, he proposed that they make Wright's case their own and pay him a staggering seven thousand dollars for the work. That was not going to happen. The AAC preferred hiring someone who commanded "proper respect at the bar in New Orleans." Wilford Smith was certainly no local, but Scott used the occasion to remind Washington of his Texas friend anyway. The AAC should consider Smith, Scott hinted, advising that "it would be well to have a man of this character co-operate." Acknowledging Scott's report, Washington wrote nothing regarding Smith and reminded his secretary to "be careful in handling the Louisiana matter to see that my name does not in any way appear." Washington appeared uninterested in Smith, but Scott continued to seek his friend's advice about the case, and Smith always obliged.[68]

By early July, Smith (who had no contact with the AAC) had prepared a brief for Scott about hypothetical plaintiffs and how they might establish facts for their hypothetical case. He did not propose a jury seating challenge. The best route, he explained, involved challenging the 1898 constitution's suffrage qualifications directly, focusing on the state's application of literacy and property qualifications. For this option, they needed a literate, propertied man who had been refused registration. An alternate course (which Smith warned against) was to have a propertyless illiterate challenge the grandfather clause. Grandfather clause challenges presented a range of traps, however, that might easily ensnare the plaintiff's attorneys.

Smith immediately understood, though most of his peers never quite grasped, how tricky direct grandfather clause challenges would be because of the legal culture within which they operated. Nineteenth-century judges and lawyers were trained in, and believed in, formalism. Legal formalism embraced strict, Aristotelian logic and divorced legal texts from social realities. Formalism disallowed arguments based upon hypotheticals, common sense, and common knowledge—especially with regard to thorny political and social issues. The Louisiana grandfather clause was designed with that in mind. By 1900 no plaintiff could use the grandfather clause. Since it was no longer in effect (it had ceased operation in September 1898), any suit against it would be moot. Alternately, they might claim that a plaintiff should have been able to use it, and that the delegates' intent and the registrars' malfeasance had rendered the grandfather clause unconstitutional. But if attorneys did that, they could only have a particular registrar's action reviewed and likely could not secure the grandfather clause's invalidation on constitutional grounds. Alternately, they could attack it as unconstitutional and try to invalidate all registrations made thereunder. The latter option, however, brought them back to mootness—they would seek the invalidation of something that effectively did not exist. Finally, there was the greatest obstacle of all: the black men who *had* been allowed to register. Those tokens would be trotted out any time that a lawyer claimed that the new southern state constitutions targeted blacks. Attacking them directly would be almost impossible, but in a subtle, indirect attack, all paths of escape might be blocked. The clause could still trap the disfranchisers, if used properly, and Wilford Smith believed he knew how.

The grandfather clause was "proof" of the Louisiana framers' intent. The clause required that illiterate, propertyless applicants prove that their father or grandfathers voted in any state before January 1, 1867. Their choice of date was deliberate: Congress passed the Reconstruction Act, which mandated black men's enfranchisement, on March 5, 1867. This way, no one could claim, technically, that the disfranchisers were targeting the act (even though they certainly were). Further, only three states had explicitly enfranchised African Americans before the Fifteenth Amendment's ratification in 1870—Tennessee in 1867 and Iowa and Minnesota in 1868—and only six others explicitly accepted black men's ballots—Maine, Massachusetts, New Hampshire, New York, Rhode Island, and Vermont—and those black voters were few and their political voices severely restricted. Of those nine states, only New York and Tennessee had sizable black populations. This all underscored a well-known fact: Southern black men who were the acknowledged descendants of voting ancestors were an extraordinarily select club.

They were so rare as to be virtually nonexistent. It was *theoretically* possible to find a black man whose free ancestors had voted *somewhere* prior to January 1, 1867, but then there was the added impracticality of proving such a thing. "The fact is notorious," Smith explained to Scott, "that the great majority of the persons affected . . . did not live in any such states prior to Jan. 1, 1867, nor did their fathers or grandfathers."[69]

One disfranchised plaintiff was not as good as any other. An attempted rapist who had been convicted of that crime such as Samuel Wright was impractical. Neither should the AAC bring a case on behalf of a propertyless illiterate, Smith implored, because the state would make his disabilities the issue. Instead, they needed a man who, though fully qualified, had been disfranchised for some reason or another. Only then would he cite the clause as evidence of the convention's malign purpose. His plan was to prevent the man's ancestry from becoming the question. With a qualified and disfranchised man as their plaintiff, the facts of the constitution's adoption, rather than the man's disabilities, "would be the pivotal point in our case," Smith advised.[70]

Wilford Smith wanted this case as badly as Scott wanted him to have it. If hired, Smith promised, he would overwhelm the courts with evidence: "I would not rest upon the judicial knowledge of the court, but would introduce proof of the fact . . . so that there would be no room for cavil." Yet despite Smith's attainments and growing renown, and Scott's endorsement, the AAC did not hire him. The council was not privy to the briefs Smith made for Scott and maybe that is why they passed over him, but the likelier reason is that AAC members took a very myopic view of the situation and never seriously looked beyond the ranks of their political club.[71]

The AAC's lack of interest in Wilford Smith seems to have been the rare thing about which they were certain. The sad truth is that their Louisiana case was a mess. They were charting a new course. No organization had ever attempted such a thing. Hitches and mistakes might prove entirely understandable and excusable. Nevertheless, if those mistakes were made, the case would fail disastrously.

In March 1900, the AAC planned to hire former U.S. senator George Edmunds of Vermont as their Supreme Court counsel, but by October the plan had changed. "Did I make it plain" that Arthur A. Birney (he of the Wright appeal) would "work up the case from the beginning?" Jesse Lawson wrote Washington in early October. Lawson had never before, in fact, mentioned Birney's involvement and the real reason for his letter was financial:

Washington had raised another one hundred dollars "from parties in the North" and Lawson wanted it for Birney. His retainer was five hundred dollars, Lawson advised, and Birney was already at work. Birney's employment was but one of a host of changes that fall. Albert Pillsbury, a former Massachusetts attorney general, was also involved in the effort and, through Richmond, Virginia, attorney Giles Jackson, urged the AAC to abandon Louisiana and instead target either North Carolina or Mississippi. The AAC could not settle the question of an attorney and council members still quibbled over the choice of target. By October 1900 they had established a "streamlined" process for bank drafts that involved five different signatures from men living in four different states. Lawson, carefully explaining all of this, estimated that it would take about four months to deliver a $250 retainer to their attorney. If Washington had lost patience, no evidence of that survives, but his days as an active participant in the Louisiana case were numbered.[72]

Organizational challenges threatened to wreck the effort, even if the participants did not realize it. That was what Washington's friend, John Milholland, feared when he wrote to him about the "proposed disfranchisement case." Milholland was tired of seeing his and others' hard work go for naught. "I am tired of these spasmodic, ill-considered efforts," he declared, "which have made the Afro-American crusades little more than things of shreds and patches." Milholland wanted strong organizations with strong leaders: a "resolute, intelligent committee." Committees were indeed what the AAC had in mind, though Milholland probably would have questioned just how well conceived they turned out to be.[73]

The test of Louisiana's 1898 constitution was not the first time that the New Orleans African American community participated in a test case, and these earlier community efforts had also followed the committee route. The Citizens Committee to Test the Constitutionality of the Separate Car Law (whose members seem not to have played any prominent law in the disfranchisement case), for example, sponsored *Plessy v. Ferguson* and had conducted a broad search for legal talent, enlisting the famed novelist, activist, and attorney Albion Tourgée as lead counsel and a local attorney, James Walker, to handle the administrative details in New Orleans. Ralph Desdunes, who led the Citizens Committee, and Tourgée had even envisioned the launch of a national organization similar to the AAC. Yet once such an organization actually existed, it still struggled to field a strong team in New Orleans. The AAC originally decided that it really wanted a local attorney to handle its case but ultimately revised its criteria. The council eventually contracted with five lawyers, four of them minor celebrities, three of them white, and only one of them a New Orleanian: Birney, Pillsbury, Frederick McGhee of St. Paul, Minnesota, former North Carolina U.S. representative George Henry White, and Armand Romain of New Orleans. Romain, a young, white Republican activist, would handle all of the actual work. There was no clear chain of command and no clearly defined strategy. This was not a recipe for success.[74]

The Afro-American Council's proposed test of Louisiana's constitution was beset by problems, most of which were the council's fault, but their internal quarrels were not the whole story. Outside events were often of greater concern and such was the case in the late summer and early fall of 1900, when the AAC reacted (or simply did not react) to Emmet Scott's efforts on Wilford Smith's behalf. More precisely, Robert Charles happened.

Robert Charles, an itinerant laborer and sometime back-to-Africa emigration agent, was the star-crossed victim and alleged instigator of the 1900 New Orleans Race Riot. The details of the Charles incident paled in comparison to their outcome. Bands of angry whites, and the city's notoriously corrupt police force, roamed the city's black neighborhoods for days in search of Charles, any suspected co-conspirators, and any other black man who stumbled across their path.

African Americans and Creoles of means, that class of blacks who had attained some measure of respectability among whites (and who were behind the AAC's planned test of Louisiana's constitution), stood aside. They feared that their "lives and property . . . might be forfeited . . . if white rage were not appeased by lesser victims." They dared not challenge the mob and they certainly dared not remind marauding whites of their plans for the 1898 constitution. Indeed, just one month after Emmet Scott's report from New Orleans, news reports revealed that "colored people [were fleeing] the city."[75]

For the rest of the summer, high-minded test cases were forgotten while New Orleans blacks worried for their lives. "Law and order" was their new preoccupation. The fear spread about the country. In Boston, the Rev. Dr. R. S. MacArthur told the congregation of Tremont Temple that the New Orleans riot showed that "law and order has become the great issue." Only Christianity held the answer, MacArthur believed, for the "great need is a pure Christianity which emphasizes liberty under law and distinguishes between liberty and license." Crescent City black leaders were desperate to quell the furor. The "colored professionals and businessmen" had formed yet another civic organization, this one "designed to stamp out lawlessness among the lower classes." They were going to assert control over lower-class men, men, of course, who could not vote.[76]

In October 1900 the U.S. Supreme Court finally decided the last of the South Carolina cases sponsored by Representative George Washington Murray's organization—*Wiley v. Sinkler*. *Wiley* involved a damages suit filed by a black man who could not vote in the 1894 congressional election and it had progressed, haltingly, through several years of appeals and rehearings. The Court dismissed Wiley's suit on the ground that it was moot. The election was over and the congressman's term had already expired. On the other hand, the Court held that disfranchised petitioners like Wiley could file money damages claims if some constitutional violation were involved. *Wiley*'s effect was extremely limited but it provided at least a little bit of good news. It surely heartened the Louisiana case's organizers, whose activities resumed that fall.[77]

Samuel Wright's case reached the U.S. Supreme Court in December 1900 and by January 1901 it was over. The Court, through Justice McKenna, rejected Gusman's plea summarily. After stating the facts and history at some length, McKenna offered a one-paragraph-long opinion. This was not a habeas corpus petition, he noted, and so Marrero had "no cause of action." "However friendly he may be to the doomed man," McKenna wrote, "however concerned he may be lest unconstitutional laws be enforced," he had no standing. The Wright case was over and Birney and the other AAC attorneys could devote themselves to their larger project.[78]

The AAC held its Louisiana project together through the winter of 1900–1901 and in early March they announced their plans for a second time: "Negroes to Test a Law," a *New York Times* headline explained. The news seeped down to rural Alabama where Evergreen's *Conecuh Record* reported that the AAC had raised a "sufficient amount of money . . . to see that it reaches the United States Supreme Court for final adjudication." Professor Jesse Lawson, representing the council in press interviews, explained that the African American community of New Orleans pursued the case because Congress had thus far failed to punish the South for disfranchisement. They were headed into court because, he wrote, "we think that this course is the only one left open to us under the circumstances." Whatever their failings as test case organizers, the AAC's Louisiana effort had already attracted far more attention than all previous cases combined. Beyond the AAC itself, some African American commentators voiced concern that intraracial rivalries might yet sink the effort, however heartened they were to learn that something was happening. The announcement pleased a guarded *A.M.E. Church Review,* which believed that too many prominent African Americans had already bowed out, to their discredit. "Were such an organization Irish, instead of negro," the editor wrote, "all the leaders would be in it." Yet despite its many weaknesses, the public announcement of the AAC's attack on Louisiana's constitution signaled that, for the first time, disfranchisement and the grandfather clause would come under full-bore assault.[79]

Smith and Scott never discussed the Louisiana case again. Smith had far bigger things on his mind and had abandoned his booming practice in Galveston for New York City. It was a stroke of luck and may have saved his life. That September, Galveston was struck by the devastating 1900 hurricane. The city was destroyed but Wilford Smith was fine. He had installed himself in a two-office suite on the thirteenth floor of the American Tract Society building, and just as in Greenville and Galveston, he flourished. From his perch above lower Manhattan and the Port of New York, he oversaw a budding admiralty practice and dabbled in real estate. "I have every reason to believe that I shall succeed here," Smith wrote to a white friend back in Galveston, "after I am known." If anything, losing out on the Louisiana case proved to be a blessing. Wilford Smith would not have that disaster hung around his neck. When disfranchisement came to Alabama in 1901, he was free to accept Booker T. Washington's call. Washington wanted to fight back against Alabama's disfranchisers, and hard, and he wanted Smith to do the lawyering. Smith's wish to become known was about to be realized.[80]

4
Negroes Have Organized
Alabama's Disfranchisers, Black Activists, and the Courts

The "literates" among them have read the hand-writing on the wall.
—*Address of the Democratic State Campaign Committee to the People of Alabama*, 1901

When disfranchisement came to Alabama, that state's African American leaders and activists were better prepared than had been their brethren in Mississippi, the Carolinas, and Louisiana. They had the benefit of those previous states' experience, after all, and in the summer of 1901, it looked as if Alabama's black community would not wait to react. They did not necessarily know how to fight, and they had no idea of either how big or sustained a fight was necessary, but they were fighting and more of them seemed to be fighting than elsewhere previously. And Alabama's activists were helped by the disfranchisers themselves, who had chosen to keep meticulous records of their debates and plans.

Alabama's 1901 convention was the first disfranchising convention that maintained a verbatim transcript of their deliberations, and the four volumes and forty-five hundred pages of the *Official Proceedings of the Constitutional Convention of the State of Alabama, May 21st, 1901, to September 3rd, 1901* is one of the most important artifacts of the disfranchisement era. The disfranchisers' intent—and whether it might be proven in court—was a constant preoccupation for disfranchisement's critics and a pressing need for antidisfranchisement litigators. The *Official Proceedings* promised to satisfy both concerns. The Alabama delegates had rambled on freely and very nearly talked themselves to death. Every brazen boast and whispered danger, every premonition and stalking nightmare from the Alabama disfranchisers' minds, was aired exhaustively and memorialized on the pages of the *Official Proceedings*.

The *Official Proceedings* was conceived amid fears that any candid, public discussion necessarily exposed the convention's work to angry constituents, hostile judges, and ambitious attorneys. Convention delegate John Ashcraft questioned the "propriety and expense" and wisdom of a stenographic record. "It is claimed," he continued, that such a record would "throw great light in the future upon the true interpretation of the Constitution." That was dangerous, Ashcraft insisted, fearing that the delegates' debates would return to haunt them: "When this work is tested before the Supreme Court of the United States, we do not want that body to search for light amid the darkness of the debates on the 14th and 15th amendments." Nor, he continued, would they want to be judged "by the bitterness which the sense of our ever pressing injury will be seen to infect our debates." Ashcraft was not alone. Fellow delegate Thomas Long wanted "a record of what we do" but not "a record of what we say." Mississippi's, South Carolina's, and Louisiana's conventions, and North Carolina's 1899 legislature, had chosen that route, maintaining nothing more than procedural journals. That rendered those states' official records practically useless for litigators. Similarly, Long did not want to make it possible for the hypothetical "Colored Cooks Union" to "get up a labor strike" and refuse employment from anyone who supported disfranchisement. But test cases were the greater threat, Long and several other delegates warned, and he maintained that a stenographic record could only hurt Alabama "when the Supreme Court of the United States comes to pass on the constitutionality of this Constitution."[1]

Ashcraft lost, and the press praised the convention's decision, dismissing naysayers' concerns. "The objection that it will offend the north to read the debates is not sound," according to the Birmingham *Daily Ledger,* skeptical that "even the most impassioned debates are going to stir the nation to any extent, or influence the supreme court in its decisions." Other journalists, including the editor of Carrollton's *West Alabamian,* naïvely predicted that hiring a stenographer at seventy dollars per day "would encourage an economy of words," that it would "be the means of cutting off a lot of unnecessary gab." Neither happened.[2]

Before the transcript was published in book form, it appeared as a daily supplement to the *Montgomery Advertiser.* The *Advertiser* published the previous day's debates each morning and even promoted a special subscription rate of $1.30 a month for the convention's duration. No American newspaper had ever attempted such a feat and in far southeastern Alabama, the *Elba Clipper* celebrated it as "an achievement in journalism second to none in the country and . . . an enterprise worthy of patronage by the citizens through-out the State everywhere." "No one," the *Vernon Courier* advised readers, "can invest a dollar and thirty cents to better advantage."[3]

The convention was praised for providing a verbatim transcript, as was the *Advertiser* for its technical achievement, but there was something still more significant about the *Official Proceedings*. It was every bit as risky as John Ashcraft and other delegates suspected. Rather than rely upon second-hand newspaper accounts and statehouse gossip, antidisfranchisement activists and civil rights attorneys could follow the proceedings word for word in an official document for only $1.30 a month. If they only had the *Advertiser*, scissors, and glue, they could cut and paste together extensive evidentiary exhibits to accompany their briefs: Voilà! The Alabama disfranchisers' legislative intent in their own officially transcribed words.

They were having the same arguments as all previous states' disfranchisers, but that did not bother Alabama Democrats. They wanted a white electorate and they wanted it legally. The hitch, all over again, was the U.S. Constitution. The *New York Times'* front-page on Sunday, June 9, 1901, summarized the situation:

ALABAMA'S NEGRO VOTE:

DIFFICULT TASK SET BEFORE THE CONSTITUTIONAL CONVENTION:

DEMAND THAT WHITE SUPREMACY BE ASSURED IS ATTENDED
BY THE DANGER OF NULLIFICATION

The "danger of nullification" had also worried officials in the five previous disfranchising states and the concern intensified dramatically with the debut of the grandfather clause. It made the Mississippi and South Carolina plans seemed positively innocent by comparison. "Few men will find fault with a law which disfranchises the negro for ignorance," Minnesota's *Duluth News Tribune* advised Alabama's delegates, but "it is these dishonest 'grandfather' clause amendments that are so odious."[4]

Southern disfranchisers complicated their work and then complained that their work was complicated. Moreover, their oft-expressed intent to evade the Fifteenth Amendment was paired with the contradictory imperative that any new restrictions on state citizenship had to be constitutional.

Alabama sustained that trend. The South's constitutional framers, noted Columbia, South Carolina's *State*, were only making things worse. "The fact of the matter," the *State* complained, "is that for the sake of buncombe," they created loopholes available to (in relative terms) "a mere handful of white men" and gave disfranchised men reason to "resort to congress and the United States courts." The *Jackson Daily Clarion-Ledger* suggested that the Alabamians would be well served to keep things simple, recognizing "at once the force of the Federal Constitution and act within its compass and limitations." However, acting within the Constitution's compass and limitations meant that they had to avoid the Fifteenth Amendment and hide that fact in plain sight. Leading convention delegates, newspaper editors, and other observers constantly reminded the convention, in mantra-like fashion, that meeting both was impossible, and that making the attempt was unwise.[5]

The grandfather clause seemed the most likely feature of the new constitution to cause trouble and, sensing that their colleagues would succumb to its sinister allure, prominent delegates issued preemptive warnings ahead of Alabama's convention. "The bare-faced violations of right and justice" seen in Mississippi, South Carolina, Louisiana, and North Carolina had "made an impression on some of the leading men of Alabama," the *Montpelier Vermont Watchman* noted. Upon his election as a convention delegate, former governor Thomas Goode Jones warned that "any scheme, no matter how fair on its face," which discriminated against blacks was "liable to bring the state in collision with Federal corrective measures, both by the courts and Congress." William C. Oates, another former governor and delegate, insisted that "intelligence and good character" should be the only tests considered, even at the peril of keeping some significant number of blacks registered as voters. The grandfather clause would not "hold water," he maintained. Oates doubted "that even the Supreme Court of Alabama would uphold such a subterfuge," according to another account of the interview. For he was certain that when it reached the U.S. Supreme Court, the grandfather clause would "go out like a rocket."[6]

Alabama's new constitution would only face judicial scrutiny upon some disfranchised voter's initiative. Those African Americans who had the will and the wherewithal to sponsor a plaintiff or plaintiffs were waiting quietly and watching. Booker T. Washington, disappointed by the Afro-American Council's faltering Louisiana project, was chief among them. On the convention's eve, Washington and twenty-three other Alabama black leaders met at J. W. Adams's dry-goods store in Montgomery to approve an official protest petition crafted by Washington himself.[7]

Within days, the document appeared on the convention floor. Alabama's boisterous delegates were in no mood to hear the complaints or pleas of the state's black population, but Booker T. Washington was a special case. On the twenty-ninth of May, at one o'clock, the appointed hour for a temporary lunchtime adjournment, the president pro tempore asked that the members linger awhile as he had before him "a communication . . . addressed" to convention president John B. Knox.[8]

The delegates, who had already begun to trickle away, protested with "cries of leave." But former state supreme court justice and delegate Thomas Coleman asked, "Who is the author of the communication?"

The chair replied, "I see it is signed by Booker T. Washington."

There was a motion to adjourn, joined by cries of "Read it." Coleman too wanted it read, insisting that "the author . . . is the most noted man of his race in the State, and perhaps in the South." "Under the circumstances," he continued, "as we are considering a question in which he and his race are vitally interested, I for one would be pleased to hear it read."

Another adjournment motion followed, whereupon Thomas G. Jones intervened with a attempt to suspend the rules, which was met by yet another adjournment motion.

The parliamentary scuffle went on for some time before Coleman rose again. "Mr. President," he insisted, "we are here, and I do not suppose it would take but a very short time to read it." At last, he prevailed.[9]

Thanks to Judge Coleman and Governor Jones, Washington's petition received a public airing over the objections of the convention's younger members. Those younger men were the sons of the old master class to which Jones and Coleman belonged and they were decidedly less impressed by the Tuskegeean. The clerk read the letter accompanying the document as well as the petition, while the unruly delegates sat twisting in their chairs, their lunches delayed, forced to hear the honeyed entreaties of the most famous man in Alabama.

Washington flattered and reassured the delegates. "I have been appointed chairman of a committee," his letter explained, "to present an address representing the feelings and wishes of the colored people." "The negro," he continued, rests "his future in a large degree upon the conscience and intelligence of a great law-making body of a great Southern State. You have the power. The world will watch while you act." There was little substantive difference between the Alabama petition and his public appeals to Ben Tillman in 1895, Georgia lawmakers in 1899, and Louisiana's 1898 constitutional convention. Take the high road, the petition implored, "It requires little thought, effort or strength to degrade and pull down a weak race, but it is a sign of great statesmanship to . . . lift up a weak and unfortunate race. Destruction is easy; construction is difficult." And having endured the reading of Washington's letter and petition, the delegates quickly scurried away.[10]

One month later, from a New York City hotel, Washington issued a press release that further stroked and flattered the Alabama delegates. "Mr. Booker T. Washington," it stated, said that the convention "is composed of some of the strongest and most conservative and wisest men" in Alabama who were "seeking to find a way to do the best and wisest thing for the interests of both races in the State." Washington acknowledged that he *might* be "disappointed" by the convention's work, but he feigned confidence that Alabama's convention "would produce the most satisfactory Constitution that any of the Southern States have recently made." He continued his kid-gloved lobbying throughout the convention. The white southern press lauded his moderation, several black newspapers ridiculed his stance, and many in the national press thought that his strategy was admirable in its intent but flawed in its execution. Reflecting upon his petition, the *Salt Lake Tribune* declared that Washington's plea was "a manly protest" but nonetheless in vain: "It will not avail anything, because the convention has met for the sole purpose of disfranchising the colored men of that State." [11]

Booker T. Washington and his co-signatories were not the only voices of black protest heard from that year—far from it. Black Alabamians began protesting early in 1901 and by June the "negroes of Alabama," reports told, were "considerably wrought up." They knew their situation was dire, but they did not necessarily view the loss of citizenship rights as either inevitable or unstoppable. In Mississippi and South Carolina, there had been African Americans seated in the convention halls as delegates, but there was little protest activity outside of the hall once the convention got underway. There had been no black delegates in Louisiana, and that convention had also moved too quickly for there to be very much protest activity. North Carolina had not staged a convention, but there had been a protracted ratification campaign, which allowed for significant protest from many quarters. The larger point is that by the time disfranchisement came to Alabama, blacks understood what was happening. Protest petitions and pleading memorials arrived from around the state, and came from prominent civic leaders and the rank and file alike. One good example came from a mass meeting in rural Hale County where "substantial colored men" prepared a petition for their county's delegates, echoing Washington's call for the just treatment of black citizens.[12]

In select instances, convention delegates offered petitions from black citizens to the entire convention and had them inserted into the *Official Proceedings.* On June 7, Gregory Smith of Mobile had "a communication from an eminent and very respectable colored man" read to the body. It was written by Rev. A. F. Owens, a Baptist minister from Mobile, who asked that delegates frame their "organic law on the suffrage and school questions [so] that the intelligent, struggling, honest, law-abiding, patriotic negro citizen will be encouraged in his efforts to elevate himself." If they did so, Owens continued, "your names will go down with honor to posterity" and "generations will rise up and call you blessed." A letter from Willis E. Sterrs, a Decatur physician, was introduced on June 18, and Sterrs began by explaining that he spoke the "sentiments of thousands of my race whose timidity locks their mouths." But Sterrs's letter went on at such length that a minor floor fight occurred over the question of whether it would even be included in the convention record. By July 12, the convention had been in session for nearly two months and the delegates had grown even more short-tempered. So the rather lengthy letter of William Holtzclaw, a young associate of Booker T. Washington's and principal of a black school at Snow Hill, was simply added to the printed record without having been read aloud. All three of these letters were temperate and conservative and did not really challenge the delegates. Even if they had, it is doubtful that any record of them would still exist.[13]

Outside of the convention hall there was heavy criticism of the delegates themselves and also of the measured stance that so many black leaders had taken. Washington's petition in particular suffered biting criticism. "The humble and unnecessary petition" of the "Baker's Dozen" as it denigrated Washington's committee, "has been read and pigeon holed," the *Mobile Southern Watchman,* an African American paper, grumbled. A delegation from Washington's committee would stand quietly and meekly in the segregated gallery, the *Watchman* explained, ridiculing those "messengers of peace" who would "watch the pigeon hole where sleepeth that immortal petition until the day of resurrection," when Christ resurrected the believing dead and ushered in the Millennium.[14]

As the convention heated up in the early summer, so did black voices of protest throughout the state at large, including general discussions of a mass exodus—a threat heard over and again in the disfranchisement era South. East of Montgomery at Camp Hill, a curious outfit called the Afro-American Exodus Union staged a mass meeting in early May to discuss "what confronts us and how to better our condition." Attendees at that meeting resolved that "the calling of a constitutional convention in the state of Alabama to disfranchise the negro is but the voice of the Almighty God summoning him to return to his native land, Africa." The Exodus Union attracted widespread attention, mainly because it amused whites. Mobile's *Daily Register* derided the meeting and its host organization as "pathetic" and "childlike," and believed that emigration agents only intended "to profit from relocation," while that city's *Daily Item* advised blacks that "past experiences with emigration orders should serve as a warning to them." The group's "Supreme President," J. R. Howard, had claimed that the constitutional convention was an act of God, an attempt to call blacks "home," but the *San Francisco Call* dismissed the notion that the "Almighty had anything whatever to do" with disfranchisement in Alabama. Even if God was pulling the strings, the *Call* opined, "it is certain he did not intend it as a voice summoning the negro to return to Africa."[15]

Everything about the Exodus Union was suspicious: Its officers included a supreme president, president, vice-president, supreme secretary, secretaries, assistant secretaries, supreme treasurer, treasurer, and assistant treasurers. In early June, Supreme President Howard issued an open letter "To the Colored People of Alabama" on behalf of a purported five hundred thousand members, all "law abiding contented domesticated and hard working people." Howard conceded half the disfranchisers' argument, agreeing "as every other intelligent man must" that "it was a mistake to have given the negro the franchise before he was old enough to know and appreciate its value." He insisted, however, that it would be a "mistake by the law makers of Alabama, after years of liberty to take it away from him now." The point is not that the Exodus Union posed a threat. It did not, but its very existence suggested that *some* Alabama blacks, in *some* areas of the state, wanted to do *something*. Other emigration outfits also operated across the South, and some blacks did leave during this period, further demonstrating African

Americans' unwillingness to endure Jim Crow without protest. That fact usually escaped white leaders. The Exodus Union was easy to dismiss, and to laugh at, and the *Montgomery Journal* plastered Howard's letter across its front page, replete with typographical errors, the better to ridicule both J. R. Howard and the organization he claimed to lead. "The pen and pencil is as dangerous in the hands of some educated negroes," the *Journal* quipped, "as a loaded gun in the hands of children."[16]

Whites could snicker at the Exodus Union, but they could not laugh away the angrier and more threatening voices emanating from the black press corps. Heaven's wrath was a popular motif. The *Richmond Planet* warned Alabama's and Virginia's disfranchisers that "principles, like God, are eternal, and the abuse of them will in time bring its own punishment." In keeping with the divine theme, it was "indeed sad," the *Washington Bee* noted of disfranchisement's spread, but insisted that "right will prevail and the lamentation of the Negro will come to an end. There is a God and a just one who will right all things."[17]

God's wrath briefly became a live issue in Alabama, courtesy of the Rev. Andrew N. Johnson, a thirty-six-year-old undertaker, Republican organizer, and part-time editor of Mobile's *Weekly Press*. Johnson shocked the convention and the state by hinting that a race war loomed on the horizon. Abandoning any semblance of deference or caution, the paper's editorial vowed that "we'd rather die, than seemingly beg for our rights." "We are citizens and not slaves," it continued, and "the negro . . . not only asks for fair play but demands it." If treated fairly, the *Press'* editors guaranteed, blacks would work for the South's material prosperity. If not, they would work to undermine the South and "weaken it so that he can destroy this system of semi-barbaric slavery." Blacks *seemed* submissive, the editorial warned, "but that submission is by force . . . a cancerous sore which will come to the surface in an eruption in years to come." Give "the negro," justice, he promised, "and he will give his life to make the south happy and prosperous."[18]

Andrew N. Johnson split the muggy haze of the Black Belt summer with a ferocious bolt, touching off peals of thunderous denunciations. The *Fort Payne Journal* missed Johnson's point entirely, warning that if blacks wanted to "receive an education and secure concessions" from whites, they should ignore the *Weekly Press* "ravings." Justice, not concessions, had been Johnson's demand. "Editors of negro papers," the *Journal* continued, "have almost without exception been violent and turbulent disturbers of the amicable relations between the races." Rev. Johnson had made himself no more popular with convention delegates. He made things harder for the convention's moderates (men such as Thomas Goode Jones and William C. Oates) and complicated the already delicate lobbying efforts of Booker T. Washington. Washington had been in constant, secret communication with Jones, Oates, and Thomas Coleman, and Johnson was not helping. "When you are doing what is wisest and best for your race," Jones wrote to Washington, "there are fools with pens" who made it nearly impossible to obtain a "wise solution to our troubles. Such a man," Jones concluded, "is the negro editor in Mobile." The governor was wrong. Andrew Johnson was no fool. He had made a greater impression than any other Alabama black activist to that point; he had reminded the convention and the rest of the state that possibly more African Americans than they cared to imagine (and who were not nearly so diplomatic as Booker T. Washington) were watching and waiting to act.[19]

There had to be an official disfranchising scheme before it could be challenged in court and the convention was slow to produce one. Judge Thomas Coleman, chair of the Suffrage and Elections Committee, finally unveiled the committee's proposal on June 29. It landed with a resounding thud. The committee's accompanying introduction noted that it had "read and considered with care" the many resolutions and ordinances recommended to it as well as "the benefit of an extensive correspondence with leading men of other States." Evidently, those leading men made incredibly persuasive arguments because the committee members appropriated everything ever included in a southern state's disfranchising constitution and then bedizened it with garish ornaments of their own design. Alabama's elaborate proposal, the *Jackson Daily Clarion-Ledger* quipped sarcastically, contained "all the good to be found in the Mississippi and Louisiana constitutions, as well as . . . bad and absurd ideas not embraced in either."[20]

The proposal contained both temporary and permanent suffrage restrictions. A voter's registration was temporary under the permanent plan. That plan, which would take effect on January 2, 1903, required that voters renew their registration each year. Registration was permanent, however, under the temporary plan. Anyone who registered before January 1, 1903, would remain registered for life. He would have to keep his poll taxes current—no small feat for a tenant farmer or sharecropper, miner, day laborer, or mill worker—but he would never again have to run the gauntlet of registration tests. The temporary and permanent plans contained the same residency requirements and good-character prohibitions against "idiots and insane" persons, and those convicted of crimes such as murder, embezzlement, wife beating, sodomy, miscegenation, the vague category of "crimes against nature," and the like. They also shared a cumulative poll tax of $1.50 per year, due from 1901 or whenever the voter reached age twenty-one. If a voter chose not to vote (and thus did not pay the tax) one year but changed his mind the next he would owe $3.00, if he missed two years and attempted to vote in the third he would owe $4.50, and so forth. A poll tax alone was troublesome and onerous enough, but this was something far nastier.

Applicants under the temporary plan could qualify in any of three categories: (1) war veterans, (2) the descendants of war veterans, or (3) "persons of good character who understand the duties and obligations of citizenship." That third subsection was a near-facsimile of Mississippi's infamous understanding clause and opened the door to a host of frauds, thus making it the biggest obstacle for prospective voters, prospective black and poor white voters especially. Despite their denunciations of Mississippi's understanding clause, Alabama's disfranchisers adopted it anyway. Few noticed, however, because it was overshadowed by the temporary plan's second subsection. Subsection two contained Alabama's version of a grandfather clause, sometimes described as the "fighting grandfather clause" or "fightin' granddaddy clause," but most often called the "descendants clause."[21]

Alabama's descendants clause, unlike Louisiana's and North Carolina's grandfather clauses, did not present itself as a direct repudiation of Reconstruction. Making 1867 the operative date for a grandfather clause (as Louisiana and North Carolina had done) was risky and just too brazen for Coleman's committee. The members were not averse to stunts; they wanted to be a bit more sophisticated about flouting the U.S. Constitution. Above all else they desired to reach their goal without appearing to have done so. By tying Alabama's descendants clause to military service—and some blacks had served in the U.S. armed forces in all military conflicts from the Revolution through the Spanish American War, the Indian Wars, and the Civil War—they believed that they had legitimized the loophole. "Such a provision" had been considered by North Carolina, that state's *Roanoke Beacon* reported, but had been abandoned because too many blacks had seemed likely to qualify. That would have threatened white supremacy in a number of eastern North Carolina counties (where black voting strength concentrated) and so the proposal was abandoned. "The constitution makers of Alabama," the *Beacon* warned, "would do well to examine the records before guaranteeing suffrage to that class of negroes."[22]

The proposal's heart was the boards of registrars. The scheme could not produce the desired result without the boards. They would administer both the temporary and permanent plans. The power of the boards, whose members were to be appointed by a committee consisting of the governor, state auditor, and agriculture commissioner, was nearly absolute and we should think of them as "registration courts." Through official foot dragging, arbitrary denial of applications, and general malfeasance, the boards could prevent anyone from registering before January 1, 1903.

The committee wrote an appeals process into the proposal, but it was a fiction. Appeals took the form of jury trials in state circuit courts, from whence plaintiffs could appeal to the state supreme court. The process was intentionally costly and time-consuming (the better to discourage actual appeals) and could not get a voter registered prior to the 1902 elections. South Carolina's Ben Tillman was one of a host of political celebrities who advised Judge Coleman's committee, and this appeals provision very much resembled one that Tillman had unsuccessfully advocated in South Carolina's 1895 constitutional convention. Tillman wanted an appeal made available in state courts in general, but South Carolina's convention confined jurisdiction to state appeals courts, of which there were few and even then met only infrequently. Seemingly minor provisions like these, Tillman insisted, were absolutely necessary; a pretended right of appeal only invited federal intervention, Tillman warned. "We are like an ostrich," he had told South Carolina's 1895 convention, "hiding its head in the sand thinking we are safe unless we put in the Constitution a provision that will give the people the idea that we are going to have fairness." Alabama's boards of registrars and the sham appeals process, superficially at least, met that ideal.[23]

Booker T. Washington advised Judge Coleman, apparently following a clandestine meeting that summer, that after gauging the sentiment on his petition committee "as well as that of other colored people," that the convention should try to "modify or leave out the . . . registrars and also what is known as the 'grandfather clause.'" Coleman ignored both requests. Around that same time, Greensboro's Addison Wimbs, an active Republican and a signatory of Washington's petition, proposed that they manipulate the boards to blacks' advantage. "The professional ballot box thief will be loath to rob himself of all power," Wimbs observed, and if they could be installed as registrars, "they will in my opinion register as many Negroes as they can and then after we get them registered we can then join with those of the citizens who want honest elections and force honest counts." Wimbs was proposing to fight fraud with fraud and that was not Booker T. Washington's sort of thing. There was also the question of what that type of man would seek in return. So Washington ignored Wimbs. Since the convention appeared set upon adopting the offensive descendants clause, he favored a more straightforward plan of attack: a legal challenge.[24]

In time there would be a black-initiated challenge to Alabama's constitution, just as the one against Louisiana's constitution, which had prompted excited news reports from New Orleans. Alabama's 1901 convention had just gotten underway when the disparate elements of the AAC's long-promised "Louisiana Case" finally coalesced. This would not slow Alabama's disfranchisement movement, but it did give Alabama's disfranchisers pause.

Early reports of the Afro-American Council's challenge to the grandfather clause in Louisiana's 1898 constitution emerged in the spring of 1901. These went largely unnoticed and the AAC quietly continued its preparations through the late spring and early summer. While the representatives of white and Democratic Alabama worried over how best to strip their black, Republican, and Populist neighbors of the ballot, black leaders worried over how to catch them. Meanwhile, Judge Coleman presented the suffrage plan on June 29, with no schedule of debate in place. The convention ground to a halt while its leaders wrestled privately over Coleman Committee's proposal. After one week, and then two, there was still no schedule of debate. Montgomery fell into a lull. Politicians simmered. The Fourth Estate fidgeted. They all worried, and waited, for something—*anything*—to happen.

The AAC's delay was similarly dramatic, but not by design. Privately, the effort teetered. Even as the first reports of the Louisiana test case emerged in March, the organization was beset with infighting and miscommunication over strategy and over who would control the case. Money was a problem as well. It certainly consumed the most time. The *New York Age*'s Timothy Fortune informed Booker T. Washington in June that the "Louisiana case is made up" but that attorney Armand Romain (the New Orleans attorney who handled the case) "wants his $500." The AAC, Fortune explained, had two hundred dollars on hand and wondered how much Washington could contribute himself. Two weeks later, Fortune advised that "Romain wants $600" and that the AAC could secure all but $175 of Romain's request. Bishop Alexander Walters wrote Washington about the case in late June and advised that he had told the council's treasurer to pay Romain whatever he needed but that Fortune had cancelled the payment. Regardless of what had come from AAC coffers, Fortune, the council, and other participants expected Washington to cover the difference personally. But Washington was not really able to do so and he did not appreciate council members' presumption that he would bear the burden of funding the work. The wrangling was interminable. Romain always wanted more money, the AAC never seemed to have enough money or to know how much had been spent, and it was never entirely clear whether anyone was really in charge.[25]

Despite the difficulties in New Orleans, the AAC announced its intention to expand the crusade. Five days before the Alabama convention's Suffrage Committee reported its proposal, the AAC held a meeting in Washington, D.C. to discuss "the proposition to test the validity of southern election laws." Professor Jesse Lawson, the council's chair, told the gathering at John Wesley AME Zion Church that Louisiana and North Carolina (both of which had adopted grandfather clauses and which he distinguished from Mississippi and South Carolina, whose understanding clauses were believed to have violated the Fourteenth Amendment and not the Fifteenth) "have adopted constitutions calculated to nullify the Fifteenth Amendment . . . and conventions are now in session in Alabama and Virginia with apparently the same end in view." Lawson pledged challenges to all of the new southern constitutions. The "ablest legal talent" had been secured, Lawson continued, and he asked for "the hearty co-operation of all law-abiding citizens of both races, north and south." Lawson had been inspired by the Louisiana effort and carried the message to Indianapolis, where the national AAC was in session. He told his audience there that he was optimistic about "securing a favorable decision on the 'grandfather clause" and asked that attendees open their wallets and contribute generously to the cause.[26]

Shortly after the John Wesley AME Zion meeting, the AAC found a plaintiff, David Jordan Ryanes, and filed its case in the Orleans Parish Civil District Court: *State ex rel. David J. Ryanes v. Jeremiah M. Gleason.* In news- and action-starved Alabama, reports of *Ryanes* gave editors new fodder. The case held particular relevance because the Alabama convention was considering a proposal very similar to Louisiana's disfranchisement scheme. Explaining the obvious, the "test of the Louisiana law," the *Mobile Daily Register* noted, "will . . . serve equally as a test of the Alabama measure." In late May an unidentified "visitor from Louisiana" had warned Chappell Cory, editor of the Democratic *Montgomery Journal,* that the case was being "ably prepared," but that was before there actually was a Louisiana Case and before Alabama had a suffrage plan of its own to debate. Two months later, however, Alabama's politicians may have thought differently about the anonymous traveler's warning. Louisiana, the visitor had confided to Cory in May, "may have it all to do over again." The sad truth, however, is that the case was neither "ably prepared" nor well executed, a fact of which neither the visitor from Louisiana nor Alabama's disfranchisers were aware.[27]

David Jordan Ryanes was sixty years old, black, a Tennessee native, and a New Orleans resident since March 1860. One news account explained that he had "an excellent reputation" and was "an elder in good standing" of the Methodist Church. He lived in the Eleventh Ward and had voted in the city for "the last thirty years or thereabouts" until, he claimed, elections officials refused him registration on July 10, 1901. On that day, Ryanes, accompanied by "a dozen . . . darkies of prominence in local politics," according to the *Times-Democrat*, appeared before Jeremiah M. Gleason, the Orleans Parish registrar of voters. Gleason proffered registration forms to Ryanes, but Ryanes did not complete them. Ryanes stated that he was illiterate and thus could not. Gleason asked whether Ryanes owned property. Ryanes stated that he did not. Gleason asked whether any of his male ancestors voted anywhere prior to January 1, 1867. Ryanes stated that they had not. According to press accounts, Gleason then stated that he could not register Ryanes if he submitted a registration form. That is exactly what they needed to happen to establish grounds for a test case, but astonishingly, Ryanes's escorts then led him away without having him file an application to register.[28]

Raleigh News and Observer editor Josephus Daniels had interviewed Gleason a year earlier during his fact-finding visit to New Orleans amid the North Carolina ratification campaign and asked, "Have any illiterate white men in New Orleans been denied the privilege of voting because they could not read and write?" No, Gleason boasted, because "every white man who wants to vote is permitted to vote. Public sentiment is such that no man in politics would attempt to throw obstacles in the way of an illiterate white man's voting." Men in politics, like Jeremiah Gleason, had no compunction about turning away illiterate black men. He would not have hesitated to turn away David Ryanes but did not have to, for Ryanes had submitted no application. Ryanes never really stood a chance, but because his organizers had failed to have him actually apply for registration, his test case did not stand one either. They were going to argue that Gleason had turned Ryanes's nonexistent application down for unconstitutional reasons. In short, they had screwed things up.[29]

Wilford Smith had briefed Emmet Scott, Booker T. Washington, and the AAC a year earlier about the type of plaintiff they ought to recruit and

David Ryanes was everything Smith did not want that plaintiff to be. Smith had made clear that the plaintiff had to be qualified (i.e., literate and propertied), yet Ryanes was illiterate and propertyless. Smith wanted an undeniably qualified plaintiff because he was concerned about unnecessary complications. By arguing on behalf of a man like Ryanes, his attorneys would have to impugn Louisiana's 1898 constitution while holding up their illiterate and impoverished client as a victim. The state would answer every attack against the 1898 constitution simply: "David Ryanes is not qualified to vote." Further, the AAC's lawyers seemed unaware of the fact that Jeremiah Gleason had allowed several black men to register as voters via the grandfather clause, including one who would later be involved in Ryanes's case. Those would be the counterarguments and would surely obscure charges and claims that Louisiana's 1898 constitution targeted blacks especially. Courts would not indulge any discussion of sociological factors and thus *Ryanes* was doomed from the start. On the other hand, if the plaintiff was the propertied and literate man that Smith had recommended, the very difficult court fight would be much easier to wage.

Evidently, AAC either could not or did not try to find the qualified man that Smith wanted in New Orleans and so they turned to Ryanes. Romain's petition demanded that Orleans Parish "show cause why [Gleason] should not inscribe his name upon the books as a voter in this parish." Without really explaining how Ryanes had been discriminated against, the document asserted that the Louisiana constitution's suffrage restrictions violated both the Fourteenth and Fifteenth Amendments. There was nothing in Ryanes's story to make his claim special or unique, or to prove either injury and causation. The petition did not contest his unsuccessful registration attempt. It alleged no malfeasance on Gleason's part. Ryanes admitted that he could not meet the 1898 constitution's voting qualifications. The petition, thus, had little to do with David Ryanes. After nearly two years of planning, the best that the AAC's committee of lawyers could come up with was a fishing expedition, a convenient way to drag the state's attorneys into court. A court hearing, a public inquiry, was what they wanted but this was not going to work. Nevertheless, Armand Romain filed the case on July 12.[30]

David Ryanes was a convenient and pliant instrument, a figurehead for the AAC's campaign. Their goal was to somehow "prove" the real intent of disfranchisement in open court, rather than force the fair application of elections rules, as Smith and Washington wished to do. The AAC's lawyers were not oblivious to the difficulties that lay along this route: "I can see a way in which the court may possibly evade the whole question," Albert Pillsbury admitted to Booker T. Washington in late July. Pillsbury also mentioned that they might decide to challenge some white man's exercise of the grandfather clause in addition to the *Ryanes* case. Why they had not settled these matters already is inexplicable. In the interim, they were left with *Ryanes.* They were asking a popularly elected parish-level civil district court judge to explore the whole of Louisiana's suffrage scheme and to then decide the case on a Fourteenth or Fifteenth Amendment question, thereby facilitating an appeal before the Louisiana Supreme Court and then the U.S. Supreme Court. "If we can get the court to go this length," Pillsbury explained to Washington, "we shall be completely successful." And they proposed that this sorrowfully inadequate vehicle could carry them on what promised to be a very rough journey.[31]

David Ryanes was a good and decent man. He had been born a slave, had endured the hardships of forced servitude for the first twenty-four year of his life, and then suffered the vicissitudes of life as a poorly equipped freedman for thirty-six more. His poverty and illiteracy were not his fault, though they did not mean that the protections of the Fourteenth and Fifteenth Amendments should be withheld. Nor did they mean that Louisiana's 1898 constitution did not violate those amendments in spirit if not in word. Ryanes's caste, never mind his race, only aggravated the difficulty of getting an antidisfranchisement case through Louisiana state courts and southern federal courts. It was just going to be far too easy for the State of Louisiana to fend off Ryanes's challenge.

"Black, ignorant, and without property," as the *New Orleans Times-Democrat* described him, David Ryanes himself created problems that were lost on no one, except, perhaps, his lawyers. Joseph Leveque, editor of *Harlequin,* a New Orleans literary magazine, was irritated that Louisiana Republicans had countenanced such an attack. Having done so, Leveque was floored that they were doing it with the "case of a darkey, so ignorant as not to be able to write his name." The *Washington Post* asked the more important question (an issue that Albert Pillsbury had floated to Booker T. Washington) of why organizers had not attacked the registration of a similarly unqualified white man, noting yet another problem with Ryanes's case: the state could simply prolong it "until the plaintiff dies of old age." Still, the grandfather clause was finally in court, which a guarded *Richmond Planet* acknowledged. "We endorse the movement and hope that it may be crowned with success," the *Planet*'s editor, and African American community leader,

John Mitchell wrote. But even if the case survived Louisiana's state courts, a U.S. Supreme Court that had upheld both slavery and polygamy in the past was "a very poor tribunal before which to secure justice." The *Planet,* like the *Post,* believed that death might play a role in the case. There was a chance, the *Planet* remarked, that some justices might die before David Ryanes's case reached Washington and be replaced by friendlier jurists: "Let us have hope." Though he ridiculed the case, Monsieur Leveque also sounded a peremptory warning, one couched in an exceptionally opaque and esoteric metaphor comparing white men to ancient warships' metal-clad bows. "Gentlemen, you will not win the battle," he insisted, and even "if you do at court, [that] victory cannot be sustained against the beak of the Caucasian."[32]

Troubled and structurally suspect though it was, *Ryanes* unsettled many of Alabama's delegates and the convention ended July with a fierce debate over the Coleman committee's proposal. The descendants clause fight was the whole argument, really, and the rhetoric was hotter than the sweltering summer air. The convention's best (and worst) talent offered able (sometimes) and florid (always) speeches on the subject. Throughout, the specter of court challenges reappeared, darting all about the delegates' deliberations.

By the time that Gregory Smith, a corporate attorney from Mobile, rose to speak, the exhausted delegates had already heard it all, several times, and from nearly everyone in attendance. It was difficult to tell whether their enthusiasm for the descendants clause had waned or if they were just bored, and Smith proposed to revive them with a legal brief. In the first weeks of the convention, Smith was rumored to be in league with former governor William C. Oates and his allies on the committee, all of whom opposed any version of the grandfather clause. Later, when the committee's proposal became public, many commentators "in the know" presumed that Gregory Smith was among the enemies of the descendants clause. Though he had not signed on with the dissenters, he was said to belong to a "knighthood" who planned to slay "the horrid shape."[33]

Sedate and unassuming, Gregory Smith was universally esteemed by the state's corporate bar, and apparently, the final version of the proposed suffrage article was drafted in his handwriting—literally. Smith was the swing vote behind the locked door of the committee room where there had been a battle for his soul. He was the proposal's handpicked defender, tapped by Thomas Coleman himself, but he could not muster a full-throated defense.

Smith gave the best justification for the descendants clause that he could, but conceded disfranchisement's vulnerabilities at several points along the way. Specifically, Gregory Smith showed just how seriously some Alabamians took the Louisiana Case.

Mobile County voters, Smith told the convention, opposed the descendants clause "because they have been taught" that it was unconstitutional. His constituents had "seen this particular clause" in Louisiana and North Carolina. "They have heard of the attack" under preparation in Washington, D.C., and "of the attack that has commenced" in New Orleans. Smith's prepared remarks were less remarkable than the answers he gave in response to questions from some of the suffrage committee's dissenters, who had published a separate "Minority Report" that denounced the descendants clause. Among that number was Frank White, who interrupted Smith to ask his opinion of Louisiana's grandfather clause. White queried, "Are you of the opinion that the grandfather clause in the Louisiana plan is constitutional?" Smith replied, simply, "I am not." Smith later volunteered that when the question had arisen during the committee's deliberations he had argued the same "in the incipiency of the Convention before I knew whether there was a man in the Convention who agreed with me or not."[34]

Smith made clear that he believed the Louisiana and North Carolina grandfather clauses—he sometimes called them "the 'sixty-seven' clauses"—were unconstitutional. He nonetheless insisted that he feared "no court's decision upon the subject" and went to great pains to allay concerns about the Louisiana Case. David Ryanes's petition asserted that he did not meet the qualifications, that the qualifications were entirely unconstitutional, and that he should be registered "under the law that he says he is an absolute nullity," Smith observed. *Ryanes* was a troubled case, as Smith correctly pointed out, but that did not mean that a stronger case could not or would not be brought. Greater significance lay in the fact that blacks were contesting disfranchisement. That fact had only heightened tensions inside the already-tense convention and Smith suggested that the Louisiana Case was just a ruse—a conspiracy even. "The petition," Smith proposed, "was therefore necessarily filed to enable the gentlemen of the views of the minority . . . to threaten" the Alabama convention and the Virginia constitutional convention, which was also underway, "with the action on the part of the negroes." The *Atlanta Constitution* buttressed Smith's suspicion in a report of two weeks earlier. "The negroes," the *Constitution* relayed, "appear to believe that the action taken might have the effect of restraining the Alabama and

Virginia conventions," the latter having just gotten underway. Nevertheless, the Alabama convention steamed forward.[35]

The convention soon approved the plan and press critics promptly resumed their denunciations of the convention and the scheme and renewed their warnings about the courts. Mississippi's *Jackson Daily Clarion-Ledger* had never thought highly of Alabama's convention delegates and their suffrage debate confirmed its reservations. The unfolding Louisiana Case was inseparable from the Alabama convention's work. "The grandfather clause is a fraud pure and simple," the *Daily Clarion-Ledger* declared, "and should it ever reach the Supreme Court . . . suits already having been begun to test its constitutionality," it would fall. That was not a concern confined to the *Daily Clarion-Ledger*. The convention's decision to privilege white illiterates "who have been brought up with fair chances to learn to read and write, while driving from the ballot boxes illiterates in black skins, who have had little opportunity to educate," the *Dallas Morning News* noted, sardonically, "marks the high water mark of Alabama statesmanship at the beginning of new century." No one, that paper continued, "will be astonished or disgruntled" if the "supreme court should hold that ignorance is ignorance," nullifying the whole project. "Alabama has decided to follow Louisiana," Georgia's *Savannah Morning News* wrote, and reminded readers that "the blacks are going to make a fight. . . . They have already started a movement to have it declared unconstitutional." If the issue were "squarely presented," the paper believed, the U.S. Supreme Court *would* strike down the grandfather clauses.[36]

If the AAC were going to get Louisiana's grandfather clause before the U.S. Supreme Court, they needed to (1) lose in civil district court, (2) appeal to the state supreme court, and lose, and then (3) appeal to Washington, D.C. That was the bare minimum, and of course they needed to lose in a particular way: The reason for defeat had to involve a federal question. A question of state law or practice more than likely would not do.

Just as Alabama's convention wound down in Montgomery, the initial phase of David Ryanes's case ended in New Orleans when Orleans Parish District Judge W. B. Somerville ruled against him, but it was the wrong kind of defeat. Attorneys for the state had not bothered with the substance of Ryanes's petition. They simply alleged that the court had no jurisdiction and that Ryanes had no valid cause of action. Judge Somerville overruled the state's jurisdictional objection, ruling that Louisiana's state courts did indeed have jurisdiction over cases such as Ryanes'—a victory, of sorts.

However, Somerville then upheld the state's "no cause of action" exception and dismissed the case. "No cause of action" meant that Ryanes did not have a case (because he had never actually applied for registration), and this could not be appealed to the U.S. Supreme Court.[37]

Judge Somerville's "no cause of action" ruling far outweighed the jurisdictional victory and spoke directly to how the AAC had managed its case. They had orchestrated Ryanes's July 12 visit to Gleason's office, and for all their planning, no one, apparently, remembered that Ryanes needed to make an application and then have it rejected if he were going to argue that it was rejected unconstitutionally. Instead, his AAC handlers walked him into Gleason's office, told him to declare himself unqualified, and then escorted him away. Gleason never rejected anything. There was no cause of action. Thus, Somerville had an easy out.

Somerville's order in no way involved federal questions and that meant that there could be no straightforward U.S. Supreme Court appeal. Still, while Somerville took care to keep federal questions out of his order, he did not exclude them from the comments he offered from the bench. Somerville reasoned that, even if Louisiana's 1898 state constitution violated the federal charter, Ryanes still could not be registered. Echoing what Gregory Smith told Alabama's convention, Somerville explained that if the Louisiana constitution was unconstitutional, no registrar could conduct voter registration anyway and thus could not register Ryanes. He also maintained that, if the grandfather clause was unconstitutional, then the remaining restrictions would be unaffected. There was no need for Somerville to comment upon the federal constitution. Still, the judge wanted to have his say, and in the process he inadvertently impugned his judicial integrity. He made the surprising admission that the suffrage provisions of Louisiana's 1898 constitution "may not be entirely within the spirit of the constitution of the United States." It was one thing for a judge to force himself to accept a constitutional juggle, but judges are not supposed to admit that their decisions are similarly contrived. That was not in southern disfranchisement's best interest. Still, Somerville's statement had no legal effect; his order meant that the case was all but dead.[38]

At a minimum, Ryanes's case faced a round in the Louisiana Supreme Court, a retrial in the civil district court, and yet another attempt at the Louisiana Supreme Court, and then maybe, just maybe, it could be appealed to the U.S. Supreme Court. That was the best case scenario and it was bad. Everything was placed on hold. Meanwhile, events rushed forward in Alabama where the campaign to ratify the proposed constitution had gotten underway.

Alabama's disfranchisers portrayed the descendants clause and the entire Temporary Plan as a gift to white men, but white men did not welcome the clause with unalloyed gladness. Critics denounced it as a ruse and interjected a number of conspiracy theories that complicated the ratification campaign. The most powerful of these involved the courts and black plaintiffs, echoing a fear that previously emerged in North Carolina. Blacks would wait for white men to ratify the descendants clause, then haul it into court, and wait for some federal judge to void it in its infancy, which, they contended, the clause's framers wished to see happen. "The grandfather clause is only a pretext," the Populist *Geneva Reaper* cautioned, and after the courts nullified it, lower-class whites and blacks would suffer as one, "with the negro holding the long end of the handstick." The Democracy was going to take white men's votes and would use "the negro" to do it. "You can vote now," the likeminded *Opelika Industrial News* noted, but asked "are you sure you can vote next year?" This was a classic bait and switch: the clause would entice poor and working-class whites, the courts would invalidate the clause, and then its supposed beneficiaries would be left in the cold.[39]

The talk of hypothetical court cases was more than mere rhetoric. Conspiracy or no, there was going to be a court fight; it had happened in Tennessee, South Carolina, Mississippi, and Louisiana. It was going to happen in Alabama, too. African Americans were totally shut out of the convention, but they did not sit by idly, even if many in the white press chose to believe otherwise. "The negro," the *Centreville Press* claimed, was little concerned about disfranchisement: "He is setting back seemingly contented and satisfied." The *Press* wanted to believe that blacks would accept disfranchisement passively. In truth, they railed against the proposed constitution. Theirs was a campaign (albeit an as yet poorly organized one) geared toward mounting a legal challenge against the unratified document. Alabama was the only state to submit its constitution for ratification, and if it were ratified, a court fight was assured. Chicago's *Broad Ax,* an African American paper, was confident that the new constitution would fail either way, and awaited "the day of its butchery with calmness."[40]

Andrew N. Johnson had roiled the convention earlier in the summer with his predictions of race war and he triggered the alarm that autumn by staging an antidisfranchisement convention in Birmingham. Attendees there urged blacks to boycott the ratification vote and focus instead on the federal courts. An official resolution adopted at the meeting admitted blacks' "utter powerlessness" over the referendum's outcome. Accordingly, redress "must be sought for in the Supreme Court of the United States." If the courts failed them, they threatened to simply leave the state (renewing a vow heard in previous states), thereby depriving the state economy of the bulk of its unskilled labor force. "We can seek homes in states, territories, or our new possessions," the document continued, "where the rights of manhood will be respected." The most important thing about that conference, however, was that it had happened at all. Responding to the Birmingham meeting, the *Indianapolis News* was struck by black southerners' resolve "to bend all energies to raising money with which to test the suffrage question in the United States Supreme Court."[41]

Black South Carolinians had tried, unsuccessfully, to derail disfranchisement in their state in 1895. That same year, and again in 1898, black Mississippians launched cases of their own. In July 1901, the Louisiana AAC began its challenge of Louisiana's 1898 "disfranchising" constitution, with promises of still more cases arriving from Virginia (though that state's constitutional convention had not yet completed its work). "The negroes of Virginia are getting ready to contest any suffrage clause which the constitutional convention may adopt," according to a wire report carried across the region in October 1901.[42]

A month later, after the Alabama convention adjourned, Governor William D. Jelks announced November 11 as the referendum date, opening the battle between the "Ratificationists" and "Antiratificationists." U.S. Representative Oscar Underwood chaired the Democratic State Campaign Committee and soon issued an *Address of the Democratic State Campaign Committee to the People of Alabama.* The *Address* provided a laundry list summary of the entire constitution, with the suffrage provisions, of course, preeminent. Discerning Representative Underwood's and his committee's greatest concerns is easy: They set them in bold type. The reason for having two registration plans, the *Address* explained, "is best shown by the two difficulties which the Convention had to meet." The first was the Fifteenth Amendment, but the second was that "**the party platform pledged that white men should not be disfranchised.**" After some further elaboration about the Democratic Party platform, the boldface returned: "**And we unqualifiedly renew our party's pledge . . . no white man who can now vote will be disfranchised.**"[43]

The committee only used extra ink for their discussion of the suffrage and elections clause of the proposed constitution. They boldfaced their declaration that "**under the temporary plan the bulk of the negroes cannot register.**" Alabama's white men had nothing to fear, the *Address* emphasized yet again, with a liberal application of ink:

> **When a man applies for registration he will not be asked to specify under which class he is entitled to register.**
>
> **The list will not show under what clause he is registered. When the party's pledge not to disfranchise any white man is remembered, it is easy to see that the above plan will effectuate it. There is a general presumption that white men are of good character and understand the duties and obligations of good citizenship; the history of the race attests to this. It is safe to say that the registrars will observe this presumption.**

Maybe it was safe to make that presumption of the registrars, but for good measure Underwood's committee explained that another safeguard remained: the appeals process. No white man would submit to disfranchisement by the registrars, they declared, and anyone who was turned away could still appeal to the state courts. However, that would never be necessary, the *Address* claimed, because "the registrars who will be appointed by high officials in the party that has always stood for white man's supremacy will be in sympathy with the best methods yet devised to secure it."[44]

White men had to set aside their personal reservations, the *Address* insisted, and unite for a common purpose. That common purpose was so serious that extra ink was not enough, and it was presented under a separate heading that warned, ominously, that the "**Negroes Have Organized.**" They had done so because the "'literates' among them have read the handwriting on the wall." Fearful of the suffrage article's operation, "they have appointed committees to raise money to defeat it." The new constitution's white opponents, who steadfastly denied any collaboration with black activists, were charlatans. There was only one explanation for their opposition, the *Address* charged: "They are fighting on the side" of "the negroes." Underwood's committee, "catching the spirit and the purpose of the new constitution," had adopted a slogan: "White Supremacy! Honest elections! And the new Constitution—One and Inseparable!" "Under this banner," the committee declared, the white men of Alabama would face down those organized black literates and all other threats.[45]

The Democratic Campaign Committee probably did not have to issue its warning about black and white collaboration; outrage over Rev. Johnson's Birmingham conference had already infuriated white Alabamians. The "insolence and bravado" displayed there had brought Monroe County's white voters "into line for ratification," Monroeville's Democratic *Monroe Journal* relayed. "They realized," the report continued, that ratification was "a fight between the Anglo-Saxon and the African." The "Antis," in an account that surfaced in Greenville's Populist *Living Truth,* charged that the Birmingham conference had been cooked up by the Ratificationists "for political effect."[46]

Fraud was presumed, even before the referendum campaign had begun. So when tales of mischief trickled in on November 11, it surprised no one. The Antis, who were led by former governor Joseph F. Johnston, believed, at least initially, that they had turned out in sufficient numbers to overcome whatever the Ratificationists threw at them. As early returns rolled in, one opposition leader, former congressman Charles Shelley, commented that "we have carried the white counties by a large majority, notwithstanding fraudulent methods in the cities." "We do not think it possible," Shelley continued, "for advocates of ratification to commit frauds in the black belt or negro counties sufficient to change the result."[47]

Shelley's underestimation of his opponents was astounding. He was not alone in that mistake. On November 12, the *New York Times* reported that the majority in favor would not be less than twenty thousand and that "the negroes [had] voted in much larger numbers than had been expected, but were unable to control the result." Again, it is surprising that the *Times* correspondent did not understand what larger-than-normal black turnout indicated: Black men were not free to cast their ballots as they wished. Blacks had indeed shown up in large numbers in some locations. Dramatizing the scene at Florence, novelist John Henry Wallace wrote that "before six o'clock in the morning, hundreds of negroes swarmed around the courthouse, eager to vote against the new constitution." They were "the crippled, the blind, the old, the infirm—every negro in the precinct was there." The *Times,* though, seemed surprised that "in many counties they turned out en masse," but the *Times* and other papers just were not looking hard enough; blacks' ballots may have been cast in large numbers, but whether black voters marked and cast those ballots is another matter entirely. The *Bessemer Weekly,* which had supported ratification, seconded the antiratificationists' charges of malfeasance, in Birmingham in particular. A "fraud of the grossest character" had been committed there, and the explanation that the "colored voters through ignorance voted for ratification . . . is . . . far from plausible or correct." Any suggestion that blacks had voted for their own disfranchisement was ridiculous, the *Weekly* fumed. The result was nothing more than "open, barefaced, unquestioned fraud, a disgrace to the state and to civilization."[48]

Two months earlier, the Populist *Columbiana People's Advocate* had satirized disfranchisement in Alabama with "A Short History." Presciently, chapter 4 foretold the result: "Fifty-thousand majority in the white counties! But, lo and behold a hundred thousand negroes have voted for the disfranchisement of their race in the black belt! The glaring fraud, the lurid lie stalks abroad to insult the intelligence of the country!" On November 20, Attorney General Charles Brown and Secretary of State Robert McDavid presented Governor William Jelks with the certified referendum results. On Thanksgiving Day, Jelks proclaimed the constitution ratified by a vote of 108,613 to 81,734. The Black Belt voted 36,224 to 5,471 for ratification. The white counties—where the ratification campaign had actually been fought— held the real surprise. Voters there were more evenly divided and just barely rejected the constitution, 76,263 to 72,389.[49]

Chapter 5 of "A Short History" predicted a federal penalty, but not the one for which blacks had organized. In this iteration, Alabama would face the wrath of U.S. Representative Edgar Crumpacker of Indiana, who had begun a congressional crusade against disfranchisement: "Two hundred representatives in congress follow the lead of Crumpacker, and constrained by the oath 'that congress shall guarantee to each State in this Union a Republican form of government,' they proceed to right the wrong and the black belt hero cries aloud in his anguish 'what fools we mortals be.'" African Americans were going to drag the constitution into court. Because that new document prescribed no specific racial discriminations, activists could not secure any preemptive injunction. They had to wait until someone was actually disfranchised and would have to wait until March for that, after voter registration began. Moreover, the state did not yet have registrars to oversee registration and disfranchisement. To the registrars' selection was where Alabama's Democratic leadership, and Alabama's small corps of African American activists, next turned.[50]

5

An Appeal to the Colored Citizens of Alabama

Registration and Resistance

Give us your hearty cooperation in this work.
—Jackson W. Giles, president, Colored Men's Suffrage Association
of Alabama

Five days after Alabama ratified its 1901 constitution, Walter Lynwood Fleming, a twenty-seven-year-old Columbia University Ph.D. student and Pike County, Alabama, native, requested copies of the document from Governor William Dorsey Jelks. The budding historian wanted them for "some rampant Republican acquaintances to whom I want to show it." Fleming considered his New York City friends misinformed about his home state's recent constitutional convention, its treatment of the suffrage in particular. "Most of them seem to think," he explained, that the new constitution disfranchised "at once and forever all negroes whether educated, or property-holders, or not."[1]

Fleming's "rampant Republican acquaintances" seem to have understood *exactly* what Alabama's constitutional framers intended: the final political emasculation of black men. It is remarkable, if not implausible, that Fleming himself would not have appreciated their true intent. In its plain text, Alabama's new constitution did not prescribe blacks' complete disfranchisement, but its purpose was no secret. Yet because the document enunciated no clear racial discrimination, Fleming and any other southern Democrat confronted by either "rampant Republicans" or some disfranchised plaintiff's counsel could contrive technically logical arguments in its defense. Additionally, some small number of African Americans would be registered so that state officials could argue that because some blacks could still vote, the new state constitution had not violated the Fifteenth Amendment. That argument was too clever by half, as anyone of Fleming's intellectual caliber should have realized. But Walter Fleming and hundreds of thousands of white Americans contented themselves with the smug and self-serving syllogisms the disfranchisers offered.

Before Alabama blacks could fight disfranchisement through the courts, someone among their number had to be disfranchised, and the registration table was where disfranchisement really happened. Legislatures and constitutional conventions merely made it possible, which the disfranchisers and their contemporaries understood. They would establish qualifications that blacks could not meet rather than exclude blacks explicitly. It was "through the anticipated inability of the negro to meet the requirements of the *registration laws*," as R. Burnham Moffat told the American Social Science Association in 1904, "that it was believed his disfranchisement would be accomplished." Those new registration laws required "proper" administration for Alabama's disfranchisers to have the white, conservative, and Democratic electorate of their Jim Crow fantasies.[2]

No sooner had Alabama's referendum ended than attention turned to the registrars. "All we ask," Bibb County's *Centreville Press* explained on November 16, is for "three registrars for this county with backbone enough to do their full duty." The *Press* insisted that only "cool intelligent men" receive consideration. The registrars would not conduct their work anonymously; they had to face each applicant personally. Poverty and shame kept most men away from the boards but for those disfavored men who fought back, for blacks and those white men suspected of Populist and Republican tendencies, there would be humiliating oral "fitness" exams and almost certain rejection. Likewise, if a particular registration board *wanted* to register blacks or Republicans or Populists, or if its members were especially warmhearted, they could do so, thereby thwarting disfranchisement. Nothing less than "the future" depended on the "honest execution" of the new suffrage regulations, U.S. Representative George Taylor reminded State Auditor Thomas Sowell, and "this work must necessarily be left to the Registrars." If the wrong men won those posts, if "weak-kneed" men populated the boards, the *Centreville Press* understood, "the labor of carrying the election . . . will be of no avail."[3]

Letter writers propagated rumors indiscriminately, panicked that their home county's registration would be overseen by recreant registrars—saboteurs who plotted the Democracy's downfall. These fears emerged in all sections, freely expressed to the Board of Appointment, consisting of State Auditor Thomas Sowell, Agriculture Commissioner Robert Ransom Poole, and Governor William Dorsey Jelks. White counties and the Black Belt alike posed threats—threats that some nascent apostate faction might fester into a full-blown antidisfranchisement movement resulting in the widespread registration of blacks, Populists, and Republicans.

The Board of Appointment's overriding concern lay in finding sturdy, cold-blooded, and conservative Democrats because the registrars could enroll nearly any voting age man they chose. Macon County, home to Booker T. Washington's Tuskegee Institute, was said to harbor a group "who would like to see a class of men made Registrars who would make our Plan fail," Congressman Charles Thompson warned. Thompson believed that the cabal was based in Tuskegee, the county seat. "The opposing faction," the new constitution's ratification-campaign opponents, "are inclined to register the negroes, and that will never do." Democrats throughout the state warned of trouble from suspicious appointees. L. A. Collier, himself a prospective Lowndes County registrar, delivered dire news about another Lowndes County candidate, E. D. Scarborough. Scarborough's nefarious scheme, he alleged, was common knowledge. He had been "rampant" against the new constitution. He and his cronies were charlatans, Collier insisted: "They pretend they want the Negroes disfranchised, but I heard one of the leading ones say he could take the negro vote and the [Antis] and defeat any one in favor." The letter writers only repeated what the Board of Appointment already well understood. "It behooves us," Poole had written to a friend in late November, "that we make no mistakes."[4]

These battles against allegedly unsuitable registration board applicants can, at times, seem like little more than a hunt for straw men, and the particular complaints described here may have been completely unfounded. Still, the fear was evident and the danger real. This is borne out by what happened in Norfolk County, Virginia in late 1903. Virginia's "disfranchising" convention dragged on through the summer of 1901 and well into 1902, lasting a year longer than Alabama's. The constitution that Virginia's convention proclaimed into effect bore a striking resemblance to Alabama's, and Virginia's elections officers were given powers as great as Alabama's. Norfolk County (which includes the city) had a long "Fusion" tradition, whereby the competing political and racial groups shared power. Fusion, though, meant that blacks could vote and hold office and Virginia's constitutional convention had intended to end all such arrangements. Nevertheless, Fusionist Democrats and Republicans won seats on the Norfolk County Registration Board and they did not merely register waves of Republicans: They registered *black* Republicans. Virginia's new suffrage provisions disfranchised scores of Norfolk County African American voters, but the county's generous and inconveniently fair-minded registrars ensured that blacks retained a political voice in local elections. In Virginia, just as in Alabama and all of the other "disfranchising" states, registrars could easily wreck the project. In Norfolk, Virginia, that possibility became real.

Norfolk County's registrars had produced a "political cancer," according to a Norfolk County Democratic Party pamphlet. Desperate, party officials called in former state senator, sitting U.S. representative, and *Lynchburg Daily News* editor Carter Glass to stir up outrage and warn others away from this mortal temptation. Norfolk County's Fusionists were "moral and political lepers," Glass railed in a November 1903 address, "who should be required, like the physical lepers of Ben Hur, to stand off the highways at the approach of decent citizens and cry out, 'Unclean! Unclean!'"[5] In one of Glass's editorials, "An Abridged History of the Norfolk County Infamy," he noted with horror that Norfolk County alone had registered more African Americans than had the entire state of Mississippi. In another, "A Political Cancer," he thundered that those blacks were on the registration books "in spite of the Constitution, because white miscreants put them there as pliable instruments in schemes of spoilation." That sort of thing is what Alabama's Board of Appointment most wanted to guard against, irrespective of looming court challenges.[6]

Jelks, Sowell, and Poole completed their work by January 1902 and attention then turned toward registration. Black Alabamians geared up to face the registrars. There were two ways to proceed: Alabama blacks could either fight the new order or ask someone else to fight for them. William Hooper Councill, president of the State Agricultural and Normal School for Negroes at Huntsville, chose the former and asked Governor Jelks for help with a memorial to "the white people of Alabama." Councill was alarmed and trembled "for the future of my people in Alabama, unless you come to our rescue." The ratification campaign had been "one of bitterness and abuse of my people," he complained. He begged for the governor's aid, taking pains to appear meek and nonthreatening: "We are in your hands as babes in the hands of giants." But the giants were little interested in what Councill had to say and so his plea passed neither comment nor any offer of aid. Part of his problem was the fact that Alabama's white elected leaders were indifferent racists. The larger part had to do with political acumen. He could have learned a lot from a fellow Alabama black educator, Booker T. Washington.[7]

Washington was no less alarmed than Councill, but he was astute enough to know that Alabama politicians did not, and would not, act in blacks' interest. Disfranchisement was a devastating setback, one which Washington hoped to ameliorate. Yet he would not waste any more time on the legislature or Governor Jelks. Instead, Washington ratcheted up the legal fight against disfranchisement and prepared to drag Alabama's 1901 constitution through the courts.

On October 2, 1901, former Alabama governor William Oates had advised Washington that "the greatest bulwark of protection to your race is to be found in the federal judiciary." U.S. District Judge John Bruce had died the day before, and Oates suggested that Washington bring his influence to bear upon President Theodore Roosevelt in the selection of Bruce's successor. Bruce had done nothing to help blacks, Oates declared, and there were no Republicans in Alabama who would improve upon Bruce's record. A dramatic change was in order. "If you could induce the President to appoint a man, a conservative democrat of large influence, courage and a high sense of justice," Oates thought, "you would do the greatest good for your people and the country." However, Washington had already told the president whom he should select. Unbeknown to Oates, Washington had already decided that a Democrat should have the seat. Roosevelt, upon assuming the presidency in September 1901, had immediately begun consulting Washington about patronage appointments in the South. The men fashioned a fast political relationship, and in federal appointments, the president did exactly as Washington advised. Washington knew who he wanted on the federal bench in Alabama when Judge Bruce retired. Bruce had already announced his retirement (he was going to leave office when he turned seventy, as was required by law), and when he died suddenly, Washington's choice got the job much sooner than planned. He was former Alabama governor, 1901 constitutional convention delegate, and arch-opponent of the descendants clause Thomas Goode Jones. Owing entirely to Washington, Jones was now the U.S. district judge for the Middle and Northern Districts of Alabama.[8]

Washington understood that courts, federal courts especially, were the most promising venues that remained open to southern blacks. Courts appeared viable, largely because they had not closed themselves to African Americans. They may not have been very welcoming, however, or terribly enthusiastic, or particularly receptive, but they remained open.

By this time Washington had already been involved in the Louisiana case, *State ex rel. Ryanes v. Gleason,* for nearly two years. The original purpose of that exercise was to yield a U.S. Supreme Court appeal, but by the spring of 1902, when voter registration opened in Alabama, *Ryanes* had not gotten beyond Orleans Parish, Louisiana. Washington quietly withdrew from the effort, although he could have demanded a reorganization of *Ryanes*. Had he done so, however, he would have alienated his allies, emboldened his critics, and his role might have become public knowledge. So he backed away and laid groundwork for a separate court challenge of his own design.

In the winter of 1901–2, while *Ryanes* languished and while Governor Jelks and the Board of Appointment struggled to populate the boards of registrars, Washington brought the antidisfranchisement legal crusade home. There would be no committees. He would hire the lawyer and pay the bills. He could not hire a local white attorney and there were few black attorneys in Alabama (none whom he would consider hiring). On that point, seven years earlier, Washington was involved in the sad saga of Thomas Harris, a black attorney who attempted to establish a practice in Tuskegee, and nearly fell victim to a lynch mob. From that and all else he had seen and experienced, Washington knew that white Alabamians were wary of black lawyers and whomever he chose needed to understand white southerners' sensibilities. So in March 1902 he traveled to New York City, where he met the Mississippi-born Wilford H. Smith for the first time.[9]

Emmet Scott had first brought Smith to Washington's attention following his *Carter v. Texas* victory and more than once recommended Smith to the *Ryanes* organizers. To their discredit, AAC leaders passed over him. That turned out to be a blessing for the Texan, because it meant that no one could blame him for *Ryanes* and it freed him to accept Booker T. Washington's call to lead the Alabama litigation. When Washington and Smith met, registration had only just opened and they would have to wait for a plaintiff. The wait was short. Roughly simultaneous to their conference, a group of Montgomery blacks formed the Colored Men's Suffrage Association of Alabama, an organization whose sole purpose was to launch a U.S. Supreme Court test of Alabama's 1901 constitution.

Disfranchisement could be either passive or active, and each disfranchised Alabama man chose the method for his civic emasculation. When voter registration opened in March 1902, most poor, illiterate, and property-less whites (the descendants clause had not impressed them) stayed away to spare themselves public humiliation. Those were *passively* disfranchised. Black voters, especially those who were literate, propertied, and tax paying (or war veterans), turned out in large numbers in most counties. Almost none succeeded. Those men were *actively* disfranchised. Some of these active victims foolishly believed the disfranchisers' insincere rhetoric about allowing "respectable" African Americans to vote and probably thought that their white neighbors might make an exception. Most of them, in all likelihood, showed up to make trouble. Each black man who submitted to rejection had lodged a protest, whether or not he understood it as such. Every time a black man forced his county's three-member board of registrars into an official rejection, he explicitly challenged the new system.

The system afforded registrars leeway to exclude nearly all black men, in nearly any manner. There were two registration plans in the new constitution. The Permanent Plan, which would take effect in 1903, contained clearly expressed tests so that satisfying it may have appeared easier. The Permanent Plan, Tuscumbia's *American Star* reminded its African American constituency, "gives an Afro-American the unquestioned right to register who can read and write or who pays taxes on $300 worth of property." However, Alabama's new suffrage regulations read like "Jabberwocky": Everything meant the opposite of what it appeared to say. Through the looking glass, registration under the Permanent Plan was only temporary and required annual renewal. Conversely, voter registration secured during the Temporary Plan's brief operation was permanent. Successful Temporary Plan applicants would comprise a "life electorate." The sixty-six county probate judges would then forward the county rolls to the secretary of state in December 1902 for inclusion in an official registry. That record amounted to Alabama's Book of Life. Blacks had to remember this, the *Star* insisted: "They should make a heroic effort to get on the [voting] roll this year. A stitch in time saves nine." Mindful of that, blacks presented themselves in large numbers.[10]

Registration under the 1901 constitution's Temporary Plan began in early March. To legitimize the new constitution, the registrars would enroll a small number of black men. A curious Texan asked Alabama Attorney General Charles Brown, "Was the negro barred from voting entirely?" White America "knew" only one black man especially well, and Brown's Texas inquisitor wanted to know whether Booker T. Washington was "a qualified voter and does he vote." Macon County's registrars would not have dared to refuse Washington's application; he had to be registered if they hoped to use him for propaganda purposes and so he and twenty-five of his faculty members received their lifetime registration certificates immediately. Washington and his faculty were not the only black men registered. White Alabamians derived much comfort, for example, from the account of how Dallas County's registrars bestowed lifetime registration upon Edward Harris, an elderly barber known for the devotion under fire he had shown his young master during the Civil War. Alabama's disfranchisers extolled men like Harris and the novelist John Henry Wallace's fictional Calvin McMillan, who gave up the vote "cause I knows dese niggers ain't got no bus'ness tryin' ter run dis country." Wallace's McMillan freely sacrificed his vote and, as his reward, "received a life certificate to vote, that he values above all his earthly possessions." These were all hollow gestures.[11]

Washington, the Tuskegee Institute faculty, and Edward Harris were rare exceptions. Being of Washington's "type" was not enough to ensure a positive registration experience, though the new constitution's defenders always claimed that educated, "respectable," propertied blacks were welcome as voters. They were not. Educated, respectable, and propertied blacks were also the men who could launch test cases and, in county after county, registrars targeted them for humiliation and exclusion. Henry Davidson's ordeal was typical. Davidson operated a school for blacks near Centreville, in his native Bibb County. Thus, he qualified as educated and propertied, but respectability was another matter. Davidson's race was not his only disability in the eyes of Bibb County's registrars. He was also a prominent local Republican. After he passed every test the registrars devised, they demanded character endorsements from three prominent white citizens. This was one of the most widely used delaying tactics available to Alabama's registrars. Davidson went in search of affidavits and, after repeated rejections, lacked a third reference. He approached a firm of lawyers, "the members of which were my staunchest friends." After two had refused, Davidson turned to a third and recounted their meeting in his memoir.

"Mr. B———," Davidson asked, "you have known me for about twenty-five years. You have known me to be an upright, loyal, and honest citizen. I have never been in the courts for a crime committed. Will you endorse me as a good citizen so that I may be given the right to vote?"

"You have heard what my partner said, Henry. I should like to help you, but my firm will not allow me."

"I don't want you to endorse me as a firm," Davidson said. "Just endorse me as an individual." Conscience would not let him hold out any longer, so he "gave in."

Davidson recalled that the man signed an affidavit "as to my good character, and I still have my certificate, of which I am very proud." His experience had been exceptional only for its outcome.[12]

The 1901 convention president, John Barnett Knox, had quipped in a ratification speech given at Centreville, Henry Davidson's hometown, that when the "ignorant, vicious, and incompetent negro" faced a registration board, "there may be some questions asked. I do not know, but I would not be surprised if there should be!" He would not have been at all surprised by what happened to sixty-three-year-old Elbert Thornton of Bullock County. Thornton faced the following questions from his county registrars, which he later described in a sworn affidavit:

—Have you ever fought in the war?
—What state do you live in?
—What relation does your state bear to the United States?
—Who is governor of your state?
—What is a republican form of government?
—What is a limited monarchy?
—What islands did the United States come in possession of by the
    Spanish American War?

Those questions were difficult and esoteric, but the examination grew odder still. Thornton recalled that the Bullock County registrars demanded to know:

—What are the differences of Jeffersonian democracy and the Calhoun
    principles as compared to the Monroe Doctrine?
—If the Nicaragua Canal is cut, what will be the effect if the Pacific
    Ocean is two feet higher than the Atlantic?

Thornton, through an attorney, recounted giving "correct answers except the one as to the principle of Jeffersonian Democracy and the Calhoun principles and the Monroe Doctrine which he declined to answer."[13]

The most galling actions on the part of Alabama's registrars was the treatment afforded to aged (and black) soldiers. They turned away black war veterans in droves. The registrars' primary weapons were the "good character" and educational tests. The character test (like that encountered by Henry Davidson) went beyond the exclusions for felonies and infamous crimes—it was so broadly construed that *anything* could be evidence of poor character. Ultimate character judgments were left solely to the registrars. To avail himself of the descendants clause (which would ostensibly "save" war veterans), an applicant first had to pass the mysterious and ever-changing character test. Derry Fonville had served in the Union Army and was enrolled as a Union pensioner, but Montgomery County's registrars demanded that he provide character references from two white men. When Fonville complied, the registrars simply declared that they were not convinced and rejected his application. Montgomery County was not exceptional. Madison County's registrars rejected James Horton and John Gipson, both of whom were Union pensioners, though each presented documentation of honorable discharge and pension receipts. Riley Clark, in Limestone County, had misplaced his discharge papers. He too was rejected, but then again, having discharge papers did not necessarily help any black veteran who went before an Alabama voter registration board.[14]

These systematic dismissals of black veterans betrayed the disfranchisers' rhetoric about honoring war veterans with the descendants clause. Herschel V. Cashin, a "well known negro politician" from Huntsville, warned that Alabama blacks would "take the new constitution before the U.S. Supreme Court." Cashin, receiver in the U.S. Land Office at Huntsville, noting the northern Alabama registration boards' treatment of black veterans, "intimated," so the *Montgomery Advertiser* reported, "that the Boards . . . violated their oath of office in refusing to register certain ex-soldiers of the Civil War." Cashin need not have intimated anything: the registrars *were* ignoring blacks' military service, justifying their malfeasance with hastily concocted character objections.[15]

Litigation was on the minds of many black Alabamians and the registrars appreciated that threat. In March, when Morgan County's registrars launched their attack upon black Union veterans, "prominent and well-to-do" African Americans in the area, Cashin among them, announced that they had hired lawyers, and the mere suggestion of litigation prompted a reversal. Three days after Cashin's threat, Morgan County's registrars decided to register him after all. Through mid-March the Morgan County Board of Registrars had registered 848 white men and 26 African Americans. Across the Tennessee River in Madison County, 963 whites and 14 blacks claimed lifetime certificates.[16]

Black Alabamians fought persistently for places in the Book of Life. Thomas Shropshire, a Cherokee County registrar who also edited Centre's *Coosa River News,* informed his readers that as of April 11, 1902, 1,710 men had been registered, "of whom exactly 20 are sons of Ham. The darkies have stood an honorable test and deserve the compliment bestowed upon them by the most scientific law ever enacted by Alabamians." Thomas and his brother Robert (they co-published the *News*) had campaigned hard for Thomas's seat on the county registration board. Partisans and businessmen in equal mea-

sure, they admittedly hoped to elevate their paper through Thomas's Democratic Party service. "We are candid that we can extend the influence of
The News," they wrote to state auditor Thomas Sowell, by strengthening the
"cause of Truth and Democracy (synonymous terms) by this small but potent office's influence."[17]

Thomas got the seat. By April 18, he and his colleagues had registered
twenty-one hundred men overall, twenty-five of whom were black. He published weekly installments of what amounted to a diary and regaled readers
with stories such as that of a "'colored genmun'" who claimed to have had
"three grandmothers 'in de wah,' and "an old darkey" who, when subjected
to an understanding test, "avowed that Uncle Sam was a bigger worthy than
the President, even giving us something of our venerated Uncle's biography,
habits of life et cetera." Thomas Shropshire had humiliated those men and
he did not care. Maybe the first really did claim to have had three grandmothers in the war; maybe the second really did offer Uncle Sam's life story.
It made no difference, however. Anecdotes like these served only one purpose: to reassure Shropshire, the other two registrars, and the citizens of
Cherokee County that this business of disfranchisement was a good thing.
Shropshire and company did their work well. By April 25 they had completed the initial round of registration. Out of twenty-eight hundred voters registered in Cherokee County, only "twenty-seven darkies" had been
granted lifetime certificates.[18]

"If there were no morals in politics," the *A.M.E. Church Review* lamented that October, "Alabama would be entitled to a Kaiser's medal for
having devised the best means for cheating American citizens out of the
suffrage." Indeed, Alabama's 198 registrars had done a remarkable job. "The
Southern disfranchisement laws," Massachusetts' *Fitchburg Daily Sentinel,*
editorialized, regretfully, "are all working beautifully." As of August, Virginia officials reported only negligible black registration and Alabama had
announced that they "are a complete success." The "annulment of the 'war
amendments' to the constitution," the *Daily Sentinel* concluded, "is practically complete." By the end of 1902, black voter registration was reduced by
98 percent. The toll upon voting generally was breathtaking. In 1900, 162,302
men cast ballots in the gubernatorial election. Two years later that number
had fallen to 91,863, a reduction of 43 percent. Alabama's registrars never
bothered to hide what they were doing.[19]

In county after county, registrars boasted of how few blacks had received,
or would receive, those coveted certificates. March 27 was a "day dedicated

to negroes" for Calhoun County's registrars, the *Advertiser* reported. One hundred applied for registration in the city of Anniston, and the Calhoun County registrars congratulated themselves for turning away 83. Sumter County, a black majority county in the western Black Belt, began registration on March 17, and at Cuba, 103 whites and 2 blacks registered; at York there were 73 whites and 1 black man enrolled; and at Livingston 135 white men received life certificates, as did 7 African Americans. Farther east, 2,400 men had registered in the city of Montgomery by late April; few of those were black and those African Americans who succeeded did so, apparently, via the descendants clause as Spanish-American War veterans. At least two counties, Crenshaw and Lee, boasted that they had registered no blacks through the end of June.[20]

The disfranchisement plan's success both pleased and alarmed white Alabamians—the registrars included. They were pleased that few blacks had registered, but mildly perturbed that relatively few white men were paying the poll taxes and claiming their lifetime certificates. By late June, an estimated two thousand Montgomery County whites had not tried to register. The county's registrars—Charles B. Teasley, Jeff Harris, and William A. Gunter Jr.—hoped "that the indifferent electors will come forward . . . and attend to this important duty." Lest white men fear derision due to poverty or illiteracy, Teasley, Harris, and Gunter wanted it known that white applicants "are not to be asked embarrassing questions" and that they were "anxious to issue certificates to the white voters of the county." Registrars and Democratic Party officials were genuinely and deeply concerned with the lower-than-expected registration. Unless something changed by July, more white voters than the disfranchisers intended would fall away. With a statewide election looming (a gubernatorial election no less), the *Sumter County Sun* warned whites that they must register and soon: "It behooves every white man in Sumter to get his name on the list before July 31st, 1902." The registrars and the county Democratic committees knew the name of every prospective white voter and at Intercourse, York, and Cuba, the *Sun* complained, "over one hundred white men" had not registered.[21]

The only humane part of this process was that the registrars made a circuit through their counties' precincts, rather than demand that voters always come to them. The registrars were paid for their trouble, of course, and spent most of their days at the county courthouse, but the 1901 constitution had provided for a few brief moments of democracy. African Americans always showed up when the registrars made precinct visits. Black federal employees, in at least three counties, were especially troublesome for their local registration boards. Postmasterships, other postal jobs, and federal patronage positions were filled by Republicans and, in the white Democratic South, U.S. post office buildings often stood as little islands of Republican Party politics and were the only places where white southerners might expect to encounter a black official. In Tallapoosa County, Alexander City's postmaster, Joseph C. Manning, led a small-scale protest against the local registration board. There, the "Colored School" principal repeatedly tried to, but never could, make his application. Tallapoosa County's board had decided to hide from the principal and all other black applicants, rather then face them personally. When Manning learned of this, he sprang into action. The white Populist legislator-turned-Republican activist was "incensed," according to his biographer. Along with a delegation of prospective black voters, he marched on the county elections registrars. They found success. Twenty or so black men got their lifetime certificates. It was an obscenely low total, but better than none.[22]

The same sad stories played out over and over that spring and summer, and the most significant of them described a group of black post office clerks and janitors, all of whom worked in Montgomery's Post Office Building. The Montgomery Post Office workers' unsuccessful registration attempts set the stage for an intricate and daring legal assault against disfranchisement. Their number included James L. Jeter, Edward Dale, and the man who emerged as their leader, Jackson W. Giles.

Jackson Giles was born a slave in 1859, had worked as a cotton sampler in his twenties, and, by his early forties, had won a coveted job as a U.S. Postal Service office clerk and mail carrier. A widowed father of three in 1902, he lived on Watts Street with his second wife, Mary, who was sixteen years his junior. In Montgomery, on March 13, 1902, Giles, age forty-three, appeared before Teasley, Harris, and Gunter. Giles had lived in Montgomery from his infancy, had kept his poll taxes current, and did not suffer from any of the character disqualifications prescribed by the 1901 constitution. He was the type of African American whom the disfranchisers claimed no animus toward during the constitutional convention, but he was also the type of man they most feared. Self-possessed, independent-minded, a Black Belt denizen, and a Republican, he and any others like him could make trouble for Democrats on election day. Thus he had to go. So they targeted him and others like him; they ought not to have, but they did.[23]

It was important that Alabama blacks file any court challenges before the

March registration ended and before the next federal elections, and Giles and his friends responded with alacrity. Joining his fellow post office employees, James Jeter and Edward Dale, were J. W. Adams (a Montgomery dry-goods dealer and confidante of Booker T. Washington) and Derry Fonville, a Union Veteran whom Montgomery County's registrars had turned away. These men, along with dozens more who were not identified by name in news accounts, established the Colored Men's Suffrage Association of Alabama (CMSAA) and chose Giles as president. They held their first meeting at Dorsette's Hall on March 25, 1902 (twelve days after the registrars refused to register Giles), and raised two hundred dollars. There was only one thing, really, on Giles's agenda: litigation. Yet litigation was going to be expensive. The CMSAA immediately issued an appeal to black Alabamians aimed at collecting at least two thousand dollars to fund their case. The African American *Savannah Tribune* was glad to hear the news from Montgomery but guarded. "It is hoped," the paper observed, "that this movement will not be spasmodic but [that] there will be a well-defined plan and it will be adhered to until the result is attained." Jackson Giles did his level best to satisfy the *Tribune*'s wish.[24]

No actual copy of the CMSAA's initial circular survives. The text survives, however, because the *Montgomery Journal* intercepted a copy and printed it verbatim, along with Giles's accompanying cover letter, on its front page. Giles and the CMSAA secretary, J. S. Julian, invited any man "interested in your own political rights and the rights of your people" to join them in a "struggle to restore our lost citizenship, wrested from us by the unjust operation of the new constitution of the State of Alabama." They wanted recipients to contribute to their test case, and wanted the circulars—*An Appeal: To the Colored Citizens of Alabama*—"distributed among your people."

The character test and the descendants clause were the primary targets of

AN APPEAL

To The Colored Citizens of Alabama

Friends and Fellow Citizens:

On the 10th day of March, 1902, and in accordance with the new constitution of our state, the registration of voters began in the court house at Montgomery county and State of Alabama. As you well know, the spirit of the constitution is to disfranchise the negroes in the State of Alabama; and, in accordance with that spirit, all negroes out of the large number that have applied for registration have been refused, except a few who have served in some war in the United States.

Among those who have applied and were refused are some of our most worthy citizens, morally, financially, an intellectually, men who pay taxes on property from $500 to $30,000. The requirements of the Board of Registrars are altogether out of harmony with law and justice, since no negro can register unless he produces two white men who are willing to make affidavit to his good character. No negro's testimony as to his good character is accepted. It seems that the presumption of the Board of Registrars is that no negro has good character. This one fact shows that the workings of the new constitution are in conflict with the Federal constitution, which declares that "the rights of suffrage of citizens shall not be abridged on account of race, color, or previous condition of servitude."

We believe, too, that the "grand father clause" in the new constitution is unconstitutional, since its provisions lets in, among the soldiers and their descendants, a large number of men entirely void of the requirements of the "good character clause" thus granting favors to one class of citizens and denying the same to others, which can be easily termed class legislation, and is unjust.

In view of these facts, and the absolute denial of our rights of suffrage we, the people of Montgomery county, in a mass meeting assembled on the 25th day of March, 1902, organized the "Colored Men's Suffrage Association" for the purpose of raising money to test in the United States district court or supreme court at Washington, D.C., the constitutionality of the Alabama constitution. We need to raise $2,000 with which to commence. To do this we must appeal to every liberty-loving patriotic colored man in this state to aid us in this struggle. You can send your contribution singly, or you can call your people together in your respective communities and organize an association, raise your money and forward same to the secretary of our association, who will turn the same over to the treasurer of our association.

Giles and Julian explained that they hoped to begin their fight in the U.S. district court (which was housed in the U.S. Post Office building where they worked) and "if necessary" make an appeal to the U.S. Supreme Court. Giles's talk of a venue was premature. Nonetheless, it showed that they had a plan and they asked recipients to "give us your hearty cooperation in this work."[25]

The CMSAA demonstrated just how ready Alabama blacks were for a fight and had provided the plaintiffs that Wilford Smith and Booker T. Washington needed. Upon learning about the association, Smith made haste to Montgomery. He sought out Giles, claiming to represent the "Citizens Protective League" of New York City and offered his services. Giles and the CMSAA accepted Smith's story at face value and hired him immediately.[26]

They were not exactly sure of his name, but Smith was black and in Montgomery and white reporters were excited that he had come. "Negroes to Test New Constitution: Milford Smith, Colored Lawyer, Here to Make Legal Fight for Black Man," was among the afternoon's banner headlines in the April 25 *Montgomery Journal*. Whether they called him Milford, Wilford, or "the colored lawyer from New York," this was big news. Montgomery's sizable legal community was abuzz over Smith's plan, wondering how the "colored New York attorney" would proceed. An enterprising *Montgomery Advertiser* reporter tracked down Smith's whereabouts and found him at a boardinghouse on Jackson Street. Smith refused to meet the reporter and the house staff only reluctantly confirmed his presence. The next day, the *Advertiser* verified what everyone already knew: Smith was in Montgomery to challenge the new state constitution. He had been "employed by a suffrage association in the East," the report divulged, and Smith "would be given assistance" by Giles's organization.[27]

Misinformation aside—and it was deliberate misinformation, after all—Smith was the man of the hour. He had been in town since mid-April, making his introductions and collecting evidence. Interest only intensified after he began preparing affidavits. Smith's first affiant was sixty-four-year-old Nelson Bibb—a carpenter and politically active member of Montgomery's black middle class—who swore his statement on April 28. Alabama was being dragged into court. A special to the next morning's *Washington Post* explained, simply and succinctly, that the "first step was taken today by the negroes of Alabama toward testing the new constitution of the state."[28]

6
The Enemies' Works
The Alabama Cases Begin

I will move on the enemies' works as soon as possible.
—Wilford H. Smith, 1902

On April 30, 1902, two days after Nelson Bibb swore his widely publicized affidavit against Montgomery County's registrars, there was a sudden and significant development in the "Louisiana Case." David Ryanes's lead attorney, Armand Romain, appeared in the Orleans Parish Civil District Court and withdrew the matter of *State ex rel. David J. Ryanes v. Jeremiah M. Gleason.* Nothing had happened in *Ryanes* following Judge W. B. Somerville's unfavorable ruling eight months earlier. Romain could have attempted an appeal to the Louisiana Supreme Court, but that seemed ill advised. Because Somerville's ruling involved no federal matter, any appeal would have been purely procedural, based solely upon questions of state law. So Romain ended the case and immediately filed a second suit of the same name. Why he had not done this sooner is a mystery.[1]

The two *Ryanes* cases compared miserably to the nascent Alabama litigation. Wilford Smith had very much wanted the "Louisiana Case" and effectively auditioned for the job in the summer of 1900. The Afro-American Council had ignored him and Alabama was his consolation prize. However, the real loser in this was the AAC. Armand Romain was just not as talented as Smith and he bore the additional burdens of an unhelpful, second-guessing gaggle of out-of-town lawyers (none of whom had either appeared alongside him in court or understood Louisiana's Napoleonic Code) and an ill-prepared organizational sponsor.

The second *Ryanes,* like the first, targeted the underlying motive for Louisiana's grandfather clause. Romain and the AAC committee hoped to force state officials to admit and defend what everyone already knew: Louisiana's constitutional framers had wanted to disfranchise David Ryanes and other similarly situated black men as well as reassure propertyless and illiterate whites that they would not suffer the same fate. Exacting such an admission was their obsession, but winning it would have meant little. As a matter of law, it would have no great effect; as a matter of politics, it offered only slight promise. It *might* have fueled some minor political agitation, but only out of all proportion to the time and money they would spend. Nevertheless, they pursued this ill-chosen goal with messianic zeal.

Time and again in the parish court, Romain had Ryanes admit his shortcomings. Time and again, Romain simply played into the state's hand, and the state's defense attorneys patiently swatted his missives away. First Louisiana Attorney General Walter Guion and 1898 constitutional convention president Ernest Kruttschnitt noted that Ryanes was unqualified. Next, Guion and Kruttschnitt pointed out that many black men had registered to vote in Orleans Parish. Then, in the second *Ryanes* case, Guion and Kruttschnitt also insisted that the court had no jurisdiction and that *res adjudicata* applied since the parish district court had already adjudicated the matter in the first case. Only then did they address the grandfather clause.

In North Carolina and Alabama, it was impossible to discern whether a particular voter registered using the grandfather clause. Louisiana, however, carefully recorded whether individual voters registered via the clause, and for Louisianans this carried no social stigma. The North Carolina and Alabama grandfather and descendants clauses were only open to poor and illiterate men who admitted their disabilities publicly. Men in those states could not use the clause without humiliating themselves, so its potential beneficiaries stayed away. Not in Louisiana. There, any man could use it. Powerful, prominent, and propertied *white* men insisted upon registering via the grandfather clause, burnishing it by their touch. The famed New Orleans attorney, Thomas J. Semmes, former Confederate States of America senator, U.S. attorney, Louisiana attorney general, law professor, and American Bar Association president, was among the first who registered under the clause, a fact that Semmes, state officials, and the disfranchisers' spokesmen broadcast proudly. The former Louisiana Democratic Party chairman, H. C. Gage, once cited Semmes's example as proof of the clause's wholesomeness. The names of grandfather clause voters, he declared, comprised "a roll of honor."[2]

Louisiana also found room for African American men on that honor roll. Statewide, some forty thousand Louisiana men (more than one hundred of whom were not white) availed themselves of the grandfather clause. In Orleans Parish and New Orleans, seven prominent black citizens registered under the grandfather clause. The seven included Walter Cohen, one of David Ryanes's escorts for his bungled appearance before Jeremiah Gleason in July 1901. The free-born Cohen, U.S. customs inspector for the Port of New Orleans, insurance executive, Republican organizer, and rumored "keeper of a saloon, gambling house, dive and dance house for Negroes and prostitutes" was hailed by Guion and Kruttschnitt as "proof" that the grandfather clause was not racially discriminatory. These were very inconvenient facts for Armand Romain, who, at the AAC's direction, framed the second *Ryanes* around the grandfather clause as blindly as he had the first.[3]

Romain, Guion, and Kruttschnitt all agreed that Ryanes's second case would be a bench trial. It took place on July 15, 1902, before Judge John St. Paul. Ryanes testified first, restating the basic details of his biography: where he lived in the city, how long he had lived there, his full name, and so on. Then Romain led Ryanes deeper into his background, a background that exposed potential new problems:

> ROMAIN: Where were you born?
> RYANES: In Tennessee.
> ROMAIN: What condition were you born in . . . so far as political and civil rights are concerned?
> RYANES: I was born a slave.
> ROMAIN: Where was your father living at the time of your birth?
> RYANES: I just cannot exactly tell that because I don't know, but I know that he was in the State before I was born. I don't recollect seeing my father but once.
> ROMAIN: Was he a free man or a slave?
> RYANES: He was a slave. I knew the people that he belonged to.

When Kruttschnitt cross-examined Ryanes, he asked but one question:

> KRUTTSCHNITT: You say that you have lived in Tennessee?
> RYANES: Yes, sir.

Kruttschnitt did not elaborate on his query, but his intent was clear. He planned to argue that Ryanes could have used the grandfather clause but had not tried.[4]

The AAC had not properly stage-managed Ryanes's registration attempt on July 12, 1901, the day of his appearance in the registration office—that is beyond dispute—and Kruttschnitt thought he had found a gaping hole. This may be called the Tennessee factor. Ryanes's Tennessee nativity seemed significant to Kruttschnitt because, first, Tennessee had not disfranchised free blacks until 1835. That was only six years before Ryanes was born, and so his father or grandfather *might* have been free. Ryanes's testimony that his father had been a slave robbed Kruttschnitt of that point. Kruttschnitt had another Tennessee angle. Tennessee ratified the Fourteenth Amendment very early (before most northern states had) and enfranchised black men on February 1, 1867, nearly three years before the Fifteenth Amendment took effect. February 1, 1867, however, was one month too late for the grandfather clause, but it seems that Kruttschnitt was unaware of that. Then again, most copies of Tennessee's constitution would have been dated simply "1867." Besides bungling Ryanes's "cause of action," the AAC had not made sure that their client was born in the right place. With thousands of disfranchised black men in New Orleans, they found one whose father or grandfather might *theoretically* have been registered to vote. The grandfather clause did not require that one's ancestor be a registered Louisiana voter. Any state's voters would do, and Ryanes could not complain about the clause's discriminatory purpose if he had been one of its potential beneficiaries.

The Tennessee factor never gained steam because the second *Ryanes* case ended as abruptly as the first, but not before New Orleans' traditionally and peculiarly blurry color line came into question. Ryanes's whole case turned on whether the grandfather clause was devised for use by white men alone, but in New Orleans, seven black men (of about one hundred statewide) used the grandfather clause. Seven is a pitifully small number, but if Armand Romain and the AAC tried to say that *only* white men could use it they would fail.

Only one other person testified: Major Jeremiah Gleason, the Orleans Parish registrar of voters. Romain called Gleason to testify and requested that he provide a variety of registration figures, including the number of men registered via Section 5 of Article 197 of the Constitution of the State of Louisiana, also known as the grandfather clause:

ROMAIN: Major, can you tell us whether there are any colored men in the Parish of Orleans registered under the provisions of section 5 of Article 197 of the Constitution?

GLEASON: There are seven—I think I have the names of seven that I know of.

Romain asked him to provide an exact total and had the major restate "seven" a few times. Gleason testified that those seven had simply filled out their registration forms as had white men. Romain could no longer argue that black men could never use the grandfather clause. He then tried leading Gleason around that inconvenient fact:

> ROMAIN: Isn't it a fact that those colored men registered under section 5 . . . registered thereunder on the ground that they were sons or grandsons of white men?
>
> GLEASON: There was no question of their father being white or black. They simply filled out the blank as the white men did.
>
> ROMAIN: They stated that their fathers or grandfathers—as the case may be—could vote and register under the laws of Louisiana?
>
> GLEASON: The question whether their father or grandfather was a white or a black man was not suggested at all in any particular case, but they filled out the blanks the same as white men did.

Judge St. Paul interjected to make sure that he had understood Gleason's testimony. Gleason reiterated that his office had not inquired as to the race of any grandfather clause applicant's father.[5]

Armand Romain was having a very bad day. Gleason had not registered Ryanes because, of course, Ryanes had never actually applied—a technicality, yes, but an inescapable one. Then, when Romain went after the grandfather clause, it turned out that seven black men had used it. That was also a technicality, and a devastating one. The only thing left was to question just how black those seven men really were. Embarrassingly, that is what Romain did:

> ROMAIN: Are any of those colored men, registered under the grandfather clause, colored men . . . or have they any mixed blood in them?
>
> GLEASON: I have no idea of the purity or ethnicity of their blood. They claim to be colored men, and are known and looked upon as colored men.

This unfortunate line of questioning continued for some time, with Romain asking Gleason to decide whether particular "colored" men were of European descent. It showed how the AAC team got all of the little things wrong, and the big ones too. If miscegenation was going to be an issue for them, they should not have staged a case in New Orleans. Testimony eventually moved away from the hue of a man's skin, but it made no difference. This case was over.[6]

The AAC's problem in the first *Ryanes* case was that the judge's decision touched upon no federal question. The organization fared no better in its second attempt. Indeed, the outcome there was actually worse. Judge St. Paul did not even rule on the evidence. He simply sustained Guion's and Kruttschnitt's *res adjudicata* claim. The AAC's lawyers committee—already a fractious bunch—could only ponder what, if anything, they should do next.[7]

David Ryanes was a good man. At no point did anyone suggest otherwise, but he was also the wrong plaintiff. Illiterate, propertyless, and poor, he was eminently dismissible. Romain could not force the state to defend why it had not registered Ryanes. Instead, he and the AAC allowed the state to demand that Ryanes show why they should. In his second case, as in the first, David Ryanes never stood a chance.

Two years earlier, Wilford Smith had told the AAC (through Emmet Scott) what kind of plaintiff they should find. David Ryanes was not him. However, Nelson Bibb, Jackson Giles, and the other disfranchised, educated, and propertied middle-class African American men Smith found in Montgomery were exactly the kind of plaintiffs the council needed down in New Orleans.

Wilford Smith was a conspicuous and fascinating figure about Montgomery in the spring of 1902. Journalists, citizens, politicians, and especially lawyers followed his comings and goings with the utmost care. Smith commanded widespread attention, yes, but relatively little press coverage. At this early stage, most editors and publishers apparently decided that the less said the better. But not every editor agreed with that policy, so we know of Smith's repeated visits to the state capitol, for example, where he met with the state's attorney general. Smith also called on the state supreme court justices and had taken pains to familiarize himself with the court's filing procedures and customs. And he needed simply to meet the court; Smith was about to become the first black attorney to have appeared before that body.

Some Montgomerians thought that Smith might begin his attack in the supreme court, but newspapermen found plenty of lawyers who questioned that. The regular procedure was to bring appeals from circuit courts, which, the *Birmingham Daily Ledger* thought, meant "a long delay." Time was short. Smith, it was known, hoped to have a verdict before the statewide general election in August. Many professed "curiosity as to what his method will be."[8]

Most of what was written about Smith's plan was purely speculative, but it was known that he was drafting affidavits and that the first had come from Nelson Bibb. Mr. Bibb was literate and propertied and enjoyed high community standing. He was everything that Smith had wanted the New Orleans plaintiff to be.

None of Alabama's major newspapers was as curious about Smith's work in Montgomery as the *Birmingham Daily Ledger*. The editor was obviously excited, not that he cheered for Smith, but because the litigation promised a conclusive judicial settlement of the disfranchisement question. Yet after reviewing what was publicly known of Smith's plans, he expressed deep dissatisfaction. For starters, Nelson Bibb was not the plaintiff that the *Daily Ledger*'s editor wanted Smith to select. He had expected a case that tested the principle of restricted suffrage and suggested that if "negroes want to get a real test" of the constitution, they should find an illiterate, ignorant, and propertyless plaintiff (someone like David Ryanes).[9]

As would emerge over the next few weeks, Wilford Smith was not fighting for the principle of universal manhood suffrage. At this stage, none of the antidisfranchisement litigators were fighting for universal manhood suffrage per se (not even the Louisiana lawyers), and none of the antidisfranchisement activists had made public calls to that effect. Instead, they fought for fairness, for fair and fairly attainable voting qualifications, fairly designed, and fairly applied. If that meant the destruction of the new southern state constitutions, all the better. The truth is that by ridding the South of understanding tests, grandfather clauses, and ill-defined literacy and character standards, and by forcing registrars to adopt and honestly administer reasonable requirements, the suffrage would be broadened dramatically. To directly raise the issue of universal manhood suffrage only complicated things, usually because it invited the southern states' defense attorneys to trot out straw men arguments about the evils of an ill-informed, easily manipulable electorate. A case built around an ignorant, illiterate, propertyless, and black plaintiff like David Ryanes (like the *Daily Ledger*'s editor wanted) would, as Wilford Smith himself predicted, get the antidisfranchisement activists nowhere.[10]

The two Ryanes cases had been more conceptual than practical. The opposite would be true of Wilford Smith's Alabama cases. Armand Romain and the AAC wanted to see the grandfather clause struck down, and wanted to force Louisiana's disfranchisers into a confessing a secret that they had never really kept. But Smith recognized that Alabama's version of a grandfather clause, the descendants clause, was the least of black men's worries. The registrars, and their limitless discretion, were the real problem. Smith's cases (as he intended for them to work) would bleed the boards' authority to death slowly, by those proverbial tiny cuts, and emasculate disfranchisement by obstructing the disfranchisers' malign intentions. The southern states' disfranchising constitutions and statutory voting restrictions were fair on their face. Smith knew that if the registrars were forced to register qualified men like Nelson Bibb, tens of thousands of black men would have to be registered statewide. So he and the Colored Men's Suffrage Association of Alabama only asked that *qualified* men be admitted to the suffrage and that the registrars be forced to follow the letter of the law, which confused the *Daily Ledger*'s editor. He wanted a spectacular court fight and complained that if Bibb or some other respectable plaintiff won, it "would only register a few more." He was wrong. Equitable, attainable, and reasonable suffrage qualifications, and fair elections conducted thereunder, would have been a stake through Jim Crow's heart.[11]

Wilford Smith never explained any of this to reporters. He never offered any explanations through intermediaries. And this was all his own design. Because we know that Booker T. Washington brought him to Alabama, it is natural to wonder whether Washington himself directed the strategy, but he seems not to have. He left it all to Smith. At the same time, the very quality that most endeared Smith to Washington—his discretion—would prove to be a disability. Though brilliant, Smith was too taciturn for his own good. Whether he realized it or not, there was a very important public relations component to this work and he ignored it. He thus missed a chance to show his strength.

Eventually, Smith ended the guessing game and brought the first of five eventual challenges to Alabama's 1901 constitution before the Alabama Supreme Court. Smith filed a mandamus petition in order to obtain an unfavorable decision, which he could then appeal to the U.S. Supreme Court. "Good lawyers" in Montgomery, the *Daily Ledger* reported on May 3 (the day after the editor had complained about Nelson Bibb), doubted that Smith's strategy would work. Montgomery's bar did not question that someone in Washington, D.C. (GOP operatives, perhaps) had choreographed all of this on Smith's behalf. They could not believe that any black lawyer could be working under his own intellectual power and presumed that Smith was taking orders from persons better qualified than either he or they. Questions were also raised—better, and loaded, questions—about his finances. Yet just as they were mistaken about his strategy, they misjudged the source of his funding. "It has been ascertained," the *Daily Ledger*'s May 3 report continued, "that he is not being paid by the local organization, but by some society in the East." East Alabama, yes, but the courthouse spectators in Montgomery really hadn't a clue.[12]

Smith filed the case on May 6. Given that he was the first affiant, many expected that Nelson Bibb would have the honor of giving his name to the case, but the petition was instead styled as *Jackson W. Giles v. Charles Teasley et al.* The petition asked that the justices compel the Montgomery County registrars' attendance at a hearing on whether the 1901 constitution violated the U.S. Constitution.[13]

Alabama's 1901 constitution did not give the state's supreme court original jurisdiction over voter registration. There was nothing unusual in that; state supreme courts typically have only appellate jurisdiction. Instead, it expressly directed unsuccessful applicants' appeals to state circuit courts. Only if a prospective voter lost that circuit court appeal (which would take the form of a civil jury trial) could he make an appeal to the Alabama Supreme Court. Wilford Smith wanted to avoid that process and so he approached the supreme court under the guise of equity, an appeal founded upon the idea that no remedy exists in law. Smith was thus arguing that there was no real appeals process in Alabama's constitution. He argued that the boards of registrars were "quasi courts" and that the prescribed appeals process was but a chimera designed "to place [the county registrars] beyond the power and control" of the Alabama Supreme Court. Alabama had only thirteen circuit courts and it would be impossible, Smith continued, for them "to hear and determine the cases of the thousands of Negroes refused registration" before the 1902 state and federal elections. Giles had no other remedy but equity, he concluded, "by which to obtain the interposition of this court . . . except the most gracious Writ of Mandamus."[14]

Alabama had disfranchised Jackson Giles and his brethren through methods that violated the Fourteenth and Fifteenth Amendments, Smith charged, and he outlined those violations. Over the summer, as he filed each successive case, Smith refined his arguments, but even in his earliest iteration of the brief, he displayed the talent and vision that had been lacking in every previous antidisfranchisement case. Specifically, he singled out the eight sections of Article VIII, which governed registration and appeals. He did not ask that the whole process be set aside, only those provisions giving the registrars their discretion. The hard and fast qualifications could remain, but the character test, the descendants clause, the suspicious residency restrictions—those had to go. As evidence, Smith offered U.S. Census tables, speeches given on the convention floor by convention president John B. Knox, a series of *Montgomery Advertiser* articles, and fourteen affidavits from disfranchised black men. The petition, which was extraordinary for its day and time, was "very elaborate," the *Daily Ledger* explained, designed as a "speedy way to get it up on appeal."[15]

The *Daily Ledger* rarely guessed correctly concerning Smith's strategy and this was yet another example of that. Smith intended to lose; he could only get to the U.S. Supreme Court if he lost. Smith's design had finally become apparent and the capital city's legal community at last appreciated the fascinating conundrum. If he lost again before the Alabama Supreme Court, he could appeal to the U.S. Supreme Court. If he won, however, there would be no appeal to Washington, D.C. Nevertheless, the latter would have created a nightmare for Alabama elections officials because they would have to register thousands of black men statewide. It seemed, for a brief while, that Smith may have bested Alabama's constitutional framers.

Smith made his public debut on May 13 before the Alabama Supreme Court and African American papers celebrated the moment as a landmark in the post-emancipation black experience. "We are rising," the *Wichita Searchlight* of Kansas announced, explaining that Smith was the "first negro to appear before" the Alabama Supreme Court. Black attorneys were rare in the early-twentieth-century South and most whites had never either seen or met one. One of those whites was a *Montgomery Advertiser* reporter who noted, with evident surprise, that Smith, "the negro lawyer of New York City," spoke in a "deep, resonant voice." Smith not only possessed the oratorical skill of a highly educated attorney but also had a well-honed scheme to attack the state's constitution. "It is believed," the account continued, that if he lost, "Smith will proceed at once to take the petition to the United States Supreme Court." The *Advertiser* was only half right, which raised yet another of the contingencies involved in Smith's plan. He wanted to lose in a particular way and on a federal question.[16]

Smith's May 13 appearance was a rule nisi proceeding, which was essentially an extended discussion of whether to have an actual hearing wherein counsel would argue and examine the contentions in Smith's brief. But if the state supreme court so ordered, it would have to base its preliminary ruling on a federal issue, one involving the constitution and laws of the United States. Unless Alabama's high court justices were somehow completely at odds with the Democratic Party (to which they all owed allegiance), they would wiggle and dance their way around federal questions for as long as humanly possible. Alternately, they could simply ignore Smith's arguments. When the court announced its decision three weeks later, Chief Justice Thomas N. McClellan revealed that they had chosen the former, writing, "This application is sui generis. . . . The supreme court has no jurisdiction." McClellan carefully confined his decision to *state* questions. If Smith wanted to enjoin the registrars, McClellan explained, "he should go before the Montgomery County circuit court or the Montgomery City Court," each of which had original jurisdiction over the board. Alabama's disfranchisement scheme thus emerged unscathed from its first courtroom attack. The *Birmingham Age-Herald* misunderstood what had happened: "There is no secret . . . that this is precisely the decision expected and desired by the colored lawyer Wilford H. Smith."[17]

This initial, hasty hearing was a momentous event in Alabama politics. Incredibly, however, politicians said very little about it. And the paucity of public comment was striking. Editors, predictably, were the only exception. Montgomery's *Advertiser* was pleased because "the decision practically puts a quietus on the case, as it now stands in practically the same shape as if no action had been taken." Some white observers, though, still could not bring themselves to take Smith seriously and sought to diminish everything he did. He was either confused, they insinuated, or an attention-seeking mountebank, or simply out his depth. The "New York negro," Cherokee County registrar and newspaper publisher Thomas Shropshire wrote, "will probably get just enough free advertisement . . . to console him for his defeat." The *Advertiser*'s reporter, however, who had never joined in the ridicule of Smith, was intrigued, and not a little suspicious, about the lack of any public response from the city's African American community: "The negroes of Montgomery . . . maintain a rigid silence" regarding the case.[18]

The silence of Montgomery's black community had as much to do with their fear of retribution as it did with the white population's ignorance, wilful and otherwise, about the black population, but Montgomery's white community was not silent. The CMSAA's "militance" had raised someone's ire, and Montgomery's postmaster, Charles W. Buckley, responded by firing three association members in his employ, including James Jeter, one of Giles's original collaborators. Buckley had come to Alabama in 1866 as a Freedmen's Bureau agent and had been a Reconstruction era Alabama U.S. representative. Yet in subsequent decades Buckley grew ever more solicitous toward white and Democratic Montgomerians. Concerned by his employees' confrontational political activities, he had "shaken up the custodial force and the heads of three negro laborers . . . have fallen in the basket." Buckley hoped to temper the association's appeal and to that end he replaced the men with Aaron Timothy, Dennis Pfeiffer, and John Wilson. Wilson was given Jeter's job. A Spanish-American War veteran and one of those precious few blacks who registered in 1902, Wilson subsequently invited himself to a CMSAA meeting, lifetime certificate in hand, and insisted that the 1901 convention had not, in fact, intended to disfranchise blacks. Little is known of Wilson and why he wanted to undermine the group is a mystery. Unmoved by Wilson's importune demonstration, the members jeered him and he "was promptly given to understand that he was without sympathy." Their heckling of Wilson aside, the association's members were coming to understand the high price of resistance.[19]

The first of the Alabama cases had faced prohibitive odds. Smith reassured Booker T. Washington in mid-June that the court's decision was "purely political, with the sole purpose, in my opinion, to delay, and thus discourage the further effort to bring the case before the U.S. Supreme Court." By this time Smith had begun to use an alias, "Filipino," in his correspondence with Washington, and Filipino explained that he had only bothered asking for rule nisi "to get the case out of the state court in the speediest way." Nothing had been lost by the attempt. He warned Washington that their work would take time. Their legal crusade faced formidable challenges. The Alabama Supreme Court would do everything possible to delay future cases, "using every device permissible under the state practice" to avoid the federal question.[20]

That last point—"permissible under the state practice"—was very important. Judges would probably do all they could to avoid Smith's argument. They would probably accept nearly any argument advanced in disfranchisement's defense. They would probably impose every sort of technical procedural delay imaginable. Nevertheless, they would not do anything that did not *appear* to comport with established practice. This suggested that eventually, at least in theory, they would have to confront Smith's legal arguments.

The value that white jurists placed upon the idea, and the appearance, of fairness was something that black attorneys could, and did, exploit, especially if they displayed a firm grounding in the law itself. "All you have to do is know the law," Smith was said to have told Thomas Dent, a young African American who practiced in Texas in the 1920s. "The judge don't care whether you're white or black," Smith reportedly advised, "just have the law for him." Dent offered that recollection more than fifty years after he had met Smith, and while it is doubtful that Smith would ever have uttered the grammatically incorrect "the judge don't care," the gist of the statement seems authentic. It is borne out by the account of Little Rock, Arkansas, attorney, Scipio Africanus Jones, another contemporary of Smith's, who recalled that he "began the practice of law in Arkansas and throughout the South at a time when the Negro lawyer was a strange creature." Reflecting on his career, Jones thought that southern judges had at least respected the ideal of fairness. "Southern men, of the Bourbon South," Jones observed, "who were elevated to the Bench and are of the Southern aristocracy" were dedicated to the "hallowed traditions of English law." They may have subscribed completely to the white supremacist system they served, but they would not destroy the judiciary in white supremacy's name; they "were unwilling" to destroy stare decisis "just to do injustice to the cases espoused by the black lawyer." What this meant for Wilford Smith in 1902 was that the Alabama courts would not dismiss his claims out of hand, but instead engage him in a waiting game. The longer the cases took, the more expensive they would become. Fund-raising would grow more difficult. Disillusionment could overwhelm the plaintiffs. Alabama judges could stall and dodge and hope that Smith's clients would abandon their fight.[21]

Abandonment is exactly what had happened in Mississippi and South Carolina in the 1890s. That is what also seemed certain to happen in Louisiana. However, Mississippi's and South Carolina's antidisfranchisement activists hadn't had the benefit of so many previous attempts guide them. They also hadn't had the promise of financial stability that Booker T. Washington seemed willing to offer (secretly) the CMSAA, and they hadn't had Wilford H. Smith.

At this time Smith was the only African American lawyer to have won a U.S. Supreme Court case. That made him, effectively, the leading civil rights attorney in the United States, though there really was not yet any such thing as a true civil rights bar. Smith was talented and motivated and possessed of a bold naïveté that allowed him to believe that he might waltz into Alabama's courts with his audacious cases and then breeze on through the appellate process. He genuinely believed that Alabama's disfranchisement scheme, and much of the South's disfranchisement regime, would be felled by a single swing of his finely honed legal axe. "We have only to get to Washington," he confidently advised his patron, "and our case will win itself."[22]

Smith laid out an ambitious strategy for the litigation, designed to force decisions on federal questions. There would be two civil cases in the Montgomery City Court, which was equivalent to a state circuit court. The first was a mandamus application asking that the black Montgomerians be registered. Second would be a damages suit against the Montgomery County registrars that sought compensation for civil rights violations. Third, Smith planned to raise the same federal questions in a city court criminal case involving an accused murderer (who had not yet been identified). He would then appeal these three anticipated city court defeats to the Alabama Supreme Court. From there he would petition the U.S. Supreme Court, asking that all three be consolidated into a single appeal. Getting through the Montgomery City Court promised to be an adventure unto itself. The Alabama judiciary would stall for as long as possible. Smith tried to prepare Booker T. Washington for the inevitable frustration that would bring: "all the state courts and court officers are in league in conspiracy to prevent our case going to the Supreme Court." Smith wrote those words on June 17, 1902, and began his assault within one week.[23]

On June 24, 1902, Smith filed the civil damages suit, for which subpoenas were issued on the same day. He filed the mandamus petition on July 1. This petition was nearly identical to that in *In re Giles,* and, true to his promise, Smith included a thick stack of evidence, including convention speeches and newspaper articles, census tables, preliminary registration figures, and affidavits, which showed intent, opportunity, and discriminatory results. He was not asking to have the entire suffrage plan set aside, only those elements he believed had produced a discriminatory result. The registrars' discretion was the real target here. Stripped of that discretion, and forced to follow the qualifications to the letter, it would be impossible to exclude thousands of Alabama blacks. Neither these briefs, nor any others that Smith ever produced, called for universal manhood suffrage. Smith, Washington, and the CMSAA were only concerned that "qualified"—that is, propertied, educated, and taxpaying—men be registered. The purpose of these cases, however, was just to create appeals, and they worked. In October 1902, Judge

Anthony Sayre ruled against Giles in each. It had been Giles's "third water haul," Georgia's *Columbus Enquirer-Sun* observer, and as far as Smith was concerned, it had succeeded.[24]

Notably absent was any targeted or extended discussion of Alabama's descendants clause. In Alabama's 1901 constitutional convention, the 1898 Louisiana constitutional convention, and the 1899 North Carolina legislative session, delegates and legislators had made much ado about grandfather clauses, but Smith's were not grandfather clause cases. The grandfather clause, in truth, was the least of southern disfranchisement's evils and undoing the clause would not undo disfranchisement; it would only close a relatively ineffective loophole intended to let in otherwise unqualified white men. As the sad story of the Louisiana litigation had shown, the grandfather clause was a moving target. What Smith did instead was use the clause and the debates surrounding its adoption as proof of something larger. Because the clause's intent and effect were virtually impossible to conceal, it was more difficult to obfuscate or dissemble about southern disfranchisement's true purpose.

The final element of Smith's city court strategy was a criminal appeal, but because he could not (legally) plan the commission of a specific felony, the criminal case was slower to develop. Smith could not have simply appealed the conviction of a man already in prison. He needed someone newly indicted by a grand jury drawn from the voter lists created according to the 1901 constitution. He would represent the accused personally to make sure that things developed according to plan. In its basics, this was identical to Cornelius Jones's Mississippi strategy. The difference, of course, was Smith himself. To Smith, a criminal appeal appeared to be a promising avenue, despite its repeated failure in Mississippi, because the U.S. Supreme Court had recently reaffirmed in *Carter v. Texas* (Smith's own case) that states could not exclude blacks from jury service because of race. There was no one better qualified than Smith to bring such an appeal. He was, after all, the attorney who had successfully argued that case.[25]

On July 8, Judge William H. Thomas of the city court's criminal division organized a grand jury. The judge summoned twenty-one men from the voter registration lists. The sheriff served notices to all but two, the judge excused two, and two failed to appear. These last two were found guilty of contempt. The remaining fifteen—white men all—were duly empaneled. One week later, on July 15, that all-white grand jury indicted Dan Rogers for the murder of Ben Howard "by shooting him with a pistol against the peace and dignity of the State of Alabama." According to a subsequent report, Rogers claimed that he and Howard were good friends and that the latter's death had been accidental. This was the inauspicious debut of Smith's accused felon.[26]

Rogers was twenty-seven years old, a butcher by trade, and a married father of three. He lived on Houston Street, his twenty-eight-year-old wife, Lucinda, was a farm laborer, his eleven-year-old daughter Annie worked as a cook, and his daughter Rosa was only three. Little else is known of him beyond the fact that he had a very good lawyer. He was arraigned on July 17, at which time Judge Thomas admitted Smith to appear before Montgomery's criminal bar. Smith, at the arraignment, moved to quash the indictment. Pending a hearing, Rogers pleaded not guilty. Trial was set for July 29.[27]

Wilford Smith was not a member of the Alabama bar and could only appear in Alabama courtrooms with judges' special permission. This was a relatively routine courtesy for out-of-town lawyers, but then nothing was routine about Wilford Smith's presence in Montgomery. Public documents record no real consternation over Wilford Smith's activities. The most likely reason for this is that, since few whites considered him to be more than a novelty, few perceived him as any sort of threat. Privately, however, it later emerged that Smith was indeed in mortal danger and that he was unaware of the threat until well after the danger had passed.

Judge Thomas abruptly canceled Dan Rogers's trial without explanation. Surviving court records do not explain the delay and nothing more happened until the city court's October term, when Smith reentered his motion to quash. An explanation finally emerged a year and a half later. During a December 1903 visit to Montgomery, Emmet Scott learned of a foiled plot to attack (and possibly murder) Smith in open court during Rogers's July 29 trial—a murder trial no less. The account came from "an attorney who was implicated," Scott told Smith, and "it was the plan for one attorney to grab you and another to search you, and another to strike you with a chair." Providentially, someone alerted Thomas, who promptly suspended the proceedings. The judge guaranteed, in open court, according to Scott's account, that "any attempt to offer [Wilford Smith] discourtesy would be followed by confinement in jail for five days, but he did not alert Smith to the prospect of any specific "discourtesy." Still, Scott concluded, "I understand that there is very great feeling against Judge Thomas because of his stand in the matter."[28]

This was dangerous work for Smith, Scott, and Washington. They might suffer public scorn, but more important, they risked physical harm. Fake names soon surfaced in their correspondence. Smith was already signing his letters as "Filipino" by mid-June and Emmet Scott had adopted "Ajax" for himself. Sometime later that summer, Washington decided that he would not correspond directly with Smith. From that point forward, Filipino and Ajax handled things by themselves, but it was not enough for Washington that the two used aliases. "Filipino" and "Ajax" were too cute: Mail carriers, telegraph operators, and Western Union couriers would be curious. So he gave them duller aliases: Wilford Smith became "J. C. May" and Emmet Scott became "R. C. Black."

With Dan Rogers's trial postponed indefinitely, and the second and third *Giles v. Teasley* cases scheduled for October, Smith focused on the continuing struggle to finance the Alabama litigation. A never-ending series of solicitations marked the litigation's course. There were delays pending payments, delays pending Jackson Giles's slow fund-raising efforts, and delays while Smith solicited various mysterious, unidentified benefactors at Washington's urging.

On June 1, 1903, Scott explained that Tuskegee Institute had spent all it could afford on the cases but enclosed "a letter of introduction to Mr. J. E. Milholland. . . . He is a man whom I want you to know, and who can be thoroughly trusted, and who is at the same time thoroughly interested in this whole matter." Scott's letter contained nothing about the litigation. He left that up to Smith and wanted to know the outcome of his meeting with Milholland. John Elmer Milholland, born in New York in 1860, was for his entire adult life a tireless promoter of the Republican Party and an advocate for the rights of African Americans. In his youth he spent twelve years as a reporter and editorial writer for the *New York Tribune*. From 1889 to 1893, he was the supervising immigration inspector for New York City and during his tenure oversaw the opening of the U.S. government's Ellis Island facility. After leaving government service, Milholland became president of the Batchelier Pneumatic Tube Company (which delivered mail throughout New York City via a series of pneumatic tubes). In his spare time, Milholland established the London-based International Union Club, which championed the Boers' cause in their revolt against British rule, and then later the Constitutional League, a genteel group that sponsored a series of investigative and legal initiatives on behalf of African Americans. Milholland's greatest legacy, however, is that he was one of the original founders of the

NAACP. But before all of that, in the hot summer of 1903, Smith found it nearly impossible to schedule a meeting with Milholland, who also had contributed to the Louisiana effort at Washington's request. "I have made several attempts to get to see him but have failed, he is a very hard man to catch," Smith explained. "His stenographer thinks he will be in the office to-morrow, and if I see him I will write you again."[29]

John Milholland (the only outside patron Smith or Scott ever mentioned by name) was both wealthy and white and eventually parted ways with Booker T. Washington, ironically, over the issue of the antidisfranchisement fight (Washington felt that Milholland was too aggressively outspoken). Whether he actually contributed remains a mystery and any donations he made were not immediately forthcoming. Smith was thoroughly irritated, notwithstanding Scott's introduction to potential third-party patrons. Test cases are not cheap, and what Tuskegee and Tuskegee's friends could not provide came out of Smith's pocket. In all Washington personally paid Smith at least three thousand dollars between 1902 and 1903. Nevertheless, even with the additional fifteen hundred dollars raised by the CMSAA, Smith struggled against funding shortfalls.[30]

The constant financial strain was not a matter of thrift or penury on Washington's part. It was a matter of propriety. He was paying Smith from Tuskegee Institute accounts, with the drafts approved by Tuskegee's treasurer. Had Washington thrown his treasury open to Smith, someone could have breached his wall of secrecy. Secrecy was always a pressing concern for Washington and that constrained Smith's fund-raising possibilities. The more money that Washington paid to Smith from Tuskegee's accounts, the greater the chance of being found out. For its part, the CMSAA (Jackson Giles, in particular) worked hard to raise funds, but their collections never covered Smith's expenses. Nor was there any institution that could direct or fund court challenges. Smith could not simply absorb the costs because he was not yet so well established in New York to handle *Giles* pro bono.

As early as the rule nisi hearing, Smith had lamented a funding shortfall. He wished, he wrote Scott, that the amount he had received "could double itself at least, but small favors thankfully received." In late June, Washington advised Scott that "Filipino desires fifteen hundred to cover all costs in addition to five hundred." Going into this project, the principals had no sense of the cost. They never satisfied one another that they had done enough to finance it or even what "enough" may have been.[31]

Smith had grown so frustrated by the autumn of 1902 that he suggested he might quit, a threat he would repeat. He did not believe he could impose additional financial demands on Giles and the CMSAA: "I am under no contract with them whatever, and was not selected by them, and must maintain the position which I took in the beginning," which apparently was a sort of pay-what-you-can arrangement. Smith did, whenever possible, help the association raise funds. For example, in October 1902, he traveled to Mobile and Birmingham for public appearances on their behalf. By the next summer, Smith was even more annoyed and Scott had seemingly grown more frugal. "What I wish," Smith demanded, "is that you place sufficient means in my hands to proceed . . . without the delays and embarrassments." He insisted that "it is useless to discuss the matter further, as it should not be expected that one can 'make bricks without straw'" Scott, in reply, advised that "we" had gone to the mat. He and Washington were no less concerned about finances than Smith and questioned Smith's personal fee: "It is a very great strain for us to make this additional outlay." Eventually, as usual, Washington and Scott came through with just enough to keep the cases going.[32]

The squabble between Smith and Scott was capped by perhaps the most heartbreaking incident in the Alabama litigation's course. In June 1903, Jackson Giles traveled the thirty or so miles east to Tuskegee and appeared at Washington's office, hat in hand. "Giles is here to-day," Scott advised Smith in May 1903, asking for Washington's aid. Scott had explained to Giles "how thoroughly impossible it is for us to contribute." Giles left without a cent and, as far as he knew, without Washington's support. However, Scott knew that he had do *something* and had suggested that Giles ask Smith to "see the Wizard in New York," who might recommend him to "some strong, influential persons." Scott desperately needed Smith to maintain the cruel charade. He implored, "Do not leave [Giles] to think at all that the interest was substantial."[33]

In the moment of Giles's rejection, Smith may have pitied his client and he may well have shared his frustration. Still, by the fall he had had enough of Jackson Giles. Giles talked a good game about fund-raising and of what he claimed to have raised, but some (and most important, Smith) evidently wondered whether it was not just theater. The case's anonymous New York City patrons (who were never named) "do not find themselves able" to make any additional remittances." Giles, Smith observed, "makes a great show of collecting funds" but mysteriously had little or no funds to show, at least none for his lawyer's fee. There is little evidence of Giles's efforts, but he may have participated in a "mass meeting of negroes" that convened in Opelika, "mostly politicians," according to the *Daily Ledger,* to "devise ways and means for fighting the new constitution." If Giles had been there, he left disappointed. Many of the participants, the report continued, "were too sharp to be caught and did not contribute."[34]

In the late summer of 1902, with the three Montgomery City Court cases (*Giles* II, *Giles* III, and *Rogers*) awaiting the court's October term, Smith undertook his fifth Alabama antidisfranchisement case. He would carry it through the federal courts. So in September Smith filed a mandamus petition with U.S. District Judge Thomas Goode Jones, a former Alabama governor, who owed his seat to Booker T. Washington. Smith brought this fifth case because of money and time. The ultimate goal was a U.S. Supreme Court hearing, and he believed Jones's court might be the fastest route. "There is every reason why matters should go to Washington [D.C.] at the earliest possible moment," he advised Scott. Indeed, he believed that he could get to Washington, D.C., in time for the October term. He was confident of a Supreme Court victory that would "settle every thing," saving "the trouble and expense of the cases in the City Court." This was a hasty, last-minute decision—and a momentous one. It soon yielded the landmark U.S. Supreme Court decision, *Giles v. Harris.*[35]

Although the last of the Giles cases to be filed, the U.S. district court case of *Giles v. Harris* would be the first to reach the Supreme Court. When he had been a delegate in the 1901 Alabama constitutional convention, Thomas Jones himself stridently insisted that attorneys would someday use the delegates' frank and honest debates against them. He was convinced that plaintiffs and their attorneys would cite the intent, and the practical effect, of the new constitution. Now the CMSAA, whose leaders worked in the very same building that housed his court, dragged disfranchisement into his courtroom. One year after the convention, Jones was now one of those federal judges about whom he had warned and counsel was asking him to enjoin Montgomery County's registrars, to order Jackson Giles's registration, and to nullify those provisions of the 1901 constitution's suffrage regulations that he considered unconstitutional.[36]

This was essentially the same brief that Smith used in the Montgomery City Court mandamus case, *Giles v. Teasley* III. He wanted the clever registrars stripped of all their clever tools. They had abused their discretion because they could and because they were supposed to do so. The hard and fast educational, property, and taxpaying qualifications, the disqualifications for felonies and "infamous crimes"—those could stay. Smith did not question, in short, any qualification that any man might reasonably meet. He did not care if a state set a high standard, since obtaining universal manhood suffrage was not his objective. But character affidavits, the distinction between the Temporary Plan and Permanent Plan, the lifetime registry, the lack of a genuine appeals process, and so on—those had to go.

No voting rights attorney or plaintiff had ever presented a federal judge with a brief this all-encompassing. This one even exceeded the arguments that Nathan Goff accepted in the South Carolina cases. No federal court, at any level, had ever taken on a state's voter registration procedures so forcibly. Smith's extraordinary petition prayed for extraordinary relief. *Wiley v. Sinkler* affirmed that federal courts had jurisdiction over personal damages suits that arose from claims of voting rights infringement, but the courts did not have jurisdiction, either by federal statute or appellate decision, over a claim such as this. Equity was his only recourse and Smith requested relief from the U.S. Circuit Court for the Middle District of Alabama "as may be in conformity with equity and good conscience."[37]

As had happened when Nelson Bibb swore the first Alabama affidavit the previous April, public and press reaction was oddly muted. It is reasonable to ask whether anyone even knew what had happened because Smith and Washington so rarely publicized anything in connection with these cases. With regard to local press coverage, it is clear that Alabama papers paid this so little attention because they did not want it to be so. The news was undeniably distributed on national news wires because Smith's Bill of Complaint showed up in Boise's *Idaho Daily Statesman* two days after it was filed. The case was of unquestioned significance, and if news of it had reached Boise, Idaho, in only two days' time, it could not have been a secret in Montgomery. The news had reached New Orleans too, where the *Southwestern Christian Advocate* noted that the case was in the hands of Wilford Smith, described by the editor as "that astute and successful race lawyer." It had to have emboldened Montgomery's black community but they rarely offered public statements and their newspapers have not survived. No recollection was recorded after the fact. Maybe they said nothing. Maybe they did not appreciate what the CMSAA's and Smith's efforts meant. Maybe they were just afraid.[38]

If Giles were to win in the federal district court, Montgomery County would then be required to enroll him on the lifetime voting registry. The county would also have to register some or all of the five thousand others alluded to in his claim. Other Alabama counties might also have added a few more black voters for good measure. Jackson Giles and a few thousand others would have enjoyed lifetime certificates, but Smith and Washington and the CMSAA were not interested in token registration. They wanted the U.S. Supreme Court to declare the suffrage article unconstitutional, thus reversing the race-based voting restrictions imposed in Alabama and other southern states. But to reach the U.S. Supreme Court, they had to lose before Judge Jones.

Judge Thomas G. Jones had been a newspaper editor, a prominent corporate attorney representing the Louisville and Northern Railroad, speaker of the state house of representatives, governor of Alabama from 1890 to 1894, the leading opponent of the descendants clause in the 1901 constitutional convention, and Booker T. Washington's handpicked choice for the U.S. district judgeship. At the time of his appointment, there was some concern that Jones was too much opposed to disfranchisement and might be too receptive of antidisfranchisement litigation. Trying to squelch such rumors, the *Atlanta Constitution,* in October 1901, sought out the opinion of an "eminent attorney" who guaranteed that Jones would never jeopardize the 1901 Alabama Constitution. This eminent attorney then hedged and advised the *Constitution* that even if Jones wanted to strike down the 1901 document, he would not have jurisdiction to do so. "The courts of the United States have no original jurisdiction to grant a mandamus" order concerning registration, he explained. Neither the U.S. circuit courts nor the district courts had "jurisdiction to enjoin" a state's voter registration laws "on the ground that they violate the constitution of the United States." Still, the *Constitution*'s legal advisor overlooked another and rather obscure possibility: that on a question of jurisdiction, Jones could vault a case into the U.S. Supreme Court. Under federal judiciary statutes, federal district and circuit court judges could send jurisdiction questions directly to the high court, bypassing a trial and foregoing a lower court ruling.[39]

During its first century, the U.S. Supreme Court had virtually no control of its docket. If a case made it up the appellate ladder, the Court could not but review the matter. This created an extraordinary case load for the justices and, in the late nineteenth century, Congress sought to alleviate that burden by creating the U.S. circuit courts of appeal. With those in place, justices no longer rode circuit, while the number of cases that reached Washington was reduced. Fewer cases made it to the supreme bench and the journey took longer, but Congress had also created an obscure mechanism that *could* get a case to the Court quickly.

The 1891 Judiciary Act created the courts of appeal and revised lower federal courts' jurisdiction. The act included a provision, in its fifth section, that district court judges could send jurisdictional questions directly to the U.S. Supreme Court, without a lower court trial and without a stop in a court of appeal, but jurisdiction had to be the *sole* question. A district court judge, say, Thomas Goode Jones, could use Section 5 to send a petition like Giles's directly to the supreme bench. This was why Smith filed a mandamus petition in district court. He did not want a district court trial. He just wanted to get before the U.S. Supreme Court by way of Section 5, saving the trouble of having to wait on the Alabama state courts to exhaust themselves with procedural delays.

Judge Jones would have to agree to this, of course, and there was at least one good (or expedient) reason why he might do so: a jurisdictional appeal would allow him to maintain his community standing, both as a jurist and as a private citizen. If *Giles v. Harris* went to trial in Jones's court, he would have to rule on the constitutional questions it contained. There would be no jury; this was neither a criminal prosecution nor a civil damages claim. If Jones ruled in Giles's favor, he faced the loss of his community standing and the public revulsion reserved for race traitors. If he ruled against Giles, he would retain his standing as a private citizen (as well as life and limb) but also be revealed as a hypocrite. He had spent the summer of 1901 denouncing the descendants clause and he surely could not simply announce that he had experienced a sudden revelation. Jones had lectured the 1901 constitutional convention about what federal judges would do and could not refuse to do. He had promised that judges "will go behind the general language, take up the operation of the statute, step to step, with its known purpose," and test its constitutionality. If a law "effects a forbidden purpose," he had insisted, "the law is void."[40]

Back in 1895, Nathan Goff reveled in the original questions that *Mills v. Green* presented, but if Thomas Goode Jones derived any pleasure from *Giles v. Harris,* he never showed it. This really was a perilous situation and the jurisdictional trick that Smith hoped to use must have made Jones think long and hard about the plan. There was, however, something that could embolden Smith and reassure Jones—a precedent case about which they were apparently unaware. Four months earlier, the U.S. Supreme Court had decided *Swafford v. Templeton,* an obscure antidisfranchisement case from Tennessee that examined this type of jurisdictional appeal.

The Swafford story unfolded in the spring of 1901, just as Alabama geared up for its disfranchising constitutional convention. Thomas Swafford—a white man—wanted to cast a vote for William McKinley in the 1900 presidential election and so he presented himself at the Rhea County courthouse, in the county seat of Dayton, on November 6, 1900. Swafford made his way to the county elections judges who, in turn, presented him with one of Tennessee's preprinted "Dortch Ballots." Then the trouble started.

Swafford was sixty years old, had served honorably in the U.S. Army's Fifth Tennessee Infantry in the Civil War, and had good eyesight and no physical infirmities, but he could neither read nor write and thus could not navigate the state's new secret ballots. Swafford later swore that he wished he could read but literacy always eluded him. He had voted regularly ever since Reconstruction and his illiteracy had never been a problem. Swafford always received election-day assistance from poll managers but that ended abruptly in 1899, when Tennessee's legislature revised the notorious Dortch Law. Swafford could not read the instructions, he could not read the candidates' names, and no one would help him. We cannot know whether he was humiliated, dumbstruck, or angry in that instant. We do know, however, that William McKinley received one less vote in Tennessee that year.[41]

The original Dortch Law, enacted in 1889, inaugurated the Disfranchisement Era in the South. Under the law, voting was to be secret. It also provided for the preparation of official, preprinted (or Australian) ballots that listed candidates alphabetically (rather than by office sought or party) and revised the election day management of polling places. Voters could no longer receive assistance while marking their ballots and they only had five minutes to do so. The coup de grâce was the Dortch Law's restricted geographic scope. It only applied to the four counties, which contained Tennessee's urban centers and had the state's highest black (and reliably Republican) populations: Knox (Knoxville), Shelby (Memphis), Hamilton (Chattanooga), and Davidson (Nashville).[42]

The 1889 Tennessee legislature was concerned with disfranchising blacks and strengthening Democrats, and it had found a successful way to achieve this, but ten years later, Democrats decided that Tennessee's Republican Party was still too strong and so they extended the Dortch Law physically. Any civil district of more than 2,500 residents in any county became subject to the statute. Rhea County, in East Tennessee, was evenly divided between the Republican and Democratic parties, court documents stated, with Republicans holding a 250-man majority. The county had a population of just over 10,000 and was traditionally apportioned into fifteen civil districts.

The 1899 legislature, after amending Dortch, consolidated Rhea County's fifteen districts into four, targeting illiterate blacks and white Republicans like Thomas Swafford.[43]

Maybe Swafford did not understand how the law had changed. Maybe he thought that someone might break the rules to help a poor old war veteran. Maybe someone staged the episode to create a test case. Whatever his reason for trying to vote that day, the ultimate result was a damages suit against Rhea County's election judges filed in federal court. Swafford's attorneys filed his claim on April 2, 1901, and within a month U.S. District Judge Charles Dickens Clark dismissed the case for want of jurisdiction. Clark noted that the Tennessee Supreme Court had already declared the Dortch Law constitutional in *Cook v. State* from 1891 and so did not think that Swafford had raised a federal question. Neither did he think that the matter fell under *Wiley v. Sinkler,* the South Carolina suit that affirmed the federal courts' jurisdiction over damages claims arising from federal elections. Thus Swafford's case remained alive.[44]

Thomas Swafford's case traveled to the U.S. Supreme Court by the same route that Wilford Smith hoped to travel with Jackson Giles's case. Ordinarily, appeals from Tennessee district courts went to the Sixth U.S. Circuit Court of Appeal, which was based in Cincinnati, Ohio. However, Congress had, in 1891, routed purely jurisdictional questions directly from district courts to the U.S. Supreme Court. If there were a question of either law or evidence involved therein, the appeal would have to take the usual route. Judge Clark certified Swafford's appeal on the narrowest evidentiary grounds, and as the spring of 1901 blazed into summer, Swafford's attorneys prepared to argue jurisdiction before the U.S. Supreme Court.

In early 1902, while Alabama's registrars busied themselves with the work of disfranchisement, and Wilford Smith and the CMSAA prepared their challenges, the Supreme Court decided *Swafford v. Templeton.* Writing for a unanimous Court, Louisiana's Edward Douglass White wrote, "The court erred in dismissing the action for want of jurisdiction, since the right which it was claimed had been unlawfully invaded was one in the very nature of things arising under the Constitution and laws of the United States, and that this inhered in the very substance of the claim." Nevertheless, Swafford had not asked for, and did not receive, a final judgment on his claim. White had only needed to address jurisdiction. Wilford Smith intended to go that extra step and hoped to persuade the justices that the voting rights of U.S. citizens merited their immediate attention.[45]

*   *   *

When Smith returned to Montgomery from his Manhattan office in early October, he tried to call on Jones but found the judge away. He would not "be able to proceed until his return," but he had made progress with his opposing counsel. William A. Gunter Sr., the father and law partner of one of the defendant registrars, William A. Gunter Jr., handled these cases for the state. Smith wanted Gunter "to demur, and have the demurrer sustained." Remarkably, Gunter agreed to speed Smith's case along. After he and Gunter had worked out their arrangement, Smith made an appointment with Judge Jones. If that meeting went as hoped, he expected that he would be able to "get my papers to Washington" in short order.[46]

All of this is very technical and dry, but it is extraordinary and highly consequential as well. The significance of Smith's and Gunter's cooperation cannot be overstated. No more than a handful of people knew what was really going on and, irrespective of position, they seemed remarkably casual and cozy. In particular, Gunter and the state's attorneys were astoundingly cooperative throughout. Gunter's confidence in his eventual victory doubtless had a lot to do with this, but his and the attorney general's placid toleration and professional embrace of Smith was simply incredible. Smith— so self-assured, so poised, so confident of his eventual victory—made it all seem so easy, much like an academic exploration of common law civil procedure.

The elaborate choreography began when Gunter submitted his very brief demurrer for the registrars. It dealt exclusively with the issue of jurisdiction, arguing that

1. Giles's suit was beyond the court's jurisdiction;
2. Giles's bill had not shown how he had suffered any injury that brought his suit "within the cognizance of a court of equity";
3. the Alabama constitution provided "a plain, adequate and complete remedy" for his complaint;
4. Giles's suit "invokes the interference by this court in the internal affairs" of the state; and
5. Giles's suit did not show why he was entitled to the relief he sought.

According to plan, Smith signed Gunter's demurrer, verifying that it was correct as to matters of established law. On Saturday, October 11, 1902, all of the principals gathered in Judge Jones's chambers in downtown Montgomery, where the judge formally sustained points one, two, and five. No actual hearing took place to discuss the merits of Giles's case. Had there been, Jones could not have ignored Gunter's third and fourth points and Smith could not have reached the U.S. Supreme Court during its October 1902 term. Within moments, Smith introduced the prearranged appeal, and then the principals departed. Jones completed the process two days later, on October 13, with a certification of Smith's writs of error to the U.S. Supreme Court. Jones has been widely criticized by historians writing about *Giles v. Harris,* who deride him as hypocritical in light of his stance in the convention and the debt he owed to Booker T. Washington. The reality, however, is that he had disposed of the matter exactly as Wilford Smith needed and desired.[47]

Thomas Goode Jones gave Wilford Smith his first U.S. Supreme Court challenge to Alabama's 1901 suffrage restrictions. The Supreme Court was set for review of Alabama's 1901 Constitution and state officials needed preparation. At long last, they showed a bit of the care and concern that the situation demanded. The U.S. Supreme Court was going to have Alabama's constitution before it and would be asked to review its design and adoption. William Gunter notified the state's attorney general, Charles Brown, that it was now his turn to act: "I enclose you a citation in the Giles suit against the registrars. The judge dismissed the bill today, and an appeal was at once filed. You can therefore go to work on *your brief.*"[48]

October 13, 1902, was a very busy day for Smith. Besides securing the long-awaited U.S. Supreme Court hearing, he appeared before Judge Anthony Sayre (a former state senator who had authored the "Sayre Law," Alabama's 1893 foray into statutory disfranchisement) in the two Montgomery City Court civil cases—*Giles v. Teasley* II and III. These were disposed on demurrers, just as had been the district court case had been. The district court proceedings, friendly though they were, had jolted the state into action. This "colored lawyer from New York" meant business. Smith informed Scott that Attorney General Charles Brown had appeared in city court on the registrars' behalf. At that hearing, Brown inexplicably reminded Sayre of Smith's victory in *Carter v. Texas,* which affirmed the principle that states could not exclude blacks from jury service, insisting that the matter was entirely different. Indeed it was. *Carter* applied to *Rogers,* but not to the *Giles v. Teasley* cases. *Carter* dealt with racial discrimination in jury selection, and jury service had nothing whatever to do with the *Giles v. Teasley* cases. Brown "could not meet the case with any sound argument," Smith boasted.[49]

Again the Alabama press said as little as possible about either the city court or U.S. district court cases in October. The *Advertiser* only noted the opening of the city court's October term and mentioned that Judge Sayre would hear Giles's civil suits. National newspapers, both black and white, saw no reason to embargo the news, so wider mention followed the Supreme Court's official certification of *Giles v. Harris* in early November. Keeping with Smith's conviction that his case was going to "win itself," Kansas City's *American Citizen* proclaimed, when it reported the district court proceedings three weeks later, that the "franchise fight will be settled for good."[50]

Meanwhile, disfranchisement continued to spread and Smith wanted to hurry his case along. Virginia completed its constitutional convention in December 1902, adopting a suffrage and elections article very similar to Alabama's, and disfranchisers were fast gaining ground in Texas. A week after the Supreme Court certified his appeal, he moved for an expedited review, forgoing oral argument, on November 10. The Court granted his request. Pressure was building rapidly. The destiny of an entire race was settling upon Smith's shoulders. The *Southwestern Christian Advocate* was relieved by the news from Alabama, especially compared to the AAC's poorly handled *Ryanes* cases. *Ryanes* only made Smith look better. "Certain citizens of Louisiana," the interracial paper of New Orleans' Methodists noted, had been working toward the same end "for many, many months" without success. The Louisiana Case, the *Advocate* continued, had "made an extremely poor showing." By contrast Smith had made it to the Supreme Court in eight months.[51]

National newspapers were awakening to the meaning of events down in Montgomery and they reflected an apparently broadening public awareness. "No little interest is being manifested" in the case, the *Atlanta Constitution* noted. The country's "ablest constitutional lawyers" agreed that the southern grandfather clauses and disfranchisement schemes were sturdy, but questioned whether they were sturdy enough. *Giles v. Harris*, however, promised a final settlement: "An opinion of the court of last resort will set at rest any doubt which may exist on the subject."[52]

Alabama's black press cheered the CMSAA and its attorney. Birmingham's *Free Speech*, whose masthead proclaimed "Freedom of Speech, Equal Rights to All, Special Privileges to None," believed that Smith and the association were "doing yeoman service on behalf of the Negro of Alabama." The paper noted the need for donations: "They have taken the fight to the courts, but it takes money to do it. Alabamians are responding encouragingly," the

Free Speech continued, "but when last heard from Birmingham and Selma were still slumbering. Wake up!" While Birmingham and Selma had been disappointments, "Mobile and Montgomery are making a very creditable showing." Black Alabamians were crushingly poor and yet, considering their material situation, they came through admirably. Mobile's *Southern Watchman* noted in the fall, as word of the Supreme Court appeal arrived, that a single suffrage meeting at that city's State Street Church yielded an offering of sixty-two dollars "to help to push the contesting case now pending in the Supreme Court of the nation."[53]

Giles v. Harris was only one prong of Smith's and the CMSAA's attack. They already had two civil appeals before the Alabama Supreme Court, and on December 8, 1902, after more than three months' delay, Judge William Thomas finally held a hearing on Smith's motion to quash Dan Rogers's indictment. Montgomery County's solicitor, former congressman Stanley Dent (one of the chief opponents of the descendants clause within the 1901 convention), moved to have Smith's motion struck from the record without a hearing. Thomas agreed. Rogers had already languished in jail for five months and was found guilty of second-degree murder at his December 9 trial. The judge sentenced him to twenty-five years in the state penitentiary. In dismissing Rogers's motion to quash, Thomas handed Smith yet another Alabama Supreme Court appeal.[54]

Smith had written Scott on November 24, just ahead of Rogers's trial, to thank him for a favor of "six Cs" (six hundred dollars). It was a considerable sum in 1902 and yet it did not satisfy all of the financial demands of these cases. He was awaiting word from Giles and hoped that the association might meet the whole of his monetary needs thenceforth. As 1902 drew to a close, his antidisfranchisement strategy was unfolding according to plan and he was excited about returning to the U.S. Supreme Court, but the Court was (and is) very particular about the form and preparation of briefs, which translates into "expensive." Expenses haunted the Alabamians throughout this entire process, and late 1902 was no different. Smith was excited and ready to do battle. As soon as the CMSAA and his Tuskegee patrons satisfied the cost of preparing and printing those briefs, he explained, "I will move on the enemies' works as rapidly as possible."[55]

7
Swords and Torches
The Virginians Enter the Fray

> The oppressing, shooting, murdering, burning, lynching, jim crow-
> ing, and disfranchising of the Negro will breed a race of Nat Turn-
> ers, and the sword and torch will devastate and dissolve the South.
> —James H. Hayes

As Wilford Smith completed his U.S. Supreme Court briefs for *Giles v. Harris,* and as he prepared the Alabama Supreme Court appeals of *Giles v. Teasley* II and III and *Rogers v. Alabama,* the Temporary Plan's third and fourth registration windows opened. The third encompassed November's third week and the fourth the six business days preceding December 20, 1902. The Temporary Plan would then expire, closing the Book of Life. Men registered thenceforth would have to register again annually.[1]

The first two registration periods had been blighted by numerous outrageous decisions against retired black soldiers from northern Alabama. Limestone County's Union veterans were particularly hard hit. Some black northern Alabama veterans—Decatur attorney Herschel Cashin, for one—threatened lawsuits and thus fought their way onto the lifetime registry. The Herschel Cashins were few, however. As the Tennessee Valley's African American leaders readied themselves for the final two registration opportunities, they prepared for a fight. The local Grand Army of the Republic (GAR) affiliate, Athens's provocatively named William Tecumseh Sherman Post, led the charge.

With an eye toward testing Alabama's descendants clause, the Sherman Post extended an invitation to Civil War and Spanish-American War veterans, and their sons and grandsons, for a September 26 meeting at the Limestone County courthouse in Athens. As was typical, white newspapers largely ignored the meeting, but the national black press was all too happy to spread the word. The "mass meeting," the *Washington Bee* reported, prepared a resolution and designated Peter J. Crenshaw as their "special messenger" to carry it to that year's GAR encampment in Washington, D.C. It asked that the GAR lobby Congress for "aggressive steps to right the wrong, unjustly practiced against the defenders of the Union." The Limestone County veterans had been "persecuted, due largely to color," and asked their comrades-in-arms for their help "to redress the grievances unjustly placed and unjustly borne by us and our descendants."[2]

Crenshaw's visit to Washington was but a beginning. During the third registration period, which began on November 20, Crenshaw appeared before Limestone County's registrars as a prospective voter. They turned him away, just as they had that spring. Crenshaw was not alone. Booker Yarbrough also appeared before the registrars that November, but the board refused to let him apply. So Yarbrough returned on December 16, armed with his discharge papers. This time the registrars allowed his application, which they promptly rejected. The Temporary Plan was due to expire two weeks later, but Crenshaw and Yarbrough were not done.[3]

There was a suspicious-looking appeals mechanism (a trap, really) built into the 1901 constitution that allowed unsuccessful applicants to make appeals in the state circuit courts. Alabama had sixty-six counties in 1902 and thus sixty-six circuit courts. With only thirteen circuit court judges dividing their time between the various county courts, appeals would have to be perfectly timed to coincide with a judge's visits. Those appeals would also take the form of inconvenient and unwieldly jury trials. Inconvenience and unwieldiness, in fact, were what sold the disfranchisers on the appeals procedure. By providing for an appeal, the disfranchisers hoped to undermine any effort to challenge the new constitution with an equity suit. Thus it could be used to derail test cases. Back in May, before Wilford Smith had filed the first Giles case in Montgomery, Birmingham's *Daily Ledger* noted that state officials might *encourage* victories for plaintiffs in registration appeals. If Smith had chosen to pursue such an appeal on Giles's behalf, he would have faced the "probable failure of the case . . . by a decision in favor of the applicant." The disfranchisers thus planned to seize victory from any nominal defeat. So Wilford Smith assiduously avoided, and repeatedly attacked, that appeals mechanism.[4]

Peter Crenshaw and Booker Yarbrough, however, availed themselves of the appellate option. They were already disfranchised, after all, and had nothing to lose. Crenshaw was widely known in northern Alabama as "a colored politician" who had "for many years lived by his powers" as a partisan and on a veteran's pension. In January 1903, Crenshaw and Yarbrough filed their appeals in the Limestone Circuit Court, requesting that Judge Osceola Kyle grant them relief and have them registered as voters. Yarbrough's claim never made it to trial, but Crenshaw's did early that April.[5]

Osceola Kyle almost became a famous man, though for the wrong reasons. A year after Crenshaw's trial, Booker T. Washington persuaded President Theodore Roosevelt and Secretary of War William Howard Taft to appoint Kyle as a U.S. judge in the newly established Panama Canal Zone. Washington thought that since "large numbers of colored people" would work on the canal, Kyle would be an excellent choice because "he is well-acquainted with the character of the colored people." Ever since Roosevelt had assumed the presidency, Washington had made most of the decisions regarding federal patronage in the South, and Judge Kyle was one of the worst choices he ever made. Kyle was popular among Republicans and was widely regarded for the kindnesses and respect he extended to blacks, but he was not a gifted jurist. After a year on the Canal Zone bench, Taft had to remove Kyle because the judge could not be bothered to learn Spanish or to study either Spanish, Columbian, or Panamanian law, all of which a Canal Zone judge had to apply (in addition to the law of the United States). But neither Kyle's disastrous tenure in the Canal Zone nor his role in Crenshaw's case, were his closest flirtation with history. That distinction came from the fact that Kyle almost had a hand in the Scottsboro Boys cases from the 1930s. By then, Kyle had returned to the circuit court bench as one of two judges for Alabama's Eighth Judicial Circuit and was defeated for reelection in 1928 by William Callahan. The other judge was James Horton, who presided over the first Scottsboro trial before being forced to recuse himself. In his stead (and from Kyle's old seat) the virulently racist Callahan oversaw the subsequent trials. In 1934, amid the furor, Kyle challenged Horton for the second judgeship but finished third in a three-man field.[6]

Thirty-one years earlier, however, *Crenshaw v. State* was the biggest thing to have happened to Osceola Kyle, and whether Crenshaw's lawyer and the registrars' counsel scripted this hearing (à la William Gunter and Wilford Smith in *Giles v. Harris*) is unclear. Yet it is certain that Judge Kyle was extremely solicitous of both Crenshaw and his attorney, W. R. Walker, and openly hostile toward the registrars, overruling their repeated, strident objections. Ignoring the state's complaints, Kyle let Walker introduce whatever evidence he wanted. He let him present Crenshaw's U.S. Army discharge papers (over the state's objection). He let him introduce Crenshaw's identity affidavit, sworn by U.S. government officials in 1867 (over the state's objection). He let him walk Crenshaw through each of the state's prescribed voter qualifications, showing how he met every one (over the state's objection). Then, after Walker rested his case, Kyle's jury charge explained that if Crenshaw had shown his fitness "by a preponderance of evidence," the jurors should order him registered. The state objected to that too.[7]

Crenshaw's case would be completely overshadowed by *Giles v. Harris*, which the U.S. Supreme Court decided soon thereafter, but in Athens, Alabama, it was the biggest thing to have happened in quite some time. "After hearing the law explained to them," a very unsympathetic *Athens Alabama Courier* reported, "the jury composed entirely of white men, whom the said Peter [the editor refused to refer to him by more than his first name] has been fighting politically since the right to vote was given him," found that he should be registered via the descendants clause. The jury was roundly criticized, but only because locals did not understand that "defeat" was really a victory for the disfranchisers. The *Courier*'s editor was disappointed in the verdict, but understood that Crenshaw's victory would have no effect on local politics. This was a singular victory in the worst sense. The jury's verdict, the editor noted, was "a victory for Peter but he will find that his opportunity to live by his political pull" had been lost. "Cuffy," he sneered, "is down and out and the 'fluence' of Peter is no longer needed in the affairs of this section."[8]

If Peter Crenshaw envisioned his appeal as a test case similar to those of Jackson Giles and the Colored Men's Suffrage Association of Alabama, that attempt had failed. He had his lifetime registration certificate and that was all; no other man would benefit from the jury's decision. Then, in a strange turn, the Limestone County registrars appealed to the Alabama Supreme Court. This could potentially undermine the pending *Giles* and *Rogers* state supreme court appeals by showing that the appeals process could work—that it was not the sham that Wilford Smith alleged it to be. The registrars got the decision they wanted. In November 1903 the Alabama Supreme Court dismissed the appeal, upholding Crenshaw's registration, the appeals process, and the descendants clause.[9]

Subsequently, *State v. Crenshaw* was widely cited by the disfranchisers and was employed to defend the new constitution against charges of racial discrimination. In a 1905 *Outlook* article titled "Reduction of Representation in the South," the 1901 constitutional convention president, John B. Knox, used *Crenshaw* as proof of how fair and just and wonderful Alabama's constitution was, a claim that Wilford Smith rebutted a few months later.[10]

Peter Crenshaw's case received relatively little attention beyond Alabama and those who noticed it were not necessarily persuaded. It was the first and only antidisfranchisement case to ever go before a jury and it yielded a very rare victory for a black plaintiff. Still, it changed nothing. It was just another "striking example," the *New York Evening Post*'s editor thought, "of the inevitable acts of injustice resulting from giving a board of white men the right to say whether colored American citizens . . . shall or shall not vote."[11]

Crenshaw shared little with the *Giles* cases down in Montgomery. W. R. Walker pursued a strategy far different from Wilford Smith's. Moreover, Crenshaw himself stood in sharp contrast to the Montgomerians. He was far more aggressive than had been Jackson Giles, the CMSAA, Wilford Smith and, it needn't be said, Booker T. Washington and Emmet J. Scott. *Crenshaw*'s closest similarity to *Giles,* however, was that it was just one of many worrisome signs for the disfranchisers in late 1902, and it reminded southern Democrats of the threatening potential of the *Giles* cases and of similar efforts developing elsewhere, namely, Virginia.

The Virginians burst onto the scene in late 1902 and they were ready for a fight. In Hampton, according to reports in the *Baltimore Afro-American Ledger,* attorney Fay S. Collier sued to compel the registration of "nine prominent colored men." Seven of those nine had been caught by a provision in Virginia's 1902 constitution requiring that poll taxes be paid before September 1, 1902. The first seven did not proffer payment by the deadline; the remaining two complained of discrimination due to the understanding clause. Collier told the *Ledger* that "both are well-educated and thoroughly competent to explain any section of the new instrument, but they were refused registration because of the questions asked by the registration board." Virginia's black activists had moved quickly and with a dramatic show of strength. Milwaukee's *Wisconsin Weekly Advocate,* a black paper, demanded that they be praised by the "Negro press and the people," promising "support from all lovers of justice." However, the Hampton effort never got very far and soon faded from view.[12]

Virginia's black voting rights activists had been threatening court challenges as early as April 1901, two months before their state's constitutional convention had even assembled. By the summer of 1902, Virginia had a new constitution and blacks escalated their campaign. Republicans subscribed to the fight as well. By July blacks were holding meetings around the state, the *New York Times* reported, where "collections are taken up and money is liberally given."[13]

The Virginia antidisfranchisement fight was initially waged under the auspices of the Negro Educational and Industrial Association of Virginia (NEIAV), founded in Charlottesville in 1900, ostensibly to promote agricultural affairs "for the benefit of the colored population." Farming, though, was but a pretext, and at the NEIAV's 1901 meeting in Staunton, members officially cast their plowshares into swords. The membership tapped James H. Hayes, a black Richmond attorney to lead them, and gave him responsibility for organizing and funding the legal assault.[14]

James H. Hayes graduated from Howard University's law school in 1885 and won election to Richmond's city council the following year. He would be active in Republican political and civil rights causes throughout his adult life. But there was more to him than office seeking, and in 1898 he and twelve other men established the *Richmond Planet*. Subsequently, he focused more intently on voting rights and by 1901 it had become a full-time occupation. For the next several years, it consumed him.[15]

The NEIAV held its 1902 meeting at Richmond, August 18–20, by which time Hayes had lined up three white attorneys, including the New York City resident and former Virginia U.S. representative John S. Wise. Wise came on board courtesy of New York City's Constitutional League (of which he was a member), which also had volunteered to pay for the Virginia antidisfranchisement litigation and had been founded by John E. Milholland (once a close friend of Booker T. Washington who helped underwrite the Louisiana and Alabama antidisfranchisement efforts). Hayes planned to retain three black attorneys, for a total of seven lawyers. As of August 1902, the NEIAV claimed to have raised three thousand dollars but more was needed. Fund-raising became the 1902 meeting's chief concern. The association announced that its goal was to raise at least fifty thousand dollars for the antidisfranchisement legal fight. Wise did not attend the August 1902 meeting, sending an open letter instead. He guaranteed that "in proper proceedings," Virginia's new constitution "will be held void."[16]

Because he was white, Wise elicited ridicule and ostracism from other white and Democratic Virginians, though he was "not ashamed of it." He insisted in an October interview that "I shall not be deterred from proceeding as I see fit." His father, Henry A. Wise, was a dominant force in antebellum Virginia politics, had served in the U.S. diplomatic corps, had been Virginia's governor in 1859 when John Brown raided Harper's Ferry, and as governor had signed Brown's death warrant. Now, forty-three years later, Governor Wise's son was fighting to keep black men enfranchised. Baltimore's *Afro-American Ledger* marveled at the irony, struck that someone connected by blood to John Brown's executioner "should be so conspicuous in his endeavor in securing the constitutional rights of Virginia Negroes." But that ironic connection only further inflamed Democrats and Democratic newspaper editors. Commenting upon a *Louisville Times* report of Wise's activities, Kentucky's *Paris Bourbon News* hinted at dire consequences, for Wise's reputation at the least. "What Mr. Wise will look at before such proceedings are even well begun," the paper speculated, "is not for ears polite."[17]

Wise was born in 1846 in Rio de Janeiro, Brazil, where his father was serving U.S. minister. The family returned to Virginia soon after, and in 1856 Henry Wise was elected governor. Young John attended the Virginia Military Institute and served as a lieutenant in the Confederate army. After the war, he studied law at the University of Virginia and practiced in Richmond. Following an unsuccessful congressional bid in 1880, he became U.S. attorney in 1882 and continued his political career. Wise left the Democratic Party to join the Readjusters, a movement that opposed the payment of the state's civil war debt in full, and promised, in the words of historian James Tice Moore, "opportunity for the able, democracy for the masses, and public education for all." Virginia had gained a new congressional seat after the 1880 census, but the legislature was slow to reapportion the state's U.S. House districts, which meant that the new district would be an at-large seat. Wise secured the Readjuster nomination and began a statewide campaign. "Brilliant and fiery" like his father, Wise was a sensation and won. The Democratic legislature, however, quickly apportioned Wise's at-large congressional seat away, and the congressman then prepared for an 1884 gubernatorial bid. He abandoned the Readjusters and won the Republican nomination to face the Democratic nominee, Fitzhugh Lee. Wise won ninety-three of Virginia's one hundred counties in a "losing" effort. Lee claimed staggering majorities in the remaining seven counties, all in Virginia's Black Belt, and took the governorship. Wise and his allies charged fraud, but with Democrats controlling the state's electoral machinery, a formal challenge was pointless.[18]

John Wise turned Republican, one biographer concluded, because of the "social schism . . . created by the Negro question." Whether it genuinely radicalized him is impossible to judge. It certainly had something to do with his rapid political conversion, while his profession of the GOP faith was the occasion for his flight from Virginia. Wise left in 1888 and took his family to New York City, where he continued to worry about America's and the South's treatment of African Americans. He also continued to seethe about the Democrats. Wise's concern for blacks was inseparable from his Democratic obsession. He never gave up his hatred for the southern Democracy. "The slavery of the body of the negro," as he wrote in a 1901 letter, congratulating Thomas Goode Jones on his appointment as U.S. district judge, "was not worse than has been, for thirty years, this slavery of the mind of the whites."[19]

John Wise hated the Democracy and its new disfranchising constitutions. Virginia's 1902 document was, he wrote in an open letter distributed to black newspapers, "a foul device . . . repugnant to every sense of manhood, of far-sightedness, or good faith." His clients in the Virginia antidisfranchisement litigation, whom he described as "a throng of 100,000 of God's creatures," were "praying and struggling and antagonizing inquiry whether they are freemen or serfs and chattels." Wise had faced severe criticism ever since his Republican conversion; his role in the antidisfranchisement fight only amplified the attacks. That only heightened the pleasure he evidently derived from the struggle and this sometimes seemed almost masochistic. "I trust to time for my vindication," he wrote, with obvious satisfaction, and "in the meantime am just as well, just as prosperous, and as happy as if the heathen did not rage furiously against me." The heathens did rage—often—and John Wise seemed to like it.[20]

The collaboration between Hayes and Wise stood in marked contrast with that of Wilford Smith, Emmet Scott, and Booker T. Washington. The Virginians were openly aggressive, bombastic, and colorful. Hayes and Wise indulged in bold, vibrant rhetoric. The Alabamians preferred pastels. Had they collaborated, the two teams could have brought brilliant public relations and legal strategies to bear against disfranchisement. Sadly, they did not work together. At times, they seemed incorrigibly disputatious and frequently competed for money and attention.

Hayes and Wise were brilliant publicists, but the finer points of legal strategy often escaped them. Privately, Hayes's friends and the influential Republicans they connected him with cautioned that this litigation had better be absolutely sound. Whitefield McKinlay, the prominent African American D.C. realtor, was among Hayes's confidants and provided an introduction to James Clarkson. Clarkson was New York's customs collector and a vital cog in the GOP's patronage machine. He knew everyone and was good to know, so McKinlay urged Hayes to seek the collector's advice. Clarkson had doubts, though he later advised McKinlay that he regarded Hayes as a "very pleasant gentleman." Clarkson had apparently told Hayes that he was not quite ready for this; it would "not do to risk this great case" without "lawyers great enough" to develop it properly. Clarkson also recalled warning Hayes that there would be but one shot: "It is better to take a little time and be sure."[21]

Writing to McKinlay several weeks later, Hayes recalled Clarkson's advice about hiring only the best lawyers and mentioned that U.S. Senator George Frisbie Hoar of Massachusetts had asked to handle the litigation. He did not recall, however, any of Clarkson's cautions or anything that suggested an appreciation for the collector's concerns. Maybe Clarkson had not offered what he claimed in his letter to McKinlay. Maybe they had escaped Hayes. Regardless, he had no qualms about himself or Wise and was overjoyed by the financial and moral support streaming his way. "We are raising money every day," he assured McKinlay. Virginia blacks would not accept disfranchisement, he continued, since "negro men, women and children are putting their dimes together in this fight, and we will raise the bulk of the money ourselves." Hayes was also wooing the *éminence grise* of the former McKinley administration, U.S. Senator Mark Hanna of Ohio. If Clarkson, Hanna, et al. publicly embraced the effort, he imagined, "we would feel all the more encouraged to fight to the death—which we intend to do help or no help." Hayes was positively ebullient.[22]

Neither dissuaded by Clarkson's misgivings, nor persuaded by the collector's strategic advice, Hayes pressed forward. This was unfortunate. Clarkson warned of the dangers of a poorly prepared and argued presentation and the Virginia cases suffered from strategic missteps throughout. This only made it easier for hostile or timid judges to reject Hayes's claims and the arguments offered by Wise.

The first misstep lay in Hayes's choice of collaborator. John Wise nearly always did the arguing, though he was ill suited for the work. While he only lost one jury trial in his entire career, his talent for swaying juries did not extend to bench trials and appellate work. Caught up in the moment or the discovery of some brilliant turn of phrase, he often lost sight of details and ignored technicalities. His "fondness for wit and raillery," a biographer noted, "would sometimes make him overplay his hand." However, details and technicalities are the stuff of which bench trials and appellate hearings are made. Consumed by the "rightness" of his cause, Wise overlooked valuable precedent, ignored key practical lessons, and imperiled the Virginia litigation from the outset.[23]

The Virginia cases unfolded concurrently with those in Alabama, yet the contrast was stark and unflattering. Jackson Giles's U.S. district court argument had cited his inability to vote in the 1902 congressional elections as justification for his petition. Wilford Smith argued that Giles's constitutional right to participate in civic affairs had been abridged when the registrars barred him from the 1902 congressional election, though he did not challenge the election itself. He knew that was pointless. Neither did he wait until the election passed. He knew that to do so would condemn his case to death by mootness.

John Wise and James Hayes, however, did challenge an election. They argued that, because blacks' constitutional rights were violated, Virginia's entire 1902 election should be set aside. That was a mistake. Additionally, Wise argued that because Virginia's 1901 constitution had been proclaimed into effect rather than ratified, it was invalid, and thus he questioned Virginia's statehood and the U.S. Constitution's demand that the "United States shall guarantee to every state in this Union a republican form of government." That too was a mistake. Regarding the first point, "setting an election aside" triggered the Political Questions Doctrine, a doctrinal obstacle that had been confronting antidisfranchisement litigators from the beginning. Political questions, the Supreme Court had declared years earlier, were "to be settled by the political power." The latter point, the "proclaimed rather than ratified" process, was simply a nonstarter. Constitutional conventions can very nearly do whatever they want, and the precedent for that was the 1787 U.S. constitutional convention. John Wise and James Hayes ignored both precedents—a formula for sure defeat.[24]

Hayes and Wise filed the first Virginia cases on November 14 at Richmond in the U.S. District Court for the Eastern District of Virginia. The first, *William Jones, John Hill, and Edgar Poe Lee v. Andrew J. Montague et al.* requested a writ of prohibition against Governor Montague and the state canvassing board to block certification of Virginia's 1902 congressional election. The second, *William S. Selden, William H. Anderson, and Clarence G. Gilpin v. Andrew J. Montague et al.,* asked for a temporary injunction against the canvassers and the invalidation of the entire 1902 constitution. Georgia's *Savannah Tribune,* an African American paper, professed optimism that segregation would eventually be struck down by the U.S. Supreme Court and, in light of the antidisfranchisement fights launched in Alabama and Virginia, believed that the Court would protect voting rights, too. "With this done," the paper predicted, "we will be able to sing more heartily: 'Praise God from whom all blessings flow.'"[25]

U.S. District Judge Edmund Waddill scheduled a preliminary hearing for November 21. On that day, Wise appeared, according to the *Afro-American Ledger*, "with two negro attorneys to make a set speech," alleging that Virginia was being run by a "rump institution." Wise explained that voting had been conducted under the state's 1902 "disfranchising" constitution, which violated the Fourteenth and Fifteenth Amendments. Tellingly, his argument had little to do with his plaintiffs. Instead, he assailed Virginia's Democratic elected officials and the 1902 constitutional convention. He charged that Virginia had no valid state government and he asked the court to invalidate the 1902 state election. These questions could hardly have been more "political." The one thing he did right was to focus on a federal election. Judge Waddill listened to Wise's arguments and did not reject them on the spot. Instead, he decided that the U.S. Court of Appeals for the Fourth Circuit should hear the two cases, bypassing a district court trial. He adjourned the proceedings pending the arrival of U.S. Chief Justice Melville Weston Fuller and Judge Nathan Goff of the U.S. Circuit Court of Appeals for the Fourth Circuit. This was the very same Nathan Goff who had adjudicated *Mills v. Green* seven years earlier and the same Melville Weston Fuller who had invalidated Goff's decision. The circuit court hearing would take place on November 28.[26]

The November 28 hearing began with the dramatic late arrivals of Fuller and Wise, the latter of whom took a sailboat across Chesapeake Bay and chartered a special train to Richmond. Goff could not attend, but as was borne out in *Mills*, Waddill and Goff could not have controlled the outcome anyway. Whenever a Supreme Court justice sat on a circuit court, his opinion prevailed. Fuller quickly and neatly dismissed the petitions for want of jurisdiction. "The matter," Fuller wrote of *Jones v. Montague*, "being political, cannot be disposed of in such a proceeding." The same judgment applied in *Selden v. Montague*.[27]

Though he could not supercede Fuller's opinion, Waddill was not bound to silence. Waddill, a recent McKinley appointee, agreed with the chief justice as to matters of established law. Yet because of the constitutional questions involved and because the matter involved alleged injuries to "one hundred thousand people," he believed that equity demanded something more:

"that technical forms and ceremonies should in large measure be dispensed with" to ensure "speedy justice." Again, however, Waddill's opinion carried no weight and even so, the PQD dictated the case's outcome. The *Atlanta Constitution* was thrilled by Waddill's commitment to precedent: "the principle . . . was so plainly reiterated by the Chief Justice," the paper concluded, "that even so strong a partisan Republican as Judge Waddill . . . was obliged to coincide in the judgement dismissing the cases." But the cases were still alive, and there would be U.S. Supreme Court appeals. "This is no time for halting effort or despair," the *Washington Colored American* urged. "Right is right, and in its face error must eventually stand humiliated and abashed," the column continued, praising the "sturdy Virginians" for their courage.[28]

Those appeals would be a while coming, so Wise immediately announced that he was not particularly worried and would go ahead and engineer a challenge to Carter Glass's election to the U.S. House of Representatives. "My defeat"—he always spoke of the fight in the first person—"affects me no more than the killing of a picket affects the result of a battle," he explained in a press statement. While awaiting the next courtroom skirmish, he targeted Virginia's congressional delegation. "I go to Washington tonight and will consult members of congress with a view" to prevent Glass "from taking his seat."[29]

"There may be a scene when Congress convenes tomorrow," the *New York Times* reported on December 1. This prospect delighted capitol observers and Wise planned to have someone introduce the federal case on the House floor as part of a seating challenge. He found a willing surrogate, and the matter prompted a brief entertainment. "Negrophiles Go Into Action on Opening Day of Congress," an *Atlanta Constitution* headline screamed, but nothing, really, came of it. The House Elections Committee dismissed Wise's claim, arguing that if Glass's election was illegal, so were the victories of "all the Virginia men elected." The committee was not ready to evict Virginia's entire House delegation. Nevertheless, they were only too happy to drop the problem in someone else's lap. They would not pass judgment on Glass's election, Chairman Robert Tayler of Ohio explained, since it was a matter for the Fifty-Eighth Congress to decide."[30]

Wise had far more planned. Ahead of the unsuccessful circuit court hearing, he trolled for plaintiffs, distributing "an unlimited number of suit forms" to black Virginians, which any attorney could file in the appropriate U.S. district court. This would save Wise and Hayes the trouble of securing clients—if they caught anyone at all. Moreover, the suit forms that blanketed Virginia each claimed damages of five thousand dollars. Those damages were incurred, the generic pleading alleged, as a result of the same grand conspiracy that Wise denounced in both *Jones* and *Selden*. Each disfranchised voter, it was hoped, would sue each constitutional convention delegate, the governor, the three registrars who denied his voting application, and the three election judges in his precinct.[31]

By December 4, the effort yielded forty-eight plaintiffs, Hayes and Wise told the press, and a reporter spotted Hayes in the U.S. district court clerk's office preparing papers. "The suits," according to the *Washington Post,* "are brought under the common law" and Hayes refused any comment on the cases. Wise and Hayes, publicity wizards that they were, made sure that newspapers followed their every move, which made Hayes's "no comment" seem even more interesting. Hayes grabbed their attention and then made good his and Wise's promise. On December 13, in U.S. courthouses at Richmond and Norfolk, they initiated new damages suits (using those preprinted suit forms) in the names of Richmond's Edgar Poe Lee and Norfolk letter carrier Anthony S. Pinner. They anticipated that more lawsuits would arise from the suit forms and enter the courts of Virginia's Western District.[32]

From all outward appearances, the Virginia litigation promised a rigorous test of Virginia's constitution and, in a rare glimmer of cooperation, Bishop Alexander Walters of the Afro-American Council appeared in Richmond to cheer Hayes, Wise, and the Virginians. The AAC, sponsor of the spectacularly lackluster Louisiana litigation, stayed out of the Virginia and Alabama efforts but supported them at least in spirit and through occasional fund-raising appearances. There was not a hint of a rivalry on that December Thursday when Walters appeared in Richmond. "Fight for your rights," he told his audience, "and do not suffer yourselves to be disfranchised."[33]

Wilford Smith had rushed Giles's federal case so that he could reach the Supreme Court before the October 1902 term expired (which all but assured a hearing and decision in 1903). The Virginia appeals were not perfected (a legalism that means prepared and filed) in time and would not be heard for some time. The appeals of *Jones v. Montague* and *Selden v. Montague* were finally filed on January 14, 1903. Many observers simply elided the two and referred to a single "Virginia case." One of these was the editor of the Olympia, Washington, *Morning Olympian,* who believed that "the suit . . . promises to be one of the most notable cases that ever went to the supreme court." In any event, there would be a very long wait for all involved: The Supreme Court did not hear arguments in the cases until April 4, 1904.[34]

The Virginians knew of Wilford Smith but seemed not to know about his intimate connection with Booker T. Washington. Smith never discussed Wise's work in his written correspondence with Emmet Scott. Nor did John Wise leave any written mention of Smith. James Hayes, however, did offer occasional, derisive observations of his Alabama counterparts.

Smith and Hayes and Wise were unfortunate rivals. They never collaborated and they never attempted to bring about coordinated region-wide challenges. It must be said, though, that Booker T. Washington would never have allowed Smith to collaborate with James Hayes even if Smith so desired (and he did not). Washington and Hayes were not close, due largely to Hayes's fraternization with Washington's nastiest critics, in particular, the *Boston Guardian*'s editor, William Monroe Trotter. Further, Hayes advocated initiatives that Washington actively opposed, namely, efforts to force a reduction southern congressional representation under the provisions of the Fourteenth Amendment.[35]

In February 1903, Hayes wrote to Washington to express his concern that the Tuskegeean was trying to undermine the Virginia litigation and Hayes's newly formed National Negro Suffrage League (NNSL), which was closely allied with William Monroe Trotter's New England Suffrage League. Washington never interfered in Hayes's litigation, but he definitely worked against the NNSL. Hayes, for his part, insisted that he was not interfering in Washington's affairs: "in me there is not the slightest desire for the usual 'killing off' business in which the Negro has become adept." As far as Hayes was concerned, his differences with Washington seemed to matters of policy, not a personal rivalry. Washington, Hayes thought, had misunderstood him, and he disavowed any desire to usurp the Tuskegeean. "Your place in history has been made," Hayes wrote, unctuously, "your name has been written where it will never be erased. Should God call you now, yours would be among the few immortal names which will never die." Nevertheless, the immortality of Washington's name was not James Hayes's to promise and flattery would not draw Washington into the NNSL.[36]

The NNSL, headquartered in Richmond, made repeated calls for national suffrage conventions, which Washington consistently undermined. He believed that such a gathering would overtly antagonize whites, while reducing southern congressional representation would harm blacks as much as it did whites. Simultaneous to (but completed disconnected from) the antidisfranchisement cases, Indiana congressman Edgar Dean Crumpacker led an ongoing, quixotic effort to reduce the congressional representation of the disfranchising states that Washington steadfastly refused to support. Washington believed that such a measure would both antagonize white southerners and inadvertently sanction disfranchisement. This inflamed critics like Trotter and frustrated men like Hayes, and Washington refused to explain himself properly. It was just one more example of the ways in which Washington and Hayes (but especially Washington) missed an opportunity to cooperate and thus strengthen both of their projects—projects, after all, that sought the same result. Hayes and Washington maintained a civil correspondence regarding the matter and in December 1904, Hayes went as far as to ask for Washington's "good counsel and advice" regarding antidisfranchisement legislation. He wanted Washington's help to persuade Congress into renewed enforcement of the Fifteenth Amendment. Lest Washington suspect that this was a trick to lure him into anything "public," Hayes insisted, "I am not writing for publicity of any kind. . . . I am not even writing this letter for the purpose of getting a reply so that I can quote you even in private, but to enlist your powerful aid." Yet the fact that Hayes had to disclaim any hidden agenda confirms the true nature of his and Washington's relationship: there wasn't one. Washington did not trust, and would not collaborate with, James H. Hayes. Neither would Wilford H. Smith.[37]

That the Alabamians did not collaborate with the Virginians was tragic. Publicity was vital to this effort but, when confronted by that task, Smith wilted. He confided as much to Booker T. Washington in June 1902. He did not know how to campaign for cash and confessed that "this kind of a fight, quasi-political, is entirely new to me, and I had no idea . . . what such a case would require." Financial crises were, however, a constant in the litigation. Smith's quiet, unassuming nature commended him to Washington, but it also explains why he so often needed additional help from his patron. Nevertheless, Smith swore to do his best as a fund-raiser because, he said, "I would like very much to have the honor of winning the case."[38]

James Hayes, Smith's rival for the "honor of winning the case," was another talented and inveterate self-promoter. He and John Wise publicized every paper that they filed and every solicitation and every contribution they received. And Hayes was not without additional rivals within Virginia's black community. Giles B. Jackson, another black Richmond attorney and sometime associate of Booker T. Washington, announced plans to defend Virginia's 1902 state constitution against Hayes's attack.[39]

Giles B. Jackson was an odd man. He was almost certainly motivated out of a "me too" spirit, an appetite for celebrity. In October 1901, for example, amidst the storm surrounding Booker T. Washington's White House dinner, Jackson claimed that he had been invited to the same dinner, but had chosen not to attend. That was a lie; Roosevelt had not invited Jackson. Then, in December 1902, Jackson announced that he would fight against his rival Hayes, even if it meant reinforcing blacks' disfranchisement. "Greek will meet Greek in the battle over the constitution of Virginia," the *Boston Guardian* reported. Jackson claimed that he had "been asked to represent the conservative Negro element of the state" against the antidisfranchisement charge led by Hayes and Wise. Despite Jackson's best efforts to steal their spotlight, Hayes and Wise made sure that the public remembered who was really the most important.[40]

Even more than Hayes (or Giles Jackson), Wise had an insatiable appetite for press attention. Utterly convinced of his own indispensability, he actually claimed aloud and in public that he was southern blacks' last best hope. A *Washington Post* gossip column, "People Met in Hotel Lobbies," caught up with Wise in late November, just after the Richmond circuit court hearing. Of his work, he explained that he felt "as though I were the administrator of the estate of Harriet Beecher Stowe." Never fear, he was ready to accept that burden and was not afraid to share his inner, most pretentious thoughts. "I guess I'm the only friend the negro has in the world," Wise revealed, "I cannot bear to see them reduced by the means resorted to in Virginia." Wise was fighting alongside the angels but his vanity made him an easy target for satirists. In early December he was the unfortunate target of several *Post* editorial jabs. On December 6, the paper noted that Wise's Virginia litigation had "started . . . with somewhat of a hurrah, but he is less vociferous now." In light of the unsuccessful federal circuit court hearing, the editor wondered "if the Virginia negroes feel that they got a sufficient run for their money . . . ?" Two days later, the *Post* goaded him again: "There is a wide and growing impression to the effect that the new Virginia constitution is John S. Wise-proof."[41]

Southern Democratic editors were particularly vexed that two native white southerners, John S. Wise and former U.S. senator and treasury secretary John G. Carlisle of Kentucky, who signed on in late 1902, had lent their talents to the initiative. Norfolk's *Virginian-Pilot* sneered that Wise had "earned and received the contempt" of all white Virginians, while Carlisle "has earned and received the cordial hate of Kentuckians." "This precious pair," the *Virginian-Pilot* continued, had agreed "to champion a new regime of Senegambianism and carpetbaggery. . . . And these, look now, are Southern men!" The *Washington Post,* however, cautioned its more rabid counterparts. "Some of our southern contemporaries," the paper believed, "are taking this matter too seriously." Though the *Post* considered Virginia's 1902 constitution "none the worse for [the] onslaught," it also recognized that the onslaught would not soon abate. Republican congressmen were agitating to unseat southern representatives and to reduce southern representation. Hayes, Wise, and Carlisle had promised forty-eight additional damages claims, and Wilford Smith had quietly perfected the first U.S. Supreme Court challenge to Alabama's 1901 constitution, which would also be the most important challenge to southern disfranchisement that the Court would hear. Still, the biggest antidisfranchisement story in early 1903 would be James H. Hayes, Esq.[42]

Bombastic and dramatic, James Hayes became disfranchisement's most widely known nemesis at the bar. Whether Hayes really helped the antidisfranchisement crusade may be questioned, but he certainly possessed a foot soldier's zeal. When Northern voting rights activists staged mass meetings throughout the winter and spring of 1903, he attended every one, and every meeting yielded collections for the Virginia litigation. In late January, for example, the AAC sponsored a meeting at Washington's Lincoln Memorial Church. There were two basic press accounts of the gathering. One casually explained that the AAC's executive council hosted a meeting that, among other things, denounced disfranchisement and endorsed the Alabama and Virginia litigation. The other, more interesting version, described an address given by James Hayes.[43]

Blacks had reached their limit, Hayes reportedly declared, and proceeded to suggest that they consider violence. They were up against the wall, he warned, and all would be lost "unless the negroes make a firm stand, contend for their rights, and, if necessary, die for them." Hayes spoke of Moses and the Israelites' Egyptian bondage, but he did not stop there. He ramped things up and remembered Joshua, his trumpet, and Jericho's destruction. Under Joshua, Hayes cried, "the children of God arose" and, with their trumpets' blast, destroyed the Canaanites and the walled city of the Jericho, which blocked the Israelites' full realization of their emancipation. If southern oppression of blacks did not abate, according to the *Washington Post*'s account of the speech, Hayes suggested that they might take up something more potent than trumpets. In the most controversial section of the address, Hayes said (again, according to the *Washington Post*):

> Negroes are leaving the State of Virginia because of the treatment they are receiving. What we want to do is to start something, and keep it up until the white people stop something. We don't intend to be oppressed any longer. We don't intend to be crushed. I am afraid we are anarchistic, that we are anarchists, and I give the warning that if this oppression in the South the negro must resort to the sword and torch, and that the Southland will become a land of blood and desolation.[44]

Hayes was not the only African American who sensed a conflagration in the offing—black women were no less concerned than were the men. There had been Rev. Andrew Johnson's warnings to Alabama's constitutional convention in 1901, and just days after the "sword and torch" speech, as it quickly became known, Miss Kate Johnson wrote in her *St. Louis Palladium* that "this country cannot exist half free and half slave. The only remedy," she continued, "is the clash of arms." Miss Stone was not alone. In the very first issue of her *Birmingham Truth*, published a week after Hayes's speech, Mrs. Carrie Tuggle declared in a powerful though simile-laden editorial that "prejudice against the negro race is like Penelope's web . . . but Ulysses-like, we will yet turn some day at the proper time and place when, Telemachus-like, where our white friends least expect us." Tuggle's erudition would have been lost on most whites, who either ignored the recently established "colored paper" or were not as well educated as she. Regardless, Hayes was giving the ladies what they wanted.[45]

Whites nationwide responded angrily to talk of fights and to the so-called sword and torch speech, while the AAC tripped over itself in flight from what one headline writer called the "Incendiary Negro." Out in Arizona, the *Tucson Citizen* warned that Hayes had been "vociferously applauded" and that the affair was the natural result of Roosevelt's magnanimity toward blacks. "Hayes," the editorial continued, and the "other negroes like him are emboldened" by the president's friendship, "and if he persists in his present course, no one need be surprised to see some of Hayes's bloody predictions fulfilled." As for the AAC, Cyrus Field Adams, who had reportedly presided over the meeting, insisted that he had not been in control of the program. Further, he insisted that the AAC did not endorse the use of either swords or torches and claimed that Hayes had never mentioned them. Hayes, Adams insisted, had only "recited what the Afro-Americans of Virginia were endeavoring to do through the courts."[46]

Hayes had triggered widespread alarm, and in Louisiana whites reportedly laid a trap. The Coliseum Club of New Orleans, according to a letter published in the *Washington Post* and *New York Times,* responded to Hayes by daring to give "Nigger Hayes $3000 and transportation to New Orleans if he will deliver in our hall his speech verbatim as delivered before [the] AAC in Washington on the 26th." Hayes, upon hearing the report, accepted the invitation and promised to pay his own expenses, but he simultaneously distanced himself from the reports of his speech, claiming to have been misquoted and disavowing any use of arms. He never went to New Orleans, and then it emerged that the letter had been a hoax. The African American journalist and activist John E. Bruce (better known by his nom de plume "Bruce Grit") wrote the *New York Times* to state that the letter was undoubtedly fake. The Coliseum Club consisted of gentlemen, Bruce explained, who would never have spelled "negro with two 'g's.'" Though it was unfortunate that Hayes had responded to the missive, Bruce thought Hayes's "courteous, dignified, and manly reply to this outburst," testified to his "good breeding" and good name.[47]

John Bruce was James Hayes's only defender in the coming weeks. Hayes's opponents and rivals within Virginia's African American community sought to use the incident to their own advantage. Giles Jackson, ever alert for ways to insinuate himself into the action, engineered a January 31 meeting in Richmond that offered an evening's program of anti-Hayes orations. The sentiment carried over to Norfolk, where a black newspaper attacked Hayes for having done more harm than good. There was also a new antidisfranchisement body in Norfolk that hoped to complement (or perhaps supplant) Hayes's. Whether this was connected to the speech is unclear, but a Republican activist named W. H. Thoroughgood announced plans for a new Virginia organization devoted to the cause of protecting blacks' rights.[48]

Just weeks later, John Wise made a similar speech before Boston's Middlesex Club, warning of a looming race war. "Some day," he predicted, "you will read . . . of a great organized outbreak of blacks, murdering white men and women, and how the infuriated whites are slaughtering in retaliation," but there was very little notice of Wise because Hayes was drawing all of the fire. Much of the fiercest antagonism came from African Americans.

Nationwide, blacks made a great show of attacking Hayes, often for the apparent benefit of whites. The Galveston, Texas, *City Times,* that city's black paper, denounced Hayes, to the smug satisfaction of the city's white organ, the *Daily News.* "GALVESTON NEGROES: What Their Paper Says of Last Week's Incendiary Utterances at Washington" was the response of the *News.* The cavalcade of condemnation rolled into Louisville, Kentucky, where the Colored Teachers Association denounced his "utterances" as "silly and treasonable." "We hold," the schoolteachers' resolution continued, "that intelligent Negroes throughout the country should denounce the man, the speech, and the Afro-American Council." Blacks throughout the country did just that. Hayes took fire from every direction. African Americans seemed unable to condemn him loudly, quickly, or often enough, all in an effort to exile him from black America. This was not simply a matter of rejecting the speech, it was also a matter of self-preservation, and it elicited defensive comparisons to white Americans generally and white America's fringe political movements. Down in New Orleans, the faithful congregants at St. James AME Church heard Bishop Charles S. Smith quickly disclaim any relationship between the "masses of the Negroes" and the "ravings of the Negro attorney Hayes." To do so, Smith insisted, according the *Colored American*'s account, would be akin to lumping all whites in with the then much-feared anarchists (one of whom had assassinated President William McKinley a year and a half earlier). Blacks were no more responsible for Hayes's "cranky utterances," he continued, "than are the entire white people . . . for the ravings of Herr [Johann] Most and Emma Goldman."[49]

The intraracial criticism of Hayes, wildly overwrought and more than a little sad, only underscored society's demand for absolute fealty from blacks. John Bruce, however, was there to defend him. Bruce lived in Yonkers, New York, and wrote a gossipy current events column, "Gotham Notes," for the *Colored American* under yet another pen name, "Dionysus III." Adding to the confusion, Bruce signed each "Dionysus III" column as "Bruce Grit." Bruce recognized that blacks were taking their attacks on Hayes too far and chided those critics for making so much of the situation. "Negroes are like a barometer," he wrote, "and a good many of us are like Judas Iscariot . . . except we do not go out and hang ourselves after we have made asses of ourselves." He indignantly denounced those who would "throw down a brave man like Hayes who has the manliness and the daring to look the devil of prejudice and oppression in the face and tell him he's a *devil.*"[50]

According to Bruce, Hayes's detractors were responding to inaccurate reports of the meetings that had been propagated by "the lying press agents who are in the conspiracy against us." Hayes had consistently maintained that his speech was misquoted without specifying what was wrong about the press accounts. John Bruce saw to it that the actual text of that controversial passage made it into print:

> I am not an anarchist, I do not believe in killing anybody, yet if necessary stand up for your rights and be killed for standing up. But the oppressing, shooting, murdering, burning, lynching, jim crowing, and disfranchising of the Negro will breed a race of Nat Turners, and the sword and torch will devastate and dissolve the South.[51]

Though this "corrected" version shows that there was no immediate threat made, it is still quite provocative. The only difference had to do with the first line, and Hayes's comments about anarchism and murder; the "sword and torch" line was not disputed. But Bruce was happy to second Hayes's sentiment. "There isn't a manly Negro from Maine to Texas," he continued, "who will not endorse this utterance." Nonetheless, Hayes's credibility took a serious hit. Whether Bruce's defense of Hayes had helped is to be doubted. The *Colored American*'s editor, for one, surely remained among the unconverted. A week earlier he had complained that Hayes had been "discredited and despised as a senseless agitator" and had "probably destroyed his utility in the anti-disfranchisement litigation." But the Virginian's outburst had nearly obscured the pending Alabama case of *Giles v. Harris*.[52]

8

The Second *Dred Scott* Case

Giles v. Harris Is Decided

> Some papers . . . have been representing me as a second Taney in
> respect of probing another Dred Scott decision.
> —Oliver Wendell Holmes Jr., 1903

James Hayes's grandstanding in early 1903 proved so fascinating that few seemed to notice when Wilford Smith filed *Giles v. Harris* with the U.S. Supreme Court on January 28. To be fair, Hayes provided a far more interesting spectacle, but *Giles v. Harris* was too important to go ignored for long. Observers—journalistic, political, and otherwise—may have been entertained and frightened by Hayes's talk of swordplay and arson, but their interest eventually swung back to Smith and *Giles.* It overwhelmed the Court's staff; they needed more briefs to satisfy public demand. The fastest way to get them was to go through the attorneys themselves, who had already hired professional printers to typeset, duplicate, and bind their pleadings, arguments, and exhibits. Joseph H. McKenney, the Supreme Court clerk, sent his request to Smith before he contacted William A. Gunter Sr. on January 27. Writing to Gunter, McKenney explained that Smith had already agreed to provide "fifty copies . . . instead of the twenty-five" required by Court rules. He hoped that Gunter could similarly oblige. The case, McKenney explained, had "attracted considerable attention."[1]

Gunter forwarded the letter to Governor William Jelks's private secretary, J. K. Jackson, along with a proposed legislative appropriation to compensate him for his work. Gunter hoped that Jackson and Jelks could persuade the legislature to fork over the tidy sum of twenty-five hundred dollars. "The case is of great importance to the state," Gunter wrote, and he supported his invoice with McKenney's request for more briefs. Jelks, however, thought Gunter's price was too high and "out of proportion to the work." He then sought Attorney General Charles Brown's opinion on "what you think the work is worth." If Gunter had been billing by the word, Jelks may have had a point; Gunter's briefs were terse and concise. But if the state itself was unable to mount an "in-house" defense, it was important to have someone like Gunter oversee things. Though Governor Jelks had doubts, Brown did not. He persuaded the governor that Gunter's charges were reasonable and the legislature eventually paid the bill.[2]

While state officials, even at this late stage, dickered over costs, Smith was calm and resolute. Speed was always his greatest concern. Accordingly, he declined the opportunity for oral argument in exchange for an expedited review. So with no hope of witnessing any public drama, curious court watchers had to content themselves with the briefs. Smith's work impressed them. Carrie Tuggle of the *Birmingham Truth* was taken by their scope and thought that they showed that "the negro is learning to present his case . . . which means a great deal in these times of caste prejudice." It did mean a great deal to a great many people, most of whom expected *Giles v. Harris* to settle the disfranchisement question. That was true of both the disfranchisers and their opponents. The stakes could not have been higher and, as Tuggle noted in late February, if Giles lost, the "door of civil and political hope is closed against the negro in the state for now."[3]

Smith opted for an expedited hearing because he expected an expedited decision, but the Court said nothing after one month and then two and three. Nearly four full months passed, in fact, before they announced a decision. Smith could only speculate over what it meant, though it clearly suggested that the justices had not dismissed *Giles* out of hand. James Hayes, meanwhile, was as busy as ever, and since Smith was not doing anything interesting, attention swung back to the Virginians.

The "sword and torch" incident had heightened James Hayes's celebrity, and his speaking tour rolled on through the deep northeastern winter. He even enlisted Wilford Smith as a supporting figure for a February 12 show at Boston's Faneuil Hall, sponsored by *Boston Guardian* editor William Monroe Trotter and the New England Suffrage League. Attendees applauded wildly, as Hayes's audiences always did, and passed a resolution denouncing the southern states' new and amended constitutions. This occasion was the only time that Hayes and Smith ever appeared together, and to mark it, the organizers did not allow Smith to speak. Audience members seem not to have known who Smith was, and besides, they were mesmerized by the speeches they did hear. After they sang "The Battle Hymn of the Republic," Albert Pillsbury, the former Massachusetts attorney general and a member of the AAC's *Ryanes* committee, rose and told the gathering, that "until every black man's rights are secure, no white man's rights are safe," and led by Trotter, the audience approved a call for a national suffrage convention. Hayes finally claimed the rostrum and closed the performance with his basic stump speech, which in its essentials mirrored Pillsbury's remarks. He brought them to their feet when he warned, "When the Negro in the canebrakes in Mississippi loses his vote you here in Massachusetts and the rest of the country may well tremble for your safety." That had always drawn ovations before and Boston was no different. The crowd roared and cheered and filled the collection plate.[4]

As long as the Supreme Court held the Alabama case in limbo, the Virginians could claim the initiative. In city after city, they attracted enthusiastic crowds who were eager to hear James Hayes and contribute to the Virginia fight. Two weeks after the Faneuil Hall meeting, the tour stopped at New York City's Cooper Union, where more than two thousand attended and gave another one thousand dollars. Atlanta's *Voice of the People,* a black emigrationist newspaper, reported that the participants made "spirited and earnest speeches" and commended "the negroes of Virginia for rendering the nation a patriotic service in contesting before the Supreme Court . . . the revolutionary constitution of Virginia." Charles William Anderson, a black leader in New York City, an officer of the New York State racing commission, and one of Booker T. Washington's closest acquaintances, spoke that evening and afterward reported to Tuskegee that the meeting had come and gone "without the least bit of dynamite."[5]

For all that was said about the Court at these mass meetings, and for all that was written in the press, little attention was paid to the nine justices individually, but two additions to the Court, announced in December 1902 and February 1903, did prompt some brief public comment. President Roosevelt tapped Boston's Oliver Wendell Holmes Jr. in December, and on the same day as the Cooper Union meeting, the White House announced former U.S. secretary of state William Rufus Day's appointment to the Court. Some North Carolina black leaders evidently believed that the appointments of Holmes and Day signaled a sea change on the supreme bench. The North Carolinians sensed that Holmes and Day were certain votes against southern disfranchisement and they rushed to join the Virginia antidisfranchisement fight. There had been no North Carolina fight like those in South Carolina, Mississippi, Louisiana, Alabama, and Virginia, but Roosevelt's appointments had inspired the Tarheel State's black leaders. Holmes and Day, they explained, would "extend to the black man, if possible, the full measure of his political as well as a civil rights, if a strong case is sent up for adjudication as a precedent."[6]

Meanwhile, James Hayes's celebrity was growing and he succeeded in persuading his audiences that his Virginia cases would finally defeat disfranchisement. He swept back into New York on April 3, when a well-primed audience of two thousand filled Brooklyn's Academy of Music and gave "a big collection" for Hayes's Virginia litigation. It had been a "monster meeting," the *Colored American* reported, moved by seeing "the northern colored [man] so closely in touch with his southern brother." Not content with simply supporting Hayes, a delegation of black leaders from Orange, New Jersey, made plans to pressure Booker T. Washington to support the Virginian. They would boycott Washington's public appearances, the *New York Sun* reported, if "he controverts the lawyer." African American women in New Jersey, too, threw themselves behind Hayes. The Women's Negro Franchise Association of New Jersey appealed to "the colored women of the state" for one thousand dollars, which they would donate to the Virginians.[7]

Big names lined up to join Hayes on stage wherever he went, such as when he stopped in Rochester, New York, in late April. There, the legendary Susan B. Anthony, age eighty-three, stood alongside the Virginian. She declared that "nothing but this outrage against the colored race could have brought me out here tonight." Other suffragists had attempted earlier to capitalize on disfranchisement, arguing that women's enfranchisement could counter the alleged "evils" of black suffrage. Anthony rejected that position, insisting that "we women are in the same boat with the disfranchised negroes." She hoped that northern men who defended blacks' voting rights might recognize their own inconsistency and demand women's enfranchisement as well. "They cannot reasonably advocate the enfranchisement of the negro while they withhold the same advantage from the women of their own part of the country," Anthony insisted. "They are really in such a muddle," she continued, "that they don't know how to get out of it."[8]

Hayes's Rochester appearance would be his last big night for quite some time, though he could not have known it. The fact that Susan B. Anthony's appearance attracted so little notice is telling, for it had been overshadowed by breaking news. Afternoon papers on April 27 ran hastily prepared reports of a U.S. Supreme Court decision in *Giles v. Harris*. Yes, the district court had jurisdiction. No, the Supreme Court would not do anything. It was murky and contradictory, did not look good, and swung the spotlight sharply away from James H. Hayes.

* * *

In purely doctrinal terms, Jackson Giles's Supreme Court case was an argument for federal intervention in state affairs and Wilford Smith had good technical reasons to believe that he would succeed. The federal courts of the period were decidedly "activist," expanding their jurisdiction as they routinely nullified those state-level economic regulations that are now identified with the Progressives.[9]

Historians have frequently characterized late-nineteenth and early-twentieth-century justices as extraordinarily conservative—concerned above all else with protecting private property from governmental regulation—but the Court was not conservative in the sense that it abhorred *all* change. It was eager to expand federal courts' power, usually at the Progressives' expense. Progressives loathed the federal courts for their interference in state regulatory matters, and lawyers and jurists among their number (such as Oliver Wendell Holmes Jr.) fought to rein in the federal judiciary, undoing the jurisdictional expansions endorsed by Justice David Josiah Brewer and others in regulatory matters, labor disputes, and the like.[10]

Giles and the voting age black men in Montgomery County stood to benefit from that expanded federal jurisdiction. Would Brewer and colleagues embrace a claim such as Giles's in order to broaden the federal courts' reach? There were recent federal cases, voting rights cases no less, which suggested that they might. *Wiley v. Sinkler,* from South Carolina, confirmed that federal courts had jurisdiction to hear voting rights cases. *Swafford v. Templeton,* from Tennessee, affirmed *Wiley* and that could only have encouraged Wilford Smith.

Beyond his claim that the district court had jurisdiction over the Giles case, Smith's petition argued that Alabama's 1901 constitution presented a "high-handed and flagrant . . . nullification of the Fourteenth and Fifteenth Amendments," a "repudiation of their solemn guarantees to the negroes of America." The federal criminal statute that Smith's brief cited to establish jurisdiction, the Ku Klux Klan Act of 1871, prescribed punishment by fine, but Smith argued that such a prescription was ridiculous. He instead demonstrated why a court of equity (the U.S. district court) should have ordered Giles registered as a voter. "It would be absurd," Smith insisted, to pretend that monetary damages "could in the least degree compensate a negro in Alabama for the deprivation of his right to vote." The thing he wanted, then, was priceless, and encouraged him to flirt with the perilous Political Questions Doctrine.[11]

The Political Questions Doctrine hung over all of the antidisfranchisement cases like Damocles' sword. Some of the antidisfranchisement litigators had eluded its clutches—namely, Cornelius Jones—but only because their cases had so many defects as to render the doctrine unnecessary. For a hundred years, the Court had cautiously avoided any overt involvement in political disputes, electoral disputes specifically, and Smith carefully disclaimed political questions. John Wise and James Hayes, conversely, confined themselves to political questions in the Virginia suits and that was a grave error. Smith did not make that mistake. He emphasized that "this case is not a suit brought to enforce a political right, but a civil right guaranteed by the Constitution of the United States." The Fifteenth Amendment, as well as the Fourteenth, addressed political rights, but in the late nineteenth century, political rights were always classed separately from civil and social rights. Smith dared not cross that line. He knew as well that the Court would try to avoid any association with elections contests and he reiterated his argument that Giles's claim was not an attempt to "control the exercise of any political function of the State of Alabama." No, *Giles v. Harris* was about protecting the legacy of Reconstruction, and Smith concluded with a plea that the Court take "judicial knowledge of the facts of history" and acknowledge the nation's "solemn constitutional guarantees made to the negro shortly after the late civil war."[12]

As James Hayes's antidisfranchisement crusade made its circuit around the northeast, Smith grew more anxious by the day and hoped "the Supreme Court . . . will dispose of our matter before the middle of [April]." Emmett J. Scott had forwarded Smith's briefs to Albert Pillsbury and Smith inquired in late March if he had yet given his opinion. Pillsbury had, in fact, replied and Scott forwarded his comments to Smith. Pillsbury evidently disagreed with Smith's strategy. Smith regretted that but was undeterred. "I have [gone] over my case a great many times," he assured Scott, "and my faith in it is strengthened each time no matter who takes a view to the contrary." Smith was firm: "If my case is not correct, then it is impossible to make one correct and we shall have to conclude that the [Fourteenth and Fifteenth Amendments] are only a myth."[13]

Smith's *Giles v. Harris* brief itself was beautifully crafted, elegant, and strong in every traditional respect, but it must be remembered that Smith's approach was decidedly unorthodox. He was not appealing the district court's ruling about disfranchisement because there had been none. Judge Thomas G. Jones had instead dismissed the case on jurisdictional grounds.

And Smith had used an obscure jurisdictional rule to get his appeal to Washington, D.C. There was a chance that the Court would examine the merits of the claim, but it was far more likely that they would either uphold Jones's ruling, thus ending the case, or rule on jurisdiction alone, and remand the case back to the district court. The former was unlikely because it would require overruling the *Swafford* decision of one year earlier.

Smith's reaction to Pillsbury was more than just defensive, self-serving rhetoric. Without knowing the particulars of Pillsbury's critique—and the actual correspondence has not survived—it is difficult to know what other course he wished Smith to pursue. However, Pillsbury may have objected simply to the novelty of Smith's approach. It was late March when Scott sent Pillsbury's critique, and Smith expressed hope in his reply that the justices would "dispose of our matter before the middle of April."[14]

Oliver Wendell Holmes Jr. was not exactly an obscure figure when Roosevelt appointed him, but neither was he famous. He was best known for being his famous father's son, and also as a teacher and judge who had written a significant book, *The Common Law,* and had published several well-regarded speeches and essays. Among practitioners, New Englanders knew him because he was Massachusetts' chief justice, but his name did not reach far beyond the region. Black activists, however, believed that the newly appointed Holmes would attack disfranchisement simply because he hailed from Massachusetts, the state most closely identified with the antebellum abolitionists. They believed much the same of William Rufus Day because he came from Ohio, the heartland of the Republican Party. This was incredibly naïve. There was nothing in either man's pedigree that augured judicial activism of any sort. Regarding Holmes in particular, had they looked up his published writings and addresses, they might have seen what was coming.

"The Path of the Law," Holmes's 1897 address before Boston University's Law School, is legendary for its introduction of the "Bad Man." Holmes wanted to "dispel a confusion between morality and law," explaining that "a bad man has as much reason as a good one for wishing to avoid an encounter with the public force." The Bad Man, "a man who cares nothing for an ethical rule . . . is likely nevertheless to care a good deal to avoid being made to pay money, and will want to keep out of jail if he can." Self-interest similarly drove lawmaking and lawgiving, Holmes insisted. Public outrage might occasionally constrain lawmakers from adopting certain laws "because the community would rise in rebellion and fight," he continued. Those were neither necessarily unconstitutional nor draconian nor retributive. Indeed, Holmes assigned them no specific classification; per his formulation, that taxonomy was not something judges should dictate. To his mind, nothing shy of a threatened "rebellion" and community outrage should set the order of things. "This limit of power," he explained, "is not coextensive with any system of morals." When dealing with bad men and bad laws, the question was not one of what they should not be allowed to do but one of determining what price (literal or figurative) they would not be willing to pay and what punishments they could not endure.[15]

Had any of the antidisfranchisement litigators or activists studied Holmes's writings, "The Path of the Law" especially, they might have rethought their approach. To Holmes, power was properly limited by "the habits of a particular people at a particular time." That a law was morally wrong did not guarantee its nullification by judges. "No one will deny that wrong statutes can be and are enforced," he told Boston University's law students and faculty, "and we should not all agree as to which ones were the wrong ones." Holmes applied this philosophy in the first Supreme Court opinion he ever wrote. *Otis v. Parker*, handed down on January 5, 1903, had included a comment on judicial power. "It is by no means true," Holmes stated, "that every law is void which may seem to the judges who pass upon it excessive, unsuited to its ostensible end, or based upon conceptions of morality with which they disagree." Wilford Smith's arguments in *Giles v. Harris* were deeply tinctured with "conceptions of morality," and had he understood the justice's philosophy, he would have wondered whether Holmes would accept them. The southern disfranchisers were indeed Bad Men, and no litigator who understood Holmes would have assumed that he would stop them.[16]

Oliver Wendell Holmes Jr. and his colleagues were confronted by a very bad man in *Giles v. Harris*. He was Jim Crow and he arrived wearing the guise of Alabama's 1901 constitution. To Holmes fell the task of explaining how the Court majority would (or would not) deal with him. Reviewing, and misconstruing, the substance of Smith's brief, Holmes concluded that, if Alabama's constitution (the Bad Man) was a fraud, then ordering that Giles be registered would make the Court party to a fraud. In that, he had misrepresented Smith, who was asking that the Court ameliorate, rather than participate in, a fraud. Continuing, Holmes then insisted that "the bill imports that the great mass of the white population intends to keep the blacks from voting. . . . If the conspiracy and the intent exist, a name on a piece of paper will not defeat them"—or the Bad Man. He simply ignored the fact that Smith had carefully framed this case to avoid any violation of the Political Questions Doctrine. Any "relief from a great political wrong, if done, as alleged, by the people of a state and the state itself," Holmes wrote, "must be given by them or by the legislative and political department of the government of the United States."[17]

Holmes and the majority simply decided their way around the issue. They had done the same thing in *Mills* and in the Mississippi cases, but in those there had been obvious technical deficiencies in the presentation. Here, Holmes and the majority ascribed difficulties to *Giles v. Harris* that did not exist.

Holmes said that Giles should have sought damages, that what he requested would make the Court party to a fraud, and that the Court could not involve itself in political disputes. Holmes seemed to view *Giles v. Harris* through his Bad Man lens, suggesting that a claim for money damages might have had a different result, but Jackson Giles did not intend to sell his ballot. As the legal scholar Louise Weinberg noted, "Holmes did not perceive that for 'great political wrongs,' compensation in damages is meaningless" and that "only injunctive relief has any utility." It was not that Holmes misunderstood Smith's argument but that he actively misrepresented the nature of Giles's claim. Smith had asserted that the registrars themselves rendered certain sections of Alabama's constitution unconstitutional by their malfeasance—malfeasance envisioned by its framers. Ordering Giles registered would have defeated that. Smith was not asking the Court to invalidate the whole of Alabama's constitution. He was trying to ensure its fair application because, unexciting though it may seem, that would have allowed tens of thousands of blacks onto the voting rolls. As for politics, Holmes brusquely dismissed Smith's contention that Giles's claim was for protection of civil, and not political, rights. In Holmes's mind, the petition was purely political.[18]

Holmes had joined "the ranks of the race's enemies," so a disgusted *Colored American* concluded. He did more than turn Jackson Giles away, he seemed to go out of his way to smash Giles's own and all future rights claims. Disfranchised men, he suggested, need not bother with the U.S. Supreme Court. The distinguished historian Lawrence Friedman said it best: Holmes's *Giles v. Harris* opinion was "both technical and smarmy."[19]

Wilford Smith had planned meticulously for this case and had exhaustively investigated why previous ones failed. In *Smith v. Mississippi* (1896) and *Gibson v. Mississippi* (1896), the Court had dodged making a direct ruling on disfranchisement on jurisdictional grounds. So Smith carefully established jurisdiction. In *Williams v. Mississippi* (1898), the Court dodged disfranchisement on evidentiary grounds. So Smith carefully amassed proof for his claims. In *Giles v. Harris,* however, jurisdiction and proof were not enough. Another problem, one that had arisen in *Mills v. Green,* had to do with proving racial animus. So Smith carefully established Giles's ancestry. The Court also could have tried to dismiss race as a motive, something that it had done more than once in the recent past, but Holmes at least had not done that. In a fascinating turn, the Court's virtuoso of that dark art, David Josiah Brewer, became the lead dissenter in *Giles.*[20]

As was noted earlier, the Fuller court was decidedly activist and the most important, and historically underappreciated, of these activist justices was David Brewer. Brewer was the most forceful advocate of an expanded federal jurisdiction and in *Giles* he chastised the majority for denying relief to the recently disfranchised black citizens of Montgomery County, Alabama. It was the only time in his long career that he sided with an African American petitioner in a civil rights or liberties claim.[21]

Brewer could not accept either Holmes's "opinion or judgement." The sole question certified by Judge Thomas G. Jones, he noted, had been one of jurisdiction. He believed that the lower court had jurisdiction, but also that the Supreme Court should not have ventured into the facts of Giles's claim. Venturing into the claim's substance, Brewer wrote, "seems to . . . practically destroy the statute." His colleagues, he feared, had invited future plaintiffs to use the jurisdictional dispute as a way to bypass lower courts, just as Wilford Smith had done. That, however, was not his biggest complaint. Though Brewer had not wanted to review the merits of the case, Holmes's majority opinion on the merits infuriated him. He took issue with Holmes's assertion that the Court could not grant the relief that Jackson Giles sought because, in part, it struck at the heart of Brewer's objective of expanding the Court's jurisdiction. That still was not his biggest complaint. Most galling, to him, was the fact that the majority opinion struck a blow against the rights of black men; it was a virtual license for southern states to run roughshod over federal citizenship protections.[22]

Holmes's profession of judicial impotence was simply too much for Brewer to stand. He was positively indignant. The majority had said that because Giles was only one of thousands of similarly situated men, the task of enforcement was greater than the Court dared to assume. That was ridiculous, Brewer stated. No matter how many men it affected, disfranchisement, as practiced by Alabama, was wrong. That Alabama's disfranchisers were Bad Men was no reason to let them alone. Neither was the fact that lots of men had been disfranchised. "That many others were similarly treated," Brewer insisted, "does not destroy [Giles's] rights. Based on Holmes's own statement of facts, Brewer wrote, the plaintiff was clearly "entitled to a place on the permanent registry." He restated Jackson Giles's rationale simply: "No one was allowed to vote who was not registered." Giles applied for registration because "he desired to vote" in the 1902 congressional election. Giles was "deprived of that right" by registrars Charles Teasley, Jeff Harris, and William A. Gunter Jr. Quoting from Justice Edward Douglass White's *Swafford v. Templeton* opinion, Brewer declared that "the right which it was claimed had been unlawfully invaded was one in the very nature of things arising under the Constitution and laws of the United States, and that this inhered in the very substance of the claim."[23]

The drama did not stop with Holmes and Brewer. There were two other significant dissenters. Henry Billings Brown offered no written explanation for his vote in Giles's favor. Yet his opinions in previous cases make his stance in *Giles* more intriguing. Brown authored the 1896 *Plessy v. Ferguson* decision, for example, and in 1901 he penned the majority opinions in the *Insular Cases,* which established a second class of U.S. citizenship based explicitly upon ethnicity.[24]

John Marshall Harlan, writing separately from Brewer, insisted that the federal courts simply did not have jurisdiction to hear Giles's claim. That was exactly how he had decided the 1896 cases of *Gibson v. Mississippi* and *Smith v. Mississippi.* Specifically, Harlan took exception to Smith's refusal (or as he saw it, failure) to claim monetary damages. The Judiciary Act of August 13, 1888, gave U.S. circuit courts jurisdiction over cases "where the matter in dispute exceeds . . . the sum or value of two thousand dollars, and arising under the Constitution or laws of the United States." The requirement for two thousand dollars was one of the jurisdictional questions that Judge Jones certified to the Supreme Court and, on that point, Harlan believed, Jones's ruling was correct, brushing aside Smith's claim that Giles's citizenship rights were priceless. The federal circuit court thus did not have jurisdiction to hear Giles's petition and so, Harlan continued, the Supreme Court should not have considered the merits of Giles's claim. He explained that he did not want "to formulate and discuss my views upon the merits of this case." Nevertheless, and to "avoid misapprehension," Harlan continued, if Jackson Giles *had* asked for the requisite money damages, he would have voted in his favor: "It is competent for the courts to give relief in such cases as this." That, however, was no comfort for Wilford Smith.[25]

Per Holmes's reasoning, Smith had asked the Court to "take judicial knowledge of the facts of history," and the Court satisfied that request. But instead of enforcing the "solemn constitutional guarantees" made after the Civil War, it hid behind history and refused to make a firm ruling on the constitutionality of disfranchisement. This led to the most disturbing and notorious aspect of Holmes's decision. In explaining why the Court had addressed the substance of Giles's petition, Holmes wrote that "we cannot forget that we are dealing with a new and extraordinary situation." If the Court ordered Giles's registration and did not nullify the Alabama constitution, Giles would probably come back before the Court "to try to overthrow the scheme." That, Holmes indicated, whether it happened sooner or later, would place federal courts in a precarious situation. Enter the Bad Man once again. The long history of American racism and the forces of proscription and segregation, Holmes declared, were simply too great for the courts to overcome. "One of the first questions," he wrote, for an equity court "is what it can do to enforce any order that it may make." *Giles v. Harris* alleged a conspiracy by the state of Alabama, but the federal courts were powerless to intervene. Holmes claimed that "the Circuit Court has no constitutional power" to compel the citizens or officers of a state "by any direct means." The Court's "lack of power" might have been a compelling argument if it had not been devoid of merit.[26]

It is tempting to read this in light of what happened in the mid-twentieth century when the Supreme Court began to strike down the legal pillars from beneath Jim Crow; specifically, there is the example of the backlash that followed *Brown v. Board of Education.* But it is important to remember that Oliver Wendell Holmes Jr. was not confronted with the same situation in the South that his successors faced at midcentury. White southerners who were poor, illiterate, Populist, or Republican suffered under disfranchisement just as much as their black neighbors. In Alabama, the fight among white men over disfranchisement was heated and a roughly even match. As well, many of those whites who were unaffected by the new rules had joined the opposition. And those white men who opposed ratification suffered no political penalty in subsequent years. Joseph Forney Johnston, the former Alabama governor who marshaled opposition forces, was elected to the U.S. Senate in 1906, defeating John B. Knox, the president of the 1901 constitutional convention and the new constitution's principal supporter.

This is not a matter of debate. As has been amply demonstrated here and by previous scholars, white southerners were not of one mind on the subject of disfranchisement. Many detested it. Barely half of Alabama's white voters supported disfranchisement in the 1901 constitutional ratification referendum, and a hefty percentage of North Carolina whites opposed that state's disfranchising amendments in 1900. Mississippi, South Carolina, Louisiana, and Virginia had not submitted their constitutions to the voters and for good reason: whites probably would have voted them down. In all of the southern states, the "Antis" (as they had been called in Alabama) were white and led by white men; they would have welcomed an alternative outcome in *Giles v. Harris*.[27]

Holmes's insistence that the Court should only issue "enforceable" orders is ultimately unconvincing. The U.S. Supreme Court *never* enforces its own orders. Enforcing a ruling in Giles's favor would have been the responsibility of President Theodore Roosevelt, Attorney General Philander Knox, and the U.S. marshals. Historians and biographers have discussed and written many things about Roosevelt, but none has yet presented evidence of his "reticence," and there is absolutely no reason to suspect, and no competent ground upon which to suggest, that he would have backed down from this fight. Only twice had presidents flatly refused to enforce Supreme Court decrees in peacetime (Thomas Jefferson in *Marbury v. Madison* and Andrew Jackson in *Worcester v. Georgia*), to the detriment of each man's reputation. Even if we were to accept Holmes's logic, it is unclear why he thought it preferable to admit institutional weakness, even allowing for his firm belief in judicial restraint. The Court, which purported to be the final arbiter of constitutional interpretation, had just declared itself impotent to sustain one of the Constitution's most significant amendments. California's *San Jose Mercury News*, a Democratic paper whose editor clearly sympathized with the disfranchisers, conceded that it would be "difficult to put up a case" that would yield a more direct ruling, one which did not involve excuses. "It is a ugly subject to handle," he wrote of disfranchisement, "and the court would rather dodge it if possible."[28]

We may parse the decision ad nauseam, but judicial impotence is really all that mattered. The Court did not *have* to make any substantive ruling, but it did, and it had arguably worsened the situation. Holmes had read his opinion from the bench and so the actual text was not immediately forthcoming. Yet Court observers knew exactly what had happened. A mournful *Indianapolis Recorder* cartoon described it all: a black man lay helpless, chained to the walls of a dank prison cell by the Supreme Court: "The Supreme Court Upholds Disfranchisement."[29]

Things worsened one week later when the court announced *James v. Bowman.* This case came from Kentucky, where Henry Bowman and Harry Weaver had allegedly, through bribery and intimidation, prevented blacks from voting in the 1898 congressional election. The Justice Department won judgments against Bowman and Weaver under the Enforcement Act of May 31, 1870, which was an enforcement mechanism for the Fifteenth Amendment. Section 5 of the act prescribed that anyone found guilty of interfering with any individual's voting would (1) pay restitution of five hundred dollars to each victim and (2) pay either an additional five-hundred-dollar fine to the court or serve a prison sentence of not less than one month and no longer than one year. After being jailed for forfeiting their bail, the pair initiated a habeas corpus proceeding, arguing that the statute itself was unconstitutional because it was not confined to state action and that their indictments had not stated race as a motive. In addition, the statute's text did not confine its scope to federal elections alone; it appeared to encompass *all* elections whether federal, state, or local, whereas the Fifteenth Amendment applied only to federal elections. Thus, Justice Brewer reasoned, to uphold the indictments would require rewriting the statute—"legislating from the bench" in modern parlance. That, Brewer insisted, courts must never do. Five other justices agreed with him. On May 4, 1903, the majority struck down Section5 because it prohibited individual action, while the Fifteenth Amendment only prohibited state action. The amendment's framers, Brewer wrote, did "not contemplate wrongful individual acts."[30]

In the span of a single week, the Court had promulgated two devastating and contradictory decisions. In *Giles v. Harris,* the Court said that it could not punish states for violating "political rights," but suggested that damages suits against individual registrars would be another matter. But, in *James v. Bowman,* it decided that the federal government could *only* punish states, not individuals, for violating black citizens' "political rights." Noting the glaring contradiction that lay between *Giles v. Harris* and *James v. Bowman,* the *New York Times* observed that the question of enforcing voting rights, whether under the Fourteenth or Fifteenth Amendments, was left "in a curious condition."[31]

James v. Bowman, so Richmond's *Planet* thought, had made plain the hypocrisy of *Giles v. Harris.* In *Giles,* the Supreme Court said that only Congress could grant the prayer for relief but in *James v. Bowman* Congress had granted relief and then the Court invalidated it. "You are told to go on with the building of your house on the same spot . . . where the old one stands, but you mustn't pull down the old house or disturb its foundation," the *Planet* complained. "You must, Shylock like, take a pound of flesh, but not a drop of blood." For the *Planet*'s editor, John Mitchell, it was clearer than ever that white America would never do right by black America. "Can the colored people see? Do they understand?" he asked. Blacks' only hope was a change in public opinion. Once public opinion became aroused, Mitchell presciently noted, no branch of the government would dare deny blacks' rights. Public outrage, he intoned, was essential to the cause of liberty and the law of the scriptures would be needed as well. Only then would blacks enjoy the justice that was demanded by the "teachings of the greatest of all law-givers, Moses; second only to the greatest, our Lord and Savior Jesus Christ. Selah."[32]

One strange twist to *Giles v. Harris* was that while the decision had made an incredible mess of things, and though it seemingly precluded any federal mandamus action, the door to the courts remained open to those money damages claims. For example, when, in the days immediately following, Alabama's white newspapers reported the good news, they were forced to recognize contradictory reports from Washington. The Supreme Court, through Holmes, had done many things but it had not endorsed Alabama's 1901 constitution. Thus, Birmingham's *Age-Herald* conceded that, while initial reports announced that the Court had upheld the constitution, "later it developed from expressions of the court that the validity of the constitution had not been touched upon." This was more than the uninformed speculation of a Birmingham editor, since the account contained a remarkable statement from an unnamed Supreme Court justice, who advised the *Chicago Record-Herald*'s Walter Wellman that "the case in point" did not address the Alabama constitution's validity. The anonymous justice insisted that the Court had neither upheld Alabama's constitution nor precluded future challenges to it. The decision "is simply to the effect," the justice continued, "that a court of equity cannot give the relief asked." Many newspapers and journals demanded further immediate action. "The court," the *Congregationalist* insisted, "may shirk the task but it cannot be evaded."[33]

A small window remained open, if only barely, but few seemed impressed. Walter Wellman's anonymous justice was really the only public figure, on either side of the issue, who derived any shred of optimism from the case. Southern editors were unhappy and so too were disfranchisement's opponents. Moorefield Storey, who would later head the NAACP's Legal Defense Fund, lamented to a friend that, "if a man deprived of his vote has no remedy except to sue for damages before a white jury in the Southern states, he is entirely without a remedy." A decision that explicitly upheld disfranchisement may have been preferable to what Holmes and five of his colleagues had done. But it was just so discouraging and disheartening. Augustus Straker, a prominent African American attorney and activist from Detroit, slammed the Court in his 1906 pamphlet *Negro Suffrage in the South*. Deriding the decision's equivocations, and its failure to settle anything conclusively, he was reminded of a popular myth about the Prophet Mohammed's tomb: "And thus Mahomet's coffin was suspended in mid air."[34]

Dissatisfaction spread and deepened, while African American and G.O.P. editors seethed, apoplectic with rage. The justices' attempt to have the matter both ways disturbed them most of all. The *New Orleans Southwestern Christian Advocate* concluded that, "whether it was intended for a dodge or not it has that appearance." The *Advocate* was, as its masthead implied, a church paper and a restrained one; the Methodist organ was disinclined to strident denunciations. Whitelaw Reid's Republican *New York Tribune*, however, recognized no such bounds. Paraphrasing the late supreme court justice, Steven J. Field (who was also Justice Brewer's uncle), the *Tribune* insisted that "it is a fundamental principle of law that what is forbidden directly cannot be done indirectly." Southern disfranchisers had devised clever but transparent discriminations, and the *Tribune* doubted that anyone was fooled (other than the U.S. Supreme Court). Justice Holmes's complaint about being party to a fraud amounted to nothing more than a distinction without a difference. "Courts," the paper complained, "are supposed to go to the heart of questions, and not be put off by transparent subterfuge." This "August tribunal," the *Richmond Planet* repeated, "is anti-Negro." The decision meant, "in the language of the plantation," that a "negro has no more show of getting his rights than a 'bob-tailed mule in fly-time.'"[35]

African American journalists were universally inflamed, none more so than William Monroe Trotter. His *Boston Guardian* headline cried, "ALABAMA'S GRANDDADDY CONSTITUTION LEGALIZED: 'JUSTICE HOLMES, MASSACHUSETTS' MEMBER ON THE U.S. SUPREME BENCH PROVES SECOND ROGER TANEY IN RENDERING THE DECISION AGAINST NEGROES." In his May 2, 1903, editorial titled "That Alabama Case," Trotter regretted that the Court had not addressed disfranchisement head-on and had chosen instead to "talk nonsense through Justice Holmes." As a result, he sputtered, a return to "slavery . . . is only a step away." He also feared that Boston's own Holmes may yet declare, as had Chief Justice Roger Taney in his *Dred Scott v. Sanford* majority opinion, that "the Negro still has no rights that white men are bound to respect."[36]

The Roger Taney and *Dred Scott* comparisons persisted for months. Holmes delivered his opinion on April 27 but withheld the printed text for one week. After reading the text, Trotter screamed on his editorial page: "THE SECOND DRED SCOTT CASE." The decision "appears even worse in the plain text." Holmes's opinion, he declared, created an extraordinary situation. The Court had proclaimed itself "lame and impotent." The Court had said it could not do what it was supposed to do, namely, guard the U.S. Constitution. Instead, it had deferred to Congress, and that body's Fourteenth Amendment–granted power to reduce the representation of state's who denied voting rights to blacks. But as Trotter astutely noted, it was unclear whether Alabama would care if it lost some portion of its congressional representation. State leaders may have been willing to accept reduction in exchange for what would have amounted to "permission" to maintain blacks' disfranchisement—the South's disfranchisers had repeatedly said as much— and this amounted to constitutional nullification. "How is Alabama to be brought to obey the Constitution of the United States if such punishment proves unavailing?" Trotter asked. This was all just too unsettling. *Giles* had made things worse—much worse. A dismayed Trotter lamented, in closing, that "Justice Taney knocked out the Missouri Compromise: Justice Holmes an act of [Congress]." Holmes, to be fair, had not struck down any congressional enactment in his turn at deciding a voting rights case. The justice who had done that was Brewer, in *James v. Bowman*. What Holmes actually did was little better. The meaning of Taney's action in *Dred Scott,* Trotter contended, had been clear, where Holmes's ruling in *Giles v. Harris* made no firm declarations and was harder to understand. Yet, and lest anyone doubt *Giles's* effect, the result was no less sinister, Trotter insisted: "Taney reasoned the Negro out of citizenship, Holmes out of his ballot."[37]

In July, the *Colored American Magazine* picked up Trotter's *Dred Scott* refrain and thought that the opinion seemed even worse with the passage of two months. Compared to the fierce reaction that greeted *Dred Scott* in 1857, the nation in 1903 received *Giles v. Harris* with relative calm: "It seems now to appeal to apathetic ears and to awaken no response in the hearts and consciences of the people." In several respects, the decision was even more deleterious to the republic's health. Justice Holmes's opinion had contained no firm pronouncements, unlike Roger Taney's of fifty-three years before. At least Taney and his colleagues had been open about their intention; Holmes and his allies admitted to no motive. The present Court, the essay continued, came "to its conclusion in such shuffling and evasive terms that one is inclined to feel only contempt." Even those rare birds who thought the opinion wise made the historical allusion. U.S. Senator George Hoar of Massachusetts jumped into the fray to heap scorn upon Holmes (who he had urged President Roosevelt not to appoint). The *Giles* decision was, in Hoar's opinion, "more far-reaching and terrible . . . than the famous judgment of Taney." Alfred Russell, an attorney addressing the Michigan State Bar Association, also offered the *Dred Scott* comparison, though he thought that the Court had correctly rejected the temptation to decide the issue. The current court, Russell concluded, "had displayed wisdom and true statesmanship in holding the powers of a court of equity unequal to the emergency."[38]

Despite Holmes's protestations that he did not read the papers, he knew exactly what they wrote of him. "Some papers," he wrote to his friend, the author Clara Stevens, "have been representing me as a second Taney in respect of probing another Dred Scott." He was not blind to the decision's effect. "I think the decision was inevitable—but it was one of those terrible questions over which one would lie awake if he had not strong nerves." It had indeed taken some nerve. Edward White has observed that Holmes's experience on Massachusetts' high court taught him that judging was sometimes an arbitrary business and imbued him with two "judicial habits," one of "deferring especially arbitrary policy choices to some other body . . . that arguably reflected community sentiment" and the other of "not agonizing over the reasoning that justified an arbitrary choice." That often yielded ugly results, and it would be many more years before the Holmes of legend supplanted the image of the man who authored *Giles v. Harris*.[39]

Holmes's dubious claim of powerlessness was something to which commentators always returned. The Court was not powerless, and it was not necessarily averse to contentious public policy issues, namely those involving business and property interests. In property's name, the justices responded consistently and with alacrity. This was not lost on the *Colored American Magazine*'s essayist. "When capital has called upon the Federal courts to protect his interests," they wrote, the justices "never skulked behind their alleged want of power to execute their process." The same question arose in other quarters. Is the Court a "Diana of the Ephesians" serving only the politically powerful and monied classes from whence its members were drawn? "Is it a wooden god?" the *Richmond Planet*'s John Mitchell asked. It claimed to be powerless to defend the Fifteenth Amendment but, the paper continued, it should recall the Pullman strike and coal strikes in Virginia and West Virginia. Who was to say that President Roosevelt would not put the power of his office behind the Court? President Grover Cleveland had the power to enforce the Court's decree at Pullman, Illinois, in 1894, Mitchell noted. If Cleveland had the power, then "why cannot President Roosevelt do it in the interest" of the Fourteenth and Fifteenth Amendments? [40]

David Brewer, the primary dissenter in *Giles v. Harris,* had always been willing to assert the Court's authority to settle disputes, most notably in *In re Debs* (1895). Brewer authored that remarkable decision by which the Court denied Eugene Debs's habeas corpus petition, thus affirming the use of federal court injunctions to thwart labor strikes—injunctions the president would have to enforce. The similarities between *Giles* and *Debs* were not lost on the *Colored American:* "As Eugene Debs and many a striker well knows," the Supreme Court justices "have been greedy and eager to enlarge their jurisdiction and to fulminate decrees which, if the subjects of them had been anything but law-abiding citizens, it would have taken grapeshot to enforce." This road always led back to *Dred Scott:* The "Alabama black man—because he is a black man and for no other reason—has no political rights which an Alabama white man is bound to respect; or, at least, if he has, the supreme court is afraid to make him respect them."[41]

Booker T. Washington's private circle of friends, acquaintances, spies, and counterspies expressed the same disappointment and outrage as seen on the pages of the *Boston Guardian,* the *Colored American,* and everywhere else. Melvin Chisum, an old Texas friend of Emmet Scott's who became one of Washington's spies, was so angry that he had decided to publish a new magazine, the *Negro.* Chisum hoped Scott would persuade Washington to contribute an article. "I concluded when I read the damnable decision of the Supreme Court on the Alabama case," Chisum explained, "that from New York ought to go a negro publication . . . that would say the things . . . that we want said, that would in other words present our side of the situation." The novelist Charles Waddell Chesnutt wrote Washington that he could no longer indulge his friend's stubborn optimism. The "policy of conciliation . . . of which you have been the most distinguished advocate," he wrote, had yielded nothing but a steady erosion of blacks' rights. This had reached its nadir in *Giles,* Chesnutt thought, where the Court declared, echoing Trotter and so many others, that "the Negro in the South has no rights which the government, as constituted, can compel Southern white men to respect." Chesnutt, it must be noted, did not know of Washington's role in the litigation. Washington, it must also be noted, made sure that Chesnutt never found out.[42]

Chesnutt continued to hammer away. In September 1903, a collection of essays, *The Negro Problem,* was published and Chesnutt contributed "The Disfranchisment of the Negro." "The right of American citizens of African descent . . . to vote upon the same terms as other citizens of the United States, is plainly declared and firmly fixed by the Constitution," Chesnutt began. That "firmly fixed" right had been eroded in the South, and federal institutions had done nothing to slow disfranchisement's march. As a result, "encouraged by the timidity of the Courts and the indifference of public opinion," southern disfranchisers were enjoying "an ominous degree of success." If it "foreshadows the attitude which the Court will take," Chesnutt continued, repeating publicly what he had already written privately to Washington, *Giles v. Harris* "is scarcely less than a reaffirmation of the *Dred Scott* decision" that "colored men in the United States have no political rights which the States are bound to respect." John Wise echoed Chesnutt that summer in an address to the Ohio State Bar Association. In *Giles v. Harris,* the Court had seemingly divorced itself from the federal government. "We have a court today," Wise complained, that "seems to seek to find how it can avoid interpretation. . . . We have a court which, when it is forced to a decision . . . scatters like a covey of quail."[43]

"Three tribunals" existed, Chesnutt observed, where blacks could appeal for protection: the U.S. courts, Congress, and public opinion. The courts and Congress would only move if public opinion demanded it, and Chesnutt wanted blacks to force a reckoning. "This Court should be bombarded with suits until it makes some definitive pronouncement" on the southern constitutions, Chesnutt demanded. Then, he continued, "the Negro and his friends" would have a "clean-cut issue" to work with. But blacks had to act on their own behalf; they could not wait for improvement. "There can be no middle ground between justice and injustice," he warned, "between the citizen and the serf."[44]

Wilford Smith too encountered scorn in the aftermath of *Giles v. Harris* and it was not helpful. The *Colored American* hoped that "the next time an important race question comes up . . . some great colored lawyer"—not

Smith, apparently—would argue the proposition. "It may be doubted," William Monroe Trotter muttered, "whether the case was stated properly to begin with." Critics had to have someone—many someones, in this case—to criticize, and Smith suffered far more than Holmes and the Court. He had already begun four *Giles* cases and the *Rogers* appeal, which were pending, but the deep secrecy surrounding the Alabama cases was working against him. Washington's need for secrecy was not an imagined one. Yet more publicity (and credit) for Smith meant more publicity for Washington, which the Tuskegee Institute principal would not risk. If Washington's role in this fight had become known, the reaction back home would have been incendiary. By this time, in fact, Washington had been forced to employ a team of Pinkerton Agency bodyguards to ensure his personal safety. Even if no harm ever befell him, whatever power he had would have drained away. This constrained Smith. He stood defenseless before the critics' ill-informed and tacky ridicule of his work, and that could not but hinder fund-raising, particularly in the northeast, where, at Washington's suggestion, Smith had solicited various unnamed private donors.[45]

Smith soldiered onward and never tried to defend himself. The attacks continued: "It is to be hoped," Trotter wrote, "that the Alabama people will secure the best legal advice and try their case again." Smith's rivals, or rather those who fancied themselves as his rivals, also capitalized upon *Giles* to aggrandize themselves. James Hayes, reacting to *Giles v. Harris*, privately sneered that Smith was "not a lawyer." Devotees of Booker T. Washington, Hayes continued, had thought Smith's case was "the strongest one pending before the Court, but [I] knew all along it was the weakest." That was nonsense. Hayes would face his own judgment day a year later.[46]

Even if Wilford Smith had wanted to brood over his defeat, there was no time to do so. *Giles v. Harris* was only one of four active Alabama cases that he was managing in the spring of 1903. *Giles v. Harris* was merely one ship from a flotilla of suits, and the others had yet to emerge from the Alabama state courts. The others were the two *Giles v. Teasley* cases (which involved both a mandamus claim and a suit for monetary damages) and the case of Dan Rogers (which would be a jury discrimination case). Smith planned to consolidate these into a single U.S. Supreme Court appeal. Consolidation held great promise, and completely unaware of Smith's plan, the editor of the *Virginia Law Register* commented in June 1903 that "just where the line of demarcation will be drawn when a case presenting the elements of *Giles v. Harris,* combined with those of *Wiley v. Sinkler,* and *Swafford v. Temple-*

ton, . . . no careful lawyer will be quick to forecast." That is, essentially, what Smith was planning.[47]

On February 28, 1903, the Alabama Supreme Court ruled in the two *Giles v. Teasley* cases. Smith lost both appeals, according to plan, but Alabama's high court refused to issue writs of error. That was definitely *not* in his plan, and so Smith would have to petition the U.S. Supreme Court directly for the writs. Specifically, he would have to pay a visit to the Supreme Court justice responsible for the Fifth Circuit, Edward Douglass White of Louisiana. Hope remained alive. The ultimate question remained unanswered, and so the *Chautauquan,* a national news magazine, optimistically offered that "it would be rash to conclude positively that the fifteenth amendment is unenforceable and futile."[48]

9
The Banner Negroes
Fighting to the End

> In the North, he said, the negroes call the members of their race in
> Alabama "the banner negroes" on account of their fight against the
> Constitution.
> —*Montgomery Advertiser* account of an address by Wilford H.
>   Smith, August 1903

Notably absent from the public coverage and the private planning of the early antidisfranchisement cases were the plaintiffs themselves. Cornelius Jones's Mississippi clients were all condemned prisoners and could play no role other than to offer testimony in court. Additionally, their cases were inseparable from Jones's congressional campaigns, and all publicity efforts revolved around him. Similarly, Congressman George Washington Murray, Senator Ben Tillman, Governor Gary Evans, and Judge Nathan Goff dominated the South Carolina litigation. Also, the South Carolina cases ended before Lawrence Mills, Daniel Wiley, and James Gowdy could become well known. David Ryanes in Louisiana was just ill suited for a public role. So the attorneys, judges, and politicians—they were the faces of all the early litigation efforts. That was also the case in Virginia. But things were different in Alabama.

Peter Crenshaw and his Grand Army of the Republic comrades made quite a showing in the Tennessee Valley, and for a moment Jackson Giles and the Colored Men's Suffrage Association of Alabama seemed poised to lead Alabama's African American community. More than any other antidisfranchisement plaintiff, Giles managed to leave some record of himself. In first week of May 1903, in the immediate aftermath of *Giles v. Harris,* he launched a renewed effort designed to raise money for his other cases and to rouse and organize the state's widely scattered activist community.

Giles no longer worked at the post office. White newspapers said he had been fired, while Giles himself maintained that he had resigned. At the time that the U.S. Supreme Court ruled against him in *Giles v. Harris,* he was tending a small store near his home and apparently had entered the newspaper business, publishing and editing the *Montgomery Negro Pilot.* In an "interview" that appeared in the *Pilot,* Giles admitted only to optimism. He was pressing forward. The next step was a CMSAA convention in Montgomery. Whether Jackson Giles understood the Supreme Court's decision cannot be determined, but many doubted that he did. He may have professed confidence, the *Mobile Daily Register* commented, "but some people would not know they were hit if a house were to fall upon them."[1]

The CMSAA convened on May 5, eight days after *Giles v. Harris* came down, with approximately 150 in attendance. Remarkably, and unlike previous CMSAA conclaves, this was a statewide affair. On five days' notice and for the first time, many of Alabama's most outspoken black activists came together. An October 1901 conference organized by Rev. Andrew Johnson of Mobile brought a large group to Birmingham, but it was neither this large nor this comprehensive.

Among those present at the May 5 CMSAA meeting were Johnson, L. H. Harrison, business manager for Carrie Tuggle's *Birmingham Truth,* and Hershel Cashin, the Decatur attorney who forced his way onto the Morgan County voting rolls by threatening litigation. Giles hummed the meeting to order with a "plaintive rendition" of "One More River to Cross" and, following an invocation, announced that he did not care to discuss either the "justice or injustice" of *Giles v. Harris.* This meeting was about the future and the three cases pending before the Alabama Supreme Court. The association's secretary, A. J. Rogers, then read a letter from Wilford Smith denouncing the U.S. Supreme Court's "cowardly yielding to the powers of the South" and reassuring the CMSAA that they had numerous northern friends and that "popular sentiment there was decidedly in their favor." Money was the main concern. Speaker after speaker called for donations to finance future appeals and to pay Giles's court costs in the city court cases. Montgomery County's sheriff was hounding him for the $119 dollars owed for filing fees and service costs from *Giles v. Teasley* II and III.[2]

There was nothing remarkable about the speeches given that day. They were no different, really, from anything said before. Still, the CMSAA had held together for a second round. It looked as if the Alabama effort was growing; the range of leaders on display testified to the organization's potential strength. After several hours and two rounds of speech making, the conference adjourned. They had only raised fifty-five dollars but went home energized and confident that they still might make things right. Massachu-setts' *Springfield Daily Republican* had seen reports of the May 5 meeting and was pleased. "It is well," the *Daily Republican* thought, "for the colored race to fight for their own rights in the matter. No race or people," the editor continued, "will long maintain itself that cannot, if necessary, work out and fight for its own salvation." The *New York Age* agreed. "We are glad to see this exhibition of pluck and determination on the part of the Alabama con-testants," the *Age* wrote, "and trust they will fight it out to the last ditch."[3]

Jackson Giles took his appeal to a national audience that summer, appear-ing at the Afro-American Press Association's convention in July in Louis-ville. "Jack is the man," a derisive *Montgomery Advertiser* account explained, "who has been butting his thick skull against the Alabama constitution." Giles asked the association for three hundred dollars, but was challenged by a New York delegate who demanded to know why Alabama blacks could not raise that relatively small sum themselves. The press convention, so the *Ad-vertiser* reported, eventually satisfied Giles's request, "notwithstanding New York's unpatriotic refusal." The *Advertiser* insisted that money was Giles's only real interest, and Democratic editors across the South had repeatedly made that charge of other similar efforts. "As long as Giles can get money," the report concluded, "he will keep up the useless contest, but if the North-ern negroes wish to invest their surplus in gold bricks, we have no protest to make."[4]

Though Giles had grabbed the spotlight, the real powers behind his cases remained staunchly silent and carefully hidden. There was nary a word from either Emmet Scott or Booker T. Washington, not even a surreptitious statement released to journalistic third parties. For his part, Smith more than once directed open letters to the CMSAA and, on occasion, appeared before them in person. In late August he addressed fifty CMSAA mem-bers at a meeting hosted by the Congregational Church on High Street in Montgomery. A *Montgomery Advertiser* reporter was in attendance, and he wrote that Smith's speech "was even-tempered and at times eloquent" and dealt largely with the strategy he had chosen for *Giles v. Harris* and for the cases yet pending. Smith was also concerned with cheering on the CMSAA and ensuring that they did not grow discouraged. They were famous and respected in the North, Smith told the CMSAA members gathered that night. Northern blacks, he said, called their Alabama brethren "the banner negroes" for their ongoing efforts to fight the Alabama constitution of 1901. But as they were the vanguard, they had only had a taste of the fight that lay ahead, Smith warned. They had seen little of what Jim Crow would do to them and thus they had to stand up to the "Supreme Court, the South, the North, [and] the world." He cautioned against putting too much faith in the Court—a reasonable but nonetheless striking statement. The Court alone could not save them, the *Advertiser* reported Smith as having said, and thus "they should stand on their own footing." CMSAA members were delighted to have had Smith with them in person and to hear from him. One elderly attendee, according to the *Advertiser,* had come "near . . . a hysterical rapture when Smith told the negroes of a probability of voting in the near future."[5]

In late February the Alabama Supreme Court denied Smith's appeals in both of the *Giles v. Teasley* cases. One of those asked for damages and the other was a mandamus petition, the same mechanism that *Giles v. Harris* had invoked. In other states, litigators sought injunctions or to have things overturned directly. In these Alabama cases, however, Smith was asking that the courts force the registrars to apply the new constitution fairly. State courts, of course, were just as hostile in Alabama as elsewhere, and the Alabama court not only denied the appeals, but went so far as to refuse writs of error (whereby a lower court certifies the issues under appeal to a higher court). A year earlier, Alabama's judicial officers were oddly cordial to Smith, but after watching him in action, they came to see him for the threat that he was. Montgomery City Court Judge William Thomas had already caught a cabal of lawyers plotting a physical assault, and they surely were not the only ones who wished Smith ill. The state supreme court would never condone venality or violence, but pettiness was a distinct possibility.[6]

Giles v. Teasley II and III and *Rogers v. Alabama* were each founded upon claims emanating from the U.S. Constitution, but the state's high court justices ignored that. Two months earlier, Oliver Wendell Holmes Jr. had said that the U.S. Supreme Court could not order Montgomery County's registrars to do anything if, as Smith alleged, they were the product of a conspiracy, Alabama's court trotted out their version of the same straw man. If the registration boards operated unconstitutionally, Justice John R. Tyson wrote, they were therefore null and a court could not order a nullity to do anything. As Wilford Smith later explained to Booker T. Washington, this was only a "trick . . . to straddle the question." Since the Alabama Supreme Court justices knew that Smith would appeal, they had decided to obstruct his path. In a strategic discussion with Washington, Smith predicted that the "state courts and court officers are in league and conspiracy to prevent our case going to the Supreme Court." That was indeed happening. The Alabama Supreme Court proceeded to dismiss Smith's request for writs. On the basis of that alone, it would seem that they were apprehensive about what the U.S. Supreme Court might do. But then the Alabama justices went even further and outright refused to certify copies of the official record. That could only mean that they were beyond apprehensive—they were plainly scared.[7]

Alabama's high court justices were clever but not clever enough. They could slow Smith's advance, but only barely and not for long. He could still get his writs, though they would have to come from the U.S. Supreme Court directly. This meant a trip to Washington for a meeting with Justice Edward Douglass White. White, a Louisiana sugar planter, was circuit justice for the Fifth Circuit, which encompassed Alabama. They met in late May, and White, evidently, wanted to accept the Alabama Supreme Court's decision. Smith informed Emmet Scott that White "did not wish to [grant the writs] after he saw that the Chief Justice . . . of Alabama had refused the application." Alabama's justices may have anticipated White's reaction. Regardless, White knew that Smith would appeal his refusal to his colleagues on the Supreme Court. Since they might reverse, and thus humiliate, him, White granted Smith his writs. However, White reached beneath his figurative robe and whipped out a stalling tactic of his own design: withholding his signature until Smith executed cost bonds of $250 for each case. Those bonds, which guaranteed that the parties would actually appear, were not unusual, but neither were they necessary. The *Giles v. Teasley* appeals had grown much more expensive, but they were back on track. Smith had them both docketed in the U.S. Supreme Court by early July.[8]

Though the two city court appeals were moving along, significant obstacles remained. Smith needed money for the cost bonds and he needed enough money to ensure briefs of the highest quality. He intended to file the writs and briefs himself and do everything possible to avoid technical delays. "They are going to do their utmost to dismiss the writ before the full court on technicalities to get around deciding the real question," he explained to Scott. "I am fully convinced now that they are playing a dodging game here as much as at Montgomery." With everything else that could go wrong, Smith did not need money trouble. His message to Scott and Washington was clear: This was no time for thrift. "You must place the necessary means in my hand," he pleaded, asking for fifteen hundred dollars "at once." "We cannot do with less than this," Smith insisted, "and it would be better to quit than to try, and fall through on account of lack of means and unreasonable delay."[9]

Smith's monetary demands were never unreasonable. The real problem was that he asked for too little and too often. Neither Booker T. Washington nor Emmet Scott ever suggested outright that Smith made unreasonable demands. If excessive costs had been the issue, he could not have remained in Washington's employ until his death in 1915. If any fault is to be found, though, it rests with Smith's piecemeal approach to finances. Scott and Washington constantly fielded pleas for one hundred dollars here, one thousand dollars there, and the bargaining never stopped. In the late spring of 1903, with three new cases queuing up, Smith and Scott dickered for the better part of a month. They finally reached an agreement in late June, whereby Scott promised to pay Smith the fifteen hundred dollars over time.

James Hayes, during this time, repeatedly denigrated Smith in northern activist circles, and that only complicated things further. He made fundraising more difficult for Smith by actively arguing that the Alabama effort was not serious. In midsummer, he "proved" the seriousness of his own work. Hayes's NEIAV announced in July that it would pay John S. Wise and John G. Carlisle ten thousand dollars each for their services. Whether this was true, and whether Wise and Carlisle ever saw this money, is unknown, but the announcement was dramatic. By comparison, Wilford Smith was a bargain. Despite Hayes's sniping, he, Wise and Carlisle had not yet argued a single Virginia antidisfranchisement case before the U.S. Supreme Court, while Smith was preparing his second, third, and fourth.[10]

Dan Rogers's case was the key component of Smith's consolidation strategy and it began to move along in mid-July. Few noticed, however, that the Alabama Supreme Court had sustained Rogers's murder conviction on July 10. Five days later, as his colleagues had done in the two *Giles v. Teasley* cases, Chief Justice Thomas N. McClellan refused a writ of error. Smith would have to call on Justice White again. Smith also intended to have Dan Rogers's case handled *forma pauperis,* requiring the Supreme Court to waive its fees on account of poverty. This, however, was not a sure bet. Just two weeks after their last round of haggling, Smith advised Scott that he would need another "D" (one thousand dollars) as soon as possible, which apparently Scott provided.[11]

Despite the obfuscations of the Alabama high court justices and despite

Smith's and Scott's inability to ever settle financial matters, the Alabama litigation was moving apace. These cases promised to be far stronger than *Giles v. Harris*, but Alabama's press corps and legal community had fallen oddly quiet. Even the *Montgomery Advertiser*, which had been so fascinated by the "negro lawyer from New York" one year earlier, said absolutely nothing. The venerable Democratic mouthpiece, Smith noted, thus far had let *Rogers* pass in "severe silence."[12]

Extended delays could be costly, in more ways than one, as Smith made clear. He had rushed off to Washington, D.C., in search of Justice White's writ in early August and then raced back to "get my man back from the penitentiary." Smith feared that state prison officials might kill Dan Rogers, or allow him to be killed, mooting his appeal. In *Rogers*, Smith reminded Scott that "we will have to be more prompt before our man is taken to The Walls [Alabama's state penitentiary] or he might be killed there in order to get rid of our appeal as the case will have to stop with his death." This was no hollow threat. Alabama's prison officials did not return Dan Rogers to the Montgomery County jail, as they should have. In September, Smith approached Attorney General Massey Wilson directly: "I would be glad if you would communicate" with the Board of Convicts and have Rogers returned. Smith and Wilson had met previously, and Smith's "recollection [was] that you agreed with me" about Rogers's transfer. Smith intimated that if the attorney general did not order Rogers's immediate return to the Montgomery County Jail, his office would face an unpleasant habeas corpus proceeding before U.S. District Judge Thomas Goode Jones. Prison officials promptly complied, no doubt at Wilson's direction. With Rogers back in the slightly safer confines of the Montgomery County Jail, Smith turned to that all-important consolidation motion. Only in late summer, after the writ was secured, did the *Montgomery Advertiser* break its silence. "Rogers, perhaps ignorant of the fact that his name is being used to test . . . the new constitution," the paper reported, dismissively, was "serving the state as a convict," while Smith was prepared "documents of legal phraseology sufficient to befuddle ordinary laymen."[13]

Seven antidisfranchisement cases had reached the nation's high court by the autumn of 1903. The three Mississippi cases (*Smith, Gibson*, and *Williams*), *Williams* especially, have subsequently attracted historians' attention, and that of some of the disfranchisers, but they had little bearing upon Smith's work. As instructive precedents, they demonstrated the importance of offering strong evidence, but then *any* Supreme Court appeal required strong evidence. *Mills v. Green,* the first disfranchisement case the Court reviewed, reminded litigators of the Political Questions Doctrine, but that constraint dated from *Marbury v. Madison.* The two antidisfranchisement cases that mattered most to Smith were *Wiley v. Sinkler* and *Swafford v. Templeton,* each of which had affirmed the federal courts' jurisdiction over voting rights claims. In neither of those cases did the plaintiff ever collect: A moot question cost Daniel Wiley two thousand dollars in damages and Thomas Swafford apparently died. But then the pendulum swung back to *Giles,* which spoke primarily to the Court's institutional unwillingness, due both to fear and recalcitrance, to engage the issue, something of which Smith was painfully aware.

Holmes, in *Giles v. Harris,* suggested that Jackson Giles look for money damages rather than a writ of mandamus. Smith did not really want to put a price upon voting rights, but Holmes's opinion suggested that the *Giles v. Teasley* damages claim held promise. *Swafford, Wiley,* and then *Giles v. Harris* had, in effect, illumined a path for plaintiffs to make disfranchisement harder and costlier for states. If Smith or anyone else were willing to "name a price" for voting rights, maybe they could bankrupt disfranchisement. At two thousand dollars a man, with court costs thrown in for good measure, disfranchisement would become expensive. Accompanying that damages suit was a *Giles v. Teasley* mandamus petition, virtually identical to *Giles v. Harris.* That the Court had rejected Giles's first mandamus petition did not mean that he could not ask again. If he could attach the mandamus to a damages claim, he might win both.

Smith, however, planned a tripartite assault, linking Dan Rogers's appeal to the two *Giles v. Teasley* cases. This arrangement held great promise, as Alabama officials seemed to have also recognized. The U.S. Supreme Court had consistently maintained that states could not exclude blacks from jury service because of race. Such exclusions violated and accused criminal's due process rights, as the Court had reaffirmed in Smith's *Carter v. Texas* case in 1900. Consolidating criminal rights and political rights cases, Smith believed, would make it harder for the Court to dodge a definitive ruling on disfranchisement. In a consolidated case, they could not reject the mandamus petition without overturning recent precedent—something courts are loath to do.[14]

By August 31, Smith's consolidation motion was ready. "Everything," he emphasized in a letter to Emmet Scott, "depends on consolidation to my mind, and the chances are if I don't consolidate, they may refuse to allow me to advance them." The likelier danger, truthfully, was that the Court would refuse consolidation and examine the cases separately. Still, there was an even greater threat: there arose, just as happened at every step, a financial crisis. The running and unfortunate money squabble proved the adage about the thin line distinguishing tragedy from farce. The problem was not that Booker T. Washington and Emmet Scott were cheap but that every draft they exchanged was another chance to be discovered. Scott and Washington drew funds from who knows where; they quite likely skimmed from Tuskegee Institute's coffers. Further, Wilford Smith had not demanded a retainer at the outset and that dictated his contacting Scott and Washington over and again, hat in hand. They would go back and forth over each latest payment (politely, of course) and then Smith would threaten a delay. Every time he made that threat, he got the money he needed. It was always unfortunate and decidedly counterproductive.[15]

Late summer's tug-of-war passed and Smith submitted the consolidation motion on October 19. The document explained that he sought consolidation because (1) all three cases involved the same question (2) the Court had refused to "pass upon the validity of the Alabama constitution" in *Giles v. Harris* and (3) "the question involved in these cases is new" and "would settle a much vexed question of law." Since this case arose from the Fifth Circuit, Justice White handled the request, and he rejected Smith's motion with astounding speed (he announced his decision on October 23) and with no explanation. "Petition Denied" was the terse headline of the *Montgomery Advertiser*'s succinct October 27 report. Actually, White had only partially rejected it. The two *Giles v. Teasley* cases were consolidated; *Rogers v. Alabama* would stand alone. So they would all be heard, but make no mistake— this was a serious blow and, in retrospect, an omen.[16]

The pending *Giles v. Teasley* appeals, like the *Giles v. Harris* appeal of one year earlier, attracted national attention, though again, it was surprisingly limited. What coverage there was tended to be perfunctory and incomplete. "Several new attempts," the *Christian Advocate* magazine editorialized, were underway to challenge Alabama's constitution, explaining only that the matter "now comes up under a new form."[17]

Wilford Smith made few appearances of any sort. Yet whenever allowed to separate his words from his person—appellate briefs, open letters, articles—he sparkled. Smith, as a public figure, shone brightest in September 1903, when he contributed an essay, "The Negro and the Law," to James Pott and Company's *The Negro Problem: A Series of Articles by Representa-*

tive American Negroes of To-day. The other contributors included Booker T. Washington ("Industrial Education for the Negro") Charles Chesnutt ("The Disfranchisement of the Negro"), Paul Laurence Dunbar ("Representative American Negroes"), and W. E. B. Du Bois, who unveiled one of his most enduring works, "The Talented Tenth." Standing alongside those giants, Smith offered the fullest philosophical exposition he ever made. Liberated from the conventions of appellate practice, Smith provided a hint of the public figure he might have become.

"The Negro and the Law" opened in the Reconstruction period with the adoption of the Thirteenth, Fourteenth, and Fifteenth Amendments. Out of the "shadow of the awful calamity and deep distress of the Civil War," Smith wrote, "the American people . . . rose to the sublime heights of doing justice to the former slaves." Nevertheless, in the years since Reconstruction, the southern states had done their level best to bring America down from that "sublime height" by undermining the Reconstruction Amendments. "They rather regard them as war measures," Smith declared, "designed . . . to humiliate and punish the people of those states lately in rebellion." There is a "distinct and positive fear on the part of the South," he continued, "that if the negro is given a man's chance . . . it will in some way lead to his social equality." Smith led readers through a review of federal civil rights legislation, Supreme Court rulings, and the South's campaign for statutory segregation from the mid-1880s forward. He placed special emphasis upon disfranchisement and the grandfather clauses, "the boldest and most open violation of the negro's rights under the Federal Constitution." These, in Smith's view, arose from another problem: the passing of a generation.[18]

Southern Democratic leaders, Smith observed, insisted that blacks should stop agitating for their rights and instead "strive to deserve the good wishes" of their white neighbors. If the South were let alone, he continued, "white leaders would ensure blacks' kindly treatment." There were problems with that, however, and the greatest was that the "old master class" was "rapidly passing away," and the new men of the New South were a colder, crasser, and more craven lot. The new men were not his only worry, for Smith also feared that new immigrants—he singled out Italians—would rise to power in the South. The Italians would multiply, the old masters would be dead, their sons and grandsons would be outnumbered, and the typical southern black man "would be wholly at the mercy of a people without sympathy for him." Whatever new group ascended, the result was the same: blacks suffered.[19]

Smith mentioned neither the CMSAA, nor the Alabama cases, nor any of the other southern antidisfranchisement organizations. True to form, he defended blacks' legal activism without appearing activist himself. Quietly and deliberately, he reassured white readers (and this essay was intended for a white audience) that blacks' quest for fair trials, the security of life and property, due process of law, and a "voice in the making and administration of those laws," would, if successful, demonstrate southern progress. He invited readers to join them and hoped that "public opinion can be awakened . . . and that it may assist [blacks] to attain" a just result. Yet even those individuals or groups who wanted to lend their aid seemed to know very little about either the shy Smith or the monumental Alabama cases he managed. The National Sociological Society, for example, was aware of *Giles v. Teasley* and wanted to help in any way it could. At the society's annual meeting in Washington, the membership asked that Attorney General Philander Knox get involved, joining the litigation "to defend the Constitution . . . against the attacks being made upon the Fifteenth Amendment." Additionally, the society decided to ask the attorneys for the Alabama case if they might want sociological help. Whether Smith entertained their offer is unknown, but also unlikely.[20]

That autumn Smith had also become concerned about Alabama blacks' apparent apathy toward the pending cases. The excitement black leaders showed back in May had not spread. Smith, predictably, worried about money too. This led him, in November, to issue another of his prepared public statements: an open letter to two Mobile pastors, Anderson N. McEwen and Andrew N. Johnson, who edited the *Southern Watchman* and *Mobile Weekly Press,* respectively. Smith reassured them that he remained enthusiastic about his overall strategy. "I have just received a letter from Mr. Giles, President of the Colored Men's Suffrage Association," Smith wrote, containing circulars "that are being sent out among the people to raise an additional $600 to assist in our cases." Smith inferred from Giles's tone, he told the ministers, that the people "were not responding as they should . . . and I fear the reason is that they are discouraged over the decision in the equity case decided last April." Smith hoped McEwen and Johnson would remind "the people" that "those who carry this fight to victory will get the honors, while those who slink away at this crucial time will be regarded as deserters."[21]

Very little is known of Smith's personality, but we can deduce that he was driven, and careful, and from flashes such this, and his consistent mar-

tial allusions, he seems passionate as well. Three cases were pending before the U.S. Supreme Court, Smith advised. We "are now playing our last
trump card and we ought to play it with boldness and effect." To that end,
he urged McEwen and Johnson to "call the leading members of your community together" and see that the CMSAA secured the six hundred dollars.
Rev. McEwen, writing in the *Southern Watchman,* thought "the letter speaks
for itself." As Smith requested, McEwen and Johnson organized a mass
meeting at McEwen's Franklin Street Baptist Church and invited "all lovers of the race and in favor of equal rights and [an] equal chance in the race
of life" to hear speeches from "the best men of the city." Of course speech
making was not that meeting's sole purpose and the *Watchman* asked readers to "come out and bring a piece of money."[22]

Smith submitted the *Rogers v. Alabama* briefs to the U.S. Supreme Court
on January 4, 1904 (there was no oral argument) and on January 6, Smith
and William Gunter argued the consolidated *Giles v. Teasley* (no account of
which survives). The wait in 1904 would be far shorter than for 1903's *Giles v.
Harris*—a mere two weeks. The Court announced *Rogers* first, on January
18. The decision was unanimous and, like *Giles v. Harris,* written by Oliver
Wendell Holmes Jr. The primary question in *Rogers* was whether the trial
court judge (William Holcombe Thomas) acted properly when he struck
Smith's motion to quash without a hearing. Holmes declared that the motion should not have been struck—it could not be "prolix," as the state alleged, because of the constitutional violations it alleged. Just as in *Giles v.
Harris* ten months earlier, he withheld a final, official judgment on Smith's
allegation that Alabama's 1901 constitutional convention conspired against
blacks. If *Rogers* was consolidated with *Giles v. Teasley* II and III, Holmes
could not have done so. If the Court had united them, he could not have
reversed the Alabama Supreme Court's jury ruling without addressing the
suffrage clause of the Alabama constitution. The inescapable conclusion is
that the Court refused consolidation for that very reason. Once again, Holmes and the Supreme Court dodged the ultimate question. They remanded
Rogers's case to the Alabama Supreme Court, which remanded it to Judge
William H. Thomas and the Montgomery City Court. Most observers did
not realize what had happened. Blinded by Rogers's personal victory, they
praised an undeserving Court. "For once," the *St. Paul Appeal* remarked, the
Supreme Court "comes up smiling."[23]

   Rogers was an extremely limited decision, yet explaining its limits was complicated, so the press had simply announced victory. The *Rogers* dodge was not readily apparent, due primarily to the fact that few people other than Washington, Smith, Scott, and the leaders of the CMSAA appreciated the connection of the *Rogers* case to the two remaining *Giles* cases. They also understood that because consolidation had failed, so too had Smith's grand strategy. Because that connection was unknown, unrecognized, or unappreciated, many in Washington's circle reacted joyfully. Charles William Anderson, for one, was thrilled. Anderson (who seems to have had some knowledge of Washington's relationship with Smith) had kept Washington updated on the behind-the-scenes bickering about whether Smith was up to the task. Many people, it seems, had insisted that Hayes's Virginia cases were stronger, though for reasons unknown and frankly unimaginable. "I have been confounding" Smith's critics, Anderson wrote Washington, "who tried to sneeze me out of court, when I told them that . . . Wilford Smith would win his case or cases, if any were won." When he learned of the *Rogers* decision, Anderson wrote, "I shouted 'glory, Hallelujah!'" *Rogers,* he observed, was "the preliminary skirmish; and we have won."[24]

Washington too seemed unaware of *Rogers*' limited effect and asked Smith to prepare a "jury decision circular" immediately. He was excited and intended to distribute the document nationally, hoping, apparently, that blacks would be spurred to action. Congratulating Smith on the "moral effect of the recent decision," Washington wondered "whether or not in any degree it reached the vital purpose which we had in mind." In his celebratory mood, Washington dispensed with code names and with indirect contact, and wrote to Smith directly and in his own name. He thought that the decision had "given the colored people a hopefulness that means a great deal" and he was advising everyone that Smith was "entitled to great credit for the victory." A Tuskegee press release, unsigned and undated, celebrated *Rogers* and praised Smith, "who has been prosecuting in the state courts an attack upon the validity of the Alabama Constitution which has fraudulently disfranchised so many of our best citizens." Emmet Scott wrote the statement: it echoed a 1900 letter to Washington complaining that "the race" would never pay Smith the "debt of gratitude" owed him following *Carter v. Texas.*[25] Scott and Washington (but Scott especially) were touchy about these unpaid debts, for self-interested reasons. The Supreme Court, Scott's release continued, had "vindicated the right of the Negroes to representation on grand juries, and our race . . . owes Mr. Smith a debt of gratitude which it will hardly be able ever to pay." When the circular appeared later that year, Kentucky's *Richmond Sentinel* reprinted it without comment, but the *Richmond Planet*'s John Mitchell understood too well *Rogers*' extremely limited effect. "Those colored folks who can extract any satisfaction out of Mr. Smith's conclusions," Mitchell advised in April, "should proceed to do so."[26]

Southern white editors, of course, tried to reject *Rogers*. Birmingham's *Free Lance,* a brand-new white supremacist and labor newspaper, decried the implications of *Rogers* for white men. Poor and working-class whites found themselves in the same boat with blacks postdisfranchisement but there would be no bonds forged through their shared suffering. Returning to a sadly familiar and Malthusian refrain, the editor insisted that blacks could only gain rights at whites' expense. "Is there no protection of a white man against trial by a jury with a negro?" the *Free Lance* whined. "Is the Caucasian not entitled to his rights?" State officials, too, received the news petulantly. Later that year, the U.S. Supreme Court sent Governor Jelks a bill for ninety-five dollars in court costs. Jelks refused to pay, and insisted that the Court could not "force the state to pay."[27]

Wilford Smith was always circumspect about *Rogers*. He was happy to oblige Washington's request for the jury decision circular, but advised that *Rogers* "can hardly be said to have any direct bearing upon the vital purpose of the litigation pending in the Supreme Court." Smith was no longer optimistic about the two *Giles v. Teasley* cases, but nonetheless felt "very much gratified," he told Washington, "to know that the result of the work so far is satisfactory to you." The *Richmond Planet*'s John Mitchell had cautioned back in January that *Rogers* "carries no ray of hope for the colored people of the Southland." Never mind that consolidation had failed; Dan Rogers had probably only "secured a lease of life or liberty for a few months." Alabama's "Negro-haters" would punish him for his success and he would be "railroaded . . . to the penitentiary or the gallows."[28]

The *Giles v. Teasley* decision came one month after *Rogers,* on February 23. This time, it was a defeat. Justice William Rufus Day produced the majority opinion. Justice Joseph McKenna concurred with Day and Justice John Marshall Harlan dissented, though neither offered written comment. First, and strangely, Day endorsed the Alabama Supreme Court's knavish denial of writs—as if that were the issue. As for the mandamus petition (*Giles v. Teasley* II), Day parroted Holmes's *Giles v. Harris* opinion. If the boards of registrars were acting unconstitutionally and had been designed to do so, as Smith insisted, they were a nullity. If they violated the Fifteenth

Amendment, his logic held, they did not exist and, therefore, could not be ordered to do anything. Just like Holmes, Day conveniently ignored and distorted what Smith asked: that the Court make voter registration "constitutional" by insisting that the state behave transparently and fairly. Addressing the money damages claim (*Giles v. Teasley* III), Day acknowledged that *Giles* charged serious constitutional violations, but insisted that the state court had not sustained a constitutional violation. The state court had, in fact, glossed over the federal issue but that did not mean it was not there. Day needed the opposite to be true and simply chose to believe it was. Alabama "has planted its decision upon a ground independent of the alleged state action," he claimed, and "its action is not reviewable here."[29]

In his bid to escape the real question, Justice Day had changed the subject. His opinion was just strange. The renowned constitutional scholars Alexander Bickel and Benno Schmidt characterized it as "bizarre" and as a "remarkable bit of Alice in Wonderland ingenuity, internal inconsistency, and practical absurdity." Smith had gone before the Alabama Supreme Court and argued that Giles's federal constitutional rights had been violated. The Alabama Supreme court rejected that claim and simply asserted, without really showing why, that his federal rights had not been violated. The U.S. Supreme Court was asked to review the Alabama Supreme Court's rejection of Giles's claim. Wilford Smith's briefs put the constitutional issue squarely before the Court and yet, Day coolly claimed: "We do not perceive how this decision involved the adjudication of a right claimed under the Federal Constitution."[30]

Most frustrating of all, the Court stubbornly refused a clear, up-or-down ruling. Instead, it left the matter in limbo, technically speaking, offering nothing to encourage southern blacks and nothing to discourage southern disfranchisers. Day claimed, solemnly, that he and his colleagues were "not unmindful of the gravity of the statements of the complainant" and that "we are of opinion" that Smith had "not brought the cases within the statute giving to this court the right of review." Regardless, the inescapable fact remained that Day had declared that a state could do virtually as it pleased just so long as it concocted trite excuses to use in its defense.[31]

Press reaction to *Giles v. Teasley* was as caustic as that which had followed *Giles v. Harris*. The decision simply proved that there had "never been a more radical and anti-Negro tribunal at Washington since the days of Chief Justice Taney," John Mitchell thought, so "death must remove eight ninths of them" before southern blacks could hope for judicial relief. In the black *At-*

lanta *Independent*'s opinion, the decision only reiterated the "oft-enunciated opinion that the Negro has no remedy at law to redress his constitutional grievances." Resurrecting the previous year's allusions to *In re Debs* and the Pullman Strike, the *Springfield Republican* noted that "our courts . . . do not hesitate to run great railroad systems in emergencies, to suppress formidable strikes by injunctions, and cast men like Debs into jail." Yet when faced with a civil rights claim from a black man, "they fall abjectly in a heap and proclaim want of jurisdiction." Less frequently, newspapers relayed franker and more unsavory reactions from whites to the Court's decision. A letter from "Countryman" to the editor of the Lee County, Alabama, *Opelika Post,* however, suggested that the Court's handling of the *Giles* cases was seen as a godsend by whites, those in rural areas especially. The pseudonymous "Countryman" wrote of the "country mother and the rural maiden" who allegedly lived in fear of sexual predation from black male neighbors. Affirming those black men's disfranchisement, he would have people believe, allayed their terror. "Oh, for a kodak to have recorded that wife's expression when she read the decision in the Giles case," Countryman wrote. "She evidently felt that the bright promise was now a reality . . . the country nigger was a nigger once more and forever."[32]

Booker T. Washington's associates responded with despair and outrage. Charles Chesnutt complained that he could "feel the foundations falling. . . . From its present attitude there seems no immediate remedy through the Supreme Court of the United States." Washington's friend, James Clarkson, New York's customs collector, was furious. Justice Day, an Ohioan, drew his particular ire. The opinion issued from "a Republican Supreme Court, with only one judge dissenting . . . and an Ohio judge . . . writing the decision," Clarkson wrote on February 26. "Ohio has been weak-backed on the cause of human rights always," Clarkson declared, though he believed that the decision had "put a great deal of fire in northern men." After reflecting on *Giles v. Teasley* for a few days more, Clarkson wrote Washington again on February 29. He was convinced that the decision would "make the question more acute and is going to arouse the wrath . . . of all people with convictions such as the Abolitionists used to have: not only a half million colored men in the North will resent it, but a million white men will be as radical as they in resenting it."[33]

There was also renewed interest, Clarkson had noted in his February 26 letter, in the Virginia cases that were managed by James Hayes and being argued by John S. Wise and (so Hayes and Wise claimed) John G. Carlisle.

The Supreme Court had scheduled arguments in the cases, *Jones v. Montague* and *Selden v. Montague,* for April 4, 1904. These were appeals of the failed November 1902 attempts to have Virginia's 1902 elections overturned. Clarkson, however, was not optimistic. He had warned Hayes directly, in 1902, to proceed cautiously with the Virginia cases, and Hayes had ignored him. Hayes subsequently hired Wise, and Clarkson strongly disapproved.[34]

Clarkson told Washington that Wise had commemorated George Washington's birthday that year with a speech at Grand Rapids, Michigan, calling for the repeal of the Fifteenth Amendment. Clarkson misunderstood Wise's comments, however. His participation in the antidisfranchisement litigation was always as much about scoring political points as it was about disfranchisement. Simultaneous to his courtroom activities, Wise also agitated for political punishment of the South. He strongly favored a reduction of southern congressional representation and did all he could to goad the GOP into action. This did not help him in the courtroom. In fact, it almost certainly hurt the Virginia litigation. But he apparently believed that an outraged Republican party could have brought the southern disfranchisers to heel and could have thus rescued both southern blacks and southern Republicans. He did indeed suggest repeal of the Fifteenth Amendment in his Grand Rapids address and in a similar appearance before Philadelphia's Young Republican Club in February 1903, but only rhetorically. He was trying to goad Republicans into action and to shame them. As he said in Philadelphia, "To maintain the statute giving suffrage to the colored man and not see that it is enforced" was holding up false hopes and encouraging lawbreaking." He challenged them to put some action behind their words. He did not care how the GOP punished southern Democrats as long as they punished them. A report from the Union League Club of New York, almost certainly penned by the club's president *ex officio,* John S. Wise, proposed a long menu of penalties, from invalidating state constitutions to reducing congressional representation to criminal prosecutions—it all sounded good to them. "A few imprisonments," his report volunteered, "a few judgements for damages collected would have a wonderfully deterrent effect."[35]

Collector Clarkson had received inaccurate information about the speech—of that there is not question. Still, he believed that the idea of John Wise leading the "great cause of suffrage in the Supreme Court is an absurdity," as he wrote to Booker T. Washington. Clarkson's concern was not unfounded. Wise was a poor appellate attorney. However, even without Wise, the Virginia effort, in Clarkson's view, was troubled. It was poorly conceived from the start and he had advised Hayes's friends back in 1902 that they needed better lawyers. Clarkson asserted that the case needed "lawyers who are themselves great enough to make the Supreme Court judges great enough to comprehend the greatness of the question." Furthermore, the lawyer or lawyers must also be "great enough to carry public opinion with them as they are fighting out the case." Naturally, Wise and Hayes did not meet his standard.[36]

Wilford Smith, by contrast, was a masterful appellate lawyer, but he lost nonetheless. He had not given up, however. Reacting to early reports of *Giles v. Teasley,* Smith wrote Washington on February 24 that the Supreme Court justices "are playing a dodging game." He was considering a reargument motion but was aware that, after experiencing three frustrating evasions, "we will have to find a way to hem them in as they do in playing checkers." Unfortunately, that would require building and launching a whole new fleet of cases. Smith expected that Washington had "gotten quite enough of the game," but Washington surprised him. They had only recently resumed direct communication and Washington was now more directly engaged than he had been since the initial stages of their two-year-old project. Perhaps a tweak of strategy would help, Washington suggested. "Would it not change the complexion of things," Washington asked Smith in another February 24 letter, "if a case were . . . founded upon an attempt to vote for a member of Congress?" "I believe there is a way to win," Washington insisted, "or at least put the Supreme Court in an awkward position." He was the only one, frankly, who seemed energized by the defeats. Defiantly, he insisted that "we must not cease our efforts."[37]

Washington had lifted Smith from a deep depression. His letter, to which Smith replied on February 26, "had the effect of making me more cheerful over the result of our recent decision." Smith had feared he would have to "sacrifice almost everything to have a chance to . . . bring the court to a fair decision, and I am glad you think the same way as to the necessity of continuing the fight." He agreed with Washington that their new case should question a black man's exclusion from the 1902 federal elections. He had, after all, avoided such a "political question" in *Giles v. Teasley* I, II, and III and in *Giles v. Harris,* but such a case might force the Court "to invent some new excuse to escape us." With characteristic optimism, he concluded, "I cannot see how this case can fail."[38]

Smith laid out a preliminary strategy in a March 1 letter to Washington. He planned a situation where the Court would "be greatly embarrassed at least, to find a way to escape us." Embarrassing the Court would provide some small measure of satisfaction and might also help improve the lot of Alabama's African American community. Writing separately to Emmet Scott that same day, however, Smith conceded that he had "lost confidence" in the Court "as regards the interests of our people, but I don't think we should give up until we have exhausted every possible remedy." Smith and Washington continued to exchange strategic notes through the month of March. Washington suggested that they craft a case around Charles O. Harris, another of the Montgomery Post Office clerks (and another CMSAA member), while Smith preferred that they stick with Jackson Giles. His doggedness, Smith supposed, "will give the race a reputation for determination that it has not heretofore had." Vanity mattered too: "Giles would be perfectly willing to lose his vote for the prestige of having his name before the country."[39]

Washington, with Smith's new proposal in hand, postponed a final decision until he could meet with Smith personally. He did, however, insist that Smith oversee Dan Rogers's second trial and he also wanted him rescued from the penitentiary—again. Montgomery County had sent him to the Walls pending retrial. "I think we ought to get him back from the penitentiary," Washington wrote, and "he should not be left to feel that we have used him and now dropped him." If Smith could no longer represent Rogers personally, Washington intended that he have competent counsel. Meanwhile, a group of "leading colored people," including Jackson Giles, contacted Julius Sternfeld of the U.S. attorney's office about Rogers's case. Sternfeld, an assistant U.S. attorney, agreed to take the case in a private capacity and Giles was to keep Smith updated on Rogers's return to the county jail. Smith also asked Attorney General Massey Wilson to intervene with prison officials again: there remained the very real possibility that Rogers might meet an unfortunate and disastrous end. "Under no circumstances," Smith told Emmet Scott, "should we desert [Rogers] or even appear to do so."[40]

On March 31, Smith advised Washington that their next case, which would be their sixth, would cost another fifteen hundred dollars. This was not enough money, but at least Smith had learned to ask up front. "This is as close as I can possibly cut the figures," he explained. Jackson Giles, too, embraced the new project. A brief announcement in his *Montgomery Negro Pilot*, which was later reprinted in May by the *Washington Colored American*, explained that there would be two more cases, that Smith was the attorney, and, of course, that they needed money. The CMSAA "appeals to every Negro of America and every lover of liberty to give some money" for the renewed fight. And then, suddenly, three weeks later, on April 22, Washington brought down the curtain. Emmet Scott notified Smith that, after considering the proposed litigation, "it will not be possible for [Washington] to do anything in this matter now." For his part, Scott wanted Smith to know that he regretted "that this should be so." Smith asked for clarification and confessed to having had "a bad case of the blues since the Supreme Court sat down on me. . . . If, however, I could have the opportunity to force them to a decision, I would greatly relieve myself as much as the people of Alabama." No such opportunity ever came. It was over.[41]

Weeks earlier, the Supreme Court had finally heard the Virginia cases. On the morning of April 4, 1904, "swarms of negroes" arrived at the Supreme Court chamber in the U.S. Capitol. Men, women, and children "clustered about the door . . . in such numbers that the passageway was blocked." In their Sunday sermons D.C. pastors had encouraged their parishioners to attend, and by twelve o'clock, when the Court's doors finally swung open, the "double line of black spectators extended through the length of the Capitol and halfway across the rotunda." Even with all the seats filled and the chamber doors locked, "the crowd . . . did not appear to diminish to any appreciable extent."[42]

That afternoon, Wise insisted that Virginia's 1902 constitution did not exist because it was not ratified but "proclaimed" into effect. The new Virginia constitution, which he declared illegitimate, was also unconstitutional. Counsel for the state insisted that Wise's arguments were directed against the state, not state officials, violating an Eleventh Amendment prohibition that had figured prominently in the *Giles* cases. The arguments that day, according to the *Planet*, "rang down the curtain in the last act of the drama in this state." Wise had "both the law and the argument on his side, but spoke to men with deaf ears." The *Planet* regarded the event as nothing but a pro forma sham: The justices, according to editor John Mitchell, simply complied with "the forms of the law by listening to Mr. Wise's speech." But the throng that crowded the capitol felt differently and, according to a news wire account, offered "an enthusiastic reception for Mr. Wise in the rotunda . . . as soon as he had concluded." After so many Supreme Court disappointments over the previous decade, the *Colored American* explained, that "colored men everywhere [seem] to regard this case as their last hope—the final stand in the great struggle which they are waging for manhood rights in this country."[43]

Decisions in *Jones v. Montague* and *Selden v. Montague* were handed down on April 25. Both were defeats. These cases had begun in the fall of 1902, when John Wise sought an injunction against Virginia's Board of Canvassers to prevent them from reporting the 1902 election results. Chief Justice Melville Fuller, sitting as circuit justice, denied the petition. That election, Wise argued, was open only to voters eligible under Virginia's 1902 "disfranchising" constitution. Since that constitution was unconstitutional, the canvassers should have been enjoined from reporting the results. Wise was not asking the Court to order anyone registered; he was asking the Court to invalidate an election as well as a state constitution. This was similar to *Mills v. Green* (which sought to void the election for delegates to South Carolina's 1895 constitutional convention). The Fuller court *was not* going to break with one hundred years of precedent and invalidate an election. Never. *Mills v. Green* was the controlling precedent here, and that decision, so Justice Brewer wrote in *Jones v. Montague,* "compels a dismissal of the writ of error." The Court would not void Virginia's 1902 election. Even if it had been so inclined, Brewer concluded, the victors were already in office. "Under those circumstances," Brewer's terse, two-paragraph-long opinion concluded, "there is nothing but a moot case remaining, and the motion to dismiss must be sustained." *Selden* merited only a two-sentence per curiam declaration.[44]

Although the Virginia cases received far less consideration than the Alabama cases, the *Planet*'s John Mitchell wrote on April 30 that "the result was the same, however." Mitchell always viewed the antidisfranchisement litigation fatalistically, but he could not stave off his frustration. "When the Negro goes to the United States Supreme Court," he noted, "that tribunal says 'Go to Congress,'" but "when he goes to Congress, he is told to go back to the United States Supreme Court"—and that was "enough to set any man to 'cussing.'" He was not alone. Two springs had come and gone and with them six major disfranchisement cases from Alabama and Virginia. Yet the only thing the Court had made clear was its reluctance to settle the issue. It had gotten so that some grew willing to accept *any* firm decision. "It is of the utmost importance," Mitchell concluded, "that the problem . . . be fundamentally considered and solved by the federal judiciary." Only if the public were to have an unequivocal Supreme Court declaration, the *Chautau-*

quan news magazine cried, only then "would come acceptance of the status quo and the cessation of a disturbing and unpleasant agitation." Very many Americans, it was clear, wanted to either hide behind, or be led by, the Supreme Court. Those who wanted to temporize with disfranchisement, and those who vowed to kill it as well, wanted the definitive judicial solution that the Court refused to provide.[45]

Even though he was abandoning the antidisfranchisement litigation, for the time being at least, Washington did not want Smith to believe that his work had been for naught. In June 1904, he reported that "a half dozen colored men in Montgomery County have been summoned for jury duty" and the sheriff had personally served the papers. "When one colored man asked a white man why it was that they were just now beginning to summon colored men, Washington recounted, the "white man replied that Negroes' names had been put into the box all along . . . but it seems that they were a long time coming out." The same thing had happened that summer in Dallas County, Alabama, where officials had summonsed Selma blacks for jury duty, the "first time since reconstruction days that the names of Negroes [had] appeared on a jury list in Dallas." Black Alabamians, Washington wanted Smith to know, "feel much elated and very grateful to you." For the rest of that summer of 1904, Smith continued to entertain the idea of a sixth Alabama disfranchisement case. Washington, though, had grown reluctant to spend more money, but he put Smith in touch with Albert Pillsbury, who was willing to consider having his own friends sponsor a new case. Nothing ever came of their discussions. But Jackson Giles, for one, wanted to keep up the fight, and by late June he had joined the executive council of James Hayes's National Negro Suffrage League, though nothing seems to have come of his activities there.[46]

Smith's victory in *Rogers v. Alabama* brought positive change to the state's juries, and the primary beneficiary was Dan Rogers himself. It seems that Rogers had actually committed the crime; there was never any suggestion that he had not stabbed and killed Ben Howard. Still, he deserved a fair trial with a fair jury. His retrial took place on December 20, 1904, and he was found guilty of first-degree manslaughter (a lesser charge than his first conviction for second-degree murder). He was sentenced to five years in prison but could be released on October 20, 1908 (it was called "short time" in Alabama), for good behavior. Dan Rogers entered the Walls on January 1, 1905. Rogers was married, had three children, was thirty years old, stood five feet eight and a half inches tall, and weighed 160 pounds. Those were the few cursory facts recorded in the prison registry that New Year's Day and they are all that is known of the man who gave his name to one of the only two successful antidisfranchisement cases, and the only one that owed to the work of Wilford Smith, Booker T. Washington, and the CMSAA. Remarkably, Dan Rogers was never leased (or rather condemned) to private industry, nor was he ever reprimanded for bad behavior. Rogers walked out of the Walls as a free man on October 20, 1908. His Supreme Court victory in January 1904 was noteworthy in itself, but in a sadder, and more significant, aspect, it attested to the lost promise of consolidation.[47]

Walter L. Fleming's November 1901 letter to Governor William Jelks, in which he described the trouble with "rampant Republican acquaintances" at Columbia University, encapsulated the dilemma confronting disfranchisers and the disfranchised alike. That year, the courts' attitude toward disfranchisement was still undetermined. The disfranchisers could believe their schemes would survive judicial review and the disfranchised could believe that they would be struck down. The defenders of Alabama's 1901 constitution and all the other southern "disfranchising" constitutions could propound syllogistic arguments that because the new southern state constitutions did not disfranchise all blacks "at once and forever" they did not violate the U.S. Constitution. The question, for lawyers such as Wilford Smith and plaintiffs such as Jackson Giles, was whether the Court would endorse the southern states' clever claims. Tragically, the Court did just that.[48]

Few black leaders realized exactly what had happened in the *Giles* cases; it took a while for the bleak reality to set in. The Supreme Court had not upheld the new southern state constitutions. Instead, the Court did something far worse. Rather than solve the disfranchisement riddle, it left the issue in limbo. Disfranchisement was neither constitutional nor unconstitutional; blacks could bring suits, but the Court would refuse to make definitive rulings. If the disfranchisers wanted to believe their handiwork was safe, they could make that assumption. If some blacks wanted to feel all hope was lost, they were entirely justified. For some, like Wilford Smith, his Virginia counterparts, and dissenting Republican congressmen such as Edgar Dean Crumpacker of Indiana, the promise of justice remained alive, but just barely.

On January 29, 1904, just after *Rogers* was announced, New York's West Side Republican Club marked the occasion of William McKinley's birthday with a dinner. The event's toastmaster was none other than John S.

Wise, and the featured speaker was Congressman Crumpacker, who attained minor renown in the 1890s and early 1900s as the leading congressional critic of disfranchisement. Held in the Waldorf-Astoria Hotel's ballroom, the event was attended by several hundred Republicans who reveled in Crumpacker's denunciations of southern whites and their new state constitutions with their "grotesque grandfather clauses." "The unmistakable tendency in the South," Crumpacker said, was to reduce blacks "to a condition of permanent servility." The Indianan concluded with a warning "that this policy in the South is destined to bring our nation into grave danger; that this deplorable policy will bring upon us a great controversy which will threaten our very foundations."[49]

In the spring of 1904 the House of Representatives was confronted with an elections contest from South Carolina (Alexander Dantzler's challenge to U.S. Representative Asbury F. Lever). At the 1902 election, Dantzler, who was black, polled only 167 votes against Lever, but he challenged the result on account of South Carolina's 1895 "disfranchising" constitution. The House Elections Committee, in a move that rivaled the U.S. Supreme Court's antidisfranchisement case dodges, declared that Dantzler had not been elected but refused to say that Lever had. Thus Lever retained his seat. The committee chairman, James Mann of Illinois, explained in the official committee report that Congress was not the "proper forum" for adjudicating the Fifteenth Amendment. This was a curious turn indeed. The Supreme Court had only recently suggested that blacks look to Congress and state legislatures for help. Mann explained that Congress would not do anything about disfranchisement "pending a final settlement of the whole question . . . by the Supreme Court of the United States." Southern House members were elated and declared that the committee's decision "means the South is to be allowed to work out the negro problem without the political interference of Congress."[50]

Just over one month after the House of Representatives dismissed Alexander Dantzler's complaint, and three weeks after the Supreme Court disposed of the Virginia cases, the Louisiana Case, or rather cases, which had been brought by the Afro-American Council in David Ryanes's name, met their final, pathetic end. Bad lawyering blighted both *State ex rel. David Ryanes v. Jeremiah Gleason* I and II. The AAC's two Louisiana cases were ill conceived, hastily filed, and horribly managed. The second case did reach the Louisiana Supreme Court and, on April 25, 1904, that body made its ruling. Louisiana's 1898 "disfranchising" constitution had prescribed which actions at law were eligible for state supreme court appeals. Voter registration was not among them. Additionally, civil appeals to the state supreme court had to involve a value or sum of at least two thousand dollars. Ryanes's case made no such claim. There had to be a federal question involved for there to be a U.S. Supreme Court appeal, so the Louisiana Supreme Court did not have to try very hard to avoid federal questions. "As we know of no authority under which the jurisdiction here invoked can be exercised," Justice Francis A. Monroe wrote, "the motion to dismiss must prevail."[51]

The Virginians fought on, though their repeated defeats had tempered their spirit considerably. For all of the publicity and fund-raising involved in the Virginia litigation, *Jones v. Montague* and *Selden v. Montague* were the only antidisfranchisement Supreme Court cases ever to ever come from the Old Dominion, but they were not the last Virginia cases attempted. There were damages suits still pending and, in February 1905, the NEIAV announced plans for a new case. Once again, the plaintiffs asked for five-thousand-dollar judgments against individual elections officials, and the NEIAV resolved to maintain their fight "till the very foundation stones of the republic tremble."[52]

Wise and Hayes filed the new suit in Rev. John E. Brickhouse's name at Norfolk's U.S. Courthouse on June 9, 1905. *Brickhouse,* the last desperate gasp of the antidisfranchisement legal assault, never traveled far. The case demanded damages from election judges, C. T. Brooks and William Jessup, who had refused to allow Brickhouse to vote in Norfolk County at the November 1902 congressional election. Counsel for Brooks and Jessup managed to delay a federal court hearing until February 1907, when arguments were finally made before Judge Nathan Goff of the Fourth Circuit, the very same Nathan Goff who had heard *Mills v. Green* twelve years earlier.[53]

In all of the Virginia cases, John S. Wise stubbornly insisted on making "political questions" claims that could not succeed. He was just too concerned with settling old political scores to wage a proper voting rights battle. Also, he genuinely preferred that Congress deal with disfranchisement by reducing representation in the House because, in part, that would affect his old Democratic nemeses personally. But the precedent for elections contests, which was the Supreme Court decision in *Luther v. Borden,* was well established. For good or ill (and more often than not ill), political questions were the exclusive province of the legislative and executive branches.

In *Brickhouse,* Wise did not ask the court to overturn an election (as he had in *Jones v. Montague* and *Selden v. Montague*). Yet as his briefs and oral arguments always wandered into political questions, there was no surprise at Goff's ruling, other than the fact that it came from the judge who had enjoined South Carolina's elections registrars in 1895. When the South Carolina activists brought Goff a companion to *Mills v. Green* later that summer (*Gowdy v. Green*), they found that stare decisis bound him. The Fourth Circuit's review of *Mills* constrained Goff's ruling in *Gowdy. Brickhouse,* like *Gowdy,* involved a clergyman plaintiff and *Brickhouse,* like *Gowdy,* ended badly. Goff was bound far more tightly than he had been in 1895. "This court will not decree concerning the policy of public measures," Goff wrote, "nor will it pass on the expediency of the action of the legislative and executive departments of the government." Wise's argument had boiled down to a question of whether the state of Virginia had ever properly adopted the 1902 instrument. That, Goff continued, "is a political question, not to be disposed of by this court." The question of whether Virginia's constitution "is consistent with the requirements of the federal constitution," Goff explained, was a question for Congress and the president to answer. "In regard to such matters," he declared, "the courts will not take the initiative, but will await the action of the departments mentioned, and when they have acted will be bound by the conclusion they have reached." When he rejected John Brickhouse's prayer for relief, Nathan Goff, the judge who, in 1895 in South Carolina, gave antidisfranchisement activists their first victory, handed them their last defeat.[54]

With Goff's decision in *Brickhouse,* African Americans' pre-NAACP voting rights efforts effectively ended. One Virginia case technically remained alive, however: *Edgar Poe Lee v. John Barbour. Lee v. Barbour* had been one of the damages claims that James Hayes filed in December 1902 using generic suit forms. A trial date had been set for January 1903 and the defendants were served with their subpoenas, but the trial never happened. The matter languished until early 1912, when the district court stenographer in Richmond notified John Wise that the case would be dismissed on April 1. Wise returned the letter with a handwritten note: "Dear Sir: Let her go— Dead horse."[55]

Booker T. Washington dabbled in civil rights litigation until early in the next decade, though not in the voting rights field. In this period, he had begun separate covert efforts to use federal courts to end peonage and to fight segregation.

As for Wilford Smith, his relationship with Washington was limited to private matters in the years ahead and he remained in Washington's employ until the latter's death in 1915. He later handled legal affairs for Marcus Garvey, serving as corporate counsel for the Black Star line of Garvey's Universal Negro Improvement Association (UNIA), and for a brief time was technically in charge of the UNIA. In 1920, he sought but did not win the Republican nomination for a seat in the U.S. House representing Harlem. Smith never again worked in civil rights litigation, though he remained in active practice until at least the 1920s. By then he had returned to Texas. It is not known when or where he died.[56]

The grass-roots antidisfranchisement protests that preceded the modern civil rights movement were over, and the participants either faded away or moved on to other things. By the time that the last of the Virginia cases— *Brickhouse*—was dismissed, the newly founded NAACP had assumed the fore. With the NAACP's inception, and the birth of its famed Legal Defense Fund, the nature and fundamental character of civil rights activism and advocacy changed.

Because Montgomery, Alabama, was the stage for so many of the modern civil rights movement's epochal events, it is tempting to seek a connection to the antidisfranchisement activists, but there is none. By 1910, Montgomery's most vocal African American activists had all either faded away or left. Oklahoma (and that territory's "black towns") was a preferred destination for defeated and disillusioned black activists. J. W. Adams, the Montgomery dry-goods dealer, Booker T. Washington associate, and CMSAA treasurer, had moved there. Mississippi's Cornelius Jones had moved there too.

For a time, it seems, Jackson Giles joined with James Hayes and the National Negro Suffrage League, but the NNSL was short lived. Giles's work on behalf of the CMSAA ruined him financially and the strain evidently wrecked his marriage. Newspaper reports of Montgomery City Court proceedings from 1905 and 1906 show that Jackson and Mary Giles had instituted alimony proceedings, though no actual divorce is noted. Eventually, they reconciled, and by the 1920s they had joined the emigration to Oklahoma. They lived out their last days quietly on a small Muskogee County farm.[57]

Acknowledgments

I wish to begin by thanking Tony Freyer and Kari Frederickson for the innumerable kindnesses they have shown me over the years. And I wish to acknowledge the influence of several professors from years ago, people who inspired (but never pushed) me to do something more with my talents—Patricia Rose, Sally Hadden, Maxine Jones, Robert Rubanowice, and Valerie Conner.

My editor at Louisiana State University Press, Rand Dotson, has been very patient for the past several years and never once questioned why I felt the need to rewrite the book completely on an annual basis. I also want thank Michael Perman, who carefully examined each year's iteration as the outside reader for the press. And though they are unaffiliated with any press, Mike Fitzgerald and Neal Hughes graciously read and critiqued an entire draft at a very early stage. At the end, Christian McWhirter not only read but also thoughtfully and meticulously edited every page of the book.

As a graduate student at the University of Alabama, fellowships from the History Department and the university's Graduate Council kept me going at a critical stage, and I am grateful for the two faculty research grants I received from the University of West Alabama.

Whether in person or by mail, the staffs of several archives and libraries made my work much easier. I wish to publicly acknowledge the Alabama Department of Archives and History, Mississippi Department of Archives and History, Hoole Special Collections Library at the University of Alabama, Bounds Library of the University of Alabama School of Law, Samford University Library, Birmingham Public Library, Athens County Archive, University of New Orleans, New Orleans Public Library, National Archives Regional Facilities in Atlanta, Forth Worth, and Philadelphia, Tennessee State Library, Texas State Library, Library of Virginia, Virginia Historical Society, West Virginia University, Schomburg Center of the New York Public Library, and the reference desks and interlibrary loan coordinators for the University of Alabama, the University of West Alabama, and the Florida State University.

Finally, when I undertook to thank all of the others who had a hand in getting me here, I found that the list grew very long and very maudlin. So it's probably best that I simply list the friends, acquaintances, and graduate assistants who helped me in any substantive way (whether they led me to a source, read a draft, made copies, tracked down documents, sat with me at a microfilm reader, commiserated with me, or listened while I talked through an idea): Neal Hughes, Paul Pruitt, William Warren Rogers Sr., Norwood Kerr, Ricki Brunner, Ed Bridges, Pat Causey, Anna Bedsole, Sheila Limerick, John Ratliff, Kathy Edwards, Merrily Harris, Al Brophy, David Beito, Anita Yesho, Drew Walters, Andrew Huebner, Mark Boulton, Cinnamon Brown, Lesa Shaul, Christina Barnes Huckabee, Joe Danielson, and Arlene Royer.

At the University of West Alabama, I've enjoyed the unflagging support of number of administrators. In particular, I wish to acknowledge the two deans I've worked under in the College of Liberal Arts, Dr. Patricia Beatty and Dr. Tim Edwards, Dr. David Taylor, Provost and Vice-President for Academic Affairs, and Dr. Richard Holland, University President.

Last, I wish to note the support and friendship of my late department chair, Dr. David Warren Bowen. Rarely did a day pass without David asking me if I'd finished the book yet, and he frequently followed that up with a brief lecture on the importance of finishing said task. I don't know whether he actually thought I might not or if he was just teasing, but it is source of deep regret that he did not live to see this book's completion.

A Note on Sources

In economy's interest, I have foregone a formal bibliography. Nevertheless, there are source materials used in this study which require some brief comment.

I did not really understand why I have spent nearly ten years on this project until I sat down to write this essay on sources. And so I thought about how it began and how it is that I birthed a book from a hastily prepared epilogue to a master's thesis on Alabama's 1901 constitutional convention.

That thesis arose from a single line in C. Vann Woodward's *Origins of the New South, 1877–1913,* which I first encountered in the fall of 1997. Explaining how the southern disfranchisers "got away with it," Woodward identified a linkage between U.S. overseas expansion and disfranchisement and segregation and tied it all together with characteristic elegance. He wrote (at page 326): "With the sections in rapport, the work of writing the white man's law for Asiatic and Afro-American went forward simultaneously." That one phrase stuck in my head, and my small project eventually became a larger study of Alabama disfranchisers' oft-expressed concerns about federal intervention—whether from the federal courts, the Republican Party, Congress, or all three. As I tutored myself in Alabama history and southern history, and the history of Alabama's 1901 constitution, book after book offered various fleeting descriptions of the same anecdote: how Thomas Goode Jones, the judge Booker T. Washington got appointed to the U.S. district court ruled against the plaintiff in a voting rights case that Washington himself had financed—*Giles v. Harris.* No one ever discussed it in any great detail, and neither did I, and I was satisfied to tack a version of the tale onto my thesis as an interesting and mildly ironic epilogue.

As I read more deeply and more broadly into all of the southern states' disfranchisement campaigns, I came across more stories like the one about Booker T. Washington and Thomas Goode Jones. There were a handful from Mississippi, one from Louisiana, three from South Carolina, and two from Virginia, and though scholars often alluded to these efforts, none had ever investigated them in any detail. So I decided to correct that, and in a few years' time I'd produced a dissertation that juxtaposed the southern disfranchisers against these early voting rights activists.

Subsequent to my dissertation defense, and after Louisiana State University Press took this manuscript under consideration, I chose to give the disfranchisement era voting rights activists a book of their own. Now that I have completed that book, I can tell you why no one wrote about this subject on this scale ever before: It is hard. Just as most earlier references to these activists and their test cases are pushed to the margins and acknowledged only in passing (if at all) in brief paragraphs or discursive notes, the source materials themselves are also often set aside. The information exists, and in very traditional places, but it must be mined from aged and forgotten court records, from fragmentary mentions in newspapers and magazines, from a letter or two in widely scattered manuscript collections, and from the footnotes and marginalia of other people's books and articles. So for ten years I've obsessively gleaned information and amassed material from which to construct a complete narrative—sometimes in big chunks but almost always in tiny bits.

The one major source I could rely upon presented a different sort of problem, that of too much information. Booker T. Washington's papers are the one indispensable source for anyone who wishes to examine black civil rights protests during this period. Nearly everyone with a protest to make or a criticism to lodge sent something about it to Booker T. Washington. If they did not correspond directly with either him or his secretary, Emmet Scott, someone else probably either discussed the matter behind their backs or on their behalf. Further, white segregationists, disfranchisers, and social reformers also corresponded endlessly with the Wizard of Tuskegee and the result is a massive trove that scholars still have only barely touched. Louis R. Harlan published fourteen edited volumes of *The Papers of Booker T. Washington* for the University of Illinois Press, but that set only includes a fraction of this vast collection. Thus I also relied upon the originals housed at the Library of Congress, available on about four hundred microfilm reels. In the notes, I have cited to the location where I first encountered an item, though many of the originals I note may also appear in the edited volumes. There is also another large collection of Washington's papers at Tuskegee University, but despite several years' of requests, I was never allowed access to them. It is to be hoped that they soon will be available for researchers' use again.

Beyond their sheer volume, Booker T. Washington's papers are time-consuming because of how he operated. Louis Harlan's indexing and cross-referencing, and the Library of Congress' recently updated finding aids, can only carry a researcher part way to their destination. Washington was so cagy, took such care to control his friends, associates, and informants, that historians find themselves quickly drawn into a thicket. One correspondent will know part of the story, and his or her letters will lead to a second participant and another piece of the tale, and then often to a third and so forth. Then a new topic or a new figure appears, often from a passing mention, and you realize that the correspondence files maintained at Tuskegee during Washington's lifetime are something akin to a rabbit warren. You come to appreciate just how great Louis Harlan's task was, and what a wonderful contribution he made to American history.

Louis Harlan is where anyone who desires to investigate any aspect of Washington's life and career must begin. Beyond the papers, there are the two volumes of biography Harlan produced in the 1970s and 1980s. Let me make clear that I do not agree with Harlan's portrayal of Washington, or the portrayals that come from most other scholars, but the craftsmanship on display in *The Making of a Black Leader, 1856–1901* (New York: Oxford University Press, 1972) and *The Wizard of Tuskegee, 1901–1915* (New York: Oxford University Press, 1983) is nothing short of masterful. I can also recommend another major biography of Washington that has only just appeared, Robert J. Norrell's *Up from History: The Life of Booker T. Washington* (Cambridge: Harvard University Press, 2009). Norrell's book is an accessible and provocative revisionist study—and a needed one—with which any future Booker T. Washington scholar must contend.

No manuscript collection other than Booker T. Washington's yielded more than a handful of useful items, but this book could not have been completed without materials found in the Whitefield McKinlay Papers, which are included in the Carter G. Woodson Collection at the Library of Congress, the Nathan Goff Papers at West Virginia University, the Oliver Wendell Holmes Jr. Papers at the Harvard University Law School, the Jones-Sadler Family Papers at the Schomburg Center of the New York Public Library, and the official correspondence of a host of governors and state agency heads in both Mississippi and Alabama, maintained by the Mississippi Department of Archives and History and the Alabama Department of Archives and History.

Court records, obviously, ground this study. Published opinions are widely used here, of course, but anyone who attempts to write legal or constitutional history must also engage the actual pleadings and briefs filed in lower and appellate courts. The Alabama, Mississippi, South Carolina, Tennessee, and Texas supreme court records have been preserved in state repositories and are open to researchers (and woefully underused). In some instances, files for a span of years or for a particular case have been lost (as was the case with the South Carolina and Texas cases I attempted to locate). Mississippi's have been indexed in a searchable database and are the easiest to locate. Alabama's and Tennessee's require a little more time and effort.

Local court records, when they can be found, are just as valuable. The Alabama cases that comprise the bulk of the foregoing narrative, with one exception, originated in the city court for Montgomery, Alabama. None of the city court records for this period survive. Conversely, the New Orleans cases from the Orleans Parish Civil District Court I examine have all survived and are housed in the New Orleans Public Library. Small towns and rural counties typically maintain their records in their county courthouses and locating those can be a touch-and-go proposition. Those with active local historical societies, however, have often established county archives that are open to researchers. For purposes of this study, the Limestone County Archive in Athens, Alabama, was a wonderful resource, and similar facilities should not be overlooked.

As one moves up the appellate and jurisdictional ladder, records collections grow larger. Thus federal court records require extra effort, not because they are inaccessible but because one cannot locate anything in them without the assistance of the skilled archivists of the NARA's regional facilities. The effort is entirely worthwhile, however, especially regarding U.S. district courts and the circuit courts of appeal, because those files will often contain correspondence between judges, attorneys, and court officials. Finally, the records of the United States Supreme Court are extensive and have been microfilmed for scholars who wish to avail themselves of this rich and underutilized resource. The microfilm collection, titled "Records and Briefs of the United States Supreme Court," is available at most schools of law. The Supreme Court justices themselves have all left behind personal papers which typically contain a great deal of information about the Court itself. Ultimately, only one justice's papers were of use to me here—those of Oliver Wendell Holmes Jr.

As for the business of disfranchisement, only two states, Alabama and Virginia, maintained a stenographic record of what they did and why. Accordingly, no one who studies the disfranchisement era should ignore the

Official Proceedings of the Constitutional Convention of the State of Alabama, May 21st, 1901, to September 3rd, 1901 (Wetumpka, Ala.: Wetumpka Printing, 1941) and the *Report of the Proceedings and Debates of the Constitution Convention of the State of Virginia, Held in the City of Richmond June 12, 1901 to June 26, 1902* (Richmond: Hermitage Press, 1906).

Studying the other disfranchising states that appear in this book is more difficult, and for those one must rely upon the official journals kept in each state (which are only good for the most rudimentary facts and figures) and the coverage provided by state newspapers. For starters, see *The Convention of '98. A Complete Work on the Greatest Political Event in Louisiana's History, and a Sketch of the Men Who Composed It, Together with a Historical Review of the Conventions of the Past, and the General Assembly Which Called the Constitutional Convention of 1898* (New Orleans: William E. Myers, 1898); *Journal of the House of Representatives of the State of Mississippi at a Regular Session Thereof, Convened in the City of Jackson, Jan. 7, 1890* (Jackson: R. H. Henry, 1890); *Journal of the Proceedings of the Constitutional Convention of the State of Mississippi, Begun at the City of Jackson on August 12, 1890, and Concluded November 1, 1890* (Jackson: E. I. Martin, 1890); *Journal of the House of Representatives of the General Assembly of the State of North Carolina at its Session of 1899* (Raleigh: Edwards & Broughton and E. M. Uzzell, 1899). For these states, scholars also must rely upon newspaper accounts of what transpired in the convention halls. While the conventions examined here (and North Carolina's 1899 legislature) opted against complete transcriptions of their debates, their doors were not closed to the public. Daily newspapers provided extensive coverage of the proceedings. For Mississippi, one should turn to the *Jackson Daily Clarion-Ledger;* for South Carolina, Columbia's *State* and the *Charleston News and Courier.* For Louisiana, all three of New Orleans' major dailies (the *Daily Picayune,* the *Daily States,* and the *Times-Democrat*) are useful; and for North Carolina, the *Raleigh News and Observer* was remarkably thorough. Daily newspapers must also be consulted when studying Alabama and Virginia. For Alabama, see the *Montgomery Daily Advertiser, Montgomery Journal, Birmingham Age-Herald, Birmingham Daily Ledger,* and *Mobile Daily Register.* For Virginia, see the *Richmond Times, Richmond Dispatch,* and *Washington Post.*

There are few published books that treat disfranchisement extensively, but several should be consulted by anyone who wishes to understand the subject. The best are V. O. Key, *Southern Politics in State and Nation* (New York: Knopf, 1949); Malcolm Cook McMillan, *Constitutional Development in Alabama : A Study in Politics, the Negro, and Sectionalism* (Chapel Hill: University of North Carolina Press, 1955); Albert B. Kirwan, *Revolt of the Rednecks: Mississippi Politics, 1876–1925* (Lexington: University of Kentucky Press, 1951); J. Morgan Kousser, *The Shaping of Southern Politics: Suffrage Restriction and the Establishment of the One-Party South, 1880–1910* (New Haven: Yale University Press, 1974); Wythe W. Holt, *Virginia's Constitutional Convention of 1901–1902* (New York: Garland, 1990); and Michael Perman, *Struggle for Mastery: Disfranchisement in the South, 1888–1908* (Chapel Hill: University of North Carolina Press, 2001). There are other studies that address disfranchisement and the disfranchisement era, of course, but any list of them will quickly devolve into pedantry.

This study could not have accomplished without years of vision-damaging toil in periodical sources—newspapers, opinion journals, and magazines. As was noted in the introduction, periodicals are often the only place where any record of these events remains. I consulted a large number of publications, a number of which were obscure niche and religious publications. These included (alphabetically) the *Albany Law Journal, American Law Review, American Lawyer, Andover Review, Arena, Atlantic Monthly, Century Illustrated Magazine, Chautauquan, Christian Advocate, Christian Observer, Congregationalist, Congregationalist and Christian World, Current Literature, Edinburgh Review, Frank Leslie's Popular Monthly, Friend's Intelligencer, Forum, Gunton's Magazine, Harlequin, Harper's Bazaar, Independent, International Monthly, Lippincott's Monthly Magazine, McClure's Magazine, Methodist Review, The Nation, New Englander and Yale Review, New York Evangelist, New York Observer and Chronicle, North American Review, Outlook, Review of Reviews, South Atlantic Quarterly, Watchman, World's Work,* and *Zion's Herald.*

When I began work a decade ago, I relied upon bound copies of regional-, state-, and county-level newspapers before moving on to microfilm versions, huddling over grainy images from county newspapers housed at the Alabama Department of Archives and History and the Birmingham Public Library or that came on loan to the University of Alabama's Amelia Gayle Gorgas Library or the Julia S. Tutwiler Library at the University of West Alabama. However, a revolution has occurred over these ten years as digital databases proliferated. I availed myself of them freely. Scholars now can peruse many of these sources in a virtual environment, one that allows them to exceed the physical capacity of the human eye and mind with a simple keyword search. The sheer volume of information that is now available (and it is constantly expanding) and the ease of accessing it has made it possible to reclaim this story from forgotten memory and faster than I otherwise might have. Digitization will in future years force us to rethink a great deal about what we "know"—and this applies, I think, to every historical subfield. Additionally, the national newspapers that everyone uses are every bit as useful as advertised. The *New York Times, Washington Post, Atlanta Constitution, New Orleans Daily Picayune, Chicago Record-Herald, Chicago Inter Ocean, San Francisco Call,* and other similar big-city papers published *something* about just about everything that was happening in the United States. One cannot stop there, however. To make newspapers "work," to overcome the particular perils that inhere in their use, scholars must also delve into lesser-known national publications as well as those published for regional, state-level, and small-town and rural-county audiences. Look at the foreign-language titles, the African American titles, the titles published by and for women, and by all means the religious newspapers. At last count, I had cited 213 separate newspapers in the notes for this book, and I consulted approximately 300 more that either had nothing relevant to offer or simply did not make it into these pages.

I used every available African American periodical that covered the time period in question here. Useful journals included the *A.M.E. Church Review,* the *A.M.E.Z. Quarterly Review, Colored American Magazine,* and *Southern Workman.* Few complete or even extensive runs of African American newspapers have survived, but those that have offer superb coverage. Again, in most instances they are the only way to find something akin to complete coverage of these early civil rights protests and initiatives. For long runs, I relied upon the *Boston Guardian, Richmond Planet, Washington Bee, Washington Colored American, New York Age, Cleveland (Ohio) Gazette, Savannah Tribune, Raleigh Gazette, Mobile Southern Watchman, New Orleans Southwestern Christian Advocate, Broad Ax* (published at different times in Salt Lake City, Chicago, and St. Paul), and *St. Paul Appeal.* For shorter runs, I relied upon the following titles (listed by state): (Alabama) *Anniston Union-Leader, Bay Minnette American Banner, Birmingham Free Speech, Birmingham Truth, Kempsville Eagle, Troy Afro-American Advocate, Tuscumbia American Star,* and *Tuskegee Alabama Headlight;* (Georgia) *Atlanta Independent, Atlanta Voice of the People;* (Indiana) *Indianapolis Freeman* and *Indianapolis Recorder;* (Kansas) *Kansas City American Citizen* and *Wichita Searchlight;* (Louisiana) *New Orleans Crusader* and *New Orleans Republican Courier;* (Maryland) *Baltimore Afro-American Ledger;* (Missouri) *Kansas City Rising*

Son and *St. Louis Palladium;* (Nebraska) *Omaha Enterprise;* (North Carolina) *Littleton True Reformer;* and (Wisconsin) *Milwaukee Wisconsin Weekly Advocate.* I also consulted the newspaper clippings files maintained and microfilmed by Hampton Institute (now Hampton University) and Tuskegee Institute (now Tuskegee University), though their coverage is best for topics from the period 1910 forward.

Any attempt to fashion a complete list of useful books would quickly grow tiresome, so I must confine myself to those which were absolutely indispensable, whether because they captured the general atmosphere of the time or because they fleshed out some aspect of the larger story. With regard to the field of African American history, see, for example, J. Clay Smith, *Emancipation: The Making of the Black Lawyer, 1844–1944* (Philadelphia: University of Pennsylvania Press, 1993); Neil McMillen, *Dark Journey: Black Mississippians in the Age of Jim Crow* (Champaign: University of Illinois Press, 1991); Vernon L. Wharton, *The Negro in Mississippi, 1865–1900* (New York: Harper Torchbooks, 1965); Jane Dailey, *Before Jim Crow: The Politics of Race in Post-Emancipation Virginia* (Chapel Hill: University of North Carolina Press, 2000); Helen Edmonds, *The Negro and Fusion Politics in North Carolina, 1894–1901* (Chapel Hill: University of North Carolina Press, 1951); Glenda Gilmore, *Gender and Jim Crow: Women and the Politics of White Supremacy in North Carolina, 1896–1920* (Chapel Hill: University of North Carolina Press, 1996); Leon F. Litwack, *Trouble in Mind: Black Southerners in the Age of Jim Crow* (New York: Alfred A. Knopf, 1998); James M. McPherson, *The Abolitionist Legacy: From Reconstruction to the NAACP* (Princeton: Princeton University Press, 1975); August Meier, *Negro Thought in America, 1880–1915: Racial Ideologies in the Age of Booker T. Washington* (Ann Arbor: University of Michigan Press, 1969); and Xi Wang, *The Trial of Democracy: Black Suffrage and Northern Republicans, 1860–1910* (Athens: University of Georgia Press, 1997).

There were also a number of significant African American autobiographies, biographies, and memoirs I found useful. See, for example, the Harlan biographies of Booker T. Washington mentioned above; John Roy Lynch, *Reminiscences of an Active Life: The Autobiography of John Roy Lynch,* ed. John Hope Franklin) (Chicago: University of Chicago Press, 1970); Ann Field Alexander, *Race Man: The Rise and Fall of the "Fighting Editor," John Mitchell, Jr.* (Charlottesville: University of Virginia Press, 2002); Mary Frances Berry, *My Face Is Black Is True: Callie House and the Struggle for Ex-Slave Reparations* (New York: Alfred A. Knopf, 2005); Thomas O. Fuller, *Twenty Years in*

Public Life, 1890–1910 (Nashville: National Baptist Publishing Board, 1910); Benjamin R. Justesen, *George Henry White: An Even Chance in the Race of Life* (Baton Rouge: Louisiana State University Press, 2001); Henry Damon Davidson, *Inching Along* (Nashville: National Publications, 1944); and John F. Marszalek, *A Black Congressman in the Age of Jim Crow: South Carolina's George Washington Murray* (Gainesville: University Press of Florida, 2006).

With regard to constitutional history, see Michael J. Klarman, *From Jim Crow to Civil Rights: The Supreme Court and the Struggle for Equality* (New York: Oxford University Press, 2004); J. Morgan Kousser, *Colorblind Injustice: Minority Voting Rights and the Undoing of the Second Reconstruction* (Chapel Hill: University of North Carolina Press, 1999); Albert W. Alschuler, *Law Without Values: The Life, Work, and Legacy of Justice Holmes* (Chicago: University of Chicago Press, 2000); Charles A. Lofgren, *The Plessy Case: A Legal-Historical Interpretation* (New York: Oxford University Press, 1987); Loren P. Beth, *The Development of the American Constitution, 1877–1917* (New York: Harper & Row, 1971); Alexander M. Bickell and Benno C. Schmidt Jr., *History of the Supreme Court of the United States: The Judiciary and Responsible Government, 1910–1921* (New York: Macmillan, 1984); Owen Fiss, *History of the Supreme Court of the United States: Troubled Beginnings of the Modern State, 1888–1910* (New York: Macmillan, 1993); Gerard Gewalt, ed., *The New High Priests: Lawyers in Post–Civil War America* (Westport, Conn.: Greenwood Press, 1984); Alexander Keyssar, *The Right to Vote: The Contested History of Democracy in the United States* (New York: Basic Books, 2000); Edward A. Purcell Jr., *Brandeis and the Progressive Constitution: Erie, the Judicial Power, and the Politics of the Federal Courts in Twentieth-Century America* (New Haven: Yale University Press, 2000); Philippa Strum, *The Supreme Court and "Political Questions": A Study in Judicial Evasion* (Tuscaloosa: University of Alabama Press, 1974); and G. Edward White, *Justice Oliver Wendell Holmes: Law and the Inner Self* (New York: Oxford University Press, 1993).

Many titles in the forgoing paragraphs could also be classed as southern history, and to those add C. Vann Woodward, *Origins of the New South, 1877–1913* (Baton Rouge: Louisiana State University Press, 1951); C. Vann Woodward, *The Strange Career of Jim Crow*, 3rd ed. (New York: Oxford University Press, 1974); Edward L. Ayers, *The Promise of the New South* (New York: Oxford University Press, 1992); Stephen Cresswell, *Multiparty Politics in Mississippi, 1877–1902* (Jackson: University Press of Mississippi, 1995); Stephen Cresswell, *Rednecks, Redeemers, and Race: Mississippi after Reconstruc-*

tion, 1877–1917 (Jackson: University of Mississippi Press, 2006); Paul D. Escott, *Many Excellent People: Power and Privilege in North Carolina, 1850–1900* (Chapel Hill: University of North Carolina Press, 1985); John Hope Franklin, ed., *Race and History: Selected Essays, 1938–1988* (Baton Rouge: Louisiana State University Press, 1989); Sheldon Hackney, *Populism to Progressivism in Alabama* (Princeton: Princeton University Press, 1969); William Ivy Hair, *Bourbonism and Agrarian Protest: Louisiana Politics 1877–1900* (Baton Rouge: Louisiana State University Press, 1969); William Ivy Hair, *Carnival of Fury: Robert Charles and the New Orleans Race Riot of 1900* (Baton Rouge: Louisiana State University Press, 1976); Stephen Kantrowitz, *Ben Tillman and the Reconstruction of White Supremacy* (Chapel Hill: University of North Carolina, 2000); Jack Temple Kirby, *Darkness at the Dawning: Race and Reform in the Progressive South* (Philadelphia: J. B. Lippincott, 1972); William Warren Rogers Sr., *The One-Gallused Rebellion: Agrarianism in Alabama, 1865–1896* (Baton Rouge: Louisiana State University Press, 1970); and Rebecca J. Scott, *Degrees of Freedom: Louisiana and Cuba after Slavery* (Cambridge: Harvard University Press, 2005).

No previous work has examined the antidisfranchisement cases as an event unto themselves, and neither can I identify any that completely capture the various state-level campaigns. I have been consistently amazed over the past several years that no one else has told this story, given that it was hiding in plain sight all the while. But I encountered a handful of theses and dissertations that came close, and while none of these offers anything like a "complete" portrait of black voting rights activism in the disfranchisement era, they did provide invaluable signposts along the way. I wish to recognize a few of the more outstanding ones and their authors here: John Sparks, "Alabama Negro Reaction to Disfranchisement, 1901–1904" (master's thesis, Samford University, 1973); Oscar S. Dooley, "The Disfranchisement of the Negro in the South: The Changing Sentiment of the North from 1870 to 1910" (master's thesis, University of Mississippi, 1936); Lewis H. Reece IV, "Pure Despotism: South Carolina's Route to Disfranchisement, 1867–1895" (Ph.D. diss., Bowling Green State University, 2001); Robert E. Martin, "Negro Disfranchisement in Virginia" (master's thesis, Howard University, 1938); and Justin Johannes Behrend, "Losing the Vote: Natchez, Mississippi, 1867–1910" (master's thesis, California State University, Northridge, 2000). Those were not the only useful ones I found; there are thirty or forty cited in this book. But the larger point is this: Do not neglect the mass of theses and dissertations moldering on university library bookshelves, especially those from the early twentieth century. They may seem obsolete, but it is rare to find one that hasn't anything useful to say.

Finally, though economy prohibited its inclusion here, I have prepared a complete, formal bibliography and will share it with anyone who wishes to utilize it. A copy has also been deposited in the Julia Tutwiler Library at the University of West Alabama in Livingston.

Notes

NOTD	*New Orleans Times-Democrat*
NYT	*New York Times*
OPCDC	Orleans Parish Civil District Court
OPCDCR	Records of the Orleans Parish Civil District Court, New Orleans Public Library
PQD	Political Questions Doctrine
Proceedings	*Official Proceedings of the Constitutional Convention of the State of Alabama, May 21st 1901, to September 3rd, 1901* (Wetumpka, Ala.: Wetumpka Printing, 1941)
RASC	Records of the Alabama Supreme Court
RBUSSC	Records and Briefs of the United States Supreme Court
RFC	Records of the Fourth U.S. Circuit Court of Appeal
RMSC	Records of the Mississippi Supreme Court
RNO	*Raleigh News and Observer*
RP	*Richmond Planet*
RUSDC	Records of the United States District Courts
SFC	*San Francisco Call*
SPA	*St. Paul Appeal*
ST	*Savannah Tribune*
SWCA	*New Orleans Southwestern Christian Advocate*
USCCDSC	United States Circuit Court for the District of South Carolina
USCCEDL	United States Circuit Court for the Eastern District of Louisiana
USCCEDT	United States Circuit Court for the Eastern District of Tennessee
USCCEDV	United States Circuit Court for the Eastern District of Virginia
USCCMDA	United States Circuit Court for the Middle District of Alabama
USCCWDNC	United States Circuit Court for the Western District of North Carolina
WB	*Washington Bee*
WCA	*Washington Colored American*
WP	*Washington Post*

PROLOGUE

1. *Giles v. Harris,* 189 U.S. 475 (1903).

2. *BG,* 2 May 1903; "The Alabama Decision," *Colored American Magazine* 6 July 1903, 536; Richard Pildes, "Democracy, Anti-Democracy, and the Canon," *Constitutional Commentary* 17, no. 2 (Summer 2000): 296.

3. *Indianapolis Freeman,* 2 May 1903; *Indianapolis Freeman,* 9 May 1903.

4. Algernon Sidney Crapsey, *A Constitutional Defense of the Negro: By Algernon Sidney*

Crapsey; delivered at a mass meeting of citizens in the Metropolitan A.M.E. Church, Washington, D.C., December 15, 1901 (Washington, D.C.: A. S. Crapsey, 1901), 7; Alexander A. Walters, "Civil and Political Status of the Negro," in *Proceedings of the National Negro Conference,* 1909 (New York: Arno Press and New York Times, 1969), 172.

5. Francis J. Grimké, "The Negro and His Citizenship," in *The Negro and the Elective Franchise,* ed. Archibald Grimké, Charles C. Cook, John Hope, John L. Love, Kelly Miller, and Francis J. Grimké, Occasional Papers no. 11, American Negro Academy (Washington, D.C.: American Negro Academy, 1905), 82–83.

6. Archibald H. Grimké, "Why Disfranchisement Is Bad," *Atlantic Monthly* 44, no. 1061 (July 1904): 75, 76; John Hope, "The Negro Vote in the States Whose Constitutions Have Not Been Specifically Revised," in Grimké et al., *Negro and the Elective Franchise,* 60.

7. Neil R. McMillen, *Dark Journey: Black Mississippians in the Age of Jim Crow* (Champaign: University of Illinois Press, 1990), 285; J. W. Hood, "The Enfranchisement of the Negro No Blunder," *Independent* 55, no. 2856 (27 August 1903): 2024.

8. Washington's address was published in the *Cleveland (Ohio) Journal,* 12 December 1903; Oswald Garrison Villard, "The Need of Organization," in *Proceedings of the National Negro Conference,* 1909 (New York: Arno Press and New York Times, 1969): 203–4.

9. Thurgood Marshall, foreword to J. Clay Smith's *Emancipation: The Making of the Black Lawyer, 1844–1944* (Philadelphia: University of Pennsylvania Press, 1993), xi.

10. See, for example, Gilbert Jonas, *Freedom's Sword: The NAACP and the Struggle Against Racism in America, 1909–1969* (New York: Routledge, 2005); Warren D. St. James, *NAACP: Triumphs of a Pressure Group, 1909–1980* (Smithtown, N.Y.: Exposition Press, 1980); Robert L. Jack, *History of the National Association for the Advancement of Colored People* (Boston: Meador, 1943).

11. W. E. B. Du Bois, "Politics and Industry" in *Proceedings of the National Negro Conference,* 1909 (New York: Arno Press and New York Times, 1969), 87; Villard, "Need of Organization," 203.

12. John Haynes Holmes, *The Disfranchisement of Negroes* (New York: National Association for the Advancement of Colored People, 1910), 16.

13. Herbert Hill, "A Record of Negro Disfranchisement" (article offprint), *Midstream: A Quarterly Jewish Review* (Autumn 1957): 49. See also Walter White, "The Negro and the Supreme Court," *Harper's Monthly* 162, no. 968 (January 1931): 243; Samuel Abrahams, "Negro Disfranchisement," *Negro History Bulletin* 12, no. 5 (February 1949): 103.

14. *BAH,* 22 June 1915; *BAH,* 27 June 1915; *Guinn v. U.S.,* 238 U.S. 347 (1915).

15. *WP,* 1 July 1901. The best-known and most thorough examinations of disfranchisement may be found in (chronologically) William Alexander Mabry, "The Disfranchisement of the Negro in the South" (Ph.D. diss., Duke University, 1933); William Alexander Mabry, "Negro Suffrage and Fusion Rule in North Carolina," *North Carolina Historical Review* 12, no. 2 (April 1935): 79–102; William Alexander Mabry, "'White Supremacy' and the North Carolina Suffrage Amendment," *North Carolina Historical Review* 13, no. 1 (January 1936): 1–24; William Alexander Mabry, "Louisiana Politics and the Grandfather Clause," *North Carolina Historical Review* 13, no. 4 (October 1936): 290–310; William Alexander Mabry, "Ben Tillman Disfranchised the Negro," *South Atlantic Quarterly* 37, no. 2 (April 1938): 170–83; William Alexander Mabry, "Disfranchisement of the Negro in Mississippi," *Journal of*

Southern History 4, no. 3 (August 1938): 318–33; William Alexander Mabry, *The Negro in North Carolina Politics since Reconstruction,* in Historical Papers of the Trinity College Historical Society, ser. 23 (Durham, N.C.: Duke University Press, 1940); V. O. Key, *Southern Politics in State and Nation* (New York: Alfred A. Knopf, 1949); C. Vann Woodward, *Origins of the New South, 1877–1913* (Baton Rouge: Louisiana State University Press, 1951); Albert Kirwan, *Revolt of the Rednecks: Mississippi Politics, 1876–1925* (Lexington: University of Kentucky Press, 1951); Malcolm Cook McMillan, *Constitutional Development in Alabama, 1798–1901: A Study in Politics, the Negro, and Sectionalism* (Chapel Hill: University of North Carolina Press, 1955); C. Vann Woodward, *The Strange Career of Jim Crow,* 3rd rev. ed. (New York: Oxford University Press, 1974); J. Morgan Kousser, *The Shaping of Southern Politics: Suffrage Restriction and the Establishment of the One-Party South, 1880–1910* (New Haven: Yale University Press, 1974); and Michael Perman, *Struggle for Mastery: Disfranchisement in the South, 1888–1908* (Chapel Hill: University of North Carolina Press, 2001). Other significant book-length studies that either address or examine disfranchisement include (chronologically) Sheldon Hackney, *Populism to Progressivism in Alabama* (Princeton: Princeton University Press, 1969); Wythe Holt, *Virginia's Constitutional Convention of 1901–1902* (New York: Garland, 1990); Glenda Elizabeth Gilmore, *Gender and Jim Crow: Women and the Politics of White Supremacy in North Carolina, 1896–1920* (Chapel Hill: University of North Carolina Press, 1996); and Glenn Feldman, *The Disfranchisement Myth: Poor Whites and Suffrage Restriction in Alabama* (Athens: University of Georgia Press, 2004).

16. *Mobile Southern Watchman,* 5 October 1901.

CHAPTER ONE

1. "Petition of Robert Sproule," in "Lower Court Record," 1–4, *Robert Sproule v. R. A. Fredericks,* case 7005, MSC, RMSC, RG 32, Box 6060, MDAH.

2. "Address of Solomon S. Calhoon," *Journal of the Proceedings of the Constitutional Convention of the State of Mississippi, Begun at the City of Jackson on August 12, 1890, and Concluded on November 1, 1890* (Jackson: E. I. Martin, 1890), 702.

3. "Brief for Appellant," *Robert Sproule v. R. A. Fredericks.*

4. "Demurrer," "Judgement on Demurrer," "Amendment to Petition," "Defendant's Answer," "Contestant's Reply," and "Judgement," in "Lower Court Record," *Robert Sproule v. R. A. Fredericks,* 4–11.

5. John Henry Wallace, *The Senator from Alabama: A Romance of the Disfranchisement of the Negro and Including a Scathing Arraignment of the White House Social-Equality Policy* (New York: Neale, 1904), 172; Theodore Rosengarten, ed., *All God's Dangers: The Life of Nate Shaw* (New York: Alfred A. Knopf, 1974), 34; interview with Louis Hamilton, Fredericktown, Missouri, WPA Slave Narrative Project, Missouri Narratives, vol. 10, p. 146, Federal Writers Project, United States Works Projects Administration, Manuscript Division, Library of Congress, digital ID 100/150145. See also, for a discussion of Ned Cobb and others, Leon Litwack, *Trouble in Mind: Black Southerners in the Age of Jim Crow* (New York: Alfred A. Knopf, 1998), 363–64.

6. *Cook v. State,* 16 S.W. 471; 90 Tenn. 407 (1891). See also *Julius Cook v. State,* Records of the Tennessee Supreme Court, Tennessee State Library and Archives, Nashville; "Brief of L. B. Eaton, for Defendant," *Julius Cook v. State.* Eaton's brief was published and circulated

in pamphlet form as *The Unconstitutionality of the Dortch Law* (publishing information unknown).

7. "Brief for Appellant," *Robert Sproule v. R. A. Fredericks.*

8. "Brief of Appellee" and "Supplement to Appellee's Brief," *Robert Sproule v. R. A. Fredericks.*

9. *Sproule v. Fredericks,* 11 So. 472 (1892), 474–75. *Sproule v. Fredericks* is largely ignored in historical accounts. There has been no mention of it since the 1920s, when Jesse Thomas Wallace noted it in his University of Chicago doctoral dissertation and in a subsequent history of Mississippi African Americans. See Jesse Thomas Wallace, "How and Why Mississippi Eliminated the Negro from State Politics" (Ph.D. diss., University of Chicago, 1923), 36; and Jesse Thomas Wallace, *A History of the Negroes of Mississippi from 1865 to 1890* (Clinton, Miss.: n.p., 1927), 166.

10. See Lewis H. Reece IV, "Pure Despotism: South Carolina's Route to Disfranchisement, 1867–1895" (Ph.D. diss., Bowling Green State University, 2001), 226–62; Michael Perman, *Struggle for Mastery: Disfranchisement in the South, 1888–1908* (Chapel Hill: University of North Carolina Press, 2001), 91–115.

11. *Ex parte Lumsden,* 19 S.E. 749, 41 S.C. 553 (1894); *Butler v. Ellerbe,* 22 S.E. 425, 44 S.C. 256 (1895). The original case files for *Ex parte Lumsden* and *Butler v. Ellerbe* have been lost. See also W. Lewis Burke, "Killing, Cheating, Legislating, and Lying: A History of Voting Rights in South Carolina after the Civil War," *South Carolina Law Review* 57 (Summer 2006): 859–87.

12. *NYT,* 5 December 1894; *NYT,* 20 December 1894; *NYT,* 23 January 1895.

13. William J. Gaboury, "George Washington Murray and the Fight for Political Democracy in South Carolina," *Journal of Negro History* 62, no. 3 (July 1977): 262–66; John F. Marszalek, *A Black Congressman in the Age of Jim Crow: South Carolina's George Washington Murray* (Gainesville: University Press of Florida, 2006); "Editorial," *Outlook* 51, no. 8 (23 February 1895): 299; *Beaufort (S.C.) New South,* 7 March 1895, as cited in Reece, "Pure Despotism," 258.

14. Burke, "Killing, Cheating, Legislating, and Lying, 870–71.

15. *WP,* 13 March 1895; *Charleston (S.C.) Weekly News and Courier,* 12 October 1898; *Wiley v. Sinkler,* 179 U.S. 58 (1900); "Notes of Recent Decisions," *American Law Review* 35 (January/February 1901): 135–36.

16. Burke, "Killing, Cheating, Legislating, and Lying," 870.

17. For further information about suffrage restriction outside the South, see Mark Wahlgren Summers, *Party Games: Getting, Keeping, and Using Power in Gilded Age Politics* (Chapel Hill: University of North Carolina Press, 2004), 229–49; Morton Keller, *Affairs of State: Public Life in Late Nineteenth Century America* (Cambridge: Belknap Press, 1977), 522–31; George Haynes, "Educational Qualifications for the Suffrage in the United States," *Political Science Quarterly* 13 (1898): 495–513; John Barnett Knox, "Reduction of Representation in the South," *Outlook* 79 (21 January 1905): 171; Francis Parkman, "The Failure of Universal Suffrage," *North American Review* 127 (1878): 1–20; J. Morgan Kousser, *The Shaping of Southern Politics: Suffrage Restriction and the Establishment of the One-Party South, 1880–1910* (New Haven: Yale University Press, 1974), 250–57; Alexander Keyssar, *The Right to Vote: The Contested History of Democracy in the United States* (New York: Basic Books, 2000), 117–71; Dudley O. McGovney, *The American Suffrage Medley: The Need for a National Uniform Suffrage* (Chicago: Uni-

versity of Chicago Press, 1949), 59–79; Arthur W. Bromage, "Literacy and the Electorate," *American Political Science Review* 24, no. 4 (November 1930): 946–62; Leslie H. Fishel Jr., "The Negro in Northern Politics, 1870–1900," *Mississippi Valley Historical Review* 42, no. 3 (December 1955): 466–89; Fishel, "Northern Prejudice and Negro Suffrage, 1865–1870," *Journal of Negro History* 39, no. 1 (January 1954): 8–26; Leo Ailunas, "A Review of Negro Suffrage Prior to 1915," *Journal of Negro History* 25, no. 2 (April 1940): 153–60; Albert Bushnell Hart, "The Exercise of the Suffrage," *Political Science Quarterly* 7, no. 2 (June 1892): 307–29; James Schouler, "Evolution of the American Voter," *American Historical Review* 2, no. 4 (July 1897): 665–74; Chilton Williamson, "American Suffrage and Sir William Blackstone," *Political Science Quarterly* 68, no. 4 (December 1953): 552–57; James Truslow Adams, "Disfranchisement of Negroes in New England," *American Historical Review* 30, no. 3 (April 1945): 543–47; Kirk H. Porter, "Suffrage Provisions in State Constitutions," *American Political Science Review* 13, no. 4 (November 1919): 577–92; Loren P. Beth, *The Development of the American Constitution, 1877–1917* (New York: Harper and Row, 1971), 116–19; Sven Beckert, "Democracy and Its Discontents: Contesting Suffrage Rights in Gilded Age New York," *Past and Present* 174 (2002): 116–57; Abram C. Bernheim, "The Ballot in New York," *Political Science Quarterly* 4, no. 1 (March 1889): 130–52; Charles Chauncey Binney, "The Australian Ballot System," *Lippincott's Monthly Magazine,* September 1889, 381–88; Joseph B. Bishop, "The Secret Ballot in Thirty-Three States," *Forum* (January 1892): 589–98; David Dudley Field, "Our Political Methods," *Forum* (November 1886): 213–22; "Further Electoral Reform," *Century Illustrated Magazine* 39, no. 4 (February 1890): 633–34; Lynde Harrison, "The Connecticut Secret Ballot Law," *New Englander and Yale Review* 16, no. 242 (May 1890): 401–9; "Honesty at Elections," *Century Illustrated Magazine* 35, no. 4 (February 1888): 648–50; "New York's Reformed Electoral System," *Century Illustrated Magazine* 40, no. 4 (July 1890): 474–76; Charles H. Phelps, "Shall Foreigners Vote?" *Californian* 5, no. 26 (February 1882): 157–64; Charles T. Saxton, "The New Method of Voting," *North American Review* 149, no. 397 (December 1889): 750–52; John Bethell Uhle, "Ballot Reform in Pennsylvania," *New Englander and Yale Review* 19, no. 260 (November 1891): 391–98; Lee J. Vance, "Different Forms of the Ballot," *Chautauquan* 23, no. 6 (September 1896): 713–17; F. I. Vassault, "Ballot Reform," *Overland Monthly and Out West Magazine* 13, no. 74 (February 1889): 134–43; John H. Wigmore, "Ballot Reform: Its Constitutionality," *American Law Review* 23 (September/October 1889): 719–32; William L. Scruggs, "Restriction of the Suffrage," *North American Review* 139, no. 336 (November 1884): 492–502; William R. Merriam, "Suffrage, North and South," *Forum* 32, no. 4 (December 1901): 460–65.

18. "No precedent," Michael Klarman has noted, "determined whether a facially race-neutral classification was in fact a racial surrogate." Michael Klarman, "The Plessy Era," in *The Supreme Court Review 1998,* ed. Dennis J. Hutchinson, David A. Strauss, and Geoffrey R. Stone (Chicago: University of Chicago Press, 1999), 361; Michael Klarman, *From Jim Crow to Civil Rights: The Supreme Court and the Struggle for Equality* (New York: Oxford University Press, 2004), 34.

19. "Bill for Injunction," *Lawrence Mills v. W. Briggs Green,* 13 April 1895, Roll 597, USC-CDSC, RUSDC, RG 21, NARA, Southeast Regional Facility, Atlanta (hereafter cited as NARA, Atlanta); Burke, "Killing, Cheating, Legislating, and Lying, 871–72.

20. Charles Simonton to Nathan Goff, 8 April 1895, NGP. The issue in the dispensary

business was whether Tillman, as governor, could punish a militia company that had refused Tillman's orders during the March 1894 dispensary riots. See Perman, *Struggle for Mastery*, 91–104; Stephen Kantrowitz, *Ben Tillman and the Reconstruction of White Supremacy* (Chapel Hill: University of North Carolina Press, 2000), 181–97; *WP*, 11 September 1894; *NYT*, 11 September 1894; *AC*, 11 September 1894; *AC*, 16 December 1894; *NYT*, 16 December 1894; *NYT*, 22 April 1895.

Federal circuit courts such as the U.S. Circuit Court for the District of South Carolina no longer exist. Prior to 1891, U.S. Supreme Court justices spent most of their time out in the country serving as circuit justices. The U.S. circuit courts were the intermediate appellate courts between the U.S. district courts and the U.S. Supreme Court. There was no separate corps of circuit judges per se. Circuit courts were comprised of district court judges and the jurisdiction's assigned Supreme Court justice. The circuit court could meet even if the Supreme Court justice was absent and likewise if no district judge was present. If the district judge or judges disagreed with the Supreme Court justice, the justice's opinion prevailed, and district judges, too, under this system, had appellate jurisdiction over their own decisions. In 1891, in consideration of the crushing case load imposed upon Supreme Court justices, Congress established the U.S. circuit courts of appeal. Supreme Court justices no longer rode circuit—though they could if they wished. And the new circuit courts of appeal judges could serve in the circuit courts within their territorial jurisdiction. Thus Nathan Goff could sit as the U.S. Fourth Circuit Court of Appeal in Richmond or, as in *Mills*, could travel southward and sit as a district judge in the Circuit Court for the District of South Carolina—the decisions of which could be appealed to the Fourth Circuit Court of Appeal, of which Nathan Goff was the only permanent member. It was a very confusing system. Goff, as the judge for the Fourth Circuit, was empowered to sit in the District Court of South Carolina because that state belonged to the Fourth Circuit. The other states in that circuit were (and remain) North Carolina, Virginia, Maryland, and West Virginia.

21. "Order—Bill of Complaint for Injunction," *Lawrence Mills v. W. Briggs Green; CS*, 19 April 1895; See also *Boise Idaho Statesman*, 19 April 1895; *Chicago Daily Inter Ocean*, 20 April 1895; *Baltimore Sun*, 20 April 1895; *Wheeling (W.Va.) Register*, 21 April 1895; *Baltimore Sun*, 22 April 1895; *BAH*, 23 April 1895; *Philadelphia Inquirer*, 24 April 1895; *Springfield (Mass.) Republican*, 24 April 1895. For coverage of Governor Evans's statement, see *Charlotte Observer*, 23 April 1895; *AC*, 23 April 1895. See also *NYT*, 23 April 1895; *RNO*, 23 April 1895; *Macon Telegraph*, 23 April 1895; *Denver Evening Post*, 23 April 1895; *Macon Weekly Telegraph*, 25 April 1895; *Worcester (Mass.) Daily Spy*, 25 April 1895. "Return to Show Cause," *Lawrence Mills v. W. Briggs Green*, 1 May 1895. For general coverage of the hearing, see *Greenville (Miss.) Times*, 11 May 1895; *NYT*, 3 May 1895; *AC*, 3 May 1895; "Federal and State Rights in South Carolina," *Independent* 47, no. 2424 (16 May 1895): 10–11; *AC*, 1 June 1895; *AC*, 4 June 1895; *AC*, 5 June 1895.

22. *Mills v. Green*, 67 F. 818 (C.C.D.S.C. 1895) 831, 832, 833.

23. *CS*, 9 May 1895; *ST*, 11 May 1895. See also, for reaction to the decision, *Charlotte Observer*, 10 May 1895; *Columbus (Ga.) Daily Enquirer-Sun*, 10 May 1895; *Knoxville (Tenn.) Journal*, 10 May 1895.

24. *NYT*, 9 May 1895; *RNO*, 11 May 1895; *Columbus (Ga.) Daily Enquirer-Sun*, 15 May 1895; *Chicago Daily Inter Ocean*, 18 May 1895; *BAH*, 19 May 1895; *Wheeling (W.Va.) Register*,

21 May 1895; *AC,* 23 May 1895; *NYT,* 26 May 1895; *AC,* 2 August 1895; *CS,* 1 December 1895. It seems that Senator Elkins (who was also a Republican) floated Goff's name for the vice presidency at least in part to get an intraparty rival out of West Virginia.

25. Gordon B. McKinney, "Southern Mountain Republicans and the Negro, 1865–1900," *Journal of Southern History* 41, no. 4 (November 1975): 505; Reece, "Pure Despotism," 271–72.

26. "Editorial," *Outlook* 51, no. 20 (18 May 1895): 807–11; *RNO,* 10 May 1895. See also, for example, "Week in Review," *Congregationalist* 80, no. 18 (2 May 1895): 676–77; *Charlotte Observer,* 3 May 1895; *Columbus (Ga.) Daily Enquirer-Sun,* 3 May 1895; *RNO,* 3 May 1895; *Philadelphia North American,* 3 May 1895; *NODP,* 3 May 1895; *Macon Telegraph,* 4 May 1895; *Charlotte Observer,* 4 May 1895; *CS,* 4 May 1895; *Wheeling (W.Va.) Register,* 4 May 1895; *Chicago Daily Inter Ocean,* 5 May 1895; *Columbus (Ga.) Enquirer-Sun,* 5 May 1895; *NODP,* 7 May 1895; *Milwaukee Sentinel,* 9 May 1895; *BAH,* 9 May 1895; *Columbus (Ga.) Daily Enquirer-Sun,* 9 May 1895; *Knoxville (Tenn.) Journal,* 9 May 1895; *Wheeling (W.Va.) Register,* 9 May 1895; *Chicago Daily Inter Ocean,* 10 May 1895; *CS,* 10 May 1895; *WP,* 10 May 1895; *NYT,* 10 May 1895; *Boston Daily Advertiser,* 10 May 1895; *Knoxville (Tenn.) Journal,* 11 May 1895; *Springfield (Mass.) Daily Republican,* 11 May 1895; *Chicago Daily Inter Ocean,* 12 May 1895; *Springfield (Mass.) Daily Republican,* 12 May 1895; *SWCA,* 16 May 1895; *Minneapolis Penny Press,* 20 May 1895; *Kansas City (Mo.) City Times,* 21 May 1895; *Greenville (Miss.) Times,* 25 May 1895.

27. Simonton to Goff, 21 May 1895, NGP. Tillman's threats and fulminations received extensive attention from national and regional newspapers. See, for example, *CS,* 11 May 1895; *BAH,* 11 May 1895; *Charlotte Observer,* 11 May 1895; *Macon Telegraph,* 11 May 1895; *NYT,* 15 May 1895; *WP,* 15 May 1895; *Denver Evening Post,* 16 May 1895; *RNO,* 17 May 1895; *Boston Daily Advertiser,* 17 May 1895; *Philadelphia North American,* 17 May 1895; *NYT,* 17 May 1895; *WP,* 17 May 1895; *Chicago Daily Inter Ocean,* 19 May 1895; *Denver Evening Post,* 20 May 1895; *Milwaukee Sentinel,* 20 May 1895; *Philadelphia North American,* 13 May 1895.

28. Melville Weston Fuller to Goff, 27 May 1895, NGP; "Citation," 23 May 1895, in *W. Briggs Green v. Lawrence Mills,* Docket no. 136, FC, RFC, RG 276, NARA, Atlanta; *NODP,* 24 May 1895; *Denver Evening Post,* 27 May 1895; *RNO,* 12 June 1895; *Philadelphia North American,* 12 June 1895; *Macon Telegraph,* 12 June 1895.

29. *WP,* 25 May 1895.

30. "Preliminary Order," 11 June 1895, *W. Briggs Green v. Lawrence Mills.* For public discussion of the order, see *AC,* 12 June 1895; *NYT,* 12 June 1895; *NYT,* 13 June 1895; "The Outlook," *Zion's Herald* 73, no. 25 (June 19, 1895): 1; "Summary of Events," *The Friend: A Religious and Literary Journal* 68, no. 48 (June 22, 1895): 384; "Record and Review: The Suffrage in South Carolina," *New York Observer and Chronicle* 73, no. 27 (4 July 1895): 13; *Central Law Journal* 41, no. 1 (5 July 1895): 1–2. As soon as the hearing in Richmond concluded, attorneys on both sides immediately wrote the court clerk, Henry Meloney, asking that they be notified as soon as a formal order was filed. See Obear and Douglass to Henry Meloney, 11 June 1895; William Barber to Meloney, 13 June 1895; Edward McGrady to Meloney, 14 June 1895; and Obear and Douglass to Meloney, 18 June 1895, all in the Fourth Circuit's case file for *W. Briggs Green v. Lawrence Mills;* "Concurring opinion of Judge Hughes," 11 June 1895, *W. Briggs Green v. Lawrence Mills.* No original copy of Hughes's concurrence survives in the case files except as part of the printed record prepared for the U.S. Supreme Court. It was published in toto, however, by the *Richmond Times* on June 12, 1895.

31. *Green v. Mills,* 69 F. 852 (4th Cir. 1895) 859. A circuit justice's opinion was always the opinion of the entire circuit court, whether or not the other judges agreed.

32. Nathan Goff to the editor of the *New York World,* 14 June 1895, as reprinted and commented upon by the *New York World* on 17 June 1895. The *Wheeling (W.Va.) Register* reprinted the exchange and remarked upon the same on June 29, 1895; Simonton to Goff, 19 June 1895, NGP.

33. *Central Law Journal* 41, no. 13 (27 September 1895): 243; See also *AC,* 12 June 1895; *St. Albans (Vt.) Daily Messenger,* 17 June 1895.

34. *CS,* 4 July 1895. See also *Springfield (Mass.) Daily Republican,* 13 June 1895; *New Haven (Conn.) Evening Register,* 13 June 1895; *CS,* 12 June 1895.

35. "Bill for Injunction and Relief," *Joseph H. Gowdy v. W. Briggs Green,* 11 July 1895, Roll 398, USCCDSC, RUSDC, RG 21, NARA, Atlanta; "Restraining Order and Order to Show Cause," *Joseph H. Gowdy v. W. Briggs Green;* AC, 26 July 1895; *NYT,* 26 July 1895; *Macon Telegraph,* 27 July 1895; *AC,* 2 August 1895; *WP,* 6 August 1895; *Philadelphia North American,* 6 and 7 August 1895; *RNO,* 7 August 1895.

36. *Gowdy v. Green,* 69 F. 865 (C.C.D.S.C. 1895) 865–67; *WP,* 6 August 1895; *AC,* 6 August 1895; *NYT,* 7 August 1895; *WP,* 7 August 1895; *AC,* 7 August 1895.

37. *CS,* 16 August 1895; *WP,* 11 September 1895; *WP,* 23 September 1895; "The Suffrage in South Carolina," *New York Observer and Chronicle* 73, no. 39 (26 September 1895): 397; "Record and Review," *New York Observer and Chronicle* 73, no. 42 (17 October 1895): 601; *WP,* 9 October 1895; *NYT,* 29 October 1895.

38. *Mills v. Green,* 159 U.S. 651 (1895).

39. *Natchez (Miss.) Brotherhood* editorial, as cited in the *NODP,* 1 October 1895; *Omaha (Neb.) Enterprise,* 14 December 1895.

40. *Marbury v. Madison,* 5 U.S. 137 (1803); *Luther v. Borden,* 48 U.S. 1 (1849). *Luther v. Borden* arose in the aftermath of Dorr's Rebellion. Dorr's Rebellion, appropriately in the current context, grew from a the popular movement for white manhood suffrage. As late as 1840, Rhode Island's constitution was, in its essentials, the 1633 charter granted by King Charles I and restricted suffrage to freeholders and their eldest sons. Rhode Island men, in 1841, produced a new constitution for Rhode Island that would ensure white manhood suffrage. They staged a referendum later that year and their constitution was ratified by the voters. However, Rhode Island's legislature—chosen by the freeholders—produced their own new constitution, which included expanded, but not universal, manhood suffrage. Each group claimed that they were Rhode Island's rightful leaders and each elected a full legislature and full slate of state officers the following spring. The universal manhood suffrage faction's leader was Thomas Dorr; his opponent was Samuel King. Both men claimed to be governor. King had been governor under the old charter and he declared Dorr to be leading a revolt, declared martial law, and called out the militia. Each side wanted President John Tyler to settle the dispute. Tyler refused but guaranteed that he would send in federal troops if disorder broke out. Eventually Dorr fled the state, but when he returned, he was tried and pardoned. The Rhode Island legislature drafted another constitution with much more liberal suffrage requirements. *Luther v. Borden* arose from the original dispute between the Dorr and King factions. See Richard B. Morris and Jeffrey B. Morris, *Encyclopedia of American History,* 7th ed. (New York: HarperCollins, 1996), 208–9; Harold M. Hyman, "Luther v.

Borden," in *The Oxford Guide to United States Supreme Court Decisions*, ed. Kermit Hall (New York: Oxford University Press, 1999), 167–68.

41. *Strauder v. West Virginia*, 100 U.S. 303 (1880); *Neal v. Delaware*, 103 U.S. 370 (1880); *Ex parte Virginia*, 100 U.S. 339 (1880); *Virginia v. Rives*, 100 U.S. 313 (1880); Benno C. Schmidt, "Juries, Jurisdiction, and Race Discrimination: The Lost Promise of *Strauder v. West Virginia*," *Texas Law Review* 61 (May 1983): 1401–99; William M. Wiecek, "*Strauder v. West Virginia*," in *The Oxford Guide to United States Supreme Court Decisions*, ed. Kermit Hall (New York: Oxford University Press, 1999), 295–96.

42. *Jackson Mississippian*, 27 May 1891. See also Robert Lowry and William B. McCardle, *A History of Mississippi from the Discovery of the Great River by Hernando DeSoto including the Earliest Settlement Made by the French under Iberville to the Death of Jefferson Davis* (Jackson, Miss.: R. H. Henry, 1891), 496.

43. Cornelius Jones Sr. and Hannah Donaldson Jones recorded their marriage with the Freedmen's Bureau on July 10, 1864. See Records of the Assistant Commissioner for the State of Mississippi Bureau of Refugees, Freedmen and Abandoned Lands, 1865–1869, Microfilm Publication M826, Roll 42, National Archives; "Obituary," Jones-Sadler Family Papers, Schomburg Center for Research in Black Culture, New York Public Library (hereafter cited as Jones-Sadler Family Papers).

44. "Obituary," Jones-Sadler Family Papers; Roster, House of Representatives, in *Journal of the House of Representatives of the State of Mississippi at a Regular Session thereof, Convened in the City of Jackson, Jan. 7, 1890* (Jackson, Miss.: R. H. Henry, 1890), 604–9.

45. Vernon L. Wharton, *The Negro in Mississippi, 1865–1900* (New York: Harper Torchbooks, 1965), 202–3; Albert D. Kirwan, "Apportionment in the Mississippi Constitution of 1890," *Journal of Southern History* 14, no. 2 (May 1948): 234–46; Albert D. Kirwan, *Revolt of the Rednecks: Mississippi Politics, 1876–1925* (Lexington: University of Kentucky Press, 1951), 78–84.

46. *JDCL*, 25 January 1900. Mississippi's legislature did not maintain a transcript of its debates—which was not unusual for that time. The state house and senate did, however, maintain journals, which recorded basic information about the bodies' activities. With only rare exceptions, neither specific speeches nor the names or inclinations of specific members were recorded—other than for motions, introductions, or votes. The house journal records how Jones voted but contains no information about his address. See *Journal of the House of Representatives of the State of Mississippi at a Regular Session Thereof, Convened in the City of Jackson, January 7, 1890* (Jackson: R. H. Henry, 1890), 85, 226, 232–35, 234.

47. As per then–U.S. representative Henry Cabot Lodge's original bill, any time that five hundred voters in a particular congressional district petitioned for federal supervision of an election, the U.S. district judge for their jurisdiction would place that district's election under the jurisdiction of federal election supervisors (that the judge would appoint). See Thomas Adams Upchurch, *Legislating Racism: The Billion Dollar Congress and the Birth of Jim Crow* (Lexington: University Press of Kentucky, 2004); "The Spectacle of Mississippi," *Independent* 42, no, 2178 (28 August 1890): 18. If the public was not interested, editors were—sometimes. See "Editorial," *Zion's Herald* 68, no. 36 (3 September 1890); "Mississippi's Problem," *Nation* (31 July 1890): 86–7; *Chicago Daily Inter Ocean*, 17 August 1890; *Denver Rocky Mountain News*, 17 August 1890; *Chicago Daily Inter Ocean*, 18 August 1890; *Boston Congregationalist*, 28 August 1890; *Denver Rocky Mountain News*, 31 August 1890; *New York Age*, 6

September 1890; *St. Paul Daily News,* 15 September 1890. For excellent secondary accounts of the Mississippi convention, its purpose, and its effects, see Perman, *Struggle for Mastery,* 70–90; Kirwan, *Revolt of the Rednecks,* 65–92; Wharton, *Negro in Mississippi,* 206–15; Stephen Cresswell, *Multiparty Politics in Mississippi, 1877–1902* (Jackson: University Press of Mississippi, 1995), 100–125; Stephen Cresswell, *Rednecks, Redeemers, and Race: Mississippi after Reconstruction, 1877–1917* (Jackson: University Press of Mississippi, 2006), 110–29. For contemporaneous accounts from the disfranchisers themselves, see S. S. Calhoon, "The Causes and Events that Led to the Calling of the Constitutional Convention of 1890," *Publications of the Mississippi Historical Society* 6, no. 1 (November 1902): 105–10; Dunbar Rowland, *A Mississippi View of Race Relations in the South: Read before the Alumni Association of the University of Mississippi, June 3rd, 1902* (Jackson, Miss.: Harmon, 1903), 12–16.

48. Neil McMillen, *Dark Journey: Black Mississippians in the Age of Jim Crow* (Champaign: University of Illinois Press, 1989), 53–54; Wharton, *Negro in Mississippi,* 210–11; *New Orleans Crusader,* 19 July 1890.

49. *SWCA,* 9 October 1890. See also *Milwaukee Sentinel,* 20 September 1890; *Portland Morning Oregonian,* 25 September 1890; *SWCA,* 30 October 1890; *New York Age,* 11 October 1890; *New York Age,* 18 October 1890; *New York Age,* 8 November 1890. Montgomery's address is mentioned in all accounts of Mississippi's 1890 constitutional convention. The most recent is Prof. Matthew Holden's revisionist treatment: *"What Answer?": Speech in Support of Franchise Committee Report, Mississippi Constitutional Convention, 1890* (Charlottesville, Va.: Isaiah T. Montgomery Studies Project, 2004). Holden's chief contribution lies in presenting the actual text of Montgomery's speech, demonstrating that it was not the surrender that his critics claim. Also see Neil McMillen's firm (though fair) critique of Montgomery's role in the convention and the context for his public career in. McMillen, *Dark Journey,* 48–57.

50. J. S. McNeilly, "History of the Measures Submitted to the Committee on Elective Franchise, Apportionment, and Elections in the Constitutional Convention of 1890," *Publications of the Mississippi Historical Society* 6, no. 1 (November 1902): 138; Johnston's observation is taken from McMillen, *Dark Journey,* 53–54, citing the *Port Gibson (Miss.) Reveille,* 23 May 1890.

51. *Brookhaven (Miss.) Leader,* 14 November 1895. For data on black legislators, see the appendices listing African American officeholders in Buford Satcher, "Blacks in Mississippi Politics, 1865–1900" (Ph.D. diss., Oklahoma State University, 1976).

52. "Brief for the State" and "Testimony of Dan Scott," in "Trial Transcript," 1–15, 16, *John Gibson v. State of Mississippi,* case 7290, RMSC, RG 32, Box 6079, MDAH.

53. "Testimony of John Gibson," in "Trial Transcript," 92, *John Gibson v. State of Mississippi.*

54. Ibid., 94, 96.

55. *Gibson v. State,* 16 So. 198 (1894).

56. "Removal Motion," "Motion to Quash," and "Order," in "Trial Transcript," *John Gibson v. State of Mississippi,* 2–7.

57. "Statement of Facts" in "Trial Transcript," *Charley Smith v. State of Mississippi,* 1–5, case 8050, RMSC, RG 32, MDAH.

58. "Motion of Quash" and "Removal Motion," in "Trial Transcript," *Charley Smith v. State of Mississippi,* 10–11, 12.

59. "Certificate of Appeal," *Charley Smith v. State of Mississippi; Smith v. State,* 18 So. 116

(1895); *Gibson v. State*, 17 So. 892 (1895). The Mississippi Supreme Court decided these cases in late May and early June 1895. See *Gibson v. State*, 17 So. 892 (Miss. 1895) (decided on 27 May 1895) and *Smith v. State*, 18 So. 116 (Miss. 1895) (decided on 3 June 1895).

60. M. Sammye Miller, "The National Archives, a Repository for Afro-Americans: Recommendations for E. M. Hewlett," *Journal of Negro History* 64, no. 4 (Autumn 1979): 391–94; J. Clay Smith, *Emancipation: The Making of the Black Lawyer, 1844–1944* (Philadelphia: University of Pennsylvania Press, 1993), 131–32. Smith, in *Emancipation* at 293–94, erroneously stated that Jones appeared before the U.S. Supreme Court with Wilford Smith on December 13, 1895, and that Smith was there to argue the case of *Gibson v. Smith*. Mary Frances Berry recently repeated the error in *My Face Is Black Is True: Callie House and the Struggle for Ex-Slave Reparations* (New York: Knopf, 2005), 174.

61. *Gibson v. Mississippi*, 162 U.S. 565 (1896); *Smith v. Mississippi*, 162 U.S. 592 (1896); *Plessy v. Ferguson*, 163 U.S. 537 (1896). *Plessy* was announced on May 18, 1896.

62. Jan Hillegas, comp., *Preliminary List of Mississippi Legal Executions*, on file with MDAH. Hillegas cites the *Greenville Times* as the source for Gibson's death date. The *Preliminary List* lists executions by date and county. These executions were not regulated by any central authority and were carried out by county sheriffs.

63. *WP*, 27 October 1895; *NODP*, 11 November 1895; *ST*, 4 January 1896.

CHAPTER TWO

1. *Indianola (Miss.) Sunflower Tocsin*, 23 August 1895.

2. John Hope Franklin, "John Roy Lynch: Republican Stalwart from Mississippi," in *Race and History: Selected Essays, 1938–1988*, ed. John Hope Franklin (Baton Rouge: Louisiana State University Press, 1989): 262.

3. *NODP*, 22 February 1892.

4. *Pascagoula (Miss.) Democrat-Star* editorial, reprinted in the *MCA*, 18 October 1895; *NODP*, 2 November 1895. The three counties that had not reported their registration figures were Coahoma (one of the river counties in the Delta), Smith (in south-central Mississippi), and Pontotoc (in north-central Mississippi); *NDD*, 5 November 1895; *Natchez (Miss.) Brotherhood* editorial, as cited by the *Indianola (Miss.) Sunflower Tocsin*, 4 October 1895. No actual issue of the *Brotherhood* has survived and it is only accessible in those instances where some other newspaper quoted from it.

5. *MCA*, 27 October 1895; *Vicksburg Commercial Herald*, as cited in the *NODP*, 12 November 1895; *Omaha (Neb.) Enterprise*, 30 November 1895; *NYT*, 28 October 1895; *NDD*, 31 October 1895; *Woodville (Miss.) Republican*, 23 November 1895; *WP*, 19 November 1895; *NYT*, 19 November 1895; *Philadelphia North American*, 19 November 1895; *Statesville (N.C.) Landmark*, 22 November 1895; *Portland Morning Oregonian*, 16 December 1895.

6. Morton Stavis, "A Century of Struggle for Black Enfranchisement in Mississippi: From the Civil War to the Congressional Challenge of 1965—and Beyond," *Mississippi Law Journal* 57 (1987): 627–40; W. Lewis Burke, "Killing, Cheating, Legislating, and Lying: A History of Voting Rights in South Carolina after the Civil War," *South Carolina Law Review* 57 (Summer 2006): 873–77.

7. *NDD*, 8 November 1895.

8. *NODP*, 2 November 1895; *Eupora (Miss.) Sun*, 19 November 1895; *Eupora (Miss.) Sun*, 29 November 1895.

9. *Sardis (Miss.) Reporter*, 22 November 1895; *NDD*, 28 December 1895. See also *Liberty (Miss.) Southern Herald*, 22 November 1895; *MCA*, 20 November 1895; *Fayette (Miss.) Chronicle*, 22 November 1895; *MCA*, 19 November 1895; *NDD*, 22 November 1895; *NODP*, 24 November 1895; *MCA*, 21 November 1895.

10. *NDD*, 8 December 1895.

11. *Hazelhurst (Miss.) Courier*, as cited by the *NODP*, 2 December 1895; *MCA*, 13 December 1895; *Vicksburg Commercial Herald*, as cited by the *NODP*, 7 October 1895; Hosea 4:17: "Ephraim is joined to idols: let him alone."

12. *NODP*, 8 October 1895; *NODP*, 19 November 1895; *NODP*, 23 November 1895; *NODP*, 11 December 1895; *MCA*, 23 November 1895; *NDD*, 3 December 1895. "The whites," the *Liberty Southern Herald* advised on December 13, 1895, about poll-tax payments, "should also take the same view of the matter."

13. *MCA*, 1 December 1895; *NODP*, 3 December 1895; *Greenville (Miss.) Times*, 13 November 1895; *NODP*, 12 December 1895.

14. *Indianola (Miss.) Sunflower Tocsin*, 20 January 1896; *NDD*, 18 January 1896.

15. *NDD*, 22 November 1896; John Roy Lynch, *Reminiscences of an Active Life: The Autobiography of John Roy Lynch*, John Hope Franklin, ed. (Chicago: University of Chicago Press, 1970), 381, 371–94; *Sardis (Miss.) Southern Reporter*, 6 March 1896. The intra party fight was well documented by the state and national press. See, for example, *NDD*, 16 January 1896; *JDCL*, 15 February 1896; *JDCL*, 17 February 1896; *JDCL*, 18 February 1896; *JDCL*, 19 February 1896; *JDCL*, 24 February 1896; *JDCL*, 25 February 1896; *JDCL*, 27 February 1896; *NDD*, 27 February 1896; *JDCL*, 2 March 1896; *JDCL*, 3 March 1896; *JDCL*, 4 March 1896; *JDCL*, 5 March 1896; *Chicago Daily Inter Ocean*, 5 March 1896; *Galveston Daily News*, 5 March 1896; *Milwaukee Sentinel*, 5 March 1896; *NYT*, 5 March 1896; *AC*, 5 March 1896; *Emporia (Kans.) Daily Gazette*, 5 March 1896; *JDCL*, 6 March 1896; *JDCL*, 7 March 1896; *AC*, 9 March 1896; *JDCL*, 10 March 1896; *JDCL*, 19 March 1896; *Lincoln (Neb.) Evening News*, 13 April 1896; *Fort Wayne (Ind.) Evening Post*, 13 April 1896; *JDCL*, 30 May 1896; *JDCL*, 12 June 1896; *Emporia (Kans.) Daily Gazette*, 12 June 1896; *JDCL*, 13 June 1896; *JDCL*, 20 June 1896; *JDCL*, 3 July 1896; *JDCL*, 6 July 1896; *JDCL*, 24 July 1896; *JDCL*, 3 September 1896; *JDCL*, 4 September 1896; *JDCL*, 7 October 1896; *JDCL*, 16 October 1896; *JDCL*, 19 October 1896; *JDCL*, 20 October 1896; *JDCL*, 22 October 1896; *JDCL*, 30 October 1896; *MCA*, 17 January 1897; *French Camp (Miss.) News*, 29 January 1897; *French Camp (Miss.) News*, 12 February 1897; *Kosciusko Mississippi Farmer*, 22 April 1897; *Kosciusko Mississippi Farmer*, 29 April 1897.

16. *JDCL*, 21 March 1896.

17. *MCA*, 4 May 1896; *Liberty (Miss.) Southern Herald*, 8 May 1896; *Grenada (Miss.) Sentinel*, 9 May 1896; *JDCL*, 11 June 1896; *JDCL*, 12 June 1896; *JDCL*, 29 June 1896; *JDCL*, 1 July 1896.

18. "Bill of Complaint," in "Lower Court Record," 1–5, *W. J. Ratliff v. Ambus Beale*, case 8520, RMSC, RG 32, Box 13533, MDAH; *Greenville (Miss.) Times*, 22 July 1896.

19. Beth Barton Schweiger has written a very persuasive article about a similar phenomenon that followed Virginia's 1902 constitution. Virginia's disfranchisers were alarmed that white voters were falling away in disfranchisement's aftermath and sought to encourage

political participation by Democratically inclined white men. See Schweiger, "Putting Politics Aside: Virginia Democrats and Voter Apathy in the Era of Disfranchisement" in *The Edge of the South: Life in Nineteenth-Century Virginia,* ed. Edward L. Ayers and John C. Willis (Charlottesville: University Press of Virginia, 1994), 194–218.

20. "J. H. Campbell, for Appellant," *W. J. Ratliff v. Ambus Beale.*

21. Solomon S. Calhoon, "Brief in Reply to Judge Campbell's Assignment," *W. J. Ratliff v. Ambus Beale.*

22. Ibid.; "Address of Solomon S. Calhoon," 703.

23. *JDCL,* 6 August 1896; *Ratliff v. Beale,* 20 So. 865 (Miss. 1896) 868–69; *Sardis (Miss.) Southern Reporter,* 11 December 1896; *French Camp (Miss.) News,* 4 December 1896; *Fayette (Miss.) Chronicle,* 4 December 1896.

24. *JDCL,* 1 December 1896. See also, for example, *JDCL,* 30 November 1896; *NDD,* 1 December 1896; *NDD,* 2 December 1896; *Greenville Times,* 2 December 1896.

25. U.S. House Committee on Elections, Report no. 1536, *A. M. Newman v. J. G. Spencer,* 54th Cong., 1st sess., 1896; U.S. House Committee on Elections, Report no. 1537, *W. P. Ratliff v. J. S. Williams,* 54th Cong., 1st sess., 1896; U.S. House Committee on Elections, Report no. 1538, *John A. Brown v. John M. Allen,* 54th Cong., 1st sess., 1896; *NODP,* 13 April 1896; *JDCL,* 17 April 1896; *JDCL,* 20 April 1896; *JDCL,* 1 May 1896. Regarding these challenges, see Stavis, "Century of Struggle," 637. For information on Lynch's dispute with Adams County officials and Governor McLaurin, see Lynch to McLaurin, 16 September 1896, Papers of Gov. Anselm J. McLaurin, Box 1129, Folder 100, MDAH (hereafter cited as McLaurin Papers); Proby & Clinton to McLaurin, 1 October 1896, Box 1129, Folder 105, McLaurin Papers; Proby & Clinton to McLaurin, 15 October 1896, Box 1129, Folder 106, McLaurin Papers; Bonner Richardson to McLaurin, 16 October 1896, Box 1129, Folder 107, McLaurin Papers. For news accounts of Lynch's battle for a place on the ballot, see, generally, *NODP,* 12 September 1896; *JDCL,* 19 September 1896; *NODP,* 20 September 1896; *NODP,* 10 October 1896; *JDCL,* 12 October 1896; *Charleston (S.C.) Weekly News and Courier,* 14 October 1896; *Woodville (Miss.) Republican,* 17 October 1896; *NODP,* 22 October 1896; *French Camp (Miss.) News,* 11 December 1896; *Liberty (Miss.) Southern Herald,* 18 December 1896.

26. *JDCL,* 4 July 1896.

27. Handbill announcing "Ratification Rally," 10 August 1896, Jones-Sadler Family Papers, Schomburg Center for Research in Black Culture, New York Public Library; *Greenville (Miss.) Times,* 5 August 1896; *Greenville (Miss.) Times,* 31 October 1896; *Greenville (Miss.) Weekly Democrat,* 29 October 1896; *MCA,* 4 December 1896; *Port Gibson (Miss.) Reveille,* 10 December 1896; *Sardis (Miss.) Southern Reporter,* 11 December 1896; Justin Johannes Behrend, "Losing the Vote: Disfranchisement in Natchez, Mississippi, 1867–1910" (master's thesis, California State University, Northridge, 2000), 59.

28. *Greenville (Miss.) Times* 18 November 1896; *Greenville (Miss.) Times,* 9 December 1896; *Greenville (Miss.) Weekly Democrat,* 10 December 1896; *NODP,* 22 December 1896; *Woodville (Miss.) Republican,* 26 December 1896; *NODP,* 29 December 1896.

29. *Vicksburg Commercial Herald,* as cited by the *MCA,* 24 January 1897; *Greenville (Miss.) Weekly Democrat,* 14 January 1897; *Indianola (Miss.) Sunflower Tocsin,* 15 January 1897.

30. *NODP,* 22 December 1896; *JDCL,* 10 June 1896.

31. "Testimony of Eliza Minor," in "Trial Transcript," *John Henry Dixon v. State of Mississippi*, 23–27, case 8504, RMSC, RG 32, Box 13533, MDAH; *Greenville (Miss.) Times*, 17 June 1896.

32. "Testimony of Theophilus Brown" and "Testimony of Dr. A. Bruce," in "Trial Transcript," *Henry Williams v. State of Mississippi*, 22, 21–25.

33. "Testimony of Ella Hicks" and "Testimony of Gus Miles," in "Trial Transcript," *Henry Williams v. State of Mississippi*, 27–30.

34. "Testimony of Henry Williams," in "Trial Transcript," *Henry Williams v. State of Mississippi*, 42, 43.

35. Ibid., 43.

36. "Motion to Quash" and "Motion for Removal," in "Trial Transcript," *Henry Williams v. State of Mississippi*," 3–12, 12–21, 49.

37. *Greenville (Miss.) Times*, 12 December 1896. Beyond this, the seating challenge received very little attention. A lone report from the *NODP* on March 3, 1898, mentioned that the congressional committee would soon announce a decision (and that Jones would surely lose).

38. "Brief for Appellee," *John Henry Dixon v. State of Mississippi*, RMSC, MDAH, 4; *Dixon v. State*, 20 So. 839 (Miss. 1896) 840.

39. *Dixon v. State*, 20 So. 841, 842; *Williams v. State*, 20 So. 1023 (Miss. 1896).

40. *JDCL*, 9 November 1896. Announcing that Williams's December 11, 1896, hanging had been postponed, the *Greenville Weekly Democrat* advised on January 14, 1897, that it was "decidedly uncertain when the Supreme Court will act upon the case"; *Henry Williams v. State of Mississippi*, United States Supreme Court, October term, 1897, case no. 531, RBUSSC; *NODP*, 15 March 1898; *WP*, 18 March 1898; *Biloxi Herald*, 19 March 1898; *NODP*, 19 March 1898.

41. "Statement of Facts," *Henry Williams v. State of Mississippi*, RBUSSC, 4; emphasis added.

42. J. Morgan Kousser, "Separate but Not Equal: The Supreme Court's First Decision on Racial Discrimination in Schools," *Journal of Southern History* 46, no. 1 (February 1980): 34n39.

43. "Statement of Facts," *Henry Williams v. State of Mississippi*, RBUSSC, 6, 11–14, 18.

44. "Brief for the State of Mississippi," *Henry Williams v. State of Mississippi*, RBUSSC, 6–7, 18; Stephen Cresswell, *Multiparty Politics in Mississippi, 1877–1902* (Jackson: University Press of Mississippi, 1995), 98; Stephen Cresswell, *Rednecks, Redeemers, and Race: Mississippi after Reconstruction, 1877–1917* (Jackson: University of Press of Mississippi, 2006), 24.

45. *Ratliff v. Beale*, 20 So. 868.

46. *Williams v. Mississippi*, 170 U.S. 213 (1898) 222, 225. The decision received relatively scant press mention. See, for example, *Grenada (Miss.) Sentinel*, 30 April 1898; *Greenwood (Miss.) Commonwealth*, 5 May 1898; *Brookhaven (Miss.) Leader*, 4 May 1898; *JDCL*, 26 April 1898; *NODP*, 26 April 1898; *Biloxi Herald*, 30 April 1898.

47. *Yick Wo v. Hopkins*, 188 U.S. 356 (1886); *Williams v. Mississippi*, 170 U.S. 225. *Yick Wo* involved a San Francisco city ordinance regulating the laundry industry. Under the ordinance, laundry operators needed special permission to operate laundries in wooden struc-

tures (and Chinese laundries were nearly always wooden). Denied this permission, Mr. Yick Wo continued to operate his laundry in a wooden building, as did many whites, and he was arrested. Yick Wo, or Yick Wo Chang, as he was also known, was not the only laundry operator jailed, but it was plainly evident that no white operator needed to fear arrest. The Court's unanimous decision, written by Justice Stanley Matthews, declared that if a law "is applied and administered by public authority with an evil eye and an unequal hand," such that it produces a discrimination, "the denial of equal justice is still within the prohibition of the Constitution." *Yick Wo v. Hopkins,* 188 U.S. 374.

48. The chief exception to the tendency to overstate *Williams* is J. Morgan Kousser. Kousser has offered the most accurate portraits of *Williams* to date, acknowledging the very circumspect view that many contemporary southerners had of the decision and its less-than-conclusive nature. See J. Morgan Kousser, *"Williams* v. *Mississippi,"* in *The Encyclopedia of Southern History,* ed. David C. Roller and Robert W. Twyman (Baton Rouge: Louisiana State University Press, 1979), 1345–46; J. Morgan Kousser, *Colorblind Injustice: Minority Voting Rights and the Undoing of the Second Reconstruction* (Chapel Hill: University of North Carolina Press, 1999), 321–23. For coverage by other historians, see, for example, Perman, *Struggle for Mastery,* 121; Alexander Keyssar, *The Right to Vote: The Contested History of Democracy in the United States* (New York: Basic Books, 2000), 115; C. Vann Woodward, *Origins of the New South, 1877–1951* (Baton Rouge: Louisiana State University Press, 1951), 322–23; C. Vann Woodward, *The Strange Career of Jim Crow,* 3rd rev. ed. (New York: Oxford University Press, 1974), 71; Sheldon Hackney, *Populism to Progressivism in Alabama* (Princeton: Princeton University Press, 1969), 160; Jack Temple Kirby, *Darkness at the Dawning: Race and Reform in the Progressive South* (Philadelphia: J. B. Lippincott, 1972), 12; Edward L. Ayers, *The Promise of the New South: Life After Reconstruction* (New York: Oxford University Press, 1992), 304; Sean Dennis Cashman, *America in the Gilded Age: From the Death of Lincoln to the Rise of Theodore Roosevelt* (New York: New York University Press, 1984), 242; Nell Irvin Painter, *Standing at Armageddon: The United States, 1877–1919* (New York: W. W. Norton, 1987), 18; Glenda Gilmore, *Gender and Jim Crow: Women and the Politics of White Supremacy in North Carolina, 1896–1920* (Chapel Hill: University of North Carolina Press, 1996), 120.

49. B. Frank Dake, "The Negro Before the Supreme Court," *Albany Law Journal* 66, no. 1 (January 1904–January 1905): 244.

50. "Disfranchising a Race," *Nation* 66, no. 1717 (16 May 1898): 398–99; *Congregationalist* 83, no. 30 (28 July 1898): 102; "Nullifying the 14th Amendment," *Zion's Herald* 1026, no. 30 (27 July 1898): 1–2; "Annus Mirabilis," *Congregationalist* 83, no. 52 (29 December 1898): 962. See also "Domestic," *Christian Observer* 86, no. 32 (3 August 1898): 751; T. Thomas Fortune, "Immorality of Southern Suffrage Legislation," *Independent* 50, no. 2609 (1 December 1898): 1576–78.

51. "Application for Reargument," n.d., *Henry Williams v. State of Mississippi,* RBUSSC; "Application for Reargument," 12 May 1898, *Henry Williams v. State of Mississippi,* RBUSSC.

52. *Belen (Miss.) Quitman Quill,* 21 October 1898; *WP,* 19 January 1899; *Contested Election of Case of Cornelius J. Jones vs. T. C. Catchings: Brief of Contestant* (Washington, D.C.: National, 1899); Cresswell, *Multiparty Politics in Mississippi,* 174; *Belen (Miss.) Quitman Quill,* 28 October 1898; *Greenwood (Miss.) Commonwealth,* 4 November 1898.

53. Hillegas, *Preliminary List of Mississippi Legal Executions*. Hillegas cites the *JDCL* as the source for Williams's date of death.

CHAPTER THREE

1. *JCDL*, 14 October 1896.

2. Alex Gates's story appeared in the *Washington Star* and was reprinted by the *Springfield (Mass.) Daily Republican*, 15 August 1897.

3. *JCDL*, 14 October 1896.

4. *Pointe à la Hâche (La.) Plaquemines Protector*, 1 January 1898.

5. *Abbeville (La.) Meridional*, 22 January 1898.

6. Constitution of the Commonwealth of Massachusetts, Article XX.

7. Louisiana Constitution of 1898, Article 197, § 5.

8. *Portland Morning Oregonian*, 2 April 1898; *Milwaukee Journal*, 25 March 1898; *Bismark (N.D.) Daily Tribune*, 28 March 1898.

9. Charles W. Chesnutt, *The Marrow of Tradition* (1901; reprint, Ann Arbor: University of Michigan Press, 1970), 240; Benno C. Schmidt Jr., "Principle and Prejudice: The Supreme Court and Race in the Progressive Era. Part 3: Black Disfranchisement from the KKK to the Grandfather Clause," *Columbia Law Review* 82 (June 1982): 836; Amasa Eaton, "The Suffrage Clause in the New Constitution of Louisiana," *Harvard Law Review* 13, no. 4 (December 1899): 293; "The Colour Question in the United States," *Edinburgh Review* 201, no. 411 (January 1905): 63. The *Albany Law Journal* also described it as an "ingenious contrivance." "Summary of Legislation by States in 1898," *Albany Law Journal* 59 (1898–99): 226.

10. *Alexandria (La.) Daily Town Talk*, 5 March 1898. This was the general reaction of Louisiana's parish-level press as well. See, for example, *Morgan City (La.) Independent Democrat*, 5 March 1898 and 12 March 1898; *Mansfield (La.) Journal*, 11 March 1898; *Opelousas (La.) Courier*, 12 March 1898; *Opelousas (La.) St. Landry Clarion*, 12 March 1898; *Shreveport (La.) Progress*, 12 March 1898; *Benton (La.) Bossier Banner*, 17 March 1898; *Natchitoches (La.) Louisiana Populist*, 18 March 1898.

11. *Monroe (La.) Bulletin*, as reprinted by the *Natchitoches Louisiana Populist*, 18 March 1898; *NODS*, 8 February 1898; *NOTD*, 8 February 1898; *NODS*, 16 February 1898.

12. *Opelousas (La.) Courier*, 26 March 1898; *NODS*, 19 March 1898.

13. *NODP*, 9 March 1898; *NODP*, 25 March 1898; *Morgan City (La.) Independent Democrat*, 26 March 1898.

14. Frank Putnam-Joseph Leveque correspondence, *Harlequin* 1, no. 49 (2 June 1900): 2–3; *Shreveport Daily Times* as reprinted by the *Colfax (La.) Chronicle*, 18 June 1898.

15. *Beaufort (N.C.) Evening Messenger*, 14 December 1898; *Dunn (N.C.) County Union*, 11 January 1899.

16. *Raleigh Gazette*, 31 October 1896.

17. *Raleigh Biblical Recorder*, 6 October 1897; *Raleigh Gazette*, 16 October 1897.

18. *Raleigh Biblical Recorder*, 10 November 1897; *Raleigh Gazette*, 17 November 1897; *Raleigh Gazette*, 20 November 1897; *Raleigh Gazette*, 19 February 1898.

19. *Greenwood (Miss.) Commonwealth*, 14 November 1898.

20. *Raleigh Biblical Recorder*, 2 November 1898; *RNO*, 1 November 1898.

21. *Henderson (N.C.) Gold Leaf*, 3 November 1898; *Raleigh Biblical Recorder*, 2 November 1898.

22. *RNO*, 13 January 1899. The North Carolina state house and senate approved the amendment on February 17 and 18, respectively. *RNO*, 18 February 1899 and *RNO*, 19 February 1899. See also, for example, "Shame on Shame," *Independent* 51, no. 2621 (23 February 1899): 567–68; Walter C. Hamm, "The Three Phases of Colored Suffrage," *North American Review* 168, no. 1008 (March 1899): 285–96.

23. *Henderson (N.C.) Gold Leaf*, 31 May 1900. For a sampling of these varied arguments See, for example, *Durham (N.C.) Daily Sun*, 30 March 1899; *Concord (N.C.) Daily Concord Standard*, 11 March 1899; *Henderson (N.C.) Gold Leaf*, 2 August 1900; *Salisbury (N.C.) Weekly Sun*, 1 August 1900; *Plymouth (N.C.) Roanoke Beacon*, 22 June 1900; *Plymouth (N.C.) Roanoke Beacon*, 29 June 1900; *Plymouth (N.C.) Roanoke Beacon*, 13 July 1900; *Plymouth (N.C.) Roanoke Beacon*, 20 July 1900; *Elizabeth City (N.C.) North Carolinian*, 5 July 1900; *Elizabeth City (N.C.) North Carolinian*, 26 July 1900.

24. *Springfield (Mass.) Republican*, 30 April 1898; *Minneapolis Journal*, 19 April 1900; *BAH*, 31 July 1900.

25. William W. Kitchin, *The North Carolina Suffrage Amendment: Speech of Hon. Wm. W. Kitchin of North Carolina, in the House of Representatives, Thursday, May 3, 1900* (Raleigh, N.C.: n.p., 1900), 17; The Louisiana Amendment the Same as Ours! anonymous broadside, 1900.

26. *Boone (N.C.) Watauga Democrat*, 13 April 1899; *Dunn (N.C.) County Union*, 5 April 1899; *Plymouth (N.C.) Roanoke Beacon*, 14 April 1899; *Greenville (N.C.) King's Weekly*, 25 April 1899.

27. *Raleigh Caucasian*, 14 June 1900; North Carolina People's Party, *The Proposed Suffrage Amendment: The Platform and Resolutions of the People's Party* (N.p.: n.p., 1900), 7; J. Fred Rippy, ed., *F. M. Simmons: Statesman of the New South: Memoirs and Addresses* (Durham, N.C.: Duke University Press, 1936), 28; North Carolina Democratic Party, *A Handbook of Republican Misrule and Negro Domination* (N.p.: n.p., 1900), 12.

28. *Elizabeth City (N.C.) North Carolinian*, 5 July 1900; *Plymouth (N.C.) Roanoke Beacon*, 18 May 1900; *Elizabeth City (N.C.) North Carolinian*, 12 July 1900.

29. *Greenville (N.C.) King's Weekly*, 23 May 1899; *Greenville (N.C.) King's Weekly*, 26 May 1899; "Indictment," in *United States v. John Thompson*, case 3818, USCCWDNC, RG 21, RUSDC, NARA, Atlanta. The case was transferred to Charlotte and the next spring the U.S. attorney dropped the charges. *AC*, 7 April 1901; *AC*, 10 April 1901. *United States v. J. L. Aiken*, case 22260, USCCWDNC, RG 21, RUSDC, NARA, Atlanta. The Swain County incident was reported in the *Raleigh Caucasian* on July 19, 1900. No records of Owl's case have been found, and it is not clear whether his suit was to be filed in federal or state court. The Jackson County incident surfaced in the *Statesville (N.C.) Landmark* on July 20, 1900, in an article reprinted from the *Charlotte Observer*. No party names were given. To date I have not located the original case files with NARA.

30. *Statesville (N.C.) Landmark*, 10 July 1900; *Rockingham (N.C.) Anglo-Saxon*, 24 August 1899; *Statesville (N.C.) Landmark*, 13 July 1900; *Statesville (N.C.) Landmark*, 20 July 1900; *WP*, 13 July 1900; *WP*, 24 July 1900.

31. *Bay Minette (Ala.) American Banner*, 16 September 1899; *Littleton (N.C.) True Reformer*, 25 July 1900; *Moravian Falls (N.C.) Yellow-Jacket*, 26 July 1900.

32. *Raleigh Biblical Recorder,* 18 July 1900.

33. *Birmingham News,* 21 May 1901; *Nashville (Tenn.) American,* 4 June 1901.

34. *Proceedings,* 12.

35. Booker T. Washington, "Atlanta Exposition Address," 18 September 1895, in *BTWPH* 4:583–87.

36. Creelman to Washington, 11 October 1895, in *BTWPH* 4:73n2.

37. BTW to Francis J. Grimké, 24 September 1895, in *BTWPH* 4:24–25.

38. "An Open Letter to Benjamin Ryan Tillman," reprinted from the *New York World,* in *BTWPH* 4:71–73.

39. Booker T. Washington, "Who Is Permanently Hurt?" in *BTWPH* 4:186–87. Originally published in *Our Day,* June 1896.

40. "An Open Letter to the Louisiana Constitutional Convention," 19 February 1898, in *BTWPH* 4:381–84.

41. Ibid.

42. Ibid.

43. John F. Patty to Washington, 4 July 1898, in *BTWPH* 4:437–38.

44. Way out in Hawaii, a month after the U.S. annexed the island nation, Honolulu's *Hawaiian Gazette* reviewed Louisiana's grandfather clause and concluded, matter of factly, that it "will soon go to the Supreme Court . . . and its decision will be of the greatest value in settling the rights of the colored men." *Honolulu Hawaiian Gazette,* 12 August 1898.

45. *Constitution and By-laws of the National Afro-American Council: Organized at Rochester, New York, September 15th, 1898* (New York: Edgar Printing and Stationery, 1898); *Official Programme: First Annual Meeting of the Afro-American Council at the Metropolitan Baptist Church, Washington, D.C., Thursday and Friday, December 29 and 30, 1898* (Washington, D.C., 1899); Cyrus Field Adams, *The National Afro-American Council, Organized in 1898: A History of the Organization, its Objects, Synopses of Proceedings, Constitution and By-Laws, Plan of Organization, Annual Topics, Etc.* (Washington: C. F. Adams, 1902); *SWCA,* 24 November 1898; *Philadelphia North American,* 30 December 1898; *Zion's Herald,* 4 January 1899; *WP,* 30 January 1899.

46. *NODP,* 12 April 1899; *Bangor (Maine) Daily Whig & Courier,* 4 May 1899; *Boston Daily Advertiser,* 4 May 1899.

47. *Macon Telegraph,* 17 October 1898.

48. *Macon Telegraph,* 18 November 1898 (reprinting Washington's statements to the *Birmingham Age-Herald* and *Montgomery Advertiser*); W. E. B. Du Bois, *The Souls of Black Folk* (New York: Modern Library, 2003), 46; *Portland Morning Oregonian,* 27 November 1898; *RNO,* 22 November 1898.

49. W. E. B. Du Bois, "The Suffrage Fight in Georgia," *Independent* 51, no. 2661 (30 November 1899): 3226–28; "Disfranchisement Defeated in Georgia," *Independent* 51, no. 2662 (7 December 1899): 3306–7; "Disfranchising the Negro," *Nation* 69, no. 1795 (23 November 1899): 384–85; Ralph Wardlaw, "Negro Suffrage in Georgia, 1867–1930" (master's thesis, University of Georgia, 1932); Clarence Bacote, "Negro Proscriptions, Protests, and Proposed Solutions in Georgia, 1880–1908," *Journal of Southern History* 25, no. 4 (November 1959): 471–98.

50. Michael Perman, *Struggle for Mastery: Disfranchisement in the South, 1888–1908* (Chapel Hill: University of North Carolina Press, 2001), 281–87.

51. Ibid.

52. MacCorkle presented the proposal at the 1900 Southern Conference on Race Problems. See William A. MacCorkle, *The Negro and the Intelligence and Property Franchise: Address of Wm. A. MacCorkle, Late Governor of West Virginia, Before the Southern Conference on Race Problems, Montgomery, Alabama, May 9, 1900* (Cincinnati: Robert Clarke, 1900); Edward Atkinson to Washington, 20 October 1899, Reel 7, BTWPLC.

53. Atkinson to BTW, 28 October 1899, Reel 7, BTWPLC.

54. BTW to Francis Jackson Garrison, 27 February 1900, in *BTWPH* 5:450–51; Richard Price Hallowell to BTW, 2 March 1900, in *BTWPH* 5:451–52; BTW to Francis Jackson Garrison, 11 March 1900, in *BTWPH* 5:458. Edmunds was an extremely vocal critic of disfranchisement and involved himself in North Carolina's ongoing ratification campaign. In a letter published in a widely distributed antiratification collection, he warned that the North Carolina grandfather clause constituted "an admission THAT A SUBTERFUGE IS NECESSARY." The device, he continued, "is MANIFESTLY REPUGNANT TO THE FIFTEENTH AMENDMENT and void" (uppercase added by publisher). Edmunds's letter appeared in *The Proposed Franchise Amendment: Some Constitutional Discussion with Declarations from Vance, Saunders, Ransom, Scales, Fowle, and Others* (N.p.: n.p., 1900), 12.

55. *A. L. Gusman, in Behalf of Nathan Wright v. L. H. Marrero,* docket no. 12849, USC-CEDL, RUSDC, RG 21, NARA, Fort Worth, Tex.; Rebecca J. Scott, *Degrees of Freedom: Louisiana and Cuba after Slavery* (Cambridge: Harvard University Press, 2005), 190–92.

56. Richard W. Thompson to BTW, 14 March 1900, in *BTWPH* 5:461–64; Thomas Robert Cripps, "The Lily White Republicans: The Negro, The Party, and the South in the Progressive Era" (Ph.D. diss., University of Maryland, 1967), 72.

57. Louis R. Harlan, "The Secret Life of Booker T. Washington," *Journal of Southern History* 37, no. 3 (August 1971): 393–416; August Meier, "Toward a Reinterpretation of Booker T. Washington," *Journal of Southern History* 23, no. 2 (May 1957): 220–27.

58. Wilford H. Smith to Emmet Scott, 24 May 1900, Reel 78, BTWPLC. Scott was Washington's private secretary and Smith had written to say that he was studying the constitutions of South Carolina, Mississippi, and Louisiana.

59. Fitzhugh Lee Styles, *Negroes and the Law: in the Race's Battle for Liberty, Equality, and Justice under the Constitution of the United States, with Causes Celebres* (Boston: Christopher Publishing House, 1937), 16; *Carter v. Texas,* 177 U.S. 442 (1900).

60. The first census record for Wilford Smith was in 1880. The 1880 U.S. census shows a twenty-year-old, black "Wilford Smith" living in Philadelphia, Pennsylvania. His occupation is listed as "farmhand," and he lived in the William Roberts household. He reappears in the 1900 and 1910 U.S. censuses. He does not appear in the 1920 U.S. census or in any other census (the 1890 U.S. census records were destroyed by fire). See 1880 U.S. census for Philadelphia, Pennsylvania, Enumeration District 467, p. 101D; 1900 U.S. census for Galveston, Texas, Enumeration District 11, sheet 7B; 1910 U.S. census for Manhattan Borough, New York City, New York, Enumeration District 1284, sheet 10A; J. Clay Smith, *Emancipation: The Making of the Black Lawyer, 1844–1944* (Philadelphia: University of Pennsylvania Press, 1993), 283; Irvin C. Mollison, "Negro Lawyers in Mississippi," *Journal of Negro History* 15, no. 1 (January 1930): 63. I would like to thank Dean Ronald Cass of the Boston University Law School and Assistant Dean Margo Hagopian for their efforts to track down Smith's aca-

demic record. It appears that those records are lost, but they were able to confirm that Smith graduated with a law degree in 1883.

61. 1880 U.S. census for Greenville, Mississippi, Enumeration District 91, p. 42B. The entry for Wilford Smith in the 1900 census shows him living in Galveston as a boarder. A second boarder in the same house was twenty-two-year-old Owen Compton. I believe that Owen Compton was Smith's brother-in-law, though he was not listed as a member of Eliza Kane's household in 1880. Though I cannot determine whether Wilford and Laura were together in Galveston, I do know that they remained married. In April 1910, according to the U.S. census, Smith reported to the census enumerator that he had been married for twenty-four years. 1910 U.S. census for Manhattan Borough, New York City, New York, Enumeration District 1284, sheet 10A.

62. Maxwell Bloomfield, "From Deference to Confrontation: The Early Black Lawyers of Galveston, Texas, 1895–1920," in *The New High Priests: Lawyers in Post–Civil War America*, ed. Gerard W. Gewalt (Westport, Conn.: Greenwood Press, 1984), 158, 161.

63. Smith to BTW, 21 February 1898, Reel 78, BTWPLC; Smith to BTW, 25 July 1898, Reel 78, BTWPLC.

64. *Carter v. State*, 46 S.W. 236 (Tex. 1898), 39 Tex.Crim. 345 (1898). The original case files for this case and its successor—*Carter v. State*, 48 S.W. 508 (Tex. 1898); 39 Tex.Crim. 345 (1898)—have been lost; *Carter v. Texas*, 177 U.S. 442 (1900). Texas has two courts of last resort: the Supreme Court of Texas, which only considers civil matters, and the Texas Court of Criminal Appeals.

65. *Carter v. Texas*, 177 U.S. 442 (1900); *Galveston Daily News*, 2 May 1900; *A.M.E. Church Review* 7, no. 4 (April 1901): 397.

66. Scott to BTW, 17 April 1900, in *BTWPH* 5:486–87; Scott to BTW, 25 July 1900, in *BTWPH* 5:592.

67. Scott to BTW, 21 June 1900, Reel 72, BTWPLC; Scott, *Degrees of Freedom*, 191.

68. Scott to BTW, 21 June 1900, Reel 72, BTWPLC; BTW to Scott, 24 June 1900, Reel 72, BTWPLC.

69. Smith to Scott, 2 July 1900, Reel 78, BTWPLC; Keyssar, 87–88, 89.

70. Ibid.

71. Ibid.

72. Lawson to BTW, 3 October 1900, in *BTWPH* 5:647–49; Lawson to BTW, 8 October 1900, in *BTWPH* 5:651–52. Lawson explained the check-drafting scheme thus: A $250 draft had been prepared and signed over to Birney by Lawson. Lawson was going to send it to St. Paul, Minnesota, for Frederick McGhee's signature. McGhee would then forward it to Bishop Alexander Walters in Jersey City, New Jersey. Walters would sign it and send it along to Frank Blagburn in Des Moines, Iowa. After adding his endorsement, Blagburn would return it to Walters, but in the meantime Walters would have left for a three-month absence and after he returned he would send it to Birney. After all that effort Birney would finally be paid his money "if there be any in the treasury."

73. John Milholland to BTW, 9 October 1900, in *BTWPH* 5:654–56.

74. Joseph Logsdon and Lawrence Powell, "Rodolphe Lucien Desdunes: Forgotten Organizer of the *Plessy* Protest," in *Sunbelt Revolution: The Historical Progression of the Civil Rights Struggle in the Gulf South, 1866–2000*, ed. Samuel C. Hyde Jr. (Gainesville: University

Press of Florida, 2003), 67–68n39; Charles A. Lofgren, *The Plessy Case: A Legal-Historical Interpretation* (New York: Oxford University Press, 1987), 28–43. McGhee was an associate of Washington but he moved in a distant orbit. He was a member of the national AAC and he and Washington collaborated on more than one civil rights fight. He later split to join the Niagra movement, which was his brainchild. See *BTWPH* 5:648n2.

75. William Ivy Hair, *Carnival of Fury: Robert Charles and the New Orleans Race Riot of 1900* (Baton Rouge: Louisiana State University Press, 1976), 188; John Smith Kendall, *History of New Orleans* (Chicago: Lewis, 1922), 538–40; "Current Events," *Friend's Intelligencer* 57, no. 31 (4 August 1900): 663. See also, for example, "Review of the Month," *Gunton's Magazine*, September 1900, 200; "Waning Respect for Law," *Congregationalist* 85, no. 35 (30 August 1900): 272; Flora McDonald Thompson, "News of the World," Harper's *Bazaar* 33, no. 32 (11 August 1900): 959; "The New Orleans Riot," *Independent* 52, no. 2696 (2 August 1900): 1881.

76. "Ministers and Churches," *Watchman* 81, no. 32 (9 August 1900): 24; Flora McDonald Thompson, "News of the World," *Harper's Bazaar* 33, no. 34 (25 August 1900): 1089.

77. *Wiley v. Sinkler,* 179 U.S. 58 (1900).

78. *Gusman v. Marerro,* 180 U.S. 81 (1901) 87; Scott, *Degrees of Freedom,* 191.

79. *NYT,* 5 March 1901; *Conecuh (Ala.) Record,* 8 March 1901; "Editorials," *A.M.E Church Review* 7, no. 4 (April 1901): 390–93; *WP,* 13 May 1901; *A.M.E. Church Review* 17, no. 4 (April 1901): 390.

80. Smith to James B. Stubbs, 9 July 1901, as cited in Bloomfield, "From Deference to Confrontation," 161.

CHAPTER FOUR

1. *Proceedings,* 54–55, 58–59

2. *BDL,* 27 May 1901; *Carrollton West Alabamian,* 29 May 1901.

3. *Elba (Ala.) Clipper,* 23 May 1901; *Vernon (Ala.) Courier,* 30 May 1901.

4. *NYT,* 9 June 1901; *Duluth (Minn.) News Tribune,* 30 May 1901. See also *Lexington (Ky.) Leader,* 26 May 1901.

5. *CS,* 26 July 1901; *JDCL,* 13 June 1901. See also *SPA,* 25 May 1901; *Every Evening, Wilmington (Del.) Commercial,* 11 June 1901; *SWCA,* 13 June 1901.

6. *Montpelier Vermont Watchman and State Journal,* 19 June 1901; *MA,* 4 June 1901; *Tuskegee (Ala.) News,* 29 May 1901. Oates's interview circulated broadly. See *Cleveland (Ohio) Plain Dealer,* 20 May 1901; *Duluth (Minn.) News Tribune,* 20 May 1901; *St. Paul (Minn.) Daily Pioneer Press,* 20 May 1901; *Chicago Daily Tribune,* 20 May 1901; *Galveston Daily News,* 20 May 1901; *SPA,* 25 May 1901; *Kansas City (Kans.) American Citizen,* 24 May 1901.

7. "Minutes of a Meeting in Montgomery," 20 May 1901, in *BTWPH* 6:117–18.

8. BTW to John B. Knox, 23 May 1901, *Proceedings,* 189.

9. *Proceedings,* 187–88.

10. *Proceedings,* 189–92. The petition was presented over twenty-four men's names: Chas. O. Boothe, D. H. Tulane, Elijah Cook, John L. Thomas, M. H. Adams, Moses Davis, H. J. A. Loveless, A. J. Wilborn, A. J. Wood, J. W. Adams, John N. Brown, Alfred C. Dungee, M.D., Booker T. Washington, S. S. H. Washington, C. F. Steers Sr., William Watkins,

Henry Todd, S. Ross, R. H. Herron, W. R. Pettiford, W. H. Council, R. B. Hudson, R. E. Lee, and Addison Wimbs.

11. "June 17, 1901 Press Release," in *BTWPH* 6:155–56; *Salt Lake City Salt Lake Tribune*, 30 May 1901. See also *Kansas City (Kans.) American Citizen*, 31 May 1901; *Tucson Daily Citizen*, 4 June 1901; *Atlanta Journal*, 28 May 1901; *Bangor (Maine) Daily News*, 29 May 1901; *Springfield Illinois State Journal*, 29 May 1901; *Davenport (Iowa) Daily Republican*, 29 May 1901; *Anaconda (Mont.) Standard*, 29 May 1901.

12. *Biloxi (Miss.) Daily Herald*, 7 June 1901; *Greensboro (Ala.) Watchman*, 20 June 1901.

13. *Proceedings*, 429, 431, 652, 2069–71.

14. *Mobile Southern Watchman*, 1 June 1901.

15. *MDR*, 12 May 1901; *Mobile Daily Item*, 12 May 1901; *SFC*, 21 May 1901.

16. *MJ*, 8 June 1901.

17. *RP*, 8 June 1901; *WB*, 22 June 1901.

18. *Mobile Weekly Press*, reprinted in the *MJ*, 3 June 1901. No copies of the *Weekly Press* survive. Reverend Johnson, the *Washington Post* reported, had promised "a day of reckoning for the South." *WP*, 4 June 1901; *Trenton (N.J.) Times*, 1 June 1901. See also David E. Alsobrook, "Mobile's Forgotten Progressive—A.N. Johnson, Editor and Entrepreneur," *Alabama Review* 32, no. 3 (July 1979): 188.

19. *Fort Payne (Ala.) Journal*, 3 June 1901; Thomas Goode Jones to BTW, 10 June 1901, in *BTWPH* 6:154. See also, for example, *Hamilton (Ala.) Marion County Democrat*, 7 June 1901; *MJ*, 4 June 1901; *Centre (Ala.) Cherokee Harmonizer*, 6 June 1901. See also *Plymouth (N.C.) Roanoke Beacon*, 14 June 1901; *Rockingham (N.C.) Anglo-Saxon*, 6 June 1901.

20. "Report of the Committee on Suffrage and Elections," Report no. 19, Records of the Alabama Constitutional Convention of 1901, Container 13075, ADAH; *Proceedings*, 1258–64; *JDCL*, 31 July 1901. Kirk Porter later described the scheme as the "most elaborate suffrage requirements in the United States." See Kirk H. Porter, *A History of Suffrage in the United States* (New York: Greenwood Press, 1969), 213.

21. The suffrage article did not clearly delineate between "permanent" and "temporary" sections. The temporary plan was contained in Sections 2, 4, and 6 (*Proceedings*, 1258, 1264). The descendants clause was imbedded in Section 4 of the proposed suffrage article:

> *Sec. 4.* The following male citizens of this State who are citizens of the United States, 21 years old or upwards, who, if their place of residence shall remain unchanged, will have, at the date of the next general election, the qualifications as to residence prescribed in Section 2 of this Article and who are not disqualified under Section 6 of this Article, shall, upon application, be entitled to register as electors prior to the first day of January 1903, namely:
>
> First—All who have honorably served in the land or naval forces of the United States in the War of 1812, or in the War with Mexico, or in any war with the Indians, or in the Civil War between the States, or in the war with Spain, or who honorably served in the land or naval forces of the Confederate States, or of the State of Alabama in the war between the States; or
>
> Second—The lawful descendants of persons who honorably served in the land or naval forces of the United States in the War of the American Revolution, or in the War of 1812, or in the War with Mexico, or in any war with the Indians, or in

the Civil War between the States, or in the land or naval forces of the Confederate States; or

Third—All persons of good character and who understand the duties and obligations of citizenship under a republican form of government. (*Proceedings,* 1258–59)

22. *Plymouth (N.C.) Roanoke Beacon,* 5 July 1901.

23. George Brown Tindall, "The South Carolina Constitutional Convention of 1895" (master's thesis, University of North Carolina–Chapel Hill, 1948), 132–33. Eufaula's *Times and News* (whose publisher, William Dorsey Jelks, became governor during the 1901 convention) advised on July 1, 1901, that "the milk in the cocoanut" of the Coleman committee's proposal was the boards of registrars. The registrars possessed incredible power and could register or not register anyone they chose. Like all the other tricks used by southern disfranchisers, this was an open secret. As the *Montgomery Journal* noted on July 1, 1901, "Even the right of appeal from the temporary registrars to the circuit and supreme courts, is a little detail thrown in to sound well."

24. BTW to Thomas Coleman, 22 July 1901, in *BTWPH* 6:179; Addison Wimbs to BTW, 6 July 1901, in *BTWPH* 6:167–68.

25. Fortune to BTW, 4 June 1901, Reel 46, BTWPLC; Fortune to BTW, 21 June 1901, Reel 46, BTWPLC; Alexander Walters to BTW, 27 June 1901, in *BTWPH* 6:160; Fortune to BTW, 27 June 1901, Reel 46, BTWPLC; Fortune to BTW, 22 July 1901, Reel 46, BTWPLC; Fortune to BTW, 27 July 1901, Reel 46, BTWPLC.

26. *Washington Evening Star,* 25 June 1901; *Indianapolis Freeman,* 29 June 1901; *RNO,* 27 June 1901.

27. *State ex rel. Ryanes v. Jeremiah Gleason,* case 65432, OPCDCR; *MDR,* 14 July 1901; *MJ,* 23 May 1901. See also *NODS,* 12 July 1901; *Forth Worth (Tex.) Register,* 12 July 1901; *NODP,* 13 July 1901; *MA,* 13 July 1901; *NODP,* 13 July 1901; *Savannah Morning News,* 16 July 1901; *CDO,* 26 July 1901.

28. *Raleigh Progressive Farmer,* 6 August 1901; "Mandamus Petition," 12 July 1901, *State ex rel. Ryanes v. Jeremiah Gleason,* case 65432, OPCDCR; NOTD as reprinted by the *WP,* 13 July 1901; *MA,* 13 July 1901.

29. Josephus Daniels interview of Jeremiah Gleason, originally published in the *Raleigh News and Observer,* reprinted in the *Rockingham (N.C.) Anglo-Saxon,* 24 May 1900.

30. *SWCA,* 18 July 1901.

31. Albert Pillsbury to BTW, 30 July 1901, in *BTWPH* 6:182–83.

32. *NOTD* editorial, as reprinted by the *WP,* 13 July 1901; "An Appalling Political Blunder," *Harlequin* 2, no. 52 (18 July 1901): 4; *RP,* 20 July 1901.

33. *Lafayette (Ala.) Sun,* 29 June 1901; *Eufaula (Ala.) Times and News,* 4 July 1901.

34. *Proceedings,* 2953, 2954–55.

35. *Proceedings,* 2959; *AC,* 12 July 1901.

36. *JDCL,* 31 July 1901; *Dallas Morning News,* 23 August 1901; *Savannah Morning News,* 4 August 1901. See also *Springfield (Mass.) Republican,* 23 August 1901.

37. "Exceptions and Answers to Petition and Amended and Supplemental Petition and Response to Writ of Mandamus," 12 August 1901, and "Judgement," 23 August 1901, *David J. Ryanes v. Jeremiah Gleason,* OPCDCR; *WP,* 25 August 1901; *SPA,* 24 August 1901. See also *MA,* 24 August 1901; *CDO,* 23 August 1901.

38. *Plymouth (N.C.) Roanoke Beacon*, 30 August 1901; *Shreveport (La.) Caucasian*, 21 August 1901.

39. *Geneva (Ala.) Reaper*, 25 September 1901; *Opelika (Ala.) Industrial News*, 25 October 1901.

40. *Centreville (Ala.) Press*, 15 August 1901; *Chicago Broad Ax*, 7 September 1901.

41. *NODS*, 6 October 1901; *NYT*, 26 September 1901; *Rockford (Ala.) Coosa Argus*, 17 October 1901; *Indianapolis News*, 7 October 1901.

42. *Houston Daily Post*, 3 October 1901; *NDD*, 3 October 1901.

43. Alabama Democratic Party State Campaign Committee, *Address of the Democratic State Campaign Committee to the People of Alabama* (Birmingham, Ala.: n.p.,1900) (copy held by New York Public Library), 5

44. Ibid., 5, 6.

45. Ibid., 7.

46. *Monroeville (Ala.) Monroe Journal*, 10 October 1901; *Greenville (Ala.) Living Truth*, 11 October 1901.

47. *Gate City (Ala.) Humming Bird*, 16 November 1901.

48. *NYT*, 12 November 1901; John Henry Wallace, *The Senator from Alabama: A Romance of the Disfranchisement of the Negro and Including a Scathing Arraignment of the White House Social-Equality Policy* (New York: Neale, 1904), 235–36; *Bessemer Weekly*, 16 November 1901.

49. *Columbiana (Ala.) People's Advocate*, 19 September 1901; Robert McDavid and Charles Brown to Jelks, 20 November 1901, Container SG23643, Folder 7, Governor William Dorsey Jelks Papers, Alabama Governors Papers, ADAH; *NYT*, 21 November 1901; Malcolm Cook McMillan, *Constitutional Development in Alabama, 1798–1901: A Study in Politics, the Negro, and Sectionalism* (Spartanburg, S.C.: Reprint Company, 1978), 350.

50. *Columbiana (Ala.) People's Advocate*, 17 October 1901.

CHAPTER FIVE

1. Walter Lynwood Fleming to William Dorsey Jelks, 16 November 1901, Container SG23643, Folder 7, Governor William Dorsey Jelks Papers, Alabama Governors Papers, ADAH (hereafter cited as Jelks Papers). Fleming was one of William A. Dunning's students. He had received his master of arts degree just a few months earlier and would receive his Ph.D. in 1904. The son of a Pike County planter, Fleming was possessed of the historical sensibilities typical of the "Dunning school." Fleming's career took him to West Virginia University, Louisiana State University, and finally to Vanderbilt University, where he spent the bulk of his career. His name is attached to the most prestigious lecture series in southern history, Louisiana State University's Walter Lynwood Fleming Lectures. Fleming's most important published contributions were *Civil War and Reconstruction in Alabama* (New York: Macmillan, 1905), and his *Documentary History of Reconstruction*, 2 vols. (Cleveland: Arthur H. Clark, 1906, 1907). For a good biography of Fleming, see Fletcher Green, "Walter Lynwood Fleming: Historian of Reconstruction," *Journal of Southern History* 2, no. 4 (November 1936): 497–521.

2. R. Burnham Moffat, "The Disfranchisement of the Negro, from a Lawyer's Standpoint," paper delivered before the American Social Science Association, published in *Journal of Social Science* 42 (September 1904): 40; emphasis added by publisher.

3. *Centreville (Ala.) Press,* 21 November 1901; George Taylor to Thomas Sowell, 6 December 1901, Alabama State Auditor, Administrative Correspondence, 1821–, Container SG21864, ADAH (hereafter cited as Sowell Papers).

4. Charles Thompson to Sowell, 10 December 1901, Container SG21864, Sowell Papers; L. A. Collier to Thomas Sowell, 18 November 1901, Container SG23691, Folder 34, Jelks Papers; Robert Ransom Poole to Samuel Blackwell, 22 November 1901, Alabama Department of Agriculture and Industries, Commissioners' Correspondence, Container SG6460 (hereafter cited as Poole Papers).

5. Democratic Executive Committee of Norfolk County, Virginia, *A Political Cancer: Being an Abridged History of the Norfolk County Conspiracy and an Incidental Personal Controversy* (Norfolk, Va.: n.p., 1904), 1. Glass's speech and subsequent barrage of *Lynchburg Daily News* editorial columns were published in *A Political Cancer.*

6. Carter Glass, "An Abridged History of the Norfolk County Infamy," *Lynchburg Daily News,* 7 November 1903, reprinted in Democratic Executive Committee of Norfolk County, *Political Cancer,* 8; Carter Glass, "Political Cancer," *Lynchburg Daily News,* 25 December 1903, reprinted in Democratic Executive Committee of Norfolk County, *Political Cancer,* 13. Norfolk newspapers devoted extensive coverage to this, and a whole series of other and related political controversies throughout 1903–1903.

7. William Councill to Jelks, 29 November 1901, Container SG23644, Folder 4, Jelks Papers.

8. William C. Oates to BTW, 2 October 1901, in *BTWPH* 6:222–23. For the full story of this episode, see R. Volney Riser, "'The Milk in the Cocoanut': Booker T. Washington, Theodore Roosevelt, and the Fear of Conspiracy in Alabama's 1901 Constitutional Ratification Referendum," *Southern Historian* 26 (Spring 2005): 30–54.

9. Louis R. Harlan and Pete Daniel, "A Dark and Stormy Night in the Life of Booker T. Washington," *Negro History Bulletin* 33, no. 7 (November 1970): 159–63; Louis R. Harlan, *Booker T. Washington: The Making of a Black Leader, 1856–1901* (New York: Oxford University Press, 1972), 171–75; Wilford H. Smith to BTW, 25 March 1902, Reel 15, BTWPLC.

10. *Tuscumbia (Ala.) American Star,* 10 April 1902; Alabama Constitution of 1901, Article 8 § 187, states: "Unless he shall become disqualified under the provisions of this article, any one who shall register prior to the first day of January, nineteen hundred and three, shall remain an elector during life, and shall not be required to register again." The boards of registrars were to submit the registration lists to the county probate judges by February 1, 1903. The judges were then to submit those lists to the secretary of state by March 1, 1903, and the secretary would collect the sixty-six lists into a single registry.

11. W. P. Guinon to Charles Brown, 2 October 1902, Alabama Attorney General's Office, Correspondence 1889–1907, Container SG10762, ADAH; Louis R. Harlan, *Booker T. Washington: Wizard of Tuskegee, 1901–1915* (New York: Oxford University Press, 1983), 245; account retold by Wilford H. Smith in "The Negro and the Law," in *The Negro Problem: A Series of Articles by Representative American Negroes of Today,* by Booker T. Washington, W. E. B. Du Bois, Charles W. Chesnutt, Wilford H. Smith, H. T. Kealing, Paul Laurence Dunbar, and T. Thomas Fortune (New York: James Pott, 1903), 153–55; John Henry Wallace, *The Senator from Alabama: A Romance of the Disfranchisement of the Negro and Including a Scathing Arraignment of the White House Social-Equality Policy* (New York: Neale, 1904), 236–37.

12. Henry Damon Davidson, *Inching Along* (Nashville: National Publications, 1944), 73–74. See also Rhoda Coleman Ellison, *Bibb County, Alabama: The First Hundred Years, 1818–1918* (Tuscaloosa: University of Alabama Press, 1984), 209–14.

13. John Barnett Knox, *Speech of Hon. John B. Knox, of Calhoun County, President of the Late Constitutional Convention of Alabama, in Closing the Campaign in Favor of Ratification, at Centreville, in Bibb County, Alabama, Nov. 9th, 1901* (N.p.: n.p., 1901), 18; Affidavit of Elbert Thornton, *In re Giles* (*Giles v. Teasley*), 3 Div. 418, 5 June 1902, RASC, ADAH.

14. Affidavit of Derry Fonville, *Jackson W. Giles v. Charles B. Teasley et al.*, 3 Div. 369, 28 February 1903, RASC, ADAH. Fonville, in this affidavit, stated that he served with the Eighty-second Regiment of the U.S. Colored Volunteer Infantry. I could not verify this, however. The only "Fonville" I found was a Zachariah Fonville, who served in the 122nd U.S. Colored Infantry. It is possible that Fonville went by another name during the war. Affidavits of James Horton and John Gipson, *Jackson W. Giles v. Charles B. Teasley*, 3 Div. 418, 5 June 1902, RASC, ADAH. James Horton served with the Forty-second Regiment, U.S. Colored Infantry. John Gipson, according to his affidavit, served with the 106th Regiment, U.S. Colored Infantry. His name is misspelled in the Civil War Soldiers and Sailors System, which records his name as "Gibson"; Affidavit of Riley Clark, *Jackson W. Giles v. Charles B. Teasley*, 3 Div. 418, 5 June 1902, RASC, ADAH. Riley Clark, according to his affidavit, served in the Fourteenth Regiment, U.S. Colored Infantry. However, Clark does not show up in *any* Fourteenth Regiment, white or colored. A Riley Clark does show up, however, in the Eighty-sixth U.S. Colored Infantry. Clark was seventy years old in 1902 and it is not improbable that he was simply mistaken. Nor is it improbable that he served with more than one regiment. He had, after all, lost his discharge papers. The Eighty-sixth saw duty in Alabama and the Florida Panhandle. Information on all three men's service records was found in "Civil War Soldiers and Sailors System," National Park Service, http://www.itd.nps.gov/cwss/.

15. *MA*, 5 May 1902. In 1899, Cashin was the lead author of *Under Fire with the Tenth U.S. Calvary*, a history of the Buffalo Soldiers and their role in the Spanish-American War. The volume is still well regarded and is considered to be one of the finest studies of the Buffalo Soldiers. Herschel V. Cashin, *Under Fire with the Tenth U.S. Calvary* (New York: F. Tennyson Neely, 1899). Cashin also held the distinction of being Decatur, Alabama's first black lawyer.

16. *AC*, 22 March 1902; *AC*, 26 March 1902; *AC*, 25 March 1902.

17. *Centre (Ala.) Coosa River News*, 11 April 1902; Thomas and Robert Shropshire to Sowell, 19 November 1901, Container SG21865, Sowell Papers.

18. *Centre (Ala.) Coosa River News*, 18 April 1902; *Centre (Ala.) Coosa River News*, 25 April 1902.

19. *African Methodist Episcopal Church Review* 19, no. 2 (October 1902): 576; *Fitchburg (Mass.) Daily Sentinel*, 23 August 1902; Malcolm C. McMillan, *Constitutional Development in Alabama, 1789–1901: A Study in Politics, the Negro, and Sectionalism* (Chapel Hill: University of North Carolina Press, 1955), 352; "Official Vote of Alabama, 1900" and "Official Vote of Alabama, 1902," in *Alabama Official and Statistical Register, 1903* (Montgomery: Brown Printing, 1903).

20. *MA*, 28 March 1902; *Livingston (Ala.) Sumter County Sun*, 27 March 1902; *MJ*, 20

April 1902. On May 3, the *Montgomery Advertiser* reported that Dallas County officials were said to be under "the strongest pressure to register the negroes" but had registered only thirty and did not expect the county's total black registration to top fifty. On June 23, the *Advertiser* reported that St. Clair County's board had accepted only twenty-three black men's applications.

21. *MA,* 29 June 1902; *Livingston (Ala.) Sumter County Sun,* 17 July 1902.

22. Paul McWhorter Pruitt Jr., "Joseph C. Manning, Alabama Populist: A Rebel Against the Solid South" (Ph.D. diss., College of William and Mary, 1980), 361.

23. 1880 U.S. census for Montgomery, Alabama, Enumeration District 129, Supervisor's District 4, p. 38; 1900 U.S. census for Montgomery, Alabama, Enumeration District 103, Supervisor's District 2, Sheet 11; "Petition of Jackson W. Giles," *Jackson W. Giles v. Charles B. Teasley,* 3 Div. 418, 5 June 1902, RASC, ADAH; Affidavit of Jackson W. Giles, *Jackson W. Giles v. Charles B. Teasley et al., Board of Registrars,* 3 Div. 369, 28 February 1903, RASC, ADAH.

24. *Huntsville Journal,* 1 May 1902, and *Huntsville Journal,* 8 May 1902, as cited in John Sparks, "Alabama Negro Reaction to Disfranchisement, 1901–1904" (master's thesis, Samford University, 1973), 81–82. Dorsette's Hall was on the third floor of a building erected by Dr. Cornelius Dorsette, Booker T. Washington's personal physician and the first black doctor licensed to practice in Alabama. Massachusetts congressman Samuel June Barrows described the building in 1891: "Dr. Dorsette had built up a thriving practice. He has erected a three-story brick building, on the lower floor of which are two stores, one of them a large and well-equipped drug store. A hall above is used for the accommodation of colored societies." See Samuel June Barrows, "What the Southern Negro Is Doing for Himself," *Atlantic Monthly* 67, no. 404 (June 1891): 813. Dorsette died in 1897. Dorsette's Hall served as the permanent meeting place of the Capitol City Guards, Montgomery's volunteer black infantry company. See *SPA,* 5 April 1902. By February 1903, the CMSAA had collected fifteen hundred dollars, according to Wilford Smith. See J. C. May (Wilford H. Smith) to R. C. Black (Emmet J. Scott), 6 February 1903, Reel 73, BTWPLC; *ST,* 29 March 1902; *Macon Telegraph,* 26 March 1902. In late summer, Giles and the CMSAA sought to broaden their appeal by creating the United Colored Men's Suffrage Association of Alabama, the ranks of which included black activists from around the state. However, it appears that this name was short lived and they simply identified themselves as the CMSAA. See *MA,* 17 August 1902.

25. Text of the Giles-Julian letter and *An Appeal: To the Colored Citizens of Alabama,* appear as published by the *MJ,* 29 April 1902. The *Journal* published the cover letter and the *Appeal* together.

26. Smith to Scott, 22 April 1901, as cited in Louis R. Harlan, *The Wizard of Tuskegee, 1901–1915* (New York: Oxford University Press, 1983), 246n29. I have cited from Harlan because I have not been able to locate the original document. See also May to Black, 15 September 1902, Reel 73, BTWPLC.

27. *BDL,* 1 May 1902; *BDL,* 3 May 1902; *MA,* 26 April 1902; *MA,* 27 April 1902.

28. "Affidavit of Nelson Bibb," *Jackson W. Giles v. Charles B. Teasley,* 3 Div. 418, 5 June 1902, RASC, ADAH; *WP,* 29 April 1902. The Bibb affidavit received nationwide attention. See, for example, *Lincoln Nebraska State Journal,* 28 April 1902; *Kansas City (Kans.) American Citizen,* 2 May 1902; *Indianapolis Freeman,* 3 May 1902.

CHAPTER SIX

1. "Motion to Discontinue," 30 April 1902, *State ex rel. Ryanes v. Jeremiah Gleason,* case 65432, OPCDCR; "Petition, Affidavit, and Order of Court," 30 April 1902, *State ex rel. Ryanes v. Jeremiah Gleason,* case 67606, OPCDCR.

2. North Carolina and Alabama did this to (1) make it impossible for any court to invalidate any grandfather clause registration without invalidating *all* voter registrations and (2) persuade white voters that the clause was not separable from the rest of the disfranchising scheme. "Separability" was a huge issue in North Carolina's ratification campaign. Louisiana's constitution did not have to be ratified, so "separability" was not as pressing a concern there. We might speculate that Louisiana's clause was deliberately "separable" so that it could be struck down without damaging the rest of the state's suffrage regulations. H. C. Gage, interviewed by Josephus Daniels of the *Raleigh News and Observer,* reprinted in the *Henderson (N.C.) Gold Leaf,* 31 May 1900.

3. William Ivy Hair, *Bourbonism and Agrarian Protest: Louisiana Politics 1877–1900* (Baton Rouge: Louisiana State University Press, 1969), 276. Hair derived these figures from the records maintained by Louisiana's secretary of state. Philip D. Uzee, "Republican Politics in Louisiana, 1877–1900" (Ph.D. diss., Louisiana State University, 1950), 172.

4. "Testimony of David Jordan Ryanes," 15 July 1902, *State ex rel. Ryanes v. Jeremiah Gleason,* case 67606, OPCDCR.

5. "Testimony of Jeremiah M. Gleason," 15 July 1902, *State ex rel. Ryanes v. Jeremiah Gleason,* case 67606, OPCDCR.

6. Ibid.

7. "Opinion of Honorable John St. Paul, Judge," 28 July 1902, *State ex rel. Ryanes v. Jeremiah Gleason,* case 67606, OPCDCR.

8. *BDL,* 3 May 1902; *AC,* 2 May 1902.

9. *BDL,* 2 May 1902.

10. Ibid.

11. Ibid.

12. *BDL,* 3 May 1902.

13. *BDL,* 6 May 1902; *Jackson W. Giles v. Charles Teasley et al.,* 5 June 1902, 3 Div. 418, RASC, ADAH; *Huntsville Tribune,* 1 May 1901, as cited by John Sparks, "Alabama Negro Reaction to Disfranchisement, 1901–1904" (master's thesis, Samford University, 1973), 81–82.

14. Alabama Constitution of 1901, Article VIII, § 186, Subsection 6; Alabama Constitution of 1901, Article VI, § 140, states: "Except in cases otherwise directed in this Constitution, the supreme court shall have appellate jurisdiction only." Voter registration was not one of the "cases otherwise directed." Indeed, an appeals framework was clearly stated in the text. However, the 1901 constitutional convention also provided that "the supreme court shall have power to issue writs of injunction, habeas corpus, quo warranto, and such other remedial and original writs as may be necessary to give it a general superintendence and control of inferior jurisdictions." In theory at least, Smith stood a chance of securing the hearing. In reality, he stood no chance at all; equity originated in England's chancery courts. By the thirteenth century, English courts adhered so rigidly to precedent that "they refused to issue

new kinds of writs, even when such writs became a matter of social necessity." In response to these denials, plaintiffs took their grievances to the king and "if he found their cause worthy of his grace, the monarch would administer justice." Eventually, the Crown delegated these appeals to the lord chancellor. See Philippa A. Strum, *The Supreme Court and "Political Questions": A Study in Judicial Evasion* (Tuscaloosa: University of Alabama Press, 1974), 8; *Jackson W. Giles v. Charles Teasley*, 5 June 1902, 3 Div. 418, RASC, ADAH.

15. *Jackson W. Giles v. Charles Teasley*, 3 Div. 418, 5 June 1902, RASC, ADAH. The affidavits were from Giles, W. J. Lawrence, James Jeter, Elbert Thornton, J. B. Dodson, Kinchin Harris, Edward Dale, Charles McKinney, Nelson Bibb, Daniel Biniard, J. S. Guthrie, James Horton, John Gipson, and Riley Clark; *BDL*, 7 May 1902; *MDR*, 9 May 1902.

16. *Wichita Searchlight*, 24 May 1902; *CG*, 14 June 1902; *MA*, 14 May 1902. Any state law or constitutional enactment is necessarily and automatically null if it confronts the constitution or laws of the United States. U.S. Constitution, Article VI, contains the supremacy clause: "This Constitution, and the laws of the United States which shall be made in pursuance thereof; and all treaties made, or which shall be made, under the authority of the United States, shall be the supreme law of the land; and the judges in every state shall be bound thereby, any thing in the Constitution or laws of any state to the contrary notwithstanding."

17. The state supreme court's ruling was published as *In re Giles*, 32 So. 167 (Ala. 1902), 133 Ala. 211 (1902); *BDL*, 5 June 1902; *BAH*, 6 June 1902.

18. *MA*, 6 June 1902; *Centre (Ala.) Coosa River News*, 9 May 1902; *Macon Telegraph*, 6 June 1902.

19. The three men were James Jeter, Jim Holmes, and Joe Goldsby. They were replaced by John Wilson, Aaron Timothy, and Dennis Pfeiffer. Timothy was described as "a Selma negro." Wilson and Pfeiffer were Montgomery residents. Giles eventually lost his job as well, but I have not ascertained exactly when that occurred. *MA*, 11 June 1902.

20. Filipino (Smith) to BTW, 17 June 1902, in *BTWPH* 6:481–84.

21. Thomas H. Dent, interview with Maxwell Bloomfield, 23 July 1981, cited in Bloomfield, "From Deference to Confrontation," 165; Scipio Africanus Jones, as quoted by Fitzhugh Lee Styles in *Negroes and the Law: in the Race's Battle for Liberty, Equality and Justice under the Constitution of the United States, with Causes Celebres* (Boston: Christopher Publishing House, 1937), 144. "Stare decisis" is the doctrine whereby courts stand by unbroken lines of precedent in order to maintain a stable legal system. Precedent is not broken casually and is only done in compelling circumstances.

22. Filipino (Smith) to BTW, 17 June 1902, in *BTWPH* 6:481–84.

23. Ibid.

24. *Jackson W. Giles v. Charles B. Teasley et al. (Giles v. Teasley* II), 3 Div. 368, 28 February 1903, RASC, ADAH; *Jackson W. Giles v. Charles B. Teasley et al. (Giles v. Teasley* III) 3 Div. 369, 28 February 1903, RASC, ADAH. The Montgomery City Court records for this period have been lost or destroyed. Accordingly, it is necessary to rely upon the manuscript records of the Alabama Supreme Court. There were, in all, three cases styled as *Giles v. Teasley*. The rule nisi proceeding was the first, the money damages suit was *Giles v. Teasley* II, and the mandamus petition was *Giles v. Teasley* III. Cases II and III were numbered 368 and 369 by the Alabama Supreme Court. *Columbus (Ga.) Enquirer-Sun*, 15 October 1902; see also *ST*, 28 June 1902; *MA*, 2 July 1902; *MA*, 14 October 1902.

25. *Carter v. Texas,* 177 U.S. 442 (1900); *Strauder v. West Virginia,* 100 U.S. 303 (1880); *Neal v. Delaware,* 103 U.S. 370 (1881).

26. *Dan Rogers v. State of Alabama,* 3 Div. 408, 10 July 1903, RASC, ADAH. The *Montgomery Advertiser* described the circumstances of Ben Howard's death a year later, on August 21, 1903, while Dan Rogers's U.S. Supreme Court appeal was pending.

27. The *Montgomery Advertiser*'s July 8 report explained that Smith appeared as a member of the Mississippi Bar. *Dan Rogers v. State of Alabama;* 1900 U.S. census for Alabama, Montgomery County, Supervisor's District 2, Enumeration District 126, Sheet 7.

28. Scott to Smith, 19 December 1903, in *BTWPH* 7:376. Though Scott had explained the threat quite clearly, Smith never acknowledged the incident in his own letters to Scott or Washington.

29. Black to May, 1 June 1903, Reel 73, BTWPLC; May to Black, 8 June 1903, Reel 73, BTWPLC.

30. Black to May, 1 June 1903, Reel 73, BTWPLC; May to Black, 8 June 1903, Reel 73, BTWPLC.

31. Filipino (Smith) to Ajax (Scott), 17 May 1902, in *BTWPH* 6:466; BTW to Scott, 23 June 1902, Reel 73, BTWPLC. Biographical information on Milholland comes from Albert Nelson Marquis and John W. Leonard, eds., *Who's Who in America: A Biographical Dictionary of Notable Living Men and Women of the United States,* vol. 6, *1910–1911* (Chicago: A. N. Marquis, 1911), 1319.

32. J. C. May to R. C. Black, 15 September 1902, Reel 73, BTWPLC; May to Black, 13 October 1902, Reel 73, BTWPLC; May to Black, 15 June 1903, Reel 73, BTWPLC; Black to May, 17 June 1903, Reel 73, BTWPLC.

33. Black to May, 25 June 1903, in *BTWPH* 7:184; Black to May, 25 June 1903, Reel 73, BTWPLC.

34. May to Black, 16 September 1903, Reel 73, BTWPLC; *BDL,* 29 September 1902. Smith and Scott corresponded more about finances than about any other issue. See, for example, Smith to BTW, 5 September 1902, Reel 78, BTWPLC; May to Black, 24 November 1902, Reel 73, BTWPLC; May to Black, 28 November 1902, Reel 73, BTWPLC; May to Black, 6 February 1903, Reel 73, BTWPLC; May to Black, 23 May 1903, Reel 73, BTWPLC; May to Black, 1 June 1903, BTWPLC, Reel 73; Black to May, 1 June 1903, BTWPLC, Reel 73; May to Black, 8 June 1903, Reel 73, BTWPLC; May to Black, 15 June 1903, BTWPLC; May to Black, 18 June 1903, Reel 73, BTWPLC; May to Black, 19 June 1903, Reel 73, BTWPLC; Black to May, 20 June 1903, Reel 73, BTWPLC; May to Black, 6 August 1903, Reel 73, BTWPLC; May to Black, 31 August 1903, Reel 73, BTWPLC; May to Black, 4 September 1903, Reel 73, BTWPLC; Smith to BTW, 31 March 1904, Reel 73, BTWPLC; Smith to BTW, 19 July 1904, Reel 79, BTWPLC.

35. Smith did not attend to the U.S. district court filing himself, entrusting the matter to "Ajax" (Emmet Scott). See Smith to BTW, 5 September 1902, Reel 78, BTWPLC; *MA,* 4 September 1902; *Salt Lake (Utah) Telegram,* 4 September 1902; *Colorado Springs Gazette,* 5 September 1902; *Anaconda (Mont.) Standard,* 5 September 1902; *Charlotte Observer,* 5 September 1902; *Boise Idaho Statesman,* 5 September 1902; *Worcester (Mass.) Spy,* 6 September 1902; *Boston Journal,* 8 September 1902; May to Black, 15 September 1902, Reel 73, BTWPLC. See also *SPA* (an African American paper that made immediate note of the action), 13 September 1902.

36. "Bill of Complaint and Exhibits," 3 September 1902, *Jackson W. Giles v. E. Jeff Harris, William A. Gunter, and Charles B. Teasley,* Equity Docket 234, USCCMDA, RG 21, RUSDC, NARA, Atlanta. Smith's brief stated that the permanent plan "was in real truth, enacted and intended to apply only to your orator and the negroes of Alabama, and was not intended to affect the rights and qualifications of the white people of Alabama, it being the intention to register only white persons under the temporary plan, and to force the negroes to wait until January first 1903."

37. *Wiley v. Sinkler,* 179 U.S. 58 (1900); "Bill of Complaint and Exhibits," 3 September 1902, *Jackson W. Giles v. E. Jeff Harris et al.*

38. *Boise Idaho Daily Statesman,* 5 September 1902; *SWCA,* 11 September 1902.

39. *AC,* 17 October 1901; For the full story of Jones's appointment, see R. Volney Riser, "'The Milk in the Cocoanut': Booker T. Washington, Theodore Roosevelt, and the Fear of Conspiracy in Alabama's 1901 Constitutional Ratification Referendum," *Southern Historian* 26 (Spring 2005): 30–54; "Judiciary Act of March 3, 1891," 15 Stat. 826 (1891).

40. *Proceedings,* 2889.

41. "Declaration," 2 April 1901, in *Thomas Swafford v. W. A. Templeton et al.,* case 698, USCCEDT, Southern Division, Chattanooga, RG 21, RUSDC, NARA, Atlanta.

42. J. Morgan Kousser, *The Shaping of Southern Politics: Suffrage Restriction and the Establishment of the One-Party South, 1880–1910* (New Haven: Yale University Press, 1974), 104–38; J. Morgan Kousser, "Post-Reconstruction Suffrage Restrictions in Tennessee: A New Look at the V. O. Key Thesis," *Political Science Quarterly* 88, no. 4 (December 1973): 655–83; Michael Perman, *Struggle for Mastery,: Disfranchisement in the South, 1888–1908* (Chapel Hill: University of North Carolina Press, 2001), 48–59.

43. "Declaration," 2 April 1901, in *Thomas Swafford v. W. A. Templeton et al.,* case 698, USCCEDT, RG 21, RUSDC, NARA, Atlanta.

44. *Cook v. State,* 16 S.W. 471 (Tenn. 1891); 90 Tenn. 407 (1891); *Julius Cook v. State,* Records of the Tennessee Supreme Court, Tennessee State Library and Archives, Nashville; "Opinion," 29 April 1901, in *Thomas Swafford v. W. A. Templeton et al.,* case 698, USCCEDT, RG 21, RUSDC, NARA, Atlanta. Clark's decision was reported as *Swafford v. Templeton,* 108 F. 309 (1901). When adjudicating a claim that involves a state statute, federal judges can (and usually do) apply and interpret state appellate decisions.

45. *Swafford v. Templeton,* 185 U.S. 487 (1902), 493.

46. May to Black, n.d., Reel 73, BTWPLC. While this letter is undated, it was certainly written just ahead of the U.S. district court proceeding.

47. "Demurrer of Defendants," 11 October 1902; "Decree Sustaining Demurrers and Dismissing Bill," 11 October 1902; "Notice of Appeal," 11 October 1902, "Certification of Appeal to U.S. Supreme Court," 13 October 1902, in *Jackson W. Giles v. E. Jeff Harris,* Equity Docket 234, USCCMDA, RG 21, RUSCD, NARA, Atlanta; *MA,* 11 October 1902. See also *Dallas Morning News,* 11 November 1902; *CDO,* 11 November 1902; *MA,* 12 October 1902; *MA,* 18 October 1902. For criticism of Jones, see, for example, J. Morgan Kousser, *Colorblind Injustice: Minority Voting Rights and the Undoing of the Second Reconstruction* (Chapel Hill: University of North Carolina Press, 1999), 322–23; Louis R. Harlan, "The Secret Life of Booker T. Washington," *Journal of Southern History* 37, no. 3 (August 1971): 398; Louis R. Harlan, *The Wizard of Tuskegee: 1901–1915* (New York: Oxford University Press, 1983), 246.

48. Gunter to Charles Brown, 11 October 1902, Alabama Attorney General's Papers,

Correspondence 1889–1903, Container SG10762, ADAH. Charles Teasley, one of the registrars, evidently paid for the litigation. A *Montgomery Advertiser* article from February 20, 1916, describing Teasley's reelection campaign for Montgomery County probate judge, mentioned that he had been a registrar in 1902 and stated that "for this legal fight Judge Teasley advanced the funds, but was letter reimbursed by the legislature."

49. May to Black, 13 October 1902, Reel 73, BTWPLC; *Giles v. Teasley* II was the money damages claim and *Giles v. Teasley* III was the mandamus petition.

50. *MA,* 12 October 1902; *Kansas City (Kans.) American Citizen,* 7 November 1902. See also "Alabama Registration Law," *Zion's Herald* 80, no. 45 (5 November 1902); *Alexander City (Ala.) Outlook,* 7 November 1902; *NYT,* 3 November 1902; *BAH,* 3 November 1902; *MA,* 4 November 1902; *AC,* 13 October 1902 and 3 November 1902; *Oshkosh (Wisc.) Daily Northwestern,* 11 November 1902; *Galveston Daily News,* 11 November 1902; *Honolulu Hawaiian Gazette,* 25 November 1902; *Syracuse (N.Y.) Post Standard,* 8 November 1902; *Phoenix Arizona Republican,* 28 November 1902; *SPA,* 22 November 1902.

51. Perman, *Struggle for Mastery,* 270–77; *SWCA,* 20 November 1902; "Motion to Advance," *Jackson W. Giles v. E. Jeff Harris,* October term, 1902, no. 493, 6 November 1902, RBUSSC. Smith submitted a copy to Alabama Attorney General Charles Brown and notified him that arguments on the motion would take place on November 10, 1902. See Alabama Attorney General's Office, correspondence, Container SG10762, ADAH; *MA,* 11 November 1902; *Anniston Evening Star,* 11 November 1902; *WP,* 11 November 1902; *CDO,* 17 December 1902; *Columbus (Ga.) Enquirer-Sun,* 17 December 1902; *MA,* 17 December 1902. Smith's motion to continue on printed briefs was made under the "Thirty-Second Rule," which was an application of Section 5 of the 1891 Judiciary Act. The rule was explained by Chief Justice Melville Weston Fuller in 1893: "Cases brought to this court by writ of error or appeal under Section 5 of the act of March 3, 1891, when the only question at issue is the question of jurisdiction of the court below, will be advanced on motion, and taken on printed briefs or arguments in accordance with the prescription of rule 6 in regard to motions to dismiss writs of error appeals." *Aspen Mining and Smelting Co. v. Billings,* 150 U.S. 31 (1893).

52. *AC,* 10 November 1902.

53. *Birmingham Free Speech,* 20 December 1902. The *Free Speech* credited this report to the *Mobile Church Observer; Mobile Southern Watchman,* 8 November 1902. The report was also picked up by the *Savannah Republican,* 13 December 1902. See also *Mobile Southern Watchman,* 24 January 1903. This sixty-two dollars was a contribution to the CMSAA.

54. *Dan Rogers v. State of Alabama.* Smith may have wanted to have his motion struck from the record, but court records and his correspondence with Emmet Scott do not indicate whether that was the case. The judge's decision did, however, arise as an issue during Rogers's U.S. Supreme Court appeal.

55. May to Black, 24 November 1902, Reel 73, BTWPLC. Smith hired Judd and Detweiler, Printers, of Washington, D.C., to prepare the briefs.

CHAPTER SEVEN

1. Alabama Constitution of 1901, Article VIII, § 186.

2. *WB,* 18 October 1902. This meeting, apparently, included white as well as black veterans. For a complete listing of Alabama's GAR posts, see Albert E. Smith Jr., "The Grand

Army of the Republic and Kindred Societies," Library of Congress online, http://www.loc. gov/rr/main/gar/garhome.html/. Crenshaw first served with the Third Alabama Colored Infantry and later the Eleventh Regiment, U.S. Colored Infantry. "Civil War Soldiers and Sailors System," National Park Service, available at: http://www.itd.nps.gov/cwss/. Crenshaw presumably made it to Washington, but what happened there is unclear. Records for the encampment do not indicate either any action on the GAR's part or that Crenshaw ever officially delivered the document. See, for example, *Official Program and Pictorial Souvenir of the 36th Annual Encampment of the Grand Army of the Republic: Washington, D.C., October 6th, 7th, 8th, 9th, 10th, and 11th, 1902* (Washington, D.C., 1902); *Journal of the National Encampment of the Grand Army of the Republic, 1902* (Washington, D.C., 1902).

3. *Peter Crenshaw v. State of Alabama*, Docket 825, Limestone County Circuit Court, January term, 1903, Records of the Limestone County Circuit Court Clerk, Final Record, 1902–1907, vol. 16, Limestone County Archives, Athens, Ala.; *Booker Yarbrough v. State of Alabama*, Limestone County Circuit Court, January term, 1903, Records of the Limestone County Circuit Court Clerk, Final Record, 1902–1907, vol. 16, Limestone County Archives, Athens, Ala. Yarbrough's case never actually went to trial and so it was never assigned a docket number.

4. *BDL*, 2 May 1902.

5. *Athens Alabama Courier*, 8 April 1903.

6. Washington to William Loeb Jr., 30 May 1904, in *BTWPH* 7:516–17; Washington to William Howard Taft, 11 June 1904, in *BTWPH* 7:529–30; *BTWPH* 7:517n1.

7. "Bill of Exceptions," *State v. Peter Crenshaw*, ASC, 8 Div. 938, November term, 1903, RASC, ADAH.

8. *Athens Alabama Courier*, 8 April 1903. See also *WB*, 9 May 1903.

9. *State v. Crenshaw*, 35 So. 456 (1903), 138 Ala. 506 (1903); *Boston Sunday Journal*, 18 October 1903; *Macon Telegraph*, 26 November 1903; *Athens Alabama Courier*, 2 December 1903; *WB*, 12 December 1903.

10. John Barnett Knox, "Reduction of Representation in the South," *Outlook* 79 (21 January 1905): 171; Wilford H. Smith, "Is the Negro Disfranchised?" *Outlook* 79 (29 April 1905): 1049. Francis Caffery was one of those Knox persuaded. *Crenshaw* was, Caffery wrote, proof of the appeals process' fairness and efficacy given that "a white jury protected a negro in his right to registration." See Francis A. Caffery, "Suffrage Limitations at the South," *Political Science Quarterly* 20, no. 1 (March 1905): 59.

11. *New York Evening Post*, reprinted by the *Mobile Southern Watchman*, 19 December 1903.

12. *Baltimore Afro-American Ledger*, 11 October 1902; *Milwaukee Wisconsin Weekly Advocate*, 20 November 1902.

13. *WP*, 12 April 1901; *NYT*, 13 July 1902.

14. *Richmond Dispatch*, 16 August 1902.

15. J. Clay Smith, *Emancipation: The Making of the Black Lawyer, 1844–1944* (Philadelphia: University of Pennsylvania Press, 1993), 264n322; "John Mitchell, Jr. and the *Richmond Planet*," Library of Virginia, http://www.lva.lib.va.us/whoweare/exhibits/mitchell/ajax. htm/.

16. *The Negro in Virginia: Compiled by Workers of the Writer's Program of the Works Projects*

Administration in the State of Virginia (New York: Hastings House, 1940); *Richmond Dispatch*, 16 August 1902; *WP*, 21 August 1902; *NYT*, 16 August 1902; *Trenton (N.J.) Times*, 19 August 1902; *SPA*, 3 August 1902; *RP*, 23 August 1902; *Savannah Republican*, 30 August 1902; *SWCA*, 25 September 1902.

17. *WP*, 17 October 1902; *Baltimore Afro-American Ledger*, 29 November 1902; *Troy (N.Y.) Semi-Weekly Times*, 21 November 1902; *Paris (Ky.) Bourbon News*, 2 December 1902.

18. James Tice Moore, *Two Paths to the New South: The Virginia Debt Controversy, 1870–1883* (Lexington: University Press of Kentucky, 1974), 112, 152, 86. See also Jane Dailey, *Before Jim Crow: The Politics of Race in Post-Emancipation Virginia* (Chapel Hill: University of North Carolina Press, 2000); Charles E. Wynes, *Race Relations in Virginia, 1870–1902* (Charlottesville: University Press of Virginia, 1961), 41.

19. Curtis Carroll Davis, "Very Well-Rounded Republican: The Several Lives of John S. Wise," *Virginia Magazine of History and Biography* 71, no. 4 (October 1963): 461–87; John S. Wise to Thomas Goode Jones, 10 October 1901, Container 2, Folder 17, Thomas Goode Jones Papers, ADAH.

20. *Kansas City (Kans.) Rising Son,* 27 February 1903.

21. James Clarkson to Whitefield McKinlay, 13 October 1902, Reel 1, Whitefield McKinlay Papers, Carter G. Woodson Collection, LOC, (hereafter cited as Whitefield McKinlay Papers).

22. Hayes to McKinlay, 7 November 1902, Reel 1, Whitefield McKinlay Papers.

23. Davis, "Very Well-Rounded Republican," 463.

24. U.S. Constitution, Article IV § 4. The PQD dated to *Marbury v. Madison* and was affirmed in *Luther v. Borden*, 48 U.S. 1 (1849).

25. *William Jones, John Hill, and Edgar Poe Lee v. Andrew J. Montague et al.*, 14 November 1902, docket no. 1759, USCCEDV. RUSDC, RG 21, NARA, Philadelphia; *William S. Selden, William H. Anderson, and Clarence G. Gilpin v. Andrew J. Montague et al.*, 14 November 1902, docket no. 538, USCCEDV, RUSDC, RG 21, NARA, Philadelphia; *ST*, 29 November 1902. See also *WP*, 17 October 1902; *Springfield (Mass.) Republican*, 17 November 1902; *CDO*, 16 November 1902; *Columbus (Ga.) Enquirer-Sun*, 16 November 1902; *CS*, 16 November 1902; *New York Sun*, 15 November 1902; *CG*, 15 November 1902; *WP*, 16 November 1902; *AC*, 16 November 1902; *AC*, 21 November 1902; *WCA*, 22 November 1902; *Washington (D.C.) Evening Times*, 25 November 1902; *SFC*, 26 November 1902.

26. *Baltimore Afro-American Ledger*, 22 November 1902; *WP*, 21 November 1902.

27. *NYT*, 29 November 1902; *WP*, 29 November 1902. Only two judges had to be present in order to hold a circuit court hearing. Judiciary Act of March 3, 1891, 15 Stat. 826, § 2; "Memorandum of Chief Justice Melville W. Fuller" and "Order Discharging Rule and Dismissing Bill," 29 November 1902, *William Jones, John Hill, and Edgar Poe Lee v. Andrew J. Montague et al; NYT*, 30 November 1902; *Lexington Morning Herald*, 27 November 1902; *MA*, 29 November 1902; *Omaha World-Herald*, 30 November 1902; *Troy (N.Y.) Semi-Weekly Times*, 2 December 1902.

28. "Memorandum of Hon. Edmund Waddill, U.S. Judge," 29 November 1902, *William S. Selden, William H. Anderson, and Clarence G. Gilpin v. Andrew J. Montague et al; BG*, 27 December 1902; *NYT*, 29 November 1902. Waddill's dissenting memorandum applied to both cases. *Atlanta Constitution* editorial (reprinted by the *WP*, 6 December 1902); *WCA*, 6 De-

cember 1902. See also *Baltimore Afro-American Ledger,* 6 December 1902; *Fort Wayne (Ind.) Journal-Gazette,* 30 November 1902; *SFC,* 30 November 1902; *SFC,* 6 December 1902; *ST,* 6 December 1902; *WCA,* 13 December 1902.

29. *AC,* 30 November 1902.

30. *NYT,* 1 December 1902; *SFC,* 1 December 1902; *AC,* 2 December 1902.

31. *NYT,* 26 November 1902; *New York Sun,* 26 November 1902; *CDO,* 26 November 1902; *Dallas Morning News,* 26 November 1902; *MA,* 26 November 1902; *Omaha World-Herald,* 26 November 1902.

32. *WP,* 8 December 1902; *Edgar Poe Lee v. John S. Barbour et al.,* 13 December 1902, docket no. 1762, USCDEDV, RUSDC, RG 21, NARA, Philadelphia; *WP,* 16 December 1902. (The files for Anthony Pinner's case were destroyed in a 1910s hurricane that struck Norfolk and flooded the federal courthouse.) See also *SPA,* 13 December 1902; *WP,* 14 December 1902; *Wichita Searchlight,* 3 January 1903; *CDO,* 7 December 1902; *CS,* 7 December 1902. Pinner's case, along with two others that were never identified by name, were transferred to the Fourth Circuit at Richmond in January 1904. See *Salt Lake Telegram,* 6 January 1904; *Olympia (Wash.) Morning Olympian,* 7 January 1904; *Boise Idaho Daily Statesman,* 8 January 1904.

33. *Florala (Ala.) News,* 19 December 1902; *WCA,* 20 December 1902; *AC,* 12 December 1902; *Philadelphia Inquirer,* 12 December 1902.

34. *Olympia (Wash.) Morning Olympian,* 12 December 1902; *CDO,* 15 January 1903; *NYT,* 15 January 1903; *WP,* 15 January 1903; *SPA,* 7 February 1903; *AC,* 15 January 1903.

35. Louis R. Harlan, *The Wizard of Tuskegee: 1901–1915* (New York: Oxford University Press, 1983), 40, 41.

36. Harlan, *Wizard of Tuskegee,* 26; Hayes to BTW, 3 February 1903, in *BTWPH* 7:30.

37. Hayes to BTW, 27 December 1904, Reel 10, BTWPLC; BTW to Hayes, 2 February 1904, Reel 10, BTW Papers, LOC; BTW to Hayes, 2 June 1904, Reel 10, BTWPLC. "Crumpackerism" was doomed on two counts. First, Republicans were scared of losing their majority. Second, it was a bad idea. Not the investigation, but the remedy Crumpacker and others hoped to pursue. Crumpacker wanted to enforce the Fourteenth Amendment's reduction of representation clause. Booker T. Washington, for one, was always an opponent of Crumpackerism because he feared that southerners might be all too willing to forgo a portion of their representation in exchange for a hands-off policy. Black southerners, in truth, were already without representation. No southern representative honestly represented their interests. A reduction in representation, meted out as punishment, would not help black southerners. See Xi Wang, *The Trial of Democracy: Black Suffrage and Northern Republicans, 1860–1910* (Athens: University of Georgia Press, 1997), 261–62; Edgar Dean Crumpacker, "Shall the Southern Delegation to Congress be Cut Down?" *Frank Leslie's Popular Monthly* 54, no. 3 (July 1902): 281–86; H. D. Money, "A Plea Against Suffrage Restriction in the South: Being an Answer to Judge Crumpacker's Article in the July Number of Leslie's Monthly," *Frank Leslie's Popular Monthly* 54, no. 6 (October 1902): 608–13.

38. Filipino (Smith) to BTW, 17 June 1902, in *BTWPH* 6:481–84.

39. J. Gordon Hylton, "The African-American Lawyer, the First Generation: Virginia as a Case Study," *University of Pittsburgh Law Review* 56 (Fall 1994): 138.

40. *WP,* 22 October 1901; *BG,* 27 December 1902.

41. *WP*, 1 December 1902; *WP*, 6 December 1902; *WP*, 8 December 1902.

42. *Norfolk Virginian-Pilot* (reprinted by the *WP*, 2 December 1902); *WP*, 2 December 1902.

43. *AC*, 27 January 1903; *Lincoln (Neb.) Evening News*, 27 January 1903; *Fort Wayne (Ind.) Journal-Gazette*, 27 January 1903; *Indiana (Pa.) Democrat*, 13 March 1903.

44. *WP*, 27 January 1903.

45. *St. Louis Palladium*, 31 January 1903; *Birmingham Truth*, 7 February 1903.

46. *Galveston Daily News*, 28 January 1903; *Tucson Daily Citizen*, 5 February 1903; *WP*, 30 January 1903. Cyrus Field Adams, a native of Louisville, Kentucky, had worked for many alongside his brother, John Quincy Adams, editor of Chicago's *Western Appeal*. Adams succeeded his brother as president of the Afro-American Press Association and was deeply involved with the AAC. In 1901 Booker T. Washington engineered his appointment as assistant registrar of the U.S. Treasury. Harlan, in *BTWPH* 6:338n4.

47. *WP*, 30 January 1903; *NYT*, 4 February 1903.

48. *MA*, 1 February 1903; *WP*, 1 February 1903; *Savannah Republican*, 7 February 1903; *Birmingham Truth*, 21 February 1903; *WP*, 7 February 1903; *Washington (D.C.) Times*, 6 February 1903.

49. *Washington (D.C.) Times*, 14 February 1903; *WB*, 21 February 1903; *Galveston Daily News*, 3 February 1903; *Birmingham Truth*, 28 February 1903; *Washington (D.C.) Colored American*, 7 February 1903.

50. *Washington (D.C.) Colored American*, 14 February 1903.

51. Ibid.

52. Ibid.; *Washington (D.C.) Colored American*, 7 February 1903.

CHAPTER EIGHT

1. "Brief for Appellant," 28 January 1903, and "Brief for Appellees," 16 February 1903, *Jackson W. Giles v. E. Jeff Harris*, October term, 1902, no. 493, RBUSC; Joseph McKenney to William A. Gunter, 27 January 1903, Container SG23645, Folder 12, Governor William Dorsey Jelks Papers, Alabama Governors Papers, ADAH (hereafter cited as Jelks Papers). William A. Gunter Sr. filed the registrars' briefs on February 24, 1903.

2. William A. Gunter to J. K. Jackson, 29 January 1903, Container SG23645, Folder 12, Jelks Papers; Jelks to Charles Brown, 30 January 1903, Container SG23645, Folder 12, Jelks Papers; *Acts of Alabama*, 1903, p. 243, no. 220.

3. *Birmingham Truth*, 7 February 1903; *Birmingham Truth*, 28 February 1903.

4. May to Black, 6 February 1903, Reel 73, BTWPLC; Smith to BTW, 13 February 1903, in *BTWPH* 7:77); *BG*, 14 February 1903; *Wichita Searchlight*, 7 March 1903.

5. *Atlanta Voice of the People*, 2 March 1903. See also *WP*, 20 February 1903; *AC*, 19 February 1903; Charles William Anderson to BTW, 25 February 1903, in *BTWPH* 7:83–84; BTW to Anderson, 28 February 1903, cited in *BTWPH* 7:84n2. See also Anderson to BTW, 13 February 1903, in *BTWPH* 7:74–75.

6. *WP*, 22 February 1903.

7. *WCA*, 25 April 1903; *New York Sun*, 7 April 1903; *New York Sun*, 13 April 1903; *NYT*, 4 April 1903; *Birmingham Truth*, 23 April 1903; *New York Sun*, 4 April 1903.

8. *Rochester (N.Y.) Union and Advertiser,* 29 April 1903.

9. This was true of federal courts in the South and the rest of the nation. See, for example, Edward Purcell, *Brandeis and the Progressive Constitution: Erie, the Judicial Power, and the Politics of the Federal Courts in Twentieth-Century America* (New Haven: Yale University Press, 2000); Tony Freyer and Timothy Dixon, *Democracy and Judicial Independence: A History of the Federal Courts of Alabama, 1820–1994* (Brooklyn: Carlson Publishing, 1995), 81.

10. Owen M. Fiss, *Troubled Beginnings of the Modern State, 1888–1910,* vol. 8 of *History of the Supreme Court of the United States* (New York: MacMillan, 1993); James W. Ely Jr., *The Chief Justiceship of Melville W. Fuller, 1888–1910* (Columbia: University of South Carolina Press, 1994); John R. Schmidhauser, *The Supreme Court as Final Arbiter in Federal-State Relations, 1789–1957* (Chapel Hill: University of North Carolina Press,1958); Peter Irons, *A People's History of the Supreme Court* (New York: Viking, 1999); Purcell, *Brandeis and the Progressive Constitution;* Robert E. Gamer, "Justice Brewer and Substantive Due Process: A Conservative Court Revisited," *Vanderbilt Law Review* 18, no. 2 (March 1965): 615–41.

11. "Brief for Appellant," 28 January 1903, United States Supreme Court, October term, 1902, no. 493, Jackson W. Giles, appellant, against E. Jeff Harris et al., Board of Registrars, Montgomery County, Alabama, appellees, RBUSC, 6–7.

12. "Brief for Appellant," 28 January 1903, 6, 16.

13. Smith to Scott, 25 March 1903, Reel 73, BTWPLC; May to Black, 30 March 1903, Reel 73, BTWPLC. I have not located any of the actual correspondence from Pillsbury regarding Smith's briefs. From Smith and Scott's correspondence it appears that Smith forwarded Pillsbury's letters to Smith and that Smith did not return them. Since Smith's own papers do not survive, neither do Pillsbury's letters.

14. Smith to Scott, 25 March 1903, Reel 73, BTWPLC.

15. Oliver Wendell Holmes Jr., "The Path of the Law," *Harvard Law Review* 10, no. 8 (25 March 1897): 459, 460.

16. Holmes, "Path of the Law," 460; *Otis v. Parker,* 187 U.S. 606 (1903) 608.

17. *Giles v. Harris,* 189 U.S. 488.

18. Louise Weinberg, "Holmes' Failure," *Michigan Law Review* 96 (1997): 695; Yosal Rogat, "Mr. Justice Holmes: A Dissenting Opinion," *Stanford Law Review* 15 (March 1963): 254–308, 262. See also, for example, Weinberg, "Holmes' Failure"; G. Edward White, *Justice Oliver Wendell Holmes: Law and the Inner Self* (New York: Oxford University Press, 1993), 333–34; Sheldon Novick, *Honorable Justice: The Life of Oliver Wendell Holmes* (Boston: Little, Brown, 1989), 459; Sheldon Novick, "Justice Holmes and the Art of Biography," *William and Mary Law Review* 33 (Summer 1992): 1219–49.

19. *WCA,* 2 May 1903. See also, for example, *Indianapolis Recorder,* 2 May 1903; *SPA,* 2 May 1903; Lawrence M. Friedman, *American Law in the Twentieth Century* (New Haven: Yale University Press, 2002), 114. Friedman's judgement, if perhaps extreme, reflects a widely accepted historical conclusion. See, for example, G. Edward White, *Justice Oliver Wendell Holmes: Law and the Inner Self* (New York: Oxford University Press, 1993), 333; Burton D. Wechsler, "Black and White Disenfranchisement: Populism, Race, and Class," *American University Law Review* 52, no. 23 (October 2002): 56; Michael Perman, *Struggle for Mastery: Disfranchisement in the South, 1888–1908* (Chapel Hill: University of North Carolina Press, 2001), 123.

20. *Gibson v. Mississippi*, 162 U.S. 565 (1896); *Smith v. Mississippi*, 162 U.S. 592 (1896); *Williams v. Mississippi*, 170 U.S. 213 (1898).

21. Michael J. Brodhead, *David J. Brewer: The Life of a Supreme Court Justice, 1837–1910* (Carbondale, Ill.: Southern Illinois University Press, 1994); Arnold M. Paul, "David J. Brewer," in *The Justices of the United States Supreme Court, 1789–1969, Their Lives and Major Opinions*, vol. 2, ed. Leon Friedman and Fred L. Israel (New York: Chelsea House, 1969), 1515–49; Gamer, "Brewer and Substantive Due Process"; Schmidhauser, *Supreme Court as Final Arbiter*, 116; Purcell, *Brandeis and the Progressive Constitution*, 51; *Giles v. Harris*, 189 U.S. 488.

22. *Giles v. Harris*, 189 U.S. 491

23. Ibid., 488, 493; *Swafford v. Templeton*, 185 U.S. 487 (1902). White sided with Holmes in *Giles v. Harris*.

24. *Plessy v. Ferguson*, 163 U.S. 537 (1896); *De Lima v. Bidwell*, 182 U.S. 1 (1901); *Downes v. Bidwell*, 182 U.S. 244 (1901). See also, for example, R. Volney Riser, "The Burdens of Being White: Empire and Disfranchisement," *Alabama Law Review* 53, no. 1 (Fall 2001): 243–272; Bartholomew H. Sparrow, *The Insular Cases and the Emergence of American Empire* (Lawrence: University Press of Kansas, 2006).

25. *Gibson v. Mississippi*, 162 U.S. 565 (1896); *Smith v. Mississippi*, 162 U.S. 592 (1896); "Judiciary Act of August 13, 1888," 25 Stat. 433; *Giles v. Harris*, 189 U.S. 504.

26. John C. Rose, "Negro Suffrage: The Constitutional Point of View." *American Political Science Review* 1, no. 1 (November 1906): 38–39; Fiss, *Troubled Beginnings of the Modern State*, 372–73, 379; White, *Justice Oliver Wendell Holmes*, 333–34; Sheldon Novick, *Honorable Justice: The Life of Oliver Wendell Holmes* (Boston: Little, Brown, 1989), 257–59; *Giles v. Harris*, 189 U.S. 488.

27. Richard Pildes has also noted the danger of looking at *Giles* backward, and the distortions thereby created. See Pildes, "Democracy, Anti-Democracy, and the Canon," *Constitutional Commentary* 17, no. 2 (Summer 2000): 301–2; Richard Pildes, "Keeping Legal History Meaningful," *Constitutional Commentary* 19, no. 3 (Winter 2002): 645–46.

28. *San Jose Mercury News*, 29 April 1903; *Dallas Morning News*, 8 May 1903. The constitutional historian Michael Klarman recently concluded that the Court's profession of judicial weakness in *Giles v. Harris* was "among the Court's most candid confessions of limited power" and that the only "analogous statements" may be found in wartime civil liberties cases. See Michael Klarman, *From Jim Crow to Civil Rights, The Supreme Court and the Struggle for Racial Equality* (New York: Oxford University Press, 2004), 36–37; Michael Klarman, "The Plessy Era," in *The Supreme Court Review, 1998*, ed. Dennis J. Hutchinson, David A. Strauss, and Geoffrey R. Stone (Chicago: University of Chicago Press, 1998), 365–66. In both pieces, Klarman draws the analogy between *Giles* and the cases of *Ex parte Milligan*, 71 U.S. 2 (1866) and *Korematsu v. United States*, 323 U.S. 214 (1944), which date from the Civil War and World War II, respectively.

29. *Indianapolis Recorder*, 2 May 1903.

30. *James v. Bowman*, 190 U.S. 127 (1903); enforcement act of 31 May 1870—"An Act to Enforce the Right of Citizens of the United States to Vote in the Several States of this Union, and for Other Reasons"—16 Stat. 140; *Chicago Record-Herald*, 6 May 1903; *WP*, 5 May 1903. Justice Brewer, significantly, made no mention whatsoever of *Ex parte Yarbrough*, the 1884

decision upholding the convictions of three *individuals* who had interfered with black vot-
ers' Fifteenth Amendment rights. *Ex parte Yarbrough,* 110 U. S. 651 (1884). See, for example,
Xi Wang, *Trial of Democracy: Black Suffrage and Northern Republicans* (Athens: University of
Georgia Press, 1997), 259; Michael J. Klarman, *From Jim Crow to Civil Rights: The Supreme
Court and the Struggle for Racial Equality* (New York: Oxford University Press, 2004), 37.

    31. *NYT,* 1 May 1903; *Rochester (N.Y.) Union and Advertiser,* 27 April 1903 and 30 April
1903; *Chicago Record-Herald,* 29 April 1903; *San Francisco Chronicle,* 28 April 1903; *Sacramento
Evening Bee,* 1 May 1903; Rogat, "Mr. Justice Holmes," 268.

    32. *RP,* 9 May 1903.

    33. *BAH,* 28 April 1903. Interestingly, the *Record-Herald* itself did not run Wellman's
piece. Instead the *Record-Herald* ran only a brief account of the decision on April 28 in a
"News of the Day" column (*Chicago Record-Herald,* 28 April 1903). The *Boston Guardian* also
mentioned Wellman's interview with the unnamed Supreme Court justice. The *Guardian*
version of May 2, 1903, however, stated that the justice was one of the majority. "Negro Suffrage and the Federal Court," *Congregationalist and Christian World* 88, no. 19 (9 May 1903):
660. See also *Anniston (Ala.) Evening Star,* 2 May 1903; *MA,* 28 April 1903; *MA,* 29 April
1903; *Fort Wayne (Ind.) Journal-Gazette,* 28 April 1903; *Phoenix Arizona Republican,* 28 April
1903; *AC,* 28 April 1903; *MDR,* 28 April 1903; *MDR,* 29 April 1903; *Grand Rapids (Mich.)
Evening Press,* 27 April 1903; *CDO,* 28 April 1903; *Aberdeen (S.D.) Daily News,* 28 April 1903;
Columbus (Ga.) Enquirer-Sun, 28 April 1903; *Columbus (Ga.) Ledger,* 28 April 1903; *Biloxi
Daily Herald,* 28 April 1903; *Boise Idaho Daily Statesman,* 28 April 1903; *Salt Lake Telegram,*
28 April 1903; *CS,* 28 April 1903; *Worcester (Mass.) Spy,* 18 April 1903; *CDO,* 29 April 1903;
Springfield (Mass.) Republican, 29 April 1903. These early reports were accounts from reporters who were present when Holmes announced the Court's decision. What he said on April
27 was not necessarily what would be written in the manuscript opinion, which was released
several days later. In the manuscript opinion, Holmes declared, "We express no opinion as to
the alleged fact of their [the sections of the Alabama constitution involved in *Giles*] unconstitutionality beyond saying that we are not willing to assume that they are valid, in the face
of the allegations and main object of the bill, for the purpose of granting the relief which it
was necessary to pray in order that that object should be secured." *Giles v. Harris,* 189 U.S.
475 (1903). Also see "The Alabama Decision," *Nation* 76, no. 1974 (30 April 1903): 346; "The
Alabama Case: Possible Remedies," *Outlook* 74, no. 2 (9 May 1903): 96; "The Alabama Case:
The Decision of the Court," *Outlook* 74, no. 2 (9 May 1903): 96; "The Alabama Case: The Case
Stated," *Outlook* 74, no. 2 (9 May 1903): 95; "The Alabama Franchise Case," *Harvard Law
Review* 17, no. 2 (December 1903): 130–31; *Washington (D.C.) National Tribune,* 21 May 1903;
MA, 28 April 1903; *AC,* 28 April 1903; *AC,* 1 May 1903; "Current Topics," *Albany Law Journal*
65, no. 5 (May 1903): 129–31; *ST,* 2 May 1903; "Negroes and the Ballot," *Zion's Herald* 81, no.
18 (6 May 1903): 547; "The Alabama Decision," *Independent* 55, no. 2840 (7 May 1903): 1104–5;
ST, 9 May 1903; *AC,* 4 June 1903; John Dos Passos, "The Negro Question," *Yale Law Journal*
12, no. 8 (June 1903): 472.

    34. Storey to Erving Winslow, 5 May 1903, Moorefield Storey Papers, Massachusetts
Historical Society, Boston, as cited in James M. McPherson, *The Abolitionist Legacy: From
Reconstruction to the NAACP* (Princeton: Princeton University Press, 1975), 355; D. Augustus
Straker, *Negro Suffrage in the South* (Detroit: Augustus Straker, 1906), 23.

35. *SWCA,* 30 April 1903; *New York Tribune* editorial, reprinted in the *Rochester (N.Y.) Union and Advertiser,* 30 April 1903; *RP,* 2 May 1903.

36. *BG,* 2 May 1903.

37. *BG,* 9 May 1903. See also *Indianapolis Freeman,* 2 May 1903; *Wichita Searchlight,* 9 May 1903; *WCA,* 9 May 1903; *WCA,* 16 May 1903; *CDO,* 1 May 1903; *Columbus (Ga.) Enquirer-Sun,* 1 May 1903; *MA,* 1 May 1903; *Portland Morning Oregonian,* 1 May 1903; *CS,* 1 May 1903; *ST,* 2 May 1903; *Springfield (Mass.) Daily Republican,* 2 May 1903; *Colorado Springs Gazette,* 6 May 1903.

38. "The Alabama Decision," *Colored American Magazine* 6 (July 1903): 536. For Senator Hoar's comments, see *Springfield (Mass.) Daily Republican,* 26 July 1903; *AC,* 30 July 1903; *WP,* 30 July 1903; Alfred Russell, "Three Constitutional Questions Decided by the Federal Supreme Court During the Last Four Months," *American Law Review* 37 (July/August 1903): 509.

39. Holmes to Clara Stevens, 12 May 1903, microfilm, Reel 14, Oliver Wendell Holmes Papers, Harvard Law School Library, Cambridge, Mass. Though Holmes is the subject of numerous major biographies penned by a number of distinguished scholars, only Liva Baker mentions the May 12, 1903, letter to Clara Stevens. See Liva Baker, *The Justice from Beacon Hill: The Life and Times of Oliver Wendell Holmes* (New York: HarperCollins, 1991), 388; G. Edward White, "The Integrity of Holmes' Jurisprudence," *Hofstra Law Review* 10 (Spring 1982): 649.

40. "Alabama Decision," 538; *RP,* 9 May 1903.

41. *In re Debs,* 158 U.S. 564 (1895); "Alabama Decision," 538, 539.

42. Melvin Chisum to Scott, 18 May 1903, Reel 73, BTWPLC; Charles Chesnutt to BTW, 2 May 1903, in *BTWPH* 7:136–37. Chesnutt and BTW corresponded along this line through the summer and fall of 1903. BTW to Chesnutt, 7 July 1903, Reel 393, BTWPLC; Chesnutt to BTW, 11 August 1903, Reel 393, BTWPLC; Chesnutt to BTW, 31 October 1903, Reel 393, BTWPLC.

43. Charles Chesnutt, "The Disfranchisement of the Negro," in *The Negro Problem: A Series of Articles by Representative American Negroes of Today,* by Booker T. Washington, W. E. B. Du Bois, Charles W. Chesnutt, Wilford H. Smith, H. T. Kealing, Paul Laurence Dunbar, and T. Thomas Fortune (New York: James Pott, 1903), 79, 91, 92; "Address of Hon. John S. Wise, before the Ohio State Bar Association, on July 19, 1903: The Constitutional View of the Race Question," in Ohio State Bar Association, *Proceedings of the Annual Meeting of the Association Held at Put-in-Bay, July 7, 8, and 9, 1903* (Toledo, Ohio: Legal News Job Rooms, Law Printers, 1903), 212, 213–14.

44. Chesnutt, "Disfranchisement of the Negro," 115–16, 118.

45. *WCA,* 2 May 1903; *BG,* 2 May 1903.

46. *BG,* 2 May 1903. The account of Hayes's comments came from Charles William Anderson, one of Washington's New York spies. The remark was made in Brooklyn, where organizers of a June antidisfranchisement meeting were finalizing plans for the event. Anderson had been at the meeting and recounted Hayes's performance in a tattletale letter to Washington. Charles William Anderson to BTW, 13 May 1903, *BTWPH* 7:138–41.

47. "Editorial," *Virginia Law Register* 9, no. 2 (June 1903): 166.

48. *Giles v. Teasley,* 33 So. 819 (Ala. 1903), 136 Ala. 164 (1903). This is the Alabama Su-

preme Court's decision in the money damages case (*Giles* II). *Giles* III, the mandamus petition, was reported as *Giles v. Teasley*, 33 So. 820 (Ala. 1903), 136 Ala. 228 (1903); "Highways and Byways," *Chautauquan* 37, no. 4 (July 1903): 332.

CHAPTER NINE

1. *MA*, 29 April 1903; *MJ*, 29 April 1903; *MDR*, 30 April 1903. I have not been able to locate any copies of the *Negro Pilot* and have tentatively established Giles's involvement with the paper from Wilford Smith's occasional references to "Giles' paper" in his correspondence with Emmet Scott and through other newspapers' fleeting references to the same effect.

2. *MA*, 6 May 1903.

3. Ibid.; *Springfield (Mass.) Daily Republican*, 3 May 1903; *New York Age*, as reprinted by the *Springfield (Mass.) Daily Republican*, 23 May 1903.

4. *MA*, 8 July 1903.

5. *MA*, 22 August 1903.

6. *MA*, 21 March 1903; *Columbus (Ga.) Enquirer-Sun*, 1 March 1903.

7. Smith to BTW, 1 March 1904, Reel 79, BTWPLC; Filipino (Smith) to BTW, 17 June 1902, in *BTWPH* 6:481–84.

8. May to Black, 23 May 1903, Reel 73, BTWPLC. At this time Smith was also preparing, at Washington's request, a circular to explain voter registration under the permanent plan. Smith to BTW, 22 May 1903, BTWPLC, Reel 78. White's decision made it onto the national news wires, though few papers ran the report. See, for example, *Duluth (Minn.) News Tribune*, 30 May 1903. Reports that Smith had docketed the cases were similarly rare. See, for example, *Columbus (Ga.) Daily Ledger*, 2 July 1903.

9. May to Black, 23 May 1903, Reel 73, BTWPLC.

10. *WP*, 15 July 1903; *NYT*, 15 July 1903.

11. May to Black, 15 July 1903, Reel 73, BTWPLC; May to Black, 17 July 1903, Reel 73, BTWPLC.

12. May to Black, 17 July 1903, Reel 73, BTWPLC.

13. May to Black, 6 August 1903, Reel 73, BTWPLC; Wilford Smith to Massey Wilson, 11 September 1903, Alabama Attorneys General Papers, Correspondence 1903–1910, Container SG10767, ADAH; *MA*, 21 August 1903.

14. *Carter v. Texas*, 177 U.S. 442 (1900); *Strauder v. West Virginia*, 100 U.S. 303 (1880); *Neal v. Delaware*, 103 U.S. 370 (1881).

15. May to Black, 31 August 1903, Reel 73, BTWPLC. In 1903 Andrew Carnegie donated $600,000 worth of U.S. Steel bonds to Tuskegee Institute with the provision that the revenue from $150,000 of the bonds go to Booker T. Washington for his personal needs and those of his widow after his death. The gift was well known publicly and widely celebrated. Louis R. Harlan, *The Wizard of Tuskegee, 1901–1915* (New York: Oxford University Press, 1983), 135. This is significant because Wilford Smith's monetary requests came with increased frequency during the spring of 1903 and some have assumed that one necessarily followed the other. Harlan suggested that the Carnegie gift might have facilitated an expansion of Washington's covert activities, the *Giles* cases among them (Harlan, *Wizard of Tuskegee*, 137). But Wash-

ington had been paying for the *Giles* cases—all five of them—for almost a year before he received the Carnegie windfall.

16. "Motion to Consolidate and Advance," 19 October 1903, *Jackson W. Giles v. Charles B. Teasley et al., Jackson W. Giles v. Charles B. Teasley et al., Rogers v. Alabama,* Alabama Attorney Generals' Office, Correspondence 1903–1910, Container SG10767, ADAH (this is the copy of the motion that Smith delivered to Attorney General Massey Wilson); *MA,* 27 October 1903. See also *AC,* 20 October 1903; *MA,* 20 October 1903; *CDO,* 20 October 1903; *Macon Weekly Telegraph,* 20 October 1903; *Dallas Morning News,* 20 October 1903; *MA,* 20 October 1903; *Columbus (Ga.) Enquirer-Sun,* 21 October 1903; *Springfield (Mass.) Daily Republican,* 22 October 1903; *WB,* 24 October 1903; *AC,* 27 October 1903; *Dallas Morning News,* 27 October 1903; *Columbus (Ga.) Enquirer-Sun,* 27 October 1903.

17. "National and International Notes: The Negro Question," *Christian Advocate* 78, no. 44 (29 October 1903): 1732.

18. Wilford Smith, "The Negro and the Law," in *The Negro Problem: A Series of Articles by Representative American Negroes of Today,* by Booker T. Washington, W. E. B. Du Bois, Charles W. Chesnutt, Wilford H. Smith, H. T. Kealing, Paul Laurence Dunbar, and T. Thomas Fortune (New York: James Pott, 1903), 127–28, 134, 142.

19. Ibid., 155–56.

20. Ibid., 159; *NYT,* 12 November 1903.

21. *Mobile Southern Watchman,* 5 December 1903.

22. Ibid. I have not found any report of this meeting's outcome. McEwen's biography is discussed in James Chapman Wilder's "History of the Alabama Negro Press, Post-Reconstruction to 1901" (master's thesis, University of Alabama, 1964), 107–8.

23. *Rogers v. Alabama,* 192 U.S. 226 (1904; *Mobile Southern Watchman,* 30 January 1904; *AC,* 6 January 1904; *MA,* 6 January 1904; *Macon Telegraph,* 6 January 1904; *Columbus (Ga.) Enquirer-Sun,* 6 January 1904; *CDO,* 6 January 1903; "Order Remanding Case to Montgomery City Court," *Dan Rogers v. State of Alabama; SPA,* 3 January 1904. The *Montgomery Advertiser* published the text of *Rogers* on March 1.

24. Charles William Anderson to BTW, 26 January 1904, in *BTWPH* 7:413–14; *Chicago Broad Ax,* 13 February 1904; *SWCA,* 21 January 1904; *NYT,* 19 January 1904; *Iowa City Daily Iowa State Press,* 18 January 1904; *Atlanta Independent,* 18 January 1904; *Galveston Daily News,* 19 January 1904.

25. BTW to Smith, 2 February 1904, in *BTWPH* 7:423; unsigned and undated press release regarding *Rogers v. Alabama,* BTW Papers, LOC, Reel 400. See also *New York Age,* 28 January 1904; *New York Tribune,* 19 January 1904. Scott had written that "the race owes Wilford H. Smith of Galveston a debt of gratitude which it will never pay, as it pays none of those who labor and sacrifice in its behalf." Scott to BTW, 25 July 1900, in *BTWPH* 5:592).

26. Unsigned and undated press release regarding *Rogers v. Alabama,* Reel 400, BTWPLC; *Richmond (Ky.) Sentinel,* 9 September 1904; *RP,* 3 April 1904. This clipping came from the Hampton University Newspaper Clippings File (available on microfilm), and it is not clear whether it is dated "1904" or "1909."

27. *Birmingham Free Lance,* 21 January 1904; *AC,* 27 August 1904.

28. Smith to BTW, 4 February 1904, Reel 79, BTWPLC. The circular eventually ap-

peared as an unsigned handbill and as a publication of Washington's "Committee of Twelve." The document's preamble asked that it be "circulated as widely as possible," through newspapers, pulpits, and word of mouth. See Committee of Twelve for the Advancement of the Interests of the Negro Race, *What a Colored Man Should Do to Vote* (Philadelphia: E. A. White, 1904); *RP*, 23 January 1904.

29. *Giles v. Teasley*, 193 U.S. 146 (1904) 164.

30. Alexander M. Bickel and Benno C. Schmidt Jr., *History of the Supreme Court of the United States*, vol 9, *The Judiciary and Responsible Government, 1910–1921* (New York: Macmillan, 198), 926; Yosal Rogat, "Mr. Justice Holmes: A Dissenting Opinion," *Stanford Law Review* 15 (March 1963): 264; *Giles v. Teasley*, 193 U.S. 165.

31. *Giles v. Teasley*, 193 U.S. 164.

32. *RP*, 27 February 1904; *Atlanta Independent*, 5 March 1904; *Springfield (Mass.) Daily Republican*, 25 February 1904; "Countryman" to the *Opelika (Ala.) Post*, reprinted by the *Columbus (Ga.) Enquirer-Sun*, 6 March 1904. See also *Salt Lake Telegram*, 23 February 1904; *Columbus Ledger-Enquirer*, 23 February 1904; *Aberdeen (S.D.) Daily News*, 23 February 1904; *MA*, 24 February 1904; *NYT*, 24 February 1904; *Anaconda (Mont.) Standard*, 24 February 1904; *Columbus (Ga.) Enquirer-Sun*, 24 February 1904; *Dallas Morning News*, 24 February 1904; *Grand Forks (N.D.) Daily Herald*, 24 February 1904; *Omaha (Neb.) World Herald*, 24 February 1904; *SWCA*, 3 March 1904; *Syracuse (N.Y.) Herald*, 23 February 1904; *Oshkosh (Wisc.) Daily Northwestern*, 23 February 1904; *Decatur (Ill.) Daily Review*, 23 February 1904; *Galveston Daily News*, 24 February 1904; *Greene Iowa Recorder*, 2 March 1904; *MA*, 3 March 1904; *Boston Journal*, 8 March 1904; *Tucson Daily Citizen*, 21 March 1904; *CG*, 30 July 1904.

33. Charles Chesnutt to BTW, 5 March 1904, Reel 8, BTWPLC; Clarkson to BTW, 26 February 1904, Reel 36, BTWPLC; Clarkson to BTW, 29 February 1904, Reel 36, BTWPLC.

34. Clarkson to BTW, 26 February 1904, BTWPLC, Reel 36.

35. Ibid.; John S. Wise, *Speech of John S. Wise at the Banquet on Lincoln's Birthday at Grand Rapids, Mich., February 12, 1904. The Republican Party and the Suffrage: What It Can Do; What It Cannot Do; What It Ought to Do* (Grand Rapids, Mich.: n.p., 1904); *Philadelphia Inquirer*, 12 February 1903; Union League Club of New York, Committee on Political Reform, *Suffrage at the South* (New York: Union League Club, 1903), 24. The Union League Club's report did not go unnoticed in the South. See, for example, *Centre (Ala.) Coosa River News*, 17 April 1903; *Lafayette (La.) Advertiser*, 20 June 1903; *Springfield (Mass.) Daily Republican*, 10 April 1903. Wise continued to give his basic, goading stump speech for quite some time. See *Fort Worth Telegram*, 3 April 1903; *Columbus (Ga.) Enquirer-Sun*, 4 April 1903; *MA*, 4 April 1903.

36. Clarkson to Whitefield McKinlay, 13 October 1902, Reel 1, Whitefield McKinlay Papers, Carter G. Woodson Collection, LOC; James Clarkson to BTW, 26 February 1904, Reel 36, BTWPLC.

37. Smith to BTW, 24 February 1904, Reel 79, BTWPLC; BTW to Smith, 24 February 1904, Reel 79, BTWPLC.

38. Smith to BTW, 26 February 1904, Reel 79, BTWPLC. Scott wrote a day later to give Washington's official go-ahead to prepare a new proposal and to offer his condolences for the *Giles* cases: "I am very much disappointed that your hard and consecrated work should have come to so ill an end." Scott to Smith, 27 February 1904, Reel 79, BTWPLC.

39. Smith to BTW, 1 March 1904, Reel 79, BTWPLC; Smith to Scott, 1 March 1904, Reel 79, BTWPLC. See also BTW to Smith, 3 March 1904, Reel 79, BTWPLC; Smith to BTW, 7 March 1904, Reel 79, BTWPLC.

40. BTW to Smith, 7 March 1904, BTWPLC, Reel 79; May to Black, 9 March 1904, Reel 73, BTWPLC.

41. Smith to BTW, 31 March 1904, Reel 79, BTWPLC; *Montgomery Negro Pilot,* reprinted in the *WCA,* 14 May 1904; Scott to Smith, 22 April 1904, Reel 79, BTWPLC; May to Black, 29 April 1904, Reel 73, BTWPLC; Smith to Scott, 2 May 1904, Reel 79, BTWPLC.

42. The Court occupied the Old Senate Chamber from 1860 (when it vacated the Old Supreme Court Chamber) until 1935, when the Court moved into a building of its own. *WP,* 5 April 1904; *New York Sun,* 5 April 1904; *SPA,* 3 April 1904.

43. *RP,* 9 April 1904; *MA,* 6 April 1904; *WCA,* 9 April 1904.

44. *Jones v. Montague,* 194 U.S. 147 (1904) 151; *Selden v. Montague,* 194 U.S. 153 (1904); *Mills v. Green,* 159 U.S. 651 (1895).

45. *RP,* 30 April 1904; "Highways and Byways," *Chautauquan* 40, no. 1 (September 1904): 11.

46. *BTW* to Smith, 16 June 1904, Reel 400, BTWPLC; *Chicago Broad Ax,* 13 February 1904; *Dallas Morning News,* 22 June 1904; BTW to Smith, 16 July 1904, Reel 79, BTWPLC; Smith to BTW, 19 July 1904, Reel 79, BTWPLC; Smith to A. E. Pillsbury, 20 July 1904, Reel 79, BTWPLC; Smith to BTW, 27 August 1904, Reel 79, BTWPLC; Smith to BTW, 22 September 1904, Reel 79, BTWPLC; BTW to Smith, 27 October 1904, Reel 79, BTWPLC. See also, regarding grand juries, Smith to BTW, 10 June 1904, Reel 400, BTWPLC; BTW to Smith, 7 June 1904, Reel 400, BTWPLC; Smith to BTW, 20 June 1904, Reel 400, BTWPLC.

47. Alabama Department of Corrections and Institutions, State Convict Record, 1903–1908, vol. 6, 204, Container SG7462, ADAH.

48. Fleming to Jelks, 16 November 1901, Container SG23643, Folder 7, Governor William Dorsey Jelks Papers, Alabama Governors Papers, ADAH.

49. *NYT,* 30 January 1904.

50. *WP,* 19 March 1904.

51. *State ex rel. Ryanes v. Gleason,* 36 So. 608 (La. 1904); 112 La. 612 (1904); Rebecca Scott, *Degrees of Freedom: Louisiana and Cuba after Slavery* (Cambridge: Harvard University Press, 2005), 192–96.

52. *WP,* 1 February 1905.

53. *WP,* 10 June 1905; *WP,* 17 June 1905; *WP,* 15 February 1907; *WP,* 16 February 1907. The original case files for *Brickhouse* were lost when a hurricane struck Norfolk in the early 1910.

54. *Brickhouse v. Brooks,* 165 F. 534 (4th Cir. 1908) 546, 547; *WP,* 16 February 1907.

55. J. W. Whittaker to John S. Wise, 16 March 1912, in *Edgar Poe Lee v. John S. Barbour et al.,* docket no. 1762, USCCEDV, RUSDC, RG 21, NARA, Philadelphia.

56. Harlan, *Wizard of Tuskegee,* 249–51. Many of the participants in *Giles* also figured prominently in the antipeonage fight, most notably Thomas Goode Jones and William Holcombe Thomas. See, for example, Pete Daniel, *The Shadow of Slavery: Peonage in the South, 1901–1969* (New York: Oxford University Press, 1973); Brent Jude Aucoin, "Thomas Goode Jones, Redeemer and Reformer: The Racial Policies of a Conservative Democrat in Pursuit

of a 'New' South" (master's thesis, Miami University, 1993), 65–83; Aucoin, "'A Rift in the Clouds': Southern Federal Judges and African American Civil Rights, 1885–1915" (Ph.D. diss., University of Arkansas, 1999), 130–47.

57. *MA*, 8 November 1905; *MA*, 19 May 1906; 1920 U.S. census for Muskogee County, Oklahoma, Supervisor's District 2, Enumeration District 57, Sheet 3A.

Index

AAC (Afro-American Council): announcement of plans for "Louisiana Case," 110; challenge to Louisiana constitution (*see* "Louisiana Case"); doubts about plans of, 100; founding of, 95; Hayes's address to, 199–200, 201, 203; importance of Washington to, 96; inability to decide on attorney, 108–9; intention to expand crusade, 125; lack of interest in Smith, 107; organizational challenges of, 108, 287n72; support of Virginia litigation, 195; Washington's relationship with, 101

Abbeville (La.) Meridional, 77

activism, antidisfranchisement: early, 19; effects of using courts in, 19–20; need for organization in, 5; political parties in, 19; steep learning curve of, 19; successes of, 6; whites in, 198–99. *See also* AAC; Colored Men's Suffrage Association of Alabama; Giles, Jackson W.; Hayes, James; Jones, Cornelius J.; Lynch, John Roy; Murray, George Washington; National Negro Suffrage League; Negro Educational and Industrial Association of Virginia; Wise, John S.

Adams, Cyrus Field, 95, 200, 303n46

Adams, J. W., 151, 252

Address of the Democratic State Campaign Committee to the People of Alabama, 134–35

affidavits, 64, 67, 72

African Americans: apparent apathy toward litigation, 236; believed to be content, 133; enfranchisement of before Fifteenth Amendment, 106; federal employees, 149–50; growing protest from in press, 120–21; opposition of to Alabama constitution, 133–34, 136; repudiation of Hayes, 201–02; warnings of violence from, 120, 200

Afro-American Council. *See* AAC

Afro-American Exodus Union, 119, 120

Afro-American Press Association, 228

Afro-American Realty Company, 102

agrarians, in Mississippi, 51

Aiken, J. L., 88

"Ajax." *See* aliases; Scott, Emmett, J.

Alabama: African Americans allowed to register in, 144–45, 147, 148, 149, 150; African Americans' attempts to register in, 143–49, 184; African Americans called to jury duty in, 247; antidisfranchisement convention (Birmingham), 133–34; "A Short History," 137; Board of Appointment, 139–40; character test in, 145, 146–47; constitution (*See* constitution, Alabama); criticism of African American leaders in, 118–19; grandfather clause in, 129–30, 133, 147, 168; lack of whites registering in, 149; Limestone County, 183–84; litigation in (*see* litigation, Alabama); plan for legal fight in, 141–43; poll taxes in, 122; preparation of activists in, 112; registrars in, 2, 122–23, 139–40, 141; registration restrictions in, 121–22, 292n10; scale of antidisfranchisement activity in, 10; threat of African American exodus in, 119–20, 134; treatment of veterans in, 146–47, 183–87. *See also* Colored Men's Suffrage Association of Alabama; Giles, Jackson W.; Washington, Booker T.

"Alabama Case." See *Giles v. Harris*